CHAMBERS CHILDREN'S POCKET DICTIONARY

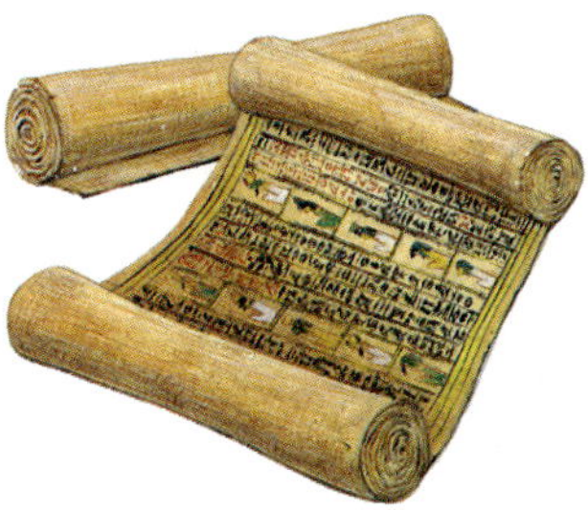

Chambers

CHAMBERS

An imprint of Larousse plc
Elsley House, 24-30 Great Titchfield Street,
London W1P 7AD

First published by Chambers 1996

2 4 6 8 10 9 7 5 3 1

A CIP catalogue record for this book is
available from the British Library.

ISBN 0 550 10671 5

Editorial team: Angela Crawley,
Andrew Delahunty, John Grisewood.

Design: Primrose Burton, Denise Gardner,
Tracey McNerney, Smiljka Surla.

Artwork research: Dawn Davies-Cook,
Janice English, Siân Williams.

Printed and bound in Hong Kong.

Making the most of your dictionary

Definitions explain what a word means.

Example sentences show how to use a word.

.**lternative forms** of a vord. Look at the next page for more information on these.

Different meanings of a word are numbered.

Words with the **same spelling** have tiny numbers after them.

Pronunciation guides for difficult words.

Usage labels show if a word is old-fashioned, slang or nformal, for example.

Related words and **phrases** are listed at the end of the entry.

winch *n* a machine for lifting things, worked by winding a rope around a revolving cylinder.

wind[1] *(rhymes with* kind*) v* (winding, wound) **1** to wrap something round and round another thing. **2** to turn a key or handle round and round to make something work. *Wind up the clock.* **3** to twist and turn. *a winding road.* **wind up** *(informal)* to annoy or tease somebody.

wind[2] *(rhymes with* tinned*) n* moving air. **windy** *adj.*

Part of speech labels show how words behave in a sentence. To find out more about each part of speech, look it up in the main part of the dictionary.

adj	adjective
adv	adverb
conj	conjunction
n	noun
prep	preposition
pron	pronoun
v	verb

rist

rist *n* a person who sells flowers.
ur *n* a powder made from grain, sed for baking.
urish *(**fluh**-rish) v* to grow well, to e successful.
w *v* to move along smoothly, as ater does in a river. **flow** *n.*
wer[1] *n* the coloured part of a plant at produces seeds.

flower

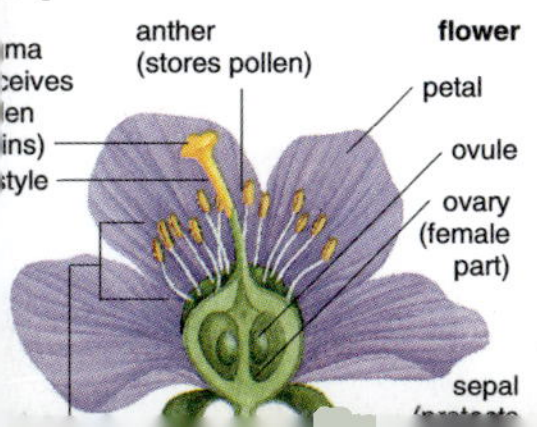

Guide words help you to find the right page.

Pictures help you to understand the meanings of words, and there are often **labels** which give you extra vocabulary.

Help with spelling

The dictionary lists words in their main form, but you will often want to know how the spelling of a word changes to make the plural or the past, for example. The information below will help you to get more from your dictionary and work out how to spell these alternative forms.

Adjectives

Using adjectives for comparing

*Amy got a **small** present, Billy's was **smaller** and Hassan's was the **smallest.***

With most adjectives of one syllable you add **-er** and **-est** to make these comparing forms. If the adjective ends in **-e**, you just add **-r** and **-st**:

small.....small**er**.....small**est**
rare..........rare**r**.....rare**st**

With most adjectives of two or more syllables, you use **more** and **most**:

more beautiful
most beautiful

However, some adjectives behave differently, and these spellings are shown in the dictionary.

big *adj* (bigger, biggest)

bad *adj* (worse, worst)

Nouns

You form the plural of most nouns by adding an **-s** to the singular:

rag.................... rag**s**
house..............house**s**

If the singular form of the noun ends in -**s, -ss, -x, -sh** or **-ch** (when it is pronounced ***ch*** as in chair), add **-es**:

bus...................bus**es**
boss................boss**es**
fox....................fox**es**
watch...............watch**es**

Many nouns ending in **-y** lose the **-y** and add **-ies** to make the plural:

fairy.................fair**ies**

Plurals that do not follow these rules are shown in the dictionary.

play *n* (*pl* plays)

child *n* (*pl* children)

Verbs

You can add **-ing** and **-ed** to many verbs without changing the spelling of the first part of the verb:

clean.......clean**ing**........clean**ed**

If a verb ends in **-e**, you take off the **-e** before adding **-ing** and **-ed**:

stare..........star**ing**...........star**ed**

Verb forms that do not follow these rules are given in the dictionary.

stop *v* (stops, stopping, stopped)

cry *v* (cries, crying, cried)

Some common verbs change their spelling when you use them in different ways. These alternative forms are shown.

wear *v* (wearing, wore, worn)

*Ben is **wearing** his blue shirt today.*
*Ben **wore** his blue shirt yesterday.*
*Ben has **worn** his blue shirt all week.*

Adverbs

You form most adverbs by adding **-ly** to the adjective:

quick.............quick**ly**

Exceptions are shown in the dictionary.

Aa

aardvark *n* an African mammal with a long, sticky tongue, that feeds on insects.

aardvark

abacus *n* a frame with rows of sliding beads, used for counting.
abandon *v* **1** to leave a place or person for ever or for a long time. *She had to abandon her car in the snow.* **2** to stop doing something before it is finished. *We abandoned the game when it started to rain.*
abbey *n* (*pl* abbeys) a group of buildings where monks or nuns live and work.
abbot *n* the man in charge of the monks in an abbey.
abbreviation *n* a short way of writing a word or group of words. *CD is an abbreviation of compact disc.*
abdicate *v* to give up the position of king or queen. **abdication** *n.*
abdomen *n* the part of the body which contains the stomach. See **insect**.
abduct *v* to take somebody away using force. **abduction** *n.*
abhor *v* (abhors, abhorring, abhorred) to hate something very much.
abhorrent *adj* horrible, disgusting.
abide *v* **cannot abide** cannot bear something. *I can't abide her!*
ability *n* the power, skill or knowledge to do something.
able *adj* having the power, skill, time, etc to do something. *I'm afraid I won't be able to come to your party.*
abnormal *adj* strange, not normal. **abnormality** *n,* **abnormally** *adv.*
aboard *adv, prep* on or in a ship, an aircraft or a train. *They went aboard the ship.*
abolish *v* to put an end to something. *When was slavery abolished?* **abolition** *n.*
abominable *adj* extremely bad or unpleasant.
aboriginal *(ab-o-**rij**-in-ul) n* one of the original inhabitants of Australia. **aboriginal** *adj.*
abortion *n* the removal of a foetus from its mother's womb in order to end a pregnancy. **abort** *v.*
about *prep, adv* **1** concerning. *a story about cats.* **2** nearly, approximately. *about two o'clock.* **3** here and there. *The children were running about in the street.* **4** near, nearby. *Is your dad about?* **about to** going to.
above *prep* **1** higher than. **2** more or greater than. *temperatures above freezing.* **above** *adv.*
abrasive *adj* **1** rough and able to wear something away by rubbing or scratching. *Sandpaper is abrasive.* **2** rude and unpleasant.
abreast *adv* side by side. *We walked three abreast.*
abridged *adj* shortened. *an abridged novel.*
abroad *adv* in or to another country.
abrupt *adj* **1** sudden and unexpected. **2** rude or sharp in the way you speak.
abscess *(**ab**-ses) n* a painful swelling on the body, containing pus.
abseil *(**ab**-sail) v* to lower yourself down a steep rock face using ropes.
absent *adj* not there, away. *Sarah is absent from school today.* **absence** *n.*
absolute *adj* complete. **absolutely** *adv.*
absorb *v* to soak up liquid. *A sponge absorbs water.* **absorbent** *adj.*
abstain *v* **1** to choose not to do something, especially something that you would like to do. **2** to choose not to vote. **abstention** *n.*

abstract *adj* based on ideas, not real things. *abstract paintings.*
absurd *adj* ridiculous or very silly. **absurdity** *n.*
abundant *adj* available in large quantities. *an abundant supply of food.* **abundance** *n.*
abuse[1] *(ab-**yooz**) v* **1** to say rude or unkind things to somebody. **2** to use something wrongly or badly. **3** to treat somebody in a cruel and violent way. **abusive** *adj.*
abuse[2] *(ab-**yoos**) n* **1** the wrong or bad use of something. *the abuse of power.* **2** insults. **3** cruel treatment.
abysmal *(a-**biz**-mul) adj* very bad.
abyss *(a-**bis**) n* a very deep hole.
academic *adj* to do with study, especially in schools or colleges.
academy *n* a school or college.
accelerate *v* to go faster and faster. **acceleration** *n.*
accelerator *n* the pedal in a motor vehicle which you press with your foot to make the vehicle go faster.
accent *n* **1** the way somebody pronounces a language. *He speaks English with an Australian accent.* **2** a mark written above a word that shows you how to say it, as in *début.*
accept *v* **1** to take something that is offered. **2** to agree to something. **acceptance** *n.*
acceptable *adj* satisfactory.
access[1] *n* a way to reach or enter somewhere. *They gained access to the house through a window.*
access[2] *v* to get information stored in a computer.
accessible *adj* easy to reach.
accessory *n* **1** an extra part that can be attached to something. *bike accessories.* **2** something such as a belt or a bag that goes with your clothes.
accident *n* an event that happens by chance, often one in which somebody gets hurt. **accidental** *adj,* **accidentally** *adv.*
accommodate *v* to provide a place for somebody to stay or live.
accommodation *n* a place to stay, live or work in.
accompany *v* (accompanies, accompanying, accompanied) **1** to go with somebody or something. **2** to happen at the same time as something. *The lightning was accompanied by a clap of thunder.* **3** to play a musical instrument along with another instrument or a voice. *Jane sang, and Michael accompanied her on the guitar.* **accompaniment** *n.*
accomplice *n* a person who helps another to commit a crime.
accomplish *v* to complete something successfully. **accomplishment** *n.*
accomplished *adj* skilled. *an accomplished musician.*
accord *n* agreement. **of your own accord** because you want to, freely.
according to *prep* as said or told by somebody. *According to Henry, this game is really good.*
accordion *n* a musical instrument like a box, played by pressing keys while squeezing the two sides together.
account *n* **1** a record of money that is owed, received or paid. **2** an arrangement to keep your money in a bank. **3** a description or report of an event.
accountant *n* a person whose job is to look after money accounts.
accumulate *v* to collect together, to pile up. **accumulation** *n.*
accurate *adj* exact, correct. **accuracy** *n.*
accuse *v* to say that somebody has done something wrong, to blame somebody. **accusation** *n.*
accustomed *adj* used to something. *She's not accustomed to waiting.*
ace *n* **1** the "one" in playing-cards. *the ace of clubs.* **2** a person who is extremely good at something. *an ace pilot.* **3** a successful unreturned serve in tennis.
ache *(rhymes with* bake*) n* a dull, steady pain, such as stomach-ache or earache. **ache** *v.*
achieve *v* to do something successfully. **achievement** *n.*
acid[1] *n* a chemical substance that can dissolve metal and that may burn your skin. **acidic** *adj.*

acid[2] *adj* sharp or sour in taste.
acid rain *n* rain that is polluted by acids in the air and that destroys plants and trees.
acknowledge *v* **1** to admit that something is true. **2** to say that you have received something. **acknowledgement** *n*.
acne *(**ak**-nee)* *n* spots on the face and neck, common in teenagers.
acorn *n* the nut of the oak tree.

acorn

acoustic guitar *n* a guitar that does not need an amplifier.
acoustics *n pl* the qualities of a room that make it easy or difficult to hear sounds in it.
acquaintance *n* a person that you only know a little.
acquire *v* to obtain something.
acquit *v* (acquits, acquitting, acquitted) to declare in a law court that somebody is not guilty. **acquittal** *n*.
acre *n* an old measure of area, equal to 4,047 square metres.
acrobat *n* a person who performs difficult balancing acts, somersaults, etc. **acrobatics** *n pl*.
acronym *n* a word made from the initial letters of other words, such as NATO, which stands for North Atlantic Treaty Organization.
across *prep*, *adv* from one side of something to the other.
act[1] *v* **1** to do something. *The doctor acted quickly to save the boy's life.* **2** to perform in a play or film. **3** to behave in a certain way. *She's acting very strangely.*
act[2] *n* **1** an action. **2** a pretence. *She's not happy really – she's just putting on an act.* **3** a part of a stage play. **4** a law passed by the government.
action *n* **1** something that you do. *a foolish action.* **2** fighting in a war.
active *adj* busy, lively.
activity *n* **1** liveliness. **2** something that you do, for example a sport or hobby.
actor *n* a person who acts in a play, a film or on television.
actress *n* a female actor.
actual *adj* real. **actually** *adv*.
acupuncture *(**ak**-yoo-punk-cher)* *n* a way of treating illness or pain by sticking thin needles into various parts of the patient's body.
acute *adj* very severe or great. *an acute shortage of teachers.*
acute accent *n* a mark (´) used in writing some words, such as *café*.
acute angle *n* an angle of less than 90º. See **triangle**.
AD *short for* Anno Domino (Latin for "in the year of Our Lord"), used with dates after the birth of Christ.
adapt *v* to change to suit a new situation. **adaptable** *adj*, **adaptation** *n*.
adaptor *n* a device for connecting two or more pieces of electrical equipment.
add *v* to put things together to make more. *If you add two and two you get four.* **addition** *n*. **additional** *adj*.
adder *n* a small, poisonous snake.
addict *n* a person who is unable to stop doing or wanting something, especially harmful drugs.
addicted *adj* unable to stop doing or wanting something. *addicted to drugs.* **addiction** *n*, **addictive** *adj*.
address *n* the number of the house and name of the street, town, etc where somebody lives. **address** *v*.
adenoids *n pl* small lumps in the back of your nose that help to prevent infection.
adequate *adj* just enough, sufficient.
adhesive[1] *n* a substance used to stick things together, glue.

adhesive[2] *adj* sticky.
adjacent *adj* next to, by the side of.
adjective *n* a word that describes something. In *a big, blue car*, the words *big* and *blue* are adjectives.
adjourn *v* to stop a meeting until a later time. **adjournment** *n.*
adjust *v* to change something slightly to make it work or fit better. **adjustment** *n.*
administration *n* controlling and managing something, such as a country or a company.
admiral *n* a senior officer in the navy.
admire *v* to like or respect somebody or something very much. *I admire her honesty.* **admirable** *adj,* **admiration** *n.*
admit *v* (admits, admitting, admitted) **1** to agree that something is true. *Jo admitted she was wrong.* **2** to allow somebody to enter. *This ticket admits one person to the museum.* **admission** *n,* **admittedly** *adv.*
ado *n* unnecessary fuss.
adolescence *n* the time of life when you change from being a child into being an adult. **adolescent** *adj, n.*
adopt *v* to take somebody else's child into your home and treat them as your own child. **adoption** *n.*
adore *v* to feel great love for somebody or something. **adoration** *n.*
adorn *v* to decorate something.
adult *n* a fully grown person or animal. **adult** *adj*, **adulthood** *n.*
advance[1] *v* to move forward.
advance[2] *n* **1** movement forwards, progress. **2** a loan of money. **in advance** before.
advanced *adj* **1** difficult, at a high level. *advanced computer studies.* **2** highly developed. *advanced technology.*
advantage *n* something that puts you in a better position than other people.
advent *n* **1** the coming or arrival of something. *the advent of computers.* **2 Advent** in the Christian Church, the four weeks before Christmas.
adventure *n* an exciting and often dangerous experience.
adverb *n* a word used to describe a verb or adjective. *Carefully*, *quickly* and *very* are adverbs.
adversary *n* an enemy or opponent.
adverse *adj* unfavourable. *adverse weather conditions.*
advertise *v* to tell people about something that you want to sell, for example on a poster, in a newspaper, or in a short film on television. **advertisement** *n.*
advice *n* a helpful suggestion.
advise *v* to tell somebody what you think they should do. *The doctor advised him to stay in bed.*
aerial *n* a device that sends out or receives television or radio signals. Aerials are often made of wire.
aerobics *n pl* physical exercises which increase the supply of oxygen to the heart. **aerobic** *adj.*
aerodynamic *adj* designed to move through the air quickly and easily.
aeronautics *n pl* the study of the design and flight of aircraft.
aeroplane *n* a vehicle that can fly, with wings and one or more engines.
aerosol *n* a small container in which a liquid, such as paint, is kept under pressure. You press a button to release the liquid as a fine spray.

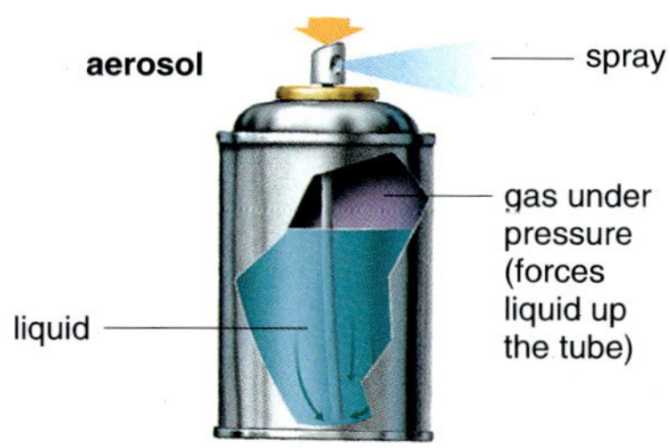

affair *n* an event or situation.
affairs *n pl* business. *financial affairs.*
affect *v* to influence or make a change in something. *What you eat affects your health.*
affection *n* a feeling of love or a strong liking for somebody. **affectionate** *adj.*
affirm *v* to state that something is definitely true.

affix *v* to attach one thing to another. *Affix a stamp to the envelope.*
afflict *v* to cause somebody pain or trouble. *afflicted with blindness.* **affliction** *n.*
affluent *adj* wealthy. **affluence** *n.*
afford *v* to have enough money to buy something. *They can't afford a holiday this year.*
afloat *adj* floating.
afraid *adj* frightened. **I'm afraid**... I am sorry. *I'm afraid I can't help.*
aft *adv* towards the back, or stern, of a ship or aircraft.
after *prep* **1** later than. **2** behind, following. *He ran after me.* **3** used with verbs: *Look after my bags* (= take care of them). *She takes after her father* (= she is like her father). **after** *conj.*
aftermath *n* the period following a disaster. *the aftermath of war.*
afternoon *n* the part of the day between morning and evening.
afterwards *adv* later.
again *adv* **1** once more. **2** as before.
against *prep* **1** next to, resting on. *Stand the ladder against the wall.* **2** in opposition to, versus. *Which team are we playing against?*
age *n* **1** the length of time that a living thing has been alive or that something has existed. **2** a period in history. *the Stone Age, the Bronze Age.* **3 ages** a long time. *I've been waiting ages.*
aged *adj* **1** *(rhymes with* caged*)* at the age of. *a child aged five.* **2** *(**ay**-jid)* very old. *an aged auntie.*
agency *n* the work or office of somebody who provides a service to others. *an advertising agency.*
agent *n* **1** a person who does business or arranges things for other people. *an actor's agent* (= a person who finds work for actors), *a travel agent.* **2** a spy. *a secret agent.*
aggravate *v* **1** to make something worse. **2** to annoy somebody. **aggravation** *n.*
aggressive *adj* always wanting to attack or argue with others. **aggression** *n,* **aggressor** *n.*
agile *adj* able to move quickly and easily. **agility** *n.*
agitate *v* to make somebody excited and worried. **agitation** *n.*
agnostic *n* a person who believes that it is not possible to know whether God exists or not. **agnostic** *adj.*
ago *adv* before now, in the past.
agony *n* great pain and suffering.
agree *v* (agreeing, agreed) **1** to say yes to something. **2** to have the same ideas as somebody. **agreement** *n.*
agriculture *n* farming. **agricultural** *adj.*
aground *adv* stranded on the bottom of the sea, a river, etc in shallow water. *The ship ran aground.*
ahead *adv* **1** in front. *We saw a light ahead.* **2** in the future. *Think ahead.*
aid[1] *n* **1** help. **2** something that gives help. *a hearing aid.* **3** money, food or equipment sent to people in need.
aid[2] *v* to help somebody.
AIDS *n* (*short for* acquired immune deficiency syndrome) a serious illness that destroys the body's ability to protect itself against infection.
ailment *n* a minor illness.
aim[1] *v* **1** to point a weapon, etc at something. **2** to plan to do something.
aim[2] *n* a plan or purpose.
air[1] *n* **1** the mixture of gases which we breathe. **2** an appearance. *The house has an air of neglect.*
air[2] *v* **1** to expose something to the air. **2** to put something in a warm place to dry. **3** to make something known. *to air your views.*
air-conditioning *n* a way of keeping the air in a building fresh and at a cool temperature. **air-conditioned** *adj.*
aircraft *n* (*pl* aircraft) a vehicle that can fly, eg a plane or a helicopter.
air-force *n* the aircraft that a country uses for fighting in the air, and the people who fly them.
airline *n* a company that owns and flies aircraft.
airliner *n* a large plane that is used for carrying passengers.
airport *n* a place where aircraft take off and land, and where people get on and off.

airship *n* a large balloon with an engine.

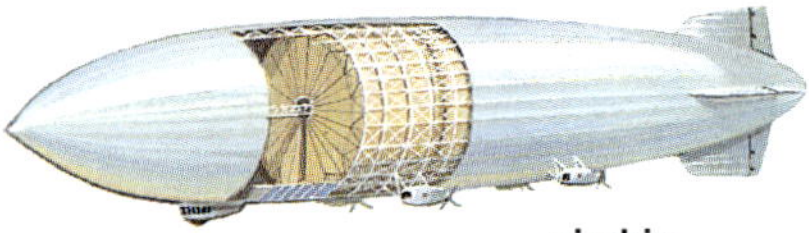

airship

airtight *adj* so tightly shut that air cannot get in or out.
aisle *(rhymes with* mile*)* *n* a long, narrow passage where people can walk between rows of seats, for example in a church or cinema.
ajar *adj* partly open. *The door is ajar.*
alarm[1] *n* **1** sudden fear. **2** something that warns you of danger. *a car alarm.*
alarm[2] *v* to frighten or disturb somebody.
alarm clock *n* a clock that makes a noise to wake you up.
albino *n* (*pl* albinos) a person or animal that has no natural colouring in their skin, hair or eyes.
album *n* **1** a book for keeping stamps or photographs in. **2** a collection of songs on a CD, record or tape.
alcohol *n* a clear liquid that is found in drinks such as whisky and beer and that can make people drunk.
alcoholic[1] *adj* containing alcohol.
alcoholic[2] *n* a person who cannot stop drinking alcohol. **alcoholism** *n.*
alcove *n* a part of a room set back into the wall.
ale *n* a type of beer.
alert[1] *adj* paying full attention, watchful. **on the alert** watchful.
alert[2] *v* to warn of danger. **alert** *n.*
algae *(**al**-gee* or ***al**-jee)* *n pl* a group of simple plants which includes seaweed.
algebra *n* a type of maths using letters and signs for numbers.
alias *(**ay**-lee-us)* *n* a false name. *The criminal had several aliases.*
alibi *(**al**-i-bye)* *n* (*pl* alibis) proof that a person was somewhere else when a crime was committed.
alien[1] *adj* foreign, strange.
alien[2] *n* **1** a creature from outer space. **2** a foreigner.

alight *adj* on fire, burning.
alike *adj* almost the same. *My mum and I look alike.* **alike** *adv.*
alive *adj* living, not dead.
alkali *(**al**-ka-lie)* *n* (*pl* alkalis) a substance that reacts with acids to form chemical salts. **alkaline** *adj.*
all *adj, adv, pron* every one, or the whole of something.
Allah *n* God, in the Islamic religion.
allege *(a-**lej**)* *v* to say that something is true without proving it. **allegation** *(a-le-**gay**-shun)* *n.*
allegiance *(a-**leej**-uns)* *n* loyalty.
allergy *n* an illness that affects you when you eat, drink, breathe or touch something that does not normally make people ill. **allergic** *adj.*
alley *n* (*pl* alleys) a narrow path or street.
alliance *n* an agreement between countries or groups.
alligator *n* an animal similar to a crocodile, found mainly in the USA and China.

alligator

allocate *v* to give a share to each person or thing. *How will the money be allocated?* **allocation** *n.*
allotment *n* a small piece of land which somebody rents for growing vegetables, fruit or flowers.
allow *v* to let somebody do something. *My parents allow me to stay up late at weekends.*
allowance *n* an amount of money that is paid regularly to somebody.
alloy *n* (*pl* alloys) a mixture of metals.
all right **1** fine or well. **2** used for saying yes.
allude *v* to refer to something in an indirect way. **allusion** *n.*
ally *n* a person or country that helps another, especially in a war.

almighty *adj* having great power.
almond *n* a type of nut.
almost *adv* nearly, not quite.
alone *adj, adv* without anybody else.
along[1] *prep* from one end to the other.
along[2] *adv* **1** forward, onwards. *to drive along.* **2** accompanying somebody. *We're going out – why don't you come along?*
aloud *adv* in a voice that can be heard.
alphabet *n* all the letters of a language arranged in order. **alphabetical** *adj.*
alpine *adj* to do with mountains.
already *adv* before now.
also *adv* as well, too
altar *n* a table in a church or temple, used in religious ceremonies.
alter *v* to change. *She altered the dress to make it fit.* **alteration** *n.*
alternate *(ol-**ter**-nat) adj* first one and then the other, in turns. *alternate stripes of red and green.* **alternate** *(**ol**-ter-nate) v.*
alternative *n* a choice between two or more things. **alternative** *adj.*
although *conj* in spite of, though.
altitude *n* the height above sea level.
altogether *adv* **1** in total. **2** completely, entirely.
aluminium *n* a light, silver-coloured metal.
always *adv* at all times, all the time.
am *form of* be.
a.m. *short for* ante meridiem (Latin for "before noon"). 9 a.m. is nine o'clock in the morning.
amalgamate *v* to join together. **amalgamation** *n.*
amateur *n* a person who does something such as a sport because they enjoy it, not for payment. **amateur** *adj.*
amaze *v* to surprise somebody very much, to astonish. **amazement** *n,* **amazing** *adj.*
ambassador *n* an important official who represents his or her own country abroad.
amber *n* **1** a hard, golden-yellow, see-through substance, used for making jewellery. **2** the golden-yellow colour of this substance.

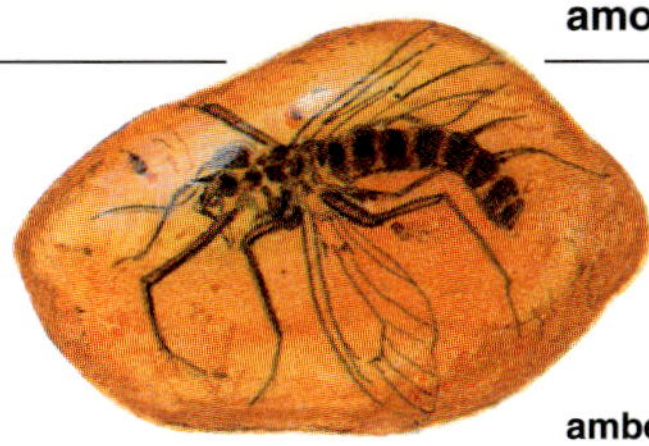

amber

ambidextrous *adj* able to use both hands equally well.
ambiguous *adj* having more than one possible meaning, not clear. **ambiguity** *n.*
ambition *n* **1** the strong desire to succeed. **2** something that a person wants to do more than anything else. *It's her ambition to become a vet.* **ambitious** *adj.*
amble *v* to walk without hurrying.
ambulance *n* a vehicle for carrying sick or injured people.
ambush *v* to hide and wait for somebody and make a surprise attack on them. **ambush** *n.*
amend *v* to correct something, to change something to make it better.
amenity *n* something that makes living in a place more pleasant or convenient. *The town has a leisure centre, a library and many other amenities.*
amid *prep* in the middle of.
ammonia *n* a sharp-smelling liquid or gas, often used for making cleaning substances.
ammunition *n* bullets and other things fired from guns.
amnesia *(am-**neez**-ya) n* loss of memory.
amnesty *n* an official pardon, especially of prisoners.
amoeba *(a-**mee**-ba) n* a one-celled animal that constantly changes its shape.
among, amongst *prep* **1** in the middle of, surrounded by. *a house among the trees.* **2** between, in shares. *He divided the money amongst his four children.*
amount[1] *n* how much of something there is.
amount[2] *v* **amount to** to add up to. *The bill amounted to £30.*

amphibian *n* an animal that lives both on land and in water. Frogs are amphibians. **amphibious** *adj*.
amphitheatre *n* an open area surrounded by rows of seats sloping upwards, used for sports events and performing plays, especially in Roman times.

amphitheatre

ample *adj* enough, plenty.
amplifier *n* a piece of electrical equipment that makes sounds louder.
amplify *v* (amplifies, amplifying, amplified) to make a sound louder. **amplification** *n*.
amputate *v* to cut off a part of the body. **amputation** *n*.
amuse *v* to make somebody smile or laugh. **amusing** *adj*.
amusement *n* **1** being amused. **2** a way of passing the time pleasantly.
anachronism *n* showing or mentioning something in a historical period in which it did not exist.
anaemia *(a-**nee**-mya) n* an illness that makes you tired and pale because your body does not have enough red blood cells. **anaemic** *adj*.
anaesthetic *(an-is-**thet**-ik) n* a substance used by doctors to prevent people feeling pain during an operation.
anagram *n* a word or phrase made from the letters of another word or phrase in a different order. *"Alps" is an anagram of "slap".*
analyse *v* to examine something closely to see what it is made of. **analysis** *n*, **analyst** *n*.
anarchy *n* a situation where nobody pays attention to any rules or laws. **anarchic** *adj*, **anarchist** *n*.
anatomy *n* the study of the structure of the body. **anatomical** *adj*.
ancestor *n* any person in your family who lived before you and from whom you are descended. **ancestral** *adj*, **ancestry** *n*.
anchor *n* a heavy, metal, hooked object on a long chain, thrown into the water to stop a boat moving. **anchor** *v*.
anchovy *n* a small fish of the herring family, with a strong taste.
ancient *adj* very old, from a time long ago.
anecdote *n* a short, interesting and often amusing account of something that happened.
anemone *(a-**nem**-uh-nee) n* a garden or woodland flower.
angel *n* a messenger from God. **angelic** *adj*.
anger *n* the strong feeling you have when you think something is unfair or wrong.
angle *n* the space between two straight lines or surfaces that meet.
angler *n* a person who goes angling.
angling *n* fishing with a rod.
angry *adj* (angrier, angriest) filled with anger. **angrily** *adv*.
anguish *n* very great suffering.
animal *n* **1** any living thing that is not a plant. **2** any mammal other than a human being.
animation *n* **1** liveliness. **2** the making of films in which puppets and drawings appear to move.
animosity *n* a feeling of strong dislike.
ankle *n* the joint connecting the foot to the leg.
annexe *n* a building added to another building to make it bigger.
anniversary *n* the day each year when a particular event is remembered. *a wedding anniversary.*
announce *v* to make something known to a lot of people. *John and Liz announced their engagement.* **announcement** *n*, **announcer** *n*.
annoy *v* to make somebody rather angry. **annoyance** *n*.
annual[1] *adj* happening every year. **annually** *adv*.

annual[2] *n* **1** a book or magazine published once a year. **2** a plant that lives for one year only.
anonymous *adj* without the name of the author being known. *an anonymous poem.* **anonymity** *n.*
anorak *n* a warm, waterproof jacket, usually with a hood.
anorexia *n* an illness that makes the sufferer refuse food, so that they may become very thin. **anorexic** *adj.*
another *adj, pron* **1** one more. **2** a different thing or person.
answer[1] *v* to say or write something when somebody has asked you a question or spoken or written to you.
answer[2] *n* **1** what you say or write to answer somebody. **2** a solution to a problem.
ant *n* a small, crawling insect that lives in large groups, called colonies.
antagonize *v* to make somebody feel angry towards you. **antagonism** *n,* **antagonistic** *adj.*
Antarctic *n* the region around the South Pole. **Antarctic** *adj.*
ante- *prefix* before.
anteater *n* a South American mammal that feeds on insects using its long snout.
antelope *n* a graceful animal like a deer, which can run very fast.
antenna *n* (*pl* antennas *or* antennae) **1** one of a pair of feelers on an insect's head. See **insect**. **2** an aerial.
anthem *n* a song or hymn written for a special occasion.
anthology *n* a collection of poems or other writings in one book.
anti- *prefix* against, opposite. *anti-terrorism.*
antibiotic *n* a drug such as penicillin which helps destroy harmful bacteria.
anticipate *v* to expect or look forward to something. **anticipation** *n.*
anticlimax *n* something that disappoints you because it is not as exciting as you expected.
anticlockwise *adj, adv* going round in the opposite direction to the hands of a clock.
antics *n pl* odd or funny behaviour. *The children laughed at the monkey's antics.*
antidote *n* something that stops a poison from working.
antiperspirant *n* a substance applied to your skin to reduce sweating.
antique *n* an old and valuable object.
antiseptic *n* a substance that kills germs.
antler *n* the branched horn of a deer.

anxiety *(ang-zye-uh-tee) n* a feeling of worry. **anxious** *adj.*
anybody *pron* any person.
anyhow *adv* **1** anyway. **2** in a careless or untidy way.
anyone *pron* any person.
anything *pron* any thing.
anyway *adv* whatever happens, in any case.
anywhere *adv* in or to any place.
apart *adv* **1** away from each other. *The two houses are a kilometre apart.* **2** into pieces. *She took the clock apart to mend it.*
apartment *n* a set of rooms, a flat.
apathy *n* a lack of interest and enthusiasm. **apathetic** *adj.*
ape *n* an animal like a monkey but without a tail. Chimpanzees and gorillas are apes.
apex *n* (*pl* apexes *or* apices) the highest point of something.
apologize *v* to say you are sorry for something. **apologetic** *adj,* **apology** *n.*
apostle *n* one of the 12 men chosen by Christ to spread his teaching.

apostrophe *(a-**pos**-tro-fee)* *n* a mark (') used in writing. It shows that letters are left out of a word (*I'm* for *I am*) or it shows ownership (*Gemma's cat*).
appal *v* (appals, appalling, appalled) to shock greatly, to horrify. **appalling** *adj*.
apparatus *n* the equipment used to do a particular job.
apparent *adj* **1** clear and obvious. **2** seeming to be true. **apparently** *adv*.
apparition *n* a ghost.
appeal *v* **1** to ask in a serious way for something. *Police appealed for witnesses to the attack.* **2** to be attractive. *The idea appeals to me.* **3** to take a legal case you have lost to a higher court to ask the judge for a new decision. **appeal** *n*.
appear *v* **1** to come into sight. *The Sun appeared from behind a cloud.* **2** to seem to be. *A microscope makes things appear bigger than they really are.*
appearance *n* **1** the appearing of somebody or something. **2** what somebody or something looks like.
appease *v* to do what somebody wants, in order to stop them being angry.
appendicitis *(a-pen-dis-**eye**-tis)* *n* a painful infection of the appendix.
appendix *n* (*pl* appendixes *or* appendices) **1** a part inside your body, attached to your intestine. **2** extra information at the end of a book.
appetite *n* the desire to eat, hunger.
applaud *v* to clap in order to show that you like something. **applause** *n*.
apple *n* a hard, round, red or green fruit.
appliance *n* a machine or device that does a particular job in the home, eg a vacuum cleaner or a washing machine.
applicant *n* a person who applies for something.
apply *v* (applies, applying, applied) **1** to ask officially for something. *apply for a job.* **2** to be relevant. *The rule applies to children under ten.* **3** to put something on something else. *Apply glue to the surface.* **application** *n*.
appoint *v* to choose somebody to do a job.
appointment *n* a time agreed for a meeting.
appreciate *v* to know the value of something, to be grateful for something. *I appreciate what you have done to help me*. **appreciation** *n*, **appreciative** *adj*.
apprehensive *adj* a little afraid.
apprentice *n* a person who works with somebody in order to learn their skill. **apprenticeship** *n*.
approach[1] *v* to come nearer.
approach[2] *n* a way leading towards something. *The approach to the house was through a wood.*
appropriate *adj* suitable.
approve *v* to be in favour of something. **approval** *n*.
approximate *adj* almost correct. *I can tell you the approximate cost.*
apricot *n* a small, soft fruit with orange-yellow flesh and a large stone inside.
April *n* the fourth month of the year.
apron *n* a piece of clothing that you wear over the front of your clothes to keep them clean, eg when cooking.
apt *adj* suitable. *an apt description.*
aptitude *n* a natural ability to do something well.
aqualung *n* breathing apparatus worn underwater by divers.
aquarium *n* (*pl* aquaria) **1** a glass tank for keeping fish in. **2** a building, especially in a zoo, where fish and other underwater animals are kept.
aquatic *adj* to do with water. *aquatic plants* (= plants that live in water).
aqueduct *n* a long bridge that carries water across a valley.

aqueduct

arable *adj* suitable for growing crops. *arable land.*
arc *n* a curved line, part of a circle.
arcade *n* **1** a covered passage where there are small shops. **2** an amusement centre with coin-operated games.
arch *n* a curved structure, for example as part of a bridge or of a door.
arch- *prefix* chief, main. *arch-enemy.*
archaeology *(ar-kee-**ol**-o-jee) n* the study of history by looking at the things that people have made and built. **archaeological** *adj,* **archaeologist** *n.*
archaic *(ar-**kay**-ik) adj* very old or old-fashioned.
archbishop *n* a chief bishop.
archery *n* the sport of shooting with a bow and arrow. **archer** *n.*
archipelago *(ar-kee-**pel**-a-go) n* (*pl* archipelagos) a group of small islands.
architect *n* a designer of buildings.
architecture *n* the style of buildings. **architectural** *adj.*
archives *n pl* a collection of historical documents and records.
Arctic *n* the region around the North Pole. **Arctic** *adj.*
ardent *adj* very enthusiastic.
arduous *adj* difficult and tiring.
are *form of* be.
area *n* **1** the size of a surface, measured in square metres, hectares, etc. If a room is 4 metres long and 3 metres wide, it has an area of 12 square metres. **2** a part of a country or of the world.
arena *n* a place where sports and other events take place.
aren't are not.
argue *v* **1** to talk angrily with somebody who you do not agree with. **2** to discuss, to give reasons for something. *She argued her point well.* **argument** *n.*
argumentative *adj* always arguing.
arid *adj* so dry that few plants can grow there. *arid desert.*
arise *v* (arising, arose, arisen) to begin to exist. *A problem has arisen.*
aristocracy *n* the highest social class, the nobility.
aristocrat *n* a member of the aristocracy. **aristocratic** *adj.*
arithmetic *n* the science of numbers, working with numbers.
ark *n* in the Bible, the vessel in which Noah escaped the Flood.
arm[1] *n* the part of the body from the shoulder to the hand.
arm[2] *v* to give weapons to somebody.
armada *n* a fleet of warships.
armadillo *n* (*pl* armadillos) a South American mammal with a shell of bony scales.

armadillo

armchair *n* a comfortable chair with parts to support your arms
armed forces *n pl* the army, navy and air force of a country.
armistice *(**ar**-mis-tis) n* an agreement between enemies to stop fighting.
armour *n* a covering, usually of metal, to protect the body in battle.

armour

arms *n pl* weapons.
army *n* a large group of people who are armed and trained to fight.
aroma *n* a pleasant smell. **aromatic** *adj.*
arose *past of* **arise**.
around *prep, adv* **1** on all sides. *We sat around the table.* **2** in different directions. *They walked around the town all morning.*
arouse *v* **1** to stir up a feeling. **2** to wake somebody. **arousal** *n.*
arrange *v* **1** to put things in a certain place or order. *I arranged the flowers in a vase.* **2** to plan or organize something. *We are arranging a party.* **arrangement** *n.*
arrest *v* to take somebody prisoner. *The police have arrested a man they believe is the robber.* **arrest** *n.*
arrive *v* **1** to reach a place. **2** to come. **arrival** *n.*
arrogant *adj* considering yourself more important than others. **arrogance** *n.*
arrow *n* **1** a pointed stick that is shot from a bow. **2** a shape like an arrow, on a sign showing direction.
arsenal *n* a place where weapons or ammunition are stored or made.
arsenic *n* a very strong poison.
arson *n* the crime of deliberately setting fire to property.
art *n* **1** the creation of drawings, paintings, sculpture, music, literature and other beautiful or interesting things. **2** a skill. *the art of conversation.*
artery *n* one of the tubes that carry blood from your heart to the rest of your body.
arthritis *n* a condition in which the joints of the body are swollen and painful. **arthritic** *adj.*
artichoke *n* **1** a round, green vegetable that looks like a thistle. **2** a whitish vegetable that grows underground.
article *n* **1** any object. **2** a piece of writing in a newspaper or magazine. **3** the word *an* or *a* (indefinite articles) or the word *the* (definite article).
articulate *adj* able to express yourself clearly.
articulated lorry *n* a lorry made in two sections so it can bend in the middle.
artificial *adj* made by people, not found in nature. **artificially** *adv.*
artillery *n* large, powerful guns used by an army.
artist *n* a person who draws, paints or makes other works of art. **artistic** *adj*, **artistically** *adv*.
ascend *(a-send)* *v* to go up. **ascent** *n.*
ash *n* **1** the powder that is left after something has burnt. **2** a tall tree with grey bark.
ashamed *adj* feeling guilty or bad about something you have done.
ashore *adv* onto the shore.
aside *adv* to or on one side. *She stepped aside to let me pass.*
ask *v* **1** to put a question to somebody because you want to know something. *I asked her what time it was.* **2** to say that you want something. *I asked for a drink.* **3** to invite. *John asked me to his party.*
asleep *adj, adv* sleeping.
aspect *n* **1** one part of a subject or problem. **2** the look or appearance of something.
aspirin *n* a drug used to reduce pain.
ass *n* a donkey.
assassinate *v* to kill an important person, such as a ruler or politician. **assassin** *n*, **assassination** *n.*
assault *v* to attack somebody violently. **assault** *n.*
assemble *v* **1** to put the parts of something together. **2** to come together in one place. *Everyone assembled for the meeting in the town hall.* **3** to bring people together in one place.
assembly *n* **1** a gathering of people, especially for a meeting. **2** putting something together.
assent *n* agreement.
assert *v* to state something clearly and firmly. **assertion** *n.*
assess *v* to decide the value or cost of something. **assessment** *n.*
assign *v* to give somebody something to do or to use. *Everyone was assigned a different job to do.*

assignment *n* a job that somebody is given to do.
assist *v* to help. **assistance** *n,* **assistant** *n.*
association *n* a group of people working together for a specific purpose.
assortment *n* a mixture of different things. **assorted** *adj.*
assume *v* **1** to accept that something is true, even though it may not be. **2** to take on power or responsibility. **assumption** *n.*
assure *v* to tell somebody something definitely. *I can assure you that the dog won't bite!* **assurance** *n.*
asterisk *n* a star-shaped mark (*) used in printing.
asteroid *n* a small planet moving around the Sun.
asthma *(ass-ma) n* an illness that makes breathing difficult. **asthmatic** *adj.*
astonish *v* to surprise somebody greatly. **astonishment** *n.*
astound *v* to astonish somebody.
astray *adv* away from the right direction, lost. *The letter must have gone astray.*
astrology *n* the study of the movements of the planets, stars, etc and how these are supposed to influence our lives. **astrologer** *n,* **astrological** *adj.*
astronaut *n* a traveller in space.
astronomy *n* the study of the Moon, Sun, stars and planets. **astronomer** *n.*
asylum *n* **1** a place to shelter, protection. *She was granted political asylum in Britain.* **2** in earlier times, a hospital for mentally ill people.
ate *past of* **eat**.
atheist *n* a person who does not believe that there is a God. **atheism** *n.*
athlete *n* a person who is good at sports such as running, jumping and throwing. **athletic** *adj.*
athletics *n pl* the sports of running, jumping and throwing.
atlas *n* a book of maps.
atmosphere *n* **1** the air around the Earth. **2** the feeling in a place. *This café has a friendly atmosphere.*
atom *n* the smallest part of a chemical element. **atomic** *adj.*

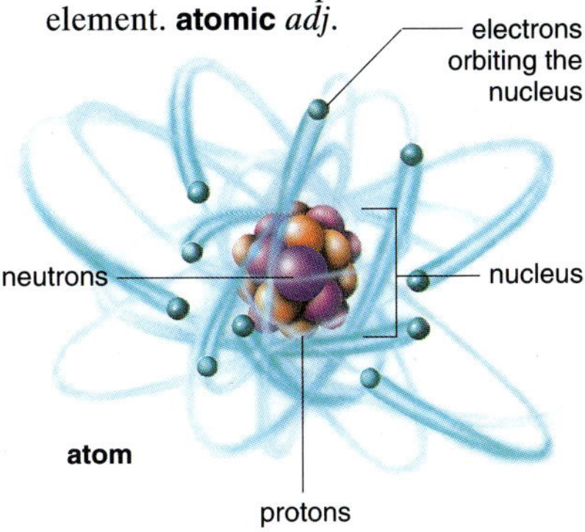

atom

atrocious *adj* very bad or very cruel.
atrocity *n* a cruel, wicked act.
attach *v* to join or fasten one thing to another. **attachment** *n.*
attack *v* to try suddenly to hurt or damage somebody or something. **attack** *n.*
attain *v* to gain or achieve something. **attainment** *n.*
attempt *v* to try to do something. **attempt** *n.*
attend *v* to be present. **attend to** to deal with something. *She has business to attend to.* **attendance** *n.*
attention *n* looking, listening or thinking carefully. *Pay attention to what you are doing.*
attic *n* a room in the roof of a house.
attire *n* clothing.
attitude *n* a way of thinking or behaving.
attract *v* **1** to make somebody like or be interested in somebody or something. **2** to pull something towards something else. *Magnets attract iron objects.* **attraction** *n.*
attractive *adj* pleasant to look at.
aubergine *(oh-bur-jheen) n* a vegetable with a smooth, dark-purple skin.
auburn *adj* (of hair) reddish-brown.
auction *n* a public sale in which each thing is sold to the person who will pay the most money for it. **auction** *v,* **auctioneer** *n.*
audible *adj* loud enough to be heard.

audience *n* a group of people watching or listening to something.
audition *n* a short performance to test the ability of an actor or musician.
auditorium *n* (*pl* auditoriums *or* auditoria) the part of a concert hall or theatre where the audience sits.
August *n* the eighth month of the year.
aunt *n* the sister of your mother or father, or your uncle's wife.
au pair *n* a young person from another country who lives with a family, helping with the housework and looking after the children.
authentic *adj* genuine, real.
author *n* a person who writes a book, article, play, etc.
authority *n* **1** the power to tell somebody what to do. **2** a person or group that tells other people what to do. **3** an expert. **authorize** *v.*
autism *n* a disability in children which affects their ability to relate to and communicate with other people. **autistic** *adj.*
autobiography *n* the story of a person's life written by that person. **autobiographical** *adj.*
autograph *n* a famous person's name, written in their own handwriting.
automatic *adj* working on its own without being looked after. *an automatic washing-machine.* **automatically** *adv.*
automation *n* the use of machines to do work in factories.
automobile *n* a car.
autumn *n* the season between summer and winter. **autumnal** *adj.*
available *adj* able or ready to be used. **availability** *n.*
avalanche *n* a sudden huge fall of snow and ice down a mountain.
avenge *v* to punish somebody in return for something bad that they have done.
avenue *n* a road, especially one with trees along both sides.
average[1] *n* the number that you get when you add together several amounts and divide the total by the number of amounts. The average of 5, 6 and 7 is 6 ($5 + 6 + 7 = 18 \div 3 = 6$).
average[2] *adj* **1** worked out as an average. **2** normal, ordinary.
aversion *n* a dislike. **averse** *adj.*
aviary *n* a place where birds are kept.
aviation *n* flying in aircraft.
avid *adj* keen, eager.
avocado *n* (*pl* avocados) a pear-shaped tropical fruit with a dark-green skin and a large stone in the middle.

avocado

avoid *v* **1** to keep out of the way of something. **2** to choose not to do something. **avoidance** *n.*
await *v* to wait for somebody or something. *A surprise awaited her.*
awake[1] *adj* not asleep.
awake[2] *v* (awaking, awoke, awoken) to wake up.
award *v* to give somebody something such as a prize or payment. **award** *n.*
aware *adj* knowing about something. **awareness** *n.*
away *adv* **1** at a distance. *a town two hours away from London.* **2** to or in another place. *She walked away.* **3** not present. *Harry is away from school because he is ill.* **4** gradually into nothing. *The music faded away.*
awe *n* respect mixed with fear.
awful *adj* very bad, very unpleasant. **awfully** *adv.*
awkward *adj* **1** uncomfortable or clumsy. **2** not convenient.
awoke *past of* awake.
awoken *past participle of* awake.
axe *n* a tool for chopping wood.
axis *n* (*pl* axes) an imaginary line through the middle of an object, around which it turns.
axle *n* the rod on which a wheel turns.

Bb

babble *v* to talk quickly in a way that is difficult to understand.
baboon *n* a large African monkey.
baby *n* a very young child.
baby-sit *v* (baby-sits, baby-sitting, baby-sat) to look after a child while its parents are out. **baby-sitter** *n*.
bachelor *n* a man who has never married.
back[1] *n* **1** the part of your body between your neck and your bottom. **2** the part of something opposite to or furthest from the front. **back** *adj*.
back[2] *adv* to the same place or person again. *Can I have my pen back?*
back[3] *v* **1** to move backwards. *She backed the car out of the garage.* **2** to support and encourage somebody. *Her parents backed her when she decided to apply for drama school.* **back down** to admit that you were wrong. **back out** not to keep to an agreement.
backbone *n* the bones that run down the back, the spine.
background *n* **1** the part of a scene or picture that is behind the most important figures or objects. **2** the things that happened before an event, that help to explain it. **3** a person's family, home and education.
backpack *n* a bag that you carry on your back.
backside *n* a person's bottom.
backstage *adj, adv* behind the scenes in a theatre.
backstroke *n* a style of swimming on your back.
backward *adj* **1** towards the back, towards where you began. **2** slow to learn or progress.
backwards *adv* **1** towards the back. **2** in the opposite way to the usual way. *Say the alphabet backwards.*
bacon *n* smoked or salted meat from a pig.
bacteria *n pl* very small living things. Some bacteria cause diseases.
bad *adj* (worse, worst) **1** not good. **2** serious. **3** (of food) rotten, not fit to eat.
badge *n* a small object that you wear on your clothes, with a picture, message or your name on it.
badger *n* an animal with a grey coat and black and white stripes on its head, that lives underground and comes out at night.
badly *adv* **1** not well. **2** seriously. **3** very much. *She badly needs help.*
badminton *n* a game similar to tennis, but played with a shuttlecock rather than a ball.
baffle *v* to puzzle somebody.
bag *n* a container made of cloth, plastic, paper, etc for carrying things.
baggage *n* bags and cases, luggage.
baggy *adj* hanging loosely, not tight.
bagpipes *n pl* a musical instrument played by blowing air through a pipe into a bag and then squeezing it out through another pipe or pipes.

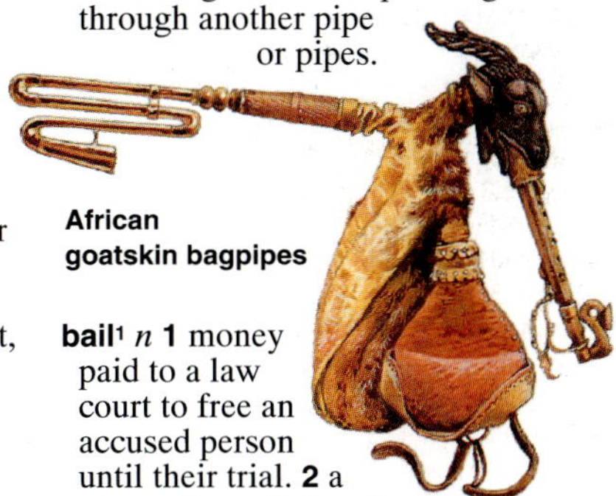

African goatskin bagpipes

bail[1] *n* **1** money paid to a law court to free an accused person until their trial. **2** a piece of wood placed across the top of the stumps in cricket.
bail[2] *v* to remove water from a boat, using a container. **bail out 1** to drop from an aircraft by parachute. **2** to get somebody out of a difficult situation.
bait *n* food put on a hook or in a trap to catch fish, animals, etc. **bait** *v*.
bake *v* to cook in an oven.
baker *n* a person whose job is to make and sell bread and cakes.

bakery *n* a place where bread and cakes are made or sold.
balance[1] *v* to keep steady, without falling. *Can you balance a book on your head?*
balance[2] *n* **1** steadiness. **2** a state in which two or more things are equal in size, weight, etc. **3** a device for weighing things.
balcony *n* a platform on the outside of a building, reached from the upstairs.
bald *adj* without hair. **baldness** *n.*
bale *n* a large bundle of something such as hay, paper or cloth.
ball *n* **1** a round object, often used in games. **2** something with a round shape. *a ball of string.* **3** a big, formal party with dancing.
ballad *n* a long, simple poem or song that tells a story.
ballerina *n* a female ballet dancer.
ballet *(bal-ay) n* a performance of dancing, often telling a story.
balloon *n* **1** a small bag made of plastic or rubber that can be filled with air or gas, used as a toy. **2** (*also* **hot-air balloon**) a large bag filled with hot air or gas, often with a basket underneath to carry passengers.

hot-air balloon

ballot *n* a way of voting in secret.
ballpoint *n* a pen with a small, metal ball as the writing point.
bamboo *n* a tropical plant with a hard, hollow stem.
ban *v* (bans, banning, banned) to forbid something. *Smoking on trains has been banned.* **ban** *n.*
banana *n* a long tropical fruit that has a yellow skin when ripe.
band *n* **1** a thin, flat strip of cloth, etc, around something. *a rubber band.* **2** a group of people. *a band of robbers.* **3** a group of musicians.
bandage *n* a strip of material for covering a wound.
bandit *n* an armed robber.
bandstand *n* a platform with a roof where a band can play in a park.
bang *n* **1** a sudden, loud noise. **2** a blow or knock. **bang** *v.*
bangle *n* a band of metal, wood or plastic worn around your arm.
banish *v* to punish somebody by ordering them to leave a place.
banisters *n pl* a rail supported by posts along the side of a staircase.
banjo *n* (*pl* banjoes *or* banjos) a string instrument played by plucking.
bank[1] *n* a business that looks after people's money for them. **banker** *n.*
bank[2] *n* the raised ground along the edge of a river or lake.
bankrupt *adj* unable to pay all your debts. **bankruptcy** *n.*
banner *n* a flag, especially one with a message on it.
banquet *n* a grand dinner for many people, a feast.
baptism *n* a Christian ceremony in which a person is sprinkled with, or dipped in, water to show that they now belong to the Christian Church. They are usually named at the same time. **baptize** *v.*
bar[1] *n* **1** a block of something hard. *a bar of chocolate.* **2** a long piece of metal. *an iron bar.* **3** a counter or room where you can buy drinks. **4** one of the short parts that a piece of music is divided into.
bar[2] *v* (bars, barring, barred) to keep somebody out.
barbarian *n* a rough, uncivilized person.
barbaric *adj* extremely cruel.
barbecue *n* **1** a grill for cooking food over a charcoal fire out of doors. **2** an

outdoor party at which food is cooked on a barbecue. **barbecue** *v*.
barbed wire *n* strong wire with sharp points along it, used for fences, etc.
barber *n* a person who cuts men's hair.
bare[1] *adj* **1** not covered by clothing. *bare feet.* **2** not decorated or covered. *bare walls.* **3** basic, just enough. *the bare necessities of life.*
bare[2] *v* to uncover or expose something. *The dog bared its teeth.*
barely *adv* only just.
bargain[1] *n* **1** an agreement to do something, especially to buy or sell something. **2** something bought cheaply that is good value for money.
bargain[2] *v* to argue over the price of something.
barge[1] *n* a flat-bottomed boat used on canals and rivers.

barge

barge[2] *v* to bump into somebody roughly or push your way roughly into a place. *He barged into the room.*
bark[1] *n* the short, loud noise made by a dog. **bark** *v*.
bark[2] *n* the rough covering of a tree.
barley *n* a cereal plant.
barmaid, **barman** *n* a person who serves drinks in a bar or pub.
bar mitzvah *n* a religious ceremony for a Jewish boy who has reached the age of 13.
barn *n* a farm building for animals or for storing crops or animal food.
barnacle *n* a shellfish that sticks to rocks and the bottom of boats.
barometer *n* an instrument that measures air pressure and that shows changes in the weather.
baron *n* a nobleman.
baroness *n* **1** a woman with the same rank as a baron. **2** the wife of a baron.
barracks *n* (*pl* barracks) a building where soldiers live.
barrel *n* **1** a container for liquids, with curved sides and flat ends. **2** the tube of a gun.
barren *adj* not able to produce crops, fruit or children. *barren soil.*
barricade *n* a barrier built quickly across a road or path to stop people passing. **barricade** *v*.
barrier *n* a fence or obstacle.
barrister *n* a lawyer who argues a case in the higher courts of law.
barrow *n* **1** a small cart. **2** a mound of earth used in prehistoric times to cover a grave.
barter *v* to exchange goods for other goods without using money.
base[1] *n* **1** the lowest part of something, which it stands on. **2** a headquarters.
base[2] *v* to develop something from another thing. *The film is based on a true story.*
baseball *n* a game played by two teams of nine players with a bat and ball.
basement *n* a level of a building below the ground.
bash *v (informal)* to hit somebody or something hard.
bashful *adj* shy.
basic *adj* **1** being the main thing on which something is based. *You need to know these basic facts before you begin.* **2** at the simplest level. *She has a basic knowledge of German.*
basically *adv*, **basics** *n pl.*
basil *n* a herb used in cooking.
basin *n* **1** a large bowl. **2** a bowl for washing yourself, fixed to a wall or floor. **3** the low, flat area beside a river, drained by the river.
basis *n* (*pl* bases) something on which another thing is based. *This idea was the basis of our plan.*
bask *v* to lie in warmth or sunshine.
basket *n* a container for holding or carrying things, made of thin strips of straw, etc woven together.
basketball *n* a game played by two teams, in which goals are scored by throwing a ball into a high net.
bass *(base) n* **1** the lowest male singing voice. **2** the low part in music. **3** an electric guitar that produces very low notes. **4** a double bass.

bat[1] *n* an animal similar to a mouse with wings, which flies at night.

bat

bat[2] *n* a piece of wood used for hitting the ball in some games, such as cricket and baseball. **bat** *v*.

batch *n* a group of things made or sent at one time. *a batch of cakes.*

bath *n* **1** a large container that you sit in to wash your whole body. **2** getting washed in a bath. **bath** *v*.

bathe *v* **1** to wash a part of your body gently. *Let me bathe that cut on your knee.* **2** to go swimming in the sea, a lake, etc. **bather** *n*.

bathroom *n* a room with a bath.

baton *n* **1** the thin stick used by the conductor of an orchestra. **2** a short stick handed from one runner to the next in a relay race. **3** a truncheon.

battalion *n* a large group of soldiers.

batter[1] *v* to hit something many times. *She battered on the door with her fists.*

batter[2] *n* a mixture of flour, eggs and water or milk, used for making pancakes or coating food for frying.

battery *n* **1** an object which stores and supplies electricity, eg for a torch or car. **2** a group of large guns. **3** a set of cages where hens are kept to lay eggs.

battle *n* a fight, especially between armies.

battlements *n pl* the top of a castle wall, with openings for shooting through.

battleship *n* a large ship used in war.

bawl *v* to shout or cry loudly.

bay *n* (*pl* bays) a part of the sea where the land curves inwards. **keep at bay** to stop somebody or something from coming any closer or affecting you.

bay window *n* a window that sticks out from the wall of a house.

bayonet *n* a long, sharp blade fixed to the end of a rifle.

bazaar *n* **1** a market, especially in the East. **2** a sale held to get money for charity.

BC (*short for* Before Christ) used with dates before the birth of Christ. *29 BC.*

beach *n* an area of sand or stones along the edge of the sea or a lake.

beacon *n* a light or fire used as a signal or warning.

bead *n* a small ball of glass or other material with a hole through it so it can be threaded on string to make necklaces or other jewellery.

beak *n* the hard, pointed part of a bird's mouth.

beaker *n* a tall cup without a handle.

beam[1] *n* **1** a long, straight piece of wood or metal supporting a roof or floor. **2** a ray of light.

beam[2] *v* to smile widely.

bean *n* **1** any plant that has seeds growing in pods. **2** the seed or pod of a bean plant, used as food. **full of beans** *(informal)* very lively.

bear[1] *n* a large, heavy wild animal with thick fur.

bear[2] *v* (bearing, bore, borne) **1** to put up with, to stand something. *She couldn't bear the pain any longer.* **2** to support or carry something. *Will this chair bear my weight?* **3** to produce fruit, children, etc. *The tree bears white flowers in summer.*

beard *n* the hair that grows on a man's chin and cheeks.

beast *n* **1** a wild animal. **2** a cruel or nasty person. **beastly** *adj*.

beat[1] *v* (beating, beat, beaten) **1** to hit many times. *Beat the drum.* **2** to defeat. **3** to stir a mixture with quick movements. *Beat the eggs and sugar well.* **4** to make a regular movement or sound. *My heart was beating fast.*

beat[2] *n* **1** a regular rhythm, for example of your heart or of music. **2** the regular round of a police officer.

beauty *n* loveliness in appearance or sound. **beautiful** *adj*, **beautifully** *adv*.

beaver *n* a wild animal with a wide, flat tail and sharp teeth that it uses to cut branches to build dams.

beaver

became *past of* become.
because *conj* for the reason that. *I was late because I missed the bus.*
beckon *v* to make a sign to somebody, asking them to come.
become *v* (becoming, became, become) to come to be, to grow to be. *She became more and more angry.*
bed *n* **1** a piece of furniture for sleeping on. **2** a place where flowers are planted. **3** the bottom of the sea or of a river.
bedclothes *n pl* sheets, blankets, duvets, etc.
bedding *n* **1** mattresses and covers for a bed. **2** straw, etc for animals to sleep on.
bedridden *adj* unable to get out of bed because you are so ill.
bedroom *n* a room for sleeping in.
bee *n* a flying insect that makes honey.
beech *n* a tree with smooth bark and shiny leaves.
beef *n* the meat from a cow, bull or ox.
beehive *n* a box for keeping bees in, so that their honey can be collected.

beehive

beer *n* an alcoholic drink made from malt and flavoured with hops.
beetle *n* an insect with hard, shiny covers for its wings.
beetroot *n* a dark-red root vegetable.
before *prep* **1** earlier than. *Please try to get here before 2 o'clock.* **2** in front of. *She was before me in the queue.* **before** *conj, adv.*
beg *v* (begs, begging, begged) **1** to ask somebody for money or food in the street. **2** to ask very eagerly or desperately for something. *He begged his captors to let him go.*
beggar *n* a person who begs for money or food in the street.
begin *v* (begins, beginning, began, begun) to start. **beginner** *n*, **beginning** *n.*
behalf *n* **on behalf of** for somebody. *Hattie thanked our teacher on behalf of the whole class.*
behave *v* **1** to act in a certain way. *Tim is behaving very oddly.* **2** to act properly, to be good.
behaviour *n* how you behave.
behead *v* to cut off somebody's head.
behind *prep* **1** at or towards the back of. *I waited behind John in the queue.* **2** on the other side of. *I hid behind the door.* **3** giving support. *She wants to become a dancer and her family are right behind her.* **4** making less progress than others. *He is behind the rest of the class with his reading.* **behind** *adv.*
beige *(bayj)* *n* a pale brown colour. **beige** *adj.*
being *n* any living person or thing.
belated *adj* arriving late.
belch *v* **1** to burp. **2** to send out fire, gases, etc. *The factory's chimneys belched out smoke.*
belief *n* what somebody believes to be true.
believe *v* **1** to feel sure that something is true or right. **2** to think something. **believer** *n.*
bell *n* a hollow, metal object that makes a ringing sound when it is struck.
bellow *v* to roar like a bull, to shout. **bellow** *n.*
bellows *n pl* an instrument for pumping air to make a fire burn better.
belly *n* the part of your body between your chest and your legs, the stomach.
belong *v* **1** to be owned by somebody. *This book belongs to me.* **2** to be a

member of a club. **3** to have a proper place somewhere. *That chair belongs in the kitchen.*

belongings *n pl* the things that somebody owns.

beloved *adj* much loved.

below *prep* **1** lower than. *Your mouth is below your nose.* **2** less than. *temperatures below zero.* **below** *adv.*

belt[1] *n* **1** a strip of leather or other material that you wear around your waist. **2** a rubber band used in a machine. *a conveyor belt.*

belt[2] *v (informal)* **1** to hit somebody hard. **2** to travel very fast. *He belted up the road.*

bench *n* **1** a long, hard seat for several people to sit on. **2** a table for somebody to work at.

bend *v* (bending, bent) **1** to make something that was straight into a curved or angled shape. *Bend your arm.* **2** to turn to the right or left. *The road bends just ahead.* **3** to lean your body in a certain direction. *She bent down to pick up the coin.* **bend** *n.*

beneath *prep, adv* **1** underneath, below. **2** not good enough for. *She felt that cleaning floors was beneath her.*

beneficial *adj* having good effects.

benefit *n* **1** something that is good to have, an advantage. **2** money paid by the government to people who need it, for example because they are ill or unemployed. **benefit** *v.*

bent *past of* bend.

bequeath *v* to leave something to somebody when you die. **bequest** *n.*

bereaved *adj* suffering from the recent death of a relative or friend. **bereavement** *n.*

beret *(**bear**-ay)* *n* a flat, round hat.

berry *n* a small fruit containing seeds.

berth *n* **1** a sleeping-place in a ship, train, etc. **2** a place in a dock where a boat is tied up.

beside *prep* next to. **be beside yourself** to lose control of yourself because of strong emotion. *She was beside herself with worry.*

besides[1] *prep* in addition to. *There are three people in my family besides me.*

besides[2] *adv* also. *These shoes are too expensive and besides, I don't even like them.*

besiege *v* to surround a place with an army, in order to force the people there to surrender.

best *adj, adv* better than all the others.

best man *n* the male friend of a bridegroom who helps him at his wedding.

bet *v* (bets, betting, bet *or* betted) to risk money on the result of a race or some other event. **I bet...** I am sure... *I bet I can run faster than you.* **bet** *n.*

betray *v* **1** to do something that will hurt somebody to whom you should be loyal. *She betrayed her own brother to the enemy.* **2** to show something that you are trying to hide. *His face betrayed his true feelings.* **betrayal** *n.*

better *adj* **1** more excellent, more suitable. **2** recovered from an illness. **better** *adv.*

between *prep* **1** in the space dividing two things. *To score, you have to kick the ball between the posts.* **2** in parts, in shares. *Divide the sweets between you.* **3** comparing one to the other. *I can't tell the difference between Lucy and her sister.*

beverage *n* a drink.

beware *v* **beware of** to watch out for something dangerous. *Beware of the dog!*

bewilder *v* to confuse or puzzle somebody. *I was bewildered by the huge choice.* **bewilderment** *n.*

beyond *prep* **1** on the far side of. *Our house is just beyond the school.* **2** more than. *They succeeded beyond all their hopes.* **be beyond somebody** be impossible for somebody to understand or do.

bi- *prefix* two or twice. *biplane* (= an aircraft with two sets of wings), *bilingual* (= speaking two languages very well).

biased *(**bye**-ust)* *adj* preferring one side to the other.

bib *n* a piece of cloth or plastic placed under a child's chin to protect their

clothes from food stains.
Bible *n* the holy book of the Christian Church. **biblical** *adj*.
bicycle *n* a two-wheeled vehicle that you ride by pedalling.
bid *v* (bids, bidding, bid) to offer a sum of money for something. **bid** *n*.
big *adj* (bigger, biggest) **1** large in size. **2** important.
bigot *n* a person who has a strong, unreasonable dislike of people of another race, religion, etc.
bigoted *adj*, **bigotry** *n*.
bike *n* a bicycle.
bikini *n* a two-piece swimming costume worn by women and girls.
bilingual *adj* speaking two languages very well.
bill *n* **1** a piece of paper showing how much money you owe for something. **2** a bird's beak. **3** an early version of a law, before it has been discussed by parliament.
billiards *n* a game in which you use a stick, called a cue, to hit balls into pockets at the edge of a long table.
billion *n* **1** one thousand million (1,000,000,000). **2** formerly, one million million (1,000,000,000,000). **billionth** *adj*.
billy-goat *n* a male goat.
bin *n* a container for rubbish or for storing something in.
binary *adj* made up of two parts or units.
binary system *n* a mathematical system using only the digits 0 and 1.
bind *v* (binding, bound) **1** to tie. *The robbers bound him to the chair with a rope.* **2** to wrap a length of material around something. *The nurse bound the wound with a bandage.* **3** to fasten together the pages of a book and put a cover on it.
bingo *n* a game in which each player covers numbers on a card as they are called out. The first player to have all or a row of their numbers called out is the winner.
binoculars *n pl* an instrument with two eyepieces that you look through to make distant objects seem closer.
biodegradable *adj* able to be broken down naturally by bacteria.
biography *n* the written story of somebody's life. **biographical** *adj*.
biology *n* the scientific study of living things. **biological** *adj*, **biologically** *adv*, **biologist** *n*.
biplane *n* an aircraft with two sets of wings.

biplane

bird *n* a creature with feathers, a beak, two legs and two wings. Most birds can fly.
birth *n* coming into life, being born.
birthday *n* the anniversary of the day that you were born.
birthmark *n* a mark on your skin that has been there since you were born.
biscuit *n* a flat, crisp type of cake.
bishop *n* **1** a senior priest in some Christian churches. **2** a chesspiece. See **chess**.
bison *n* (*pl* bison) a large, hairy ox.
bit *n* **1** a small piece or amount. **2** the metal part of a bridle that the horse holds in its mouth. **3** the smallest unit of information used by a computer. **4** the end part of a drill.
bitch *n* a female dog, wolf or fox.
bite *v* (biting, bit, bitten) **1** to cut something with your teeth. **2** to sting. **bite** *n*.
bitter *adj* **1** sharp and unpleasant in taste, not sweet. *This coffee is very bitter.* **2** angry and upset. **3** (of the weather) very cold. **bitterness** *n*.
bizarre *adj* very strange.
black[1] *n* the darkest of all colours.
black[2] *adj* **1** black in colour. **2** (of people) dark-skinned.
blackberry *n* a small, juicy, black fruit that grows on a thorny bush.
blackbird *n* a black bird that sings beautifully.

blackboard *n* a board with a black surface that you write on with chalk.
blackcurrant *n* a small, black fruit that grows on a bush.
blacken *v* to make or become black.
black hole *n* an area in space, where a star has collapsed, that sucks everything into it, even light.
blackmail *n* threatening to tell a secret unless somebody pays you money. **blackmail** *v*, **blackmailer** *n.*
blacksmith *n* a person who makes or repairs iron goods, such as horseshoes.
bladder *n* the organ of your body where waste liquid is stored before it is passed out of your body.
blade *n* **1** the sharp cutting edge of a knife, sword, etc. **2** a leaf of grass. **3** anything shaped like a blade.
blame *v* to say that somebody is the cause of something bad. *I didn't break it – don't blame me!* **blame** *n.*
blancmange *(bluh-**monj**)* *n* a dessert like a jelly, made with milk.
bland *adj* mild and dull. *This food tastes a bit bland.*
blank *adj* with nothing on it. *a blank sheet of paper.*
blanket *n* **1** a thick, woollen cover for a bed. **2** a thick layer of something. *A blanket of snow covered the ground.*
blare *v* to make a very loud, unpleasant sound. *I can't hear you with that radio blaring!*
blaspheme *(blas-**feem**)* *v* to speak about God or religion without respect. **blasphemous** *adj*, **blasphemy** *n.*
blast *n* **1** a sudden rush of air. **2** an explosion. **3** a sudden loud noise. **blast** *v.*
blast-off *n* the moment when a rocket is launched.
blaze *v* to burn with a strong flame. **blaze** *n.*
blazer *n* a smart jacket, often worn as part of a uniform.
bleach[1] *n* a strong liquid used for bleaching and cleaning.
bleach[2] *v* to remove the colour from something, especially with bleach.
bleak *adj* **1** cold and bare. *a bleak landscape.* **2** without hope. *The future looks bleak.*
bleat *v* to cry like a sheep. **bleat** *n.*
bleed *v* (bleeding, bled) to lose blood.
bleep *v* to make a short, high sound. **bleep** *n.*
blend *v* to mix together. **blend** *n.*
bless *v* to ask God to look after somebody or something. *The priest blessed the children.* **blessing** *n.*
blew *past of* blow.
blind[1] *adj* not able to see. **blindness** *n.*
blind[2] *v* to make somebody blind.
blind[3] *n* a covering that can be pulled down over a window.
blindfold *n* a piece of cloth tied over your eyes to prevent you from seeing.
blink *v* to close and open your eyes quickly.
bliss *n* very great happiness. **blissful** *adj*, **blissfully** *adv.*
blister *n* a small bubble under your skin, filled with a watery liquid.
blizzard *n* a heavy snowstorm.
bloated *adj* swollen, especially as a result of eating too much.
blob *n* a drop of a thick liquid.
block[1] *n* **1** a big, solid piece of something. *a block of wood.* **2** a large building of flats or offices. **3** a group of buildings with streets on four sides. **4** a barrier. *a road block.*
block[2] *v* to get in the way, so that people or things cannot get past.
block letters *n pl* capital letters.
blond *adj* (of a man or boy) having light-coloured hair.
blonde *adj* (of a woman or girl) having light-coloured hair.
blood *n* the red liquid that flows around our bodies. **bloody** *adj.*
blood-vessel *n* one of the tubes that carries blood around inside your body.
bloom[1] *v* to flower.
bloom[2] *n* a flower.
blossom[1] *n* the flowers on trees in spring.
blossom[2] *v* **1** to produce blossom. **2** to develop. *She blossomed into a fine musician.*
blot *n* a spot or stain made by ink or paint. **blot** *v.*

blouse *n* a shirt worn by women and girls.
blow[1] *v* (blowing, blew, blown) **1** (of the wind) to move. **2** to let air out through your mouth. **3** to move by blowing. *The wind blew the fence down.* **4** to be moved by the wind. *The door blew shut.* **blow up** to destroy something by an explosion.
blow[2] *n* **1** a hard knock. *a blow to the head.* **2** a sudden piece of bad luck. *His wife's death was a terrible blow.*
blubber[1] *n* the fat of whales and some other sea animals.
blubber[2] *v* to cry noisily.
blue[1] *n* the colour of a clear sky. **out of the blue** suddenly, without warning.
blue[2] *adj* **1** of the colour of a clear sky. **2** sad or depressed.
blues *n pl* a type of slow, sad jazz. **the blues** a feeling of sadness.
bluff *v* to try to trick somebody by pretending to be stronger, cleverer, etc than you really are or by pretending to be somebody else. *He bluffed his way into the palace by pretending to be a police officer.* **bluff** *n.*
blunder *n* a stupid mistake. **blunder** *v.*
blunt *adj* **1** having an edge or point that is not sharp. **2** saying honestly and plainly what you think, without being polite. **bluntness** *n.*
blur *v* (blurs, blurring, blurred) to make something unclear. *The rain blurred our view out of the window.* **blur** *n.*
blush *v* to become red in the face, usually because you are embarrassed. **blush** *n.*
boa constrictor *n* a large snake that kills its prey by winding itself around it and crushing it.
boar *n* **1** a male pig. **2** a wild pig.
board[1] *n* **1** a long, flat piece of wood. **2** a flat piece of stiff card, etc used for a particular purpose. *a notice-board, a chess-board.* **3** a group of people who run a business. *the board of directors.* **4** meals. *He pays for his board and lodging.* **on board** on a ship, plane or train.
board[2] *v* **1** to go on to a ship, plane or train. **2** to live and have your meals somewhere.
boarding-school *n* a school where you sleep and eat as well as have lessons. **boarder** *n.*
boast *v* to talk proudly about how good you think you are, or about something of yours. **boast** *n*, **boastful** *adj*, **boastfully** *adv*.
boat *n* a vehicle for travelling on water.
bob[1] *v* (bobs, bobbing, bobbed) to move up and down quickly. *The cork was bobbing about in the water.*
bob[2] *n* a short hairstyle in which the hair is all one length.
bobsleigh *n* a long sledge for two or more people, used for racing.
body *n* **1** the whole of a person or an animal. **2** a dead person or animal. **3** the main part of a thing. *a car-body.*
bodyguard *n* a person whose job is to protect somebody else from attacks.
bog[1] *n* an area of very wet ground. **boggy** *adj.*
bog[2] *v* (bogs, bogging, bogged) **bog down** to prevent somebody from making progress.
bogus *adj* false. *She entered the country using a bogus passport.*
boil[1] *v* **1** (of a liquid) to become so hot that it bubbles and produces steam. **2** to cook something in boiling water.
boil[2] *n* a painful swelling under the skin.
boiler *n* a tank in which water is heated to supply a building.
boiling *adj (informal)* very hot.
boiling-point *n* the temperature at which a liquid boils.
boisterous *adj* noisy and lively.
bold *adj* **1** brave and confident. **2** standing out clearly, easy to see. *bold colours.* **boldness** *n.*
bollard *n* a short, concrete post placed in a road to stop traffic from passing.
bolt[1] *n* **1** a sliding metal bar used for fastening a door. **2** a thick metal pin used with a nut for fastening things together.
bolt[2] *v* **1** to fasten with a bolt. **2** to rush away, to escape. *The horse has bolted.* **3** to swallow food quickly.

bomb *n* a container filled with explosives, used to blow things up. **bomb** *v*, **bomber** *v*.
bombard *v* **1** to attack with bombs or heavy gunfire. **2** to attack with questions, abuse, etc. **bombardment** *n*.
bombshell *n* a great, usually unpleasant, surprise.
bond[1] *n* **1** a feeling that unites people or groups. *a bond of friendship.* **2 bonds** ropes or chains used to hold somebody prisoner.
bond[2] *n* to stick together.
bondage *n* slavery.
bone *n* one of the hard, white parts that make up a skeleton. **bony** *adj*.

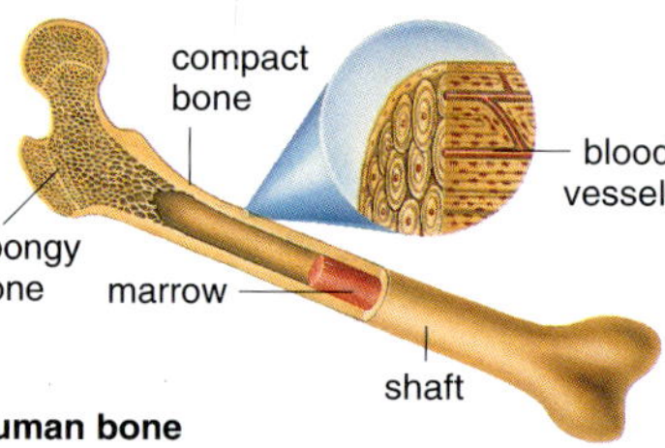

human bone

bonfire *n* a large fire out-of-doors.
bonnet *n* **1** the cover of a car engine. **2** a baby's or a woman's hat fastened under the chin.
bonny *adj* (bonnier, bonniest) pretty or good-looking.
bonus *n* an extra payment or reward.
booby trap *n* a hidden bomb or trap intended to hurt the person who comes near it.
book[1] *n* a number of sheets of paper fastened together inside a cover, for reading or for writing in.
book[2] *v* to order something before the time you need it. *We have booked a table in the restaurant.*
booklet *n* a small book with a paper cover.
bookmaker *n* a person who takes bets on horse races, etc and pays out money to the winners.
bookworm *n* a person who loves reading books.
boom *n* **1** a loud, deep sound, like the sound of cannons. **2** a sudden increase in something. *There has been a boom in sales of ice-cream this summer.* **3** a pole along which a sail is stretched. **boom** *v*.
boomerang *n* a curved piece of wood which, when thrown, returns to the thrower. They were used as hunting weapons by Australian aboriginals.

boomerang
(with aboriginal shield)

boost *v* to increase the power or amount of something. *We need to boost our sales figures.* **boost** *n*.
boot[1] *n* **1** a heavy shoe that covers the foot and lower part of the leg. **2** the storage space at the back of a car.
boot[2] *v* to kick. **boot up** to start a computer working by loading a start-up program.
booty *n* goods that have been stolen, especially in a war.
border *n* **1** the line that divides two countries. **2** a decorative strip along the edge of something. **3** a long flowerbed.
bore[1] *v* **1** to make a hole through something, especially with a drill. **2** to make somebody tired and uninterested. *I was really bored by that film.* **bored** *adj*, **boredom** *n*, **boring** *adj*.
bore[2] *n* **1** an uninteresting person or thing. **2** the size of the barrel of a gun.
bore[3] *past of* bear.
born *v* **be born** to come into the world. *What year were you born?*
borne *past participle of* bear.
borough ***(buh-ruh)*** *n* a town or an area that has its own local government.

borrow *v* to take something away for a while, intending to return it.
bosom *n* a person's breast.
boss *n* a manager, the person in charge.
bossy *adj* (bossier, bossiest) liking to tell other people what to do. **bossiness** *n.*
botany *n* the study of plants. **botanical** *adj*, **botanist** *n.*
both *adj, adv, pron* the two, the one and the other. *Both of my brothers are older than me.*
bother[1] *v* **1** to worry, annoy or disturb somebody. *Don't bother me now – I'm busy.* **2** to take the time or trouble to do something. *You needn't bother to clear up – I'll do it later.*
bother[2] *n* trouble or inconvenience.
bottle *n* a narrow-necked glass or plastic container for liquids.
bottom *n* **1** the lowest part of something. **2** the part of your body that you sit on. **bottom** *adj.*
bough *(rhymes with* cow*)* *n* a tree branch.
bought *past of* buy.
boulder *n* a large stone.
bounce *v* to spring up again, as a ball does when it hits the ground. **bounce** *n,* **bouncy** *adj.*
bound[1] *past of* bind.
bound[2] *v* to leap or jump. **bound** *n.*
bound[3] *adj* **bound to** certain to.
boundary *n* a line that separates one place from another.
bouquet *(boo-**kay**)* *n* a bunch of flowers.
bout *n* **1** a period of illness. *a bout of flu.* **2** a contest in wrestling or boxing. **3** a short period of something. *a bout of hard work.*
boutique *n* a small shop, especially one selling clothes.
bow[1] *(rhymes with* no*)* *n* **1** a weapon for shooting arrows, made of a stick of wood bent by a string. **2** a wooden rod with strings stretched along it, used for playing musical instruments such as the violin. **3** a looped knot, used for tying shoelaces, etc.
bow[2] *(rhymes with* now*)* *v* to bend your head and the upper part of your body forwards, as actors do at the end of a play.
bow[3] *(rhymes with* now*)* *n* **1** bowing. **2** the front part of a ship.
bowels *n pl* the long tubes through which food passes after it leaves your stomach.
bowl[1] *n* a deep, round dish.
bowl[2] *v* to throw the ball in a game such as cricket.
bowler *n* **1** a person who bowls in cricket. **2** a person who plays bowls. **3** a hat with a rounded top.
bowling *n* an indoor game in which you roll a large, heavy ball along tracks to try to knock down skittles.
bowls *n* an outdoor game played on a flat lawn, called a green, with very heavy balls which are rolled.
box[1] *n* a hollow container, especially one with straight sides made of wood or cardboard.
box[2] *v* to fight with your fists as a sport.
boxer *n* **1** a person who boxes as a sport. **2** a large, short-haired dog.
boxing *n* the sport of fighting with your fists.
Boxing Day *n* the first weekday after Christmas Day.
box office *n* a place in a theatre or cinema where you can buy tickets.
boy *n* (*pl* boys) a male child or young man.
boycott *v* to refuse to take part in something or to do business with somebody, as a protest. **boycott** *n.*
bra *n* (*short for* brassiere) a garment which women wear under their other clothes to support their breasts.
brace[1] *n* **1** a piece of wire fitted over teeth to straighten them. **2** a device which holds things together or in place. **3 braces** shoulder-straps for holding up a pair of trousers.
brace[2] *v* **brace yourself** to prepare yourself for something difficult or unpleasant.
bracelet *n* a piece of jewellery that you wear around your wrist.
bracket *n* **1** a support for something fixed to a wall. **2 brackets** the marks ( ) in writing, used to enclose words.

brag *v* (brags, bragging, bragged) to boast.
braid *n* **1** a plait of hair. **2** a narrow strip of woven threads, used to decorate something.
Braille *(brayl) n* a system of raised dots on paper which blind people can read by feeling.
brain *n* the part of your body inside your head which controls the rest of your body and with which you think.

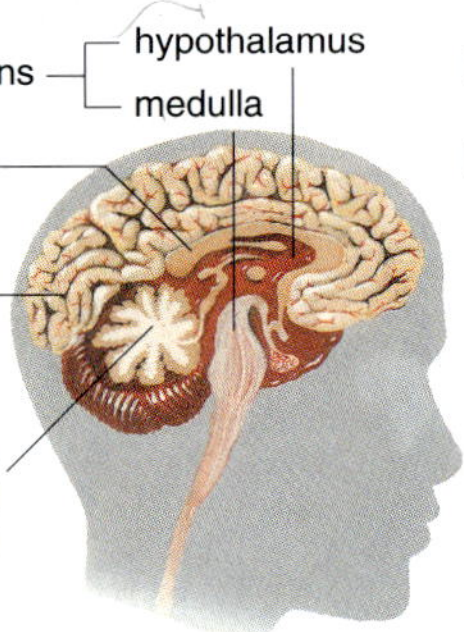

human brain

brainwash *v* to force somebody to have a particular view by repeating something to them over and over.
brainwave *n* a sudden good idea.
brainy *adj* (brainier, brainiest) clever.
brake *n* a part of a vehicle used for stopping or slowing down. **brake** *v.*
bramble *n* a thorny bush that blackberries grow on.
bran *n* the outer covering of grain.
branch[1] *n* **1** one of the arm-like parts growing out from the trunk of a tree. **2** an office or shop belonging to a larger organization. *The bank has four branches in the city.*
branch[2] *v* to separate into smaller parts like branches. *The railway line branches here.*
brand[1] *n* a particular make of goods.
brand[2] *v* **1** to mark cattle with a hot piece of metal to show who they belong to. **2** to give somebody a bad reputation. *She was branded a thief.*
brand-new *adj* absolutely new.
brandy *n* a strong, alcoholic drink made from wine.
brass *n* **1** a yellowish metal made by mixing copper and zinc. **2 the brass** the musical instruments made of brass that form part of an orchestra.
brave *adj* able to face danger without fear, or to suffer pain without complaining. **bravery** *n.*
brawl *n* a fight. **brawl** *v.*
bray *n* (*pl* brays) the harsh sound that a donkey makes. **bray** *v.*
bread *n* food made from flour, water and often yeast, and baked in an oven.
breadth *n* the distance from one side of something to the other.
break[1] *v* (breaking, broke, broken) **1** to divide into pieces, especially with force. *The thief got in by breaking a window.* **2** to stop working. *My watch has broken.* **3** to fail to keep something. *You broke your promise.* **break down 1** (of machinery) to stop working. *Our car broke down on the motorway.* **2** to become very upset. **breakdown** *n.* **break in** to enter a building by force. *Thieves broke in and stole her jewellery.* **break-in** *n.* **break out** to appear or start suddenly. *War has broken out.* **break up** to finish or end. *School breaks up soon.*
break[2] *n* **1** a rest from working. **2** an opening. *a break in the clouds.* **3** a change. *a break in the weather.*
breakage *n* the breaking of something.
breaker *n* a large sea wave.
breakfast *n* the first meal of the day.
breakthrough *n* an important development or discovery.
breakwater *n* a wall built out into the sea to protect the shore from strong waves.
breast *n* **1** one of the two parts on a woman's chest that can produce milk. **2** a person's or an animal's chest.
breaststroke *n* a style of swimming on your front.
breath *n* the air taken into and sent out from your lungs.
breathalyser *n* a device used by the police to measure the amount of alcohol in a person's blood.
breathe *v* to take air into your lungs and let it out again.

breather *n (informal)* a short rest.
breed[1] *v* (breeding, bred) **1** (of animals) to produce young. **2** to keep animals and allow them to breed so that you can sell them.
breed[2] *n* a particular type of an animal. *The spaniel is a breed of dog.*
breeze *n* a gentle wind. **breezy** *adj.*
brew *v* **1** to make beer. **2** to make tea or coffee. **3** to start to develop. *There's a storm brewing.*
brewery *n* a place where beer is made.
bribe[1] *n* money or a gift given to persuade somebody to do something.
bribe[2] *v* to offer somebody a bribe. **bribery** *n.*
brick *n* **1** a block of baked clay for building. **2** a toy building-block.
bride *n* a woman who is about to get married, or who has just married.
bridegroom *n* a man who is about to get married or who has just married.
bridesmaid *n* a girl or woman who helps a bride at her wedding.
bridge[1] *n* **1** a structure built to allow people and vehicles to cross a road, river, etc.

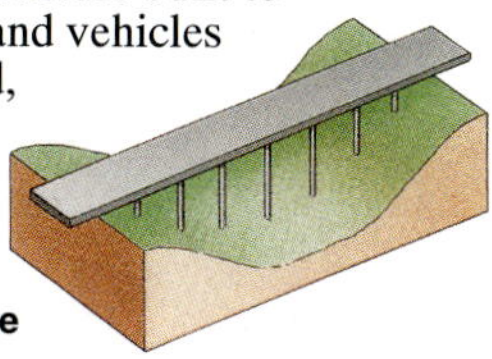

beam bridge

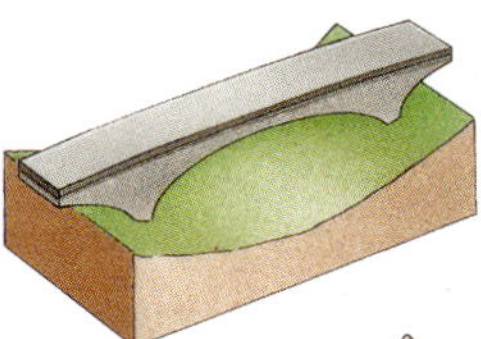

arch bridge

suspension bridge

2 the captain's platform on a ship. **3** a card game for four players. **4** the bony part of your nose. **5** a thin piece of wood over which the strings are stretched on a violin, guitar, etc.
bridge[2] *v* to build or form a bridge over something.
bridle *n* the harness on a horse's head to which the reins are attached.
brief[1] *adj* short. *a brief visit.*
brief[2] *v* to give somebody instructions so they can do something. **brief** *n.*
briefcase *n* a flat case used for carrying documents.
briefs *n pl* underpants or knickers.
brigade *n* **1** a large unit in the army. **2** a group of people with a particular job. *the fire brigade.*
brigadier *n* a senior army officer.
bright *adj* **1** shining strongly, full of light. *bright sunshine.* **2** strong and clear. *bright red.* **3** cheerful. *a bright smile.* **4** clever. **brightness** *n.*
brighten *v* to make or become brighter.
brilliant *adj* **1** very clever. **2** very bright. **3** very good. **brilliance** *n.*
brim *n* **1** the edge of a hat. **2** the edge of a cup or glass.
brine *n* salty water.
bring *v* (bringing, brought) **1** to come carrying something or accompanying somebody. *Can I bring a friend to your party?* **2** to cause to come. *The news brought great happiness.* **bring about** to cause. **bring up 1** to care for a child until it is an adult. **2** to mention something.
brink *n* the edge of a cliff, etc. **on the brink of** just about to do something.
brisk *adj* moving quickly.
bristle *n* a short, stiff hair. **bristly** *adj.*
brittle *adj* hard but easily broken. *Eggshells are brittle.*
broad *adj* wide.
broadcast *v* (broadcasting, broadcast) to send out a programme on radio or television. **broadcast** *n.*
broaden *v* to make or become broader.
broccoli *n* a vegetable with small, green flower heads.
brochure *(broh-shoor) n* a magazine or booklet giving information about something. *a holiday brochure.*
broke *past of* break.
broken *past participle of* break.
broker *n* a person who buys and sells stocks and shares for other people.

brolly *n (informal)* an umbrella.
bronchitis *(bron-**kye**-tis) n* an illness that makes it difficult to breathe and that makes you cough a lot.
bronze *n* a golden-brown metal made from a mixture of copper and tin. **bronze** *adj.*
brooch *(rhymes with* coach*) n* a piece of jewellery that you can pin to your clothes.
brood[1] *v* **1** (of a bird) to sit on eggs to hatch them. **2** to worry for a time about something.
brood[2] *n* a group of birds or other creatures hatched or born at one time.
brook *n* a small stream.
broom *n* a long-handled brush for sweeping.
broth *n* a thin soup.
brother *n* a boy or man who has the same parents as you.
brought *past of* bring.
brow *n* **1** a forehead. **2** an eyebrow. **3** the top of a hill.
brown *n* the colour of coffee and wood. **brown** *adj.*
browse *v* to look casually, especially at goods in a shop.
bruise *n* a dark mark on your skin where it has hit against something. **bruise** *v.*
brush[1] *n* an object with short, stiff hairs, used for making your hair tidy, cleaning something, painting, etc
brush[2] *v* **1** to use a brush. **2** to touch lightly while moving close to something. *She brushed past him.*
brutal *adj* cruel and violent. *a brutal attack.* **brutally** *adv.*
brute *n* **1** an animal. **2** a cruel and violent person.
bubble *n* a thin ball of liquid with air or gas inside. *soap bubbles.* **bubble** *v,* **bubbly** *adj.*
buccaneer *n* in earlier times, a pirate.
buck[1] *n* **1** the male of the deer, rabbit, hare and some other animals. **2** *(informal)* a US dollar.
buck[2] *v* (of a horse) to jump into the air with all four feet together.
bucket *n* an open container with a handle, for carrying liquids.
buckle *n* a fastening for joining the ends of a belt or strap. **buckle** *v.*
bud *n* a shoot on a plant or tree that will develop into a leaf or flower.
Buddhism *n* an Asian religion that teaches spiritual purity and freedom from human concerns, founded in India by Buddha in the fifth century BC. **Buddhist** *adj, n.*

statue of Buddha

budge *v* to move.
budgerigar *n* a type of small parrot often kept as a pet.
budget *n* a plan of how money will be spent. **budget** *v.*
buffalo *n (pl* buffaloes*)* **1** a large Asian ox. **2** a North American bison.
buffer *n* something which lessens the force of a crash or blow.
buffet *(**buh**-fay) n* **1** a counter where you can buy food and drink, especially on a train or at a station. **2** a meal where you help yourself from different dishes of food set out on a table.
bug *n* **1** an insect. **2** a minor illness. *a tummy bug.* **3** a mistake in a computer program. **4** a tiny, hidden microphone for recording conversations secretly. **bug** *v.*
buggy *n* a seat on wheels for pushing young children along.
bugle *n* a brass musical instrument like a small trumpet.
build[1] *v* (building, built) to make something by putting parts together.
build[2] *n* the shape and size of a person's body. *He is of average build.*

building *n* a structure with a roof and walls.
building society *n* an organization where you can keep your savings and that lends money to people to buy homes.
bulb *n* **1** the round part of some plants that grows underground. **2** the round, glass part of an electric light.

bulb 1

bulb 2

bulge *n* a swelling. *The apple made a bulge in her pocket.* **bulge** *v.*
bulky *adj* (bulkier, bulkiest) large and difficult to carry.
bull *n* the male of the cow, elephant, whale and some other animals.
bulldog *n* a type of strong, fierce-looking dog.
bulldozer *n* a machine for moving earth and clearing land.
bullet *n* a small piece of metal fired from a gun.
bulletin *n* a news announcement.
bull-fight *n* a traditional public entertainment in Spain and South America in which men fight bulls.
bullion *n* bars of silver or gold.
bullock *n* a castrated bull.
bull's-eye *n* the centre of a target.
bully *n* a person who uses their strength or power to hurt or frighten others. **bully** *v.*
bumble-bee *n* a type of large bee.
bump[1] *v* to knock against something.
bump[2] *n* **1** a lump or swelling. **2** a loud, heavy blow, or the sound this makes.
bumper *n* a bar fixed to the front and back of a car to protect it from damage.
bumpy *adj* (bumpier, bumpiest) uneven, having bumps. *a bumpy road.*
bun *n* **1** a small, round, sweet bread roll or cake. **2** hair twisted into a round shape and fastened at the back of the head.
bunch *n* **1** a number of things growing or fastened together. *a bunch of bananas, a bunch of flowers.* **2** a group of people.
bundle *n* a number of things tied up together. *a bundle of sticks.*
bungalow *n* a house built on one level.
bunkbeds *n pl* a pair of narrow beds one above the other.
bunker *n* **1** a strongly built underground shelter. **2** an area filled with sand on a golf course. **3** a large box for keeping coal in.
buoy *(boy) n* a floating marker used as a guide or warning for ships.
buoyant *adj* able to float. **buoyancy** *n.*
burden *n* **1** a heavy load. **2** something that is difficult to do or bear. *She worried about becoming a burden to her children in her old age.* **burden** *v.*
bureau *(**byoor**-oh) n* (*pl* bureaux *or* bureaus) an office.
burger *n* a hamburger.
burglar *n* a person who breaks into a house to steal. **burglary** *n,* **burgle** *v.*
burial *n* the burying of a dead body.
burn[1] *v* (burning, burnt *or* burned) **1** to destroy or damage something by heat or fire. **2** to be on fire.
burn[2] *n* an injury or mark caused by heat or fire.
burp *v* to make a sudden, loud noise in your throat, as air rises from your stomach.
burrow *n* a hole or tunnel made in the ground by an animal for use as a shelter. **burrow** *v.*
burst[1] *v* (bursting, burst) **1** to break open or apart suddenly, to explode. **2** to start doing something suddenly. *He burst into tears.*
burst[2] *n* **1** a break. *a burst in the pipe.* **2** a sudden, short period of something. *a burst of applause.*
bury *v* (buries, burying, buried) **1** to put a dead body in the ground. **2** to hide something under the ground or under something else.

bus *n* a large road vehicle used for carrying a lot of people.
bush *n* **1** a large plant with a lot of thick stems. **2 the bush** an area of wild land in Africa or Australia.
bushy *adj* (bushier, bushiest) growing thickly. *bushy eyebrows.*
business *(biz-nis)* *n* **1** making, selling or buying something to get money. **2** a company that makes, buys or sells things. **3** a thing that concerns you. *What I do is none of your business.*
busker *n* a person who plays or sings in the street for money. **busk** *v.*
bust[1] *n* **1** a woman's breasts. **2** a statue of a person's head and shoulders.
bust[2] *v (informal)* to break.
bustle *v* to rush about in a busy way.
busy *adj* (busier, busiest) **1** having a lot to do. **2** full of traffic, people, etc. *a busy street.* **busily** *adv.*
butcher *n* a person whose job is cutting up and selling meat.
butler *n* the chief male servant of a house.
butt[1] *n* **1** a barrel. *a water-butt.* **2** the handle end of a gun. **3** the end of a cigarette left after it has been smoked.
butt[2] *v* to hit with the head or horns. *The goat butted him in the stomach.*
butter *n* a soft, yellow food made from cream, used for cooking and for spreading on bread.
buttercup *n* a small, yellow wild flower.
butterfly *n* an insect with large, often patterned, wings.

Camberwell Beauty

buttocks *n pl* the two fleshy parts of your bottom.
button *n* **1** a small, round object used for fastening parts of clothing together. **2** a thing that you press to make a machine work.
buy *v* (buying, bought) to get something by paying money for it.
buzz *v* to make a humming noise like bees. **buzz** *n.*
buzzard *n* a large bird of prey.
by-election *n* an election of an MP in a single area, to replace somebody who has died or resigned.
bypass *n* a road that goes round a town instead of passing through it.
byte *n* a unit for measuring the amount of memory or information in a computer.

Cc

cab *n* **1** a taxi. **2** the part of a lorry, bus or train where the driver sits.
cabbage *n* a large, round vegetable with large green or purple leaves.
cabin *n* **1** a room in a ship, or a section of an aircraft. **2** a small, simple house, usually wooden.
cabinet *n* a cupboard. **the Cabinet** the senior members of a government.
cable *n* **1** strong, thick rope or wire. **2** a set of wires carrying electricity or telephone signals.
cable car *n* a box-shaped vehicle hanging from a moving cable, for carrying people up and down mountains or across valleys.
cable television *n* television programmes sent along cables, rather than transmitted by radio signals.
cackle *n* **1** the sound made by a hen. **2** a loud, unpleasant laugh. **cackle** *v.*
cactus *n* (*pl* cactuses *or* cacti) a prickly desert plant with a thick stem.
cadet *n* a person training to become a member of the armed forces or the police.
cadge *v* to ask for something and succeed in getting it.

café *(**kaf**-ay) n* a small restaurant where drinks and quick meals or snacks are served.
cage *n* a box with bars, in which birds or animals are kept.
cake *n* **1** a sweet food made from flour, butter, eggs, sugar, etc and baked in an oven. **2** a block of soap.
caked *adj* covered with a thick layer of something that gets hard when it dries.
calamity *n* a disaster.
calcium *n* a chemical element found in minerals such as limestone and chalk, as well as in teeth and bones.
calculate *v* to work out an answer by using maths. **calculation** *n.*
calculator *n* an electronic machine for doing sums.
calendar *n* a list of the days, weeks and months of the year.
calf *(rhymes with* laugh*) n (pl* calves) **1** a young cow, seal, elephant or whale. **2** the back part of your leg below the knee.
call *v* **1** to shout to somebody to get them to come to you. **2** to give a name to somebody. *They called the baby Jack.* **3** to telephone. **4** to visit. *I'll call at your house later.* **call off** to cancel. **call** *n*, **caller** *n.*
call-box *n* a telephone-box.
calligraphy *(ka-**lig**-raf-ee) n* handwriting as an art.
calling *n* a profession or occupation.
callous *adj* cruel and heartless.
calm *(rhymes with* arm*) adj* **1** quiet, still. *a calm sea.* **2** not excited or anxious. *Please keep calm!* **calm** *v*, **calm** *n.*
calorie *n* a unit for measuring the amount of energy provided by food.
calves *plural of* calf.
camcorder *n* a portable video camera and sound recorder.
came *past of* come.
camel *n* an animal with one or two humps on its back, used in desert countries for carrying goods and people.
camera *n* an instrument for taking still or moving photographs.

camouflage *v* to disguise something by making it look like other things that are around it. Animals in the wild are camouflaged so that they can hide from other creatures. **camouflage** *n.*
camp[1] *n* a place where people stay in tents or huts for a while.
camp[2] *v* to live in a tent for a while.
campaign *n* an organized series of actions planned in order to achieve a particular result. *a campaign to ban smoking in public places.*
campus *n* the grounds of a college or university.
can[1] *v* (could) **1** to be able to. *Can you swim?* **2** to be allowed to. *You can borrow my bike.*
can[2] *n* a metal container for food or drink, a tin.
canal *n* an artificial waterway for boats, or for taking water to fields.
canary *n* a small, yellow song-bird which is often kept in a cage as a pet.
cancel *v* (cancels, cancelling, cancelled) to stop something that has been arranged from happening. *The football match was cancelled.* **cancellation** *n.*
cancer *n* a serious disease which makes some body cells grow too fast.
candid *adj* saying openly what you think, honest. **candour** *n.*
candidate *n* **1** a person who takes part in a competition, especially for election to parliament or for a job. **2** a person taking a test or an exam.
candle *n* a stick of wax with a wick through the middle, burned to give light.
candlestick *n* a holder for a candle.
candy *n* a sweet.
cane *n* **1** a long, hollow stem of a plant such as bamboo. **2** a walking stick.

canine *adj* to do with dogs.
cannabis *n* a drug that is smoked or chewed.
canned *adj* put in cans. *canned peas.*
cannibal *n* a person who eats human flesh. **cannibalism** *n*.
cannon *n* a big, heavy gun.
cannot can not.
canoe *n* a light, narrow boat moved through the water by paddles.
canopy *n* a cloth covering hung over a throne, bed, etc.
can't can not.
canteen *n* a restaurant in a factory or other place of work.
canter *v* to gallop at an easy pace. **canter** *n*.
canvas *n* a coarse cloth used for tents, sails, shoes, etc and for painting on.
canvass *v* to go round asking people to vote for your political party.
canyon *n* a long valley with very steep sides, usually with a river flowing through it.
cap *n* **1** a soft, flat hat with a peak at the front. **2** a lid.
capable *adj* able to do something. **capability** *n*.
capacity *n* **1** the amount that something can hold. **2** the power or ability to do something.
cape *n* **1** a short cloak. **2** a piece of land that juts out into the sea.
capital *n* **1** the city where the government of a country is. **2** (*also* **capital letter**) a large letter. Capitals are used at the beginning of names and sentences. A, B, and C are capitals. **3** money invested to make more money or to start a business.
capital punishment *n* punishment of a crime by legally killing the criminal.
capsize *v* to turn upside down in the water. *The dinghy capsized.*
capsule *n* **1** a small pill containing medicine, which you swallow whole. **2** a part of a spacecraft which is designed to separate and travel on its own.
captain *n* **1** the officer in charge of a ship or aircraft. **2** a senior army officer. **3** the leader of a sports team.
caption *n* the words near a picture which explain what it is.
captivate *v* to fascinate somebody.
captive *n* a prisoner, a captured person or animal. **captivity** *n*.
captor *n* a person who captures another person or an animal.
capture *v* **1** to take somebody prisoner. **2** to take something by force. *Enemy forces captured the castle.*
car *n* **1** a vehicle with an engine and four wheels, for carrying four or five people. **2** a railway carriage.
caramel *n* **1** a type of soft toffee. **2** burnt sugar used as a flavouring.
carat *n* **1** a unit for measuring the purity of gold. **2** a unit for measuring the weight of precious stones.
caravan *n* **1** a home on wheels, pulled by a car or, previously, a horse. **2** a group of people and animals travelling together across a desert.

caravan

carbon *n* a chemical element found in diamonds, charcoal and in all living things.
carbon dioxide *n* a gas that is present in the air, breathed out by humans and animals.
carbon monoxide *n* a poisonous gas with no smell, found in car exhaust fumes.
carburettor *n* the part of a vehicle's engine where petrol is mixed with air.
carcass *n* the body of a dead animal.
card *n* **1** thick, stiff paper. **2** a piece of stiff paper with a picture or message on it. *a birthday card.* **3** a piece of

plastic with your name or other information on it. *a credit card.* **4** a playing-card. **5** a postcard.
cardboard *n* thick, stiff paper.
cardiac *adj* to do with the heart.
cardigan *n* a knitted woollen jacket.
cardinal *n* a senior priest in the Roman Catholic Church.
care[1] *v* **1** to think that something is important or interesting, to feel concerned about something. **2** to mind or be upset about something. *I don't care what you say.* **care for 1** to look after somebody or something. **2** to love somebody.
care[2] *n* **1** caring. **2** great attention. *The label on the box says "Handle with care".* **3** a worry. **take care** to be careful. **take care of** to look after.
career[1] *n* a job or profession that a person has for a long time. *a career in teaching.*
career[2] *v* to move fast and in an uncontrolled way.
careful *adj* taking great care, paying attention. **carefully** *adv.*
careless *adj* not paying enough attention to what you do, not careful. **carelessness** *n.*
caress *v* to touch gently and lovingly.
caretaker *n* a person who looks after a large building such as a school.
cargo *n* (*pl* cargoes) goods carried by a ship, truck, train or aircraft.
caricature *n* a drawing of somebody with their most distinctive features exaggerated in an amusing way.
carnation *n* a garden flower.
carnival *n* a public festival with street processions, colourful costumes and singing and dancing.
carnivore *n* an animal that eats meat. **carnivorous** *adj.*
carol *n* a Christian religious song of joy, especially sung at Christmas.
carp *n* a large freshwater fish.
car park *n* an area where people may park their cars.
carpenter *n* a person who makes things from wood. **carpentry** *n.*
carpet *n* a thick, soft floor covering, made of wool or a similar material.
carriage *n* **1** one of the parts of a train, in which the passengers travel. **2** a vehicle pulled by horses.
carrion *n* the dead and decaying body of an animal.
carrot *n* an orange-coloured root vegetable.
carry *v* (carries, carrying, carried) **1** to hold something and take it to another place. **2** (of a sound) to be able to be heard at a distance. **carry on** to continue. **carry out** to succeed in doing something.
cart *n* a wooden vehicle pulled by a horse, an ox or some other animal.
cartilage *(**kar**-til-ij)* *n* a strong, flexible material in your body, found especially around your joints.
carton *n* a plastic or cardboard box, especially for food or drink.
cartoon *n* **1** a funny drawing, in a newspaper or magazine. **2** a film made by photographing a series of drawings, in which the characters appear to move. **cartoonist** *n.*
cartridge *n* **1** a case containing the explosive that fires a bullet from a gun. **2** a small, closed container for ink.
cartwheel *n* a somersault in which you fall sideways, stand on your hands and then bring your legs over, finally returning to a standing position.
carve *v* **1** to shape a piece of wood or stone. **2** to slice meat to serve at a meal. **carving** *n.*

cartwheel

cascade[1] *n* a waterfall.
cascade[2] *v* to pour down like a waterfall.
case *n* **1** a box for carrying things or storing them. **2** an example, an instance. *a case of mistaken identity.* **3** a matter that needs to be investigated, especially one to be decided in a court of law.
cash[1] *n* money in paper notes and coins.

cash[2] *v* to exchange a cheque for money.
cashier *n* a person who receives and pays out money in a bank, shop or other business.
cashmere *n* very fine, soft wool from goats.
casino *n* (*pl* casinos) a building where people play gambling games.
cask *n* a wooden barrel, often used for storing alcoholic drinks.
casket *n* a small box for jewels.
casserole *n* **1** a dish made by cooking meat or vegetables in liquid inside an oven. **2** a container with a lid, in which food is cooked.
cassette *n* a plastic case containing magnetic tape used for recording and playing back sounds and music.
cassock *n* a long robe, usually black, worn by some Christian priests.
cast[1] *v* (casting, cast) **1** to throw or direct something. *The Moon cast a pale light over the garden.* **2** to give somebody a part in a play. **3** to pour liquid metal into a mould.
cast[2] *n* **1** all the people in a play or film. **2** something made in a mould.
castanets *n pl* a Spanish wooden percussion instrument which makes a clicking sound.
castaway *n* (*pl* castaways) a person whose boat has been shipwrecked.
castle *n* **1** a large building with thick, high walls, fortified against attack. **2** a chesspiece, also called a rook. See **chess**.
castrate *v* to remove a male animal's testicles so that it cannot reproduce.
casual *adj* **1** relaxed, careless or not serious. *She has a casual attitude towards work.* **2** not smart or formal. *casual clothes.* **3** not planned, happening by chance. *a casual meeting.*
casualty *n* a person who is killed or injured in a war or an accident.
casualty department *n* a part of a hospital where people with injuries or sudden illnesses go for treatment.
cat *n* **1** a furry animal often kept as a pet. **2** one of the group of large wild animals that includes lions and tigers.
catacombs *(**kat**-a-kooms) n pl* an underground burial chamber.
catalogue *n* a list of things, such as the books in a library or the items in a shop.
catalyst *(**kat**-a-list) n* **1** a substance that speeds up a chemical reaction. **2** something that causes a change.
catamaran *n* a boat that looks like two boats joined together side by side.
catapult *n* a Y-shaped stick with a piece of elastic fixed to it, for shooting stones.
cataract *n* **1** a condition of the eye, which causes blindness. **2** a waterfall.
catarrh *(kat-**ar**) n* the thick liquid that forms in your nose and throat when you have a cold.
catastrophe *(kat-**as**-trof-ee) n* a great disaster. **catastrophic** *(kat-a-**strof**-ik) adj.*
catch[1] *v* (catching, caught) **1** to get hold of something that is moving. *I caught the ball.* **2** to be early enough for a bus, train, etc. **3** to get an illness. *catch a cold.* **4** to notice somebody doing something wrong. *The store detective caught her stealing.* **5** to hit something hard. *The tennis racquet caught her on the chin.* **6** to hear something. *I didn't catch what he said.* **catch on** to become popular. **catch up 1** to reach or pass somebody in front, after following. **2** to spend time doing something that you should have done before. *She has a lot of school work to catch up on.*
catch[2] *n* **1** catching something. **2** a small device for keeping a door, box, etc closed. **3** a hidden difficulty.
catch-phrase *n* a phrase that becomes popular for a time, usually because a famous person has said it.
catchy *adj* (catchier, catchiest) easy to remember. *a catchy tune.*
category *n* a class or group.
caterpillar *n* the larva stage in the growth of a butterfly or moth.

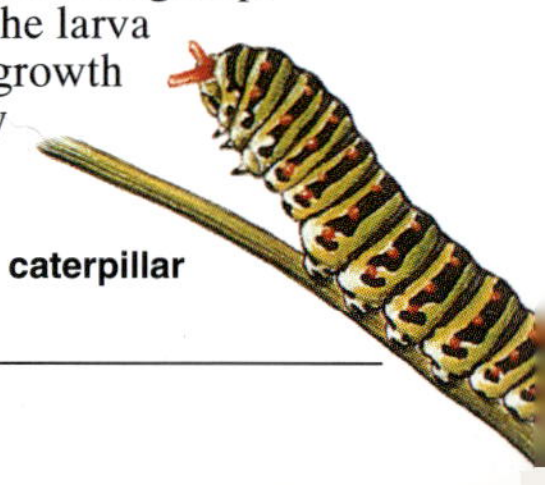

caterpillar

cathedral *n* the main church of an area, that has a bishop in charge of it.

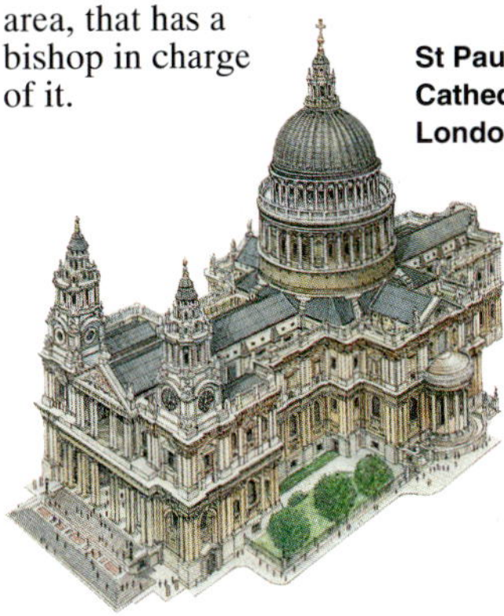

St Paul's Cathedral, London

Catholic *n* a member of the part of the Christian Church that has the Pope as its leader. **Catholic** *adj*.
catkin *n* the hanging, fluffy flower of the hazel and some other trees.
cattle *n* cows, bulls and oxen.
caught *past of* catch.
cauliflower *n* a vegetable with large, green leaves surrounding the edible round, white part in the middle.
cause¹ *v* to make something happen.
cause² *n* **1** what makes something happen. *Have they found the cause of the explosion?* **2** an aim which a person or group supports. *The money was donated to a good cause.*
causeway *n* (*pl* causeways) a raised path crossing marshland or water.
caution¹ *n* care, being careful. *Proceed with caution.*
caution² *v* to give somebody a formal warning.
cautious *adj* careful.
cavalry *n* soldiers on horseback.
cave *n* a large hole in the side of a hill or cliff, or under the ground.
caveman *n* (*pl* cavemen) a person who lived in a cave in prehistoric times.
cavern *n* a large, deep cave.
caviar *n* the salted eggs of a large fish called a sturgeon, eaten as a delicacy.
cavity *n* a space or hole in something solid.
CD *short for* compact disc.
CD-ROM (*short for* compact disc, read-only memory) a disk that stores large amounts of information which you can see on a computer screen but not alter.
cease *v* to stop.
cedar *n* a large evergreen tree.
ceiling *n* the inner roof of a room.
celebrate *v* to have a party or do something else to show that it is a special occasion. *We went to a restaurant to celebrate my birthday.* **celebration** *n*.
celebrity *n* a famous person.
celery *n* a vegetable with long, crisp stalks, usually eaten raw in salads.
cell *n* **1** a very small unit of living matter in animals and plants. **2** a small room in a prison, monastery or convent.

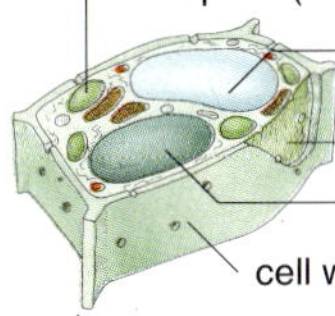

plant cell

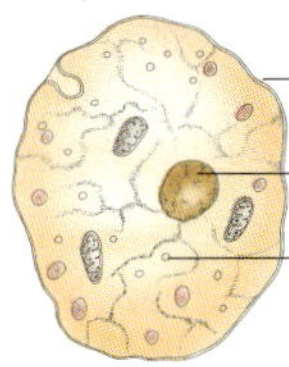

animal cell

cellar *n* an underground room for storing things.
cello *(chel-o)* *n* (*pl* cellos) a stringed instrument like a large violin. **cellist** *n*.
cellular *adj* **1** to do with cells. **2** with many holes.
cellulose *n* the substance present in the cell walls of plants.
Celsius *another word for* centigrade.
cement *n* a grey powder that becomes hard when mixed with water. Cement is used in building.
cemetery *n* a place where dead people are buried.
censor *v* to remove from books, films, etc any part that might offend people. **censorship** *n*.

census *n* an official counting of all the people in a country or in an area.
cent *n* a coin used in many countries of the world, such as the USA and Australia. *There are 100 cents in a US dollar.*
centenary *n* the hundredth anniversary of something.
centi- *prefix* one hundred, one hundredth. *centimetre* (= one hundredth of a metre).
centigrade *adj* measured on the temperature scale where water freezes at 0 degrees and boils at 100 degrees. *Twenty degrees centigrade can be written as 20ºC.*
centimetre *n* a measure of length. There are 100 centimetres in a metre.
centipede *n* a small creature with a long body and many legs.

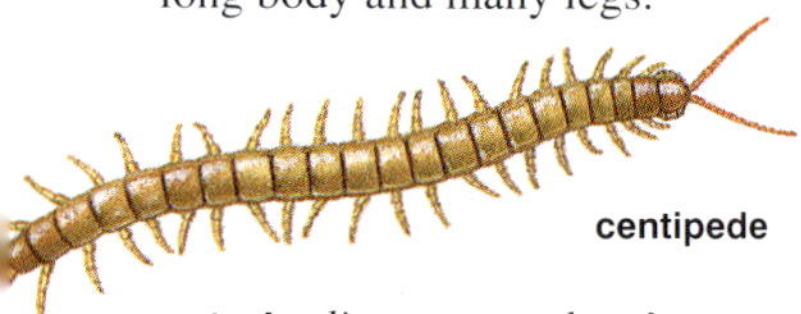

centipede

central *adj* at or near the centre. **centrally** *adv*.
centre *n* **1** the middle part or point of something. **2** a building where people meet for an activity of a particular kind. *a sports centre.*
centurion *n* an officer in the ancient Roman army.
century *n* **1** one hundred years. **2** a score of 100 runs in cricket.
ceramic *adj* made of baked clay.
ceramics *n pl* ceramic objects.
cereal *n* **1** grain crops such as maize, rice or wheat used for food. **2** a breakfast food made from grain.
ceremonial *adj* with ceremony, formal.
ceremony *n* a formal event such as a wedding, funeral, coronation, etc.
certain *adj* **1** sure. *Are you certain you locked the door?* **2** particular and, though known, not named. *a certain person I know.* **certainty** *n*.
certificate *n* a piece of paper that is official proof of something. *a birth certificate.*
CFC *short for* chlorofluorocarbon, a gas which damages the ozone layer.
chaff *n* the outer parts of grain which need to be removed before the grain is used as food.
chaffinch *n* small song-bird.
chain *n* a line of rings, called links, joined together.
chair *n* a piece of furniture for sitting on.
chalet *(**shall**-ay)* *n* a small, wooden house, found especially in Alpine regions.
chalk *n* **1** a soft white rock. **2** a piece of a substance like this, used for writing on blackboards.
challenge *v* **1** to invite somebody to take part in a fight or contest. *challenge somebody to a duel.* **2** to test or question somebody or something. *She challenged my statement.* **challenge** *n*.
chamber *n* a room.
chameleon *(ka-**mee**-lee-un)* *n* a lizard that changes colour to match its surroundings.**champagne** *(sham-**pain**)* *n* white wine with lots of bubbles in it.
champion[1] *n* a person who has beaten all others in a game, competition, etc.
champion[2] *v* to strongly support a particular cause.
championship *n* a competition to find the best person or team.
chance *n* **1** a possibility of something happening. *They have no chance of winning.* **2** an opportunity to do something. *She had a chance to meet the president.* **3** luck, something that happens that you cannot control. *We met by chance.* **take a chance** to take a risk.
chancellor *n* the head of an organization or of a country.
Chancellor of the Exchequer *n* the minister in the British government who is in charge of finance.
chancy *adj* (chancier, chanciest) risky.
change[1] *v* **1** to become different or make something different. **2** to exchange one thing for another. *If it doesn't work, take it back to the shop*

and change it. **3** to put on different clothes. **4** to get off one train, bus, etc and get on another.

change[2] *n* **1** changing something. **2** the money given back when you give too much money for something. **3** something different from what is usual. *We usually go to school by car, but today we're walking for a change.* **changeable** *adj*.

channel *n* **1** a narrow stretch of water joining two seas. **2** a narrow passage for water to run through. **3** a television station.

chant *n* **1** a word or group of words repeated over and over again. **2** a religious song or prayer. **chant** *n.*

chaos *(**kay**-os) n* complete confusion. **chaotic** *adj*.

chapel *n* a small church, or part of a larger church.

chaplain *n* a clergyman or clergywoman who works in a school, hospital, prison, etc.

chapter *n* one section of a book.

char *v* (charring, charred) to burn something until it is black.

character *n* **1** what sort of person you are. **2** one of the people in a book or play. *Mowgli is a character in* The Jungle Book. **3** a letter, number or other symbol used in printing.

characteristic[1] *n* a quality or feature that is typical of something and that makes it different from other things.

characteristic[2] *adj* typical.

charcoal *n* a black substance made by burning wood without much air.

charge[1] *v* **1** to ask a certain price for something. **2** to rush forwards in an aggressive way. *She charged into the shop and demanded her money back.* **3** to formally accuse somebody of doing something wrong. *He was arrested and charged with murder.* **4** to pass an electrical current through a battery, etc to give it power.

charge[2] *n* **1** a price or fee. **2** formally accusing somebody of a crime. **3** an attack. **4** the electricity carried by something. **in charge of** in control of and responsible for something.

chariot *n* a horse-drawn vehicle used for fighting and racing long ago.

chariot

charity *n* **1** an organization that raises money to help people in need. **2** help given to people in need.

charm *n* **1** the power of attracting, delighting, etc. **2** an object that is believed to have magic power. **3** a magic spell. **charm** *v.*

charming *adj* pleasant and attractive.

chart *n* **1** a table that gives information about something. **2** a map for sailors. **chart** *v.*

charter *n* a written statement of rights or permission to do something.

chase *v* to run after and try to catch somebody or something.

chasm *(**kaz**-um) n* a deep gap in the ground.

chat *v* (chats, chatting, chatted) to talk in a friendly way. **chat** *n*, **chatty** *adj.*

château *(**sha**-toe) n* (*pl* châteaux) a castle or mansion in France.

chatter *v* **1** to talk quickly and continuously about unimportant things. **2** (of teeth) to knock together repeatedly because of fear or cold.

chauffeur *(**show**-fur) n* a person paid to drive their employer's car.

cheap *adj* not expensive, low in price.

cheat[1] *v* to act dishonestly in order to get something for yourself.

cheat[2] *n* a person who cheats.

check[1] *v* **1** to make sure that something is right. *Check your spelling.* **2** to stop or hold back for a short time. *He nearly screamed, but checked himself in time.*

check² *n* **1** the checking of something. **2** a pattern made up of squares.
check-in *n* a desk at an airport where you go to show your ticket, etc before getting on a flight. **check in** *v*.
checkout *n* a counter in a supermarket where you pay for what you buy.
check-up *n* an examination by a doctor to make sure you are healthy.
cheek *n* **1** the side of your face, below your eye. **2** rude and disrespectful behaviour. *She had the cheek to ask me for money.*
cheeky *adj* (cheekier, cheekiest) rude and disrespectful. **cheekily** *adv*.
cheer *v* **1** to shout encouragement or approval. **2** to make somebody happier or less worried. **cheer up** to make or become happier.
cheerful *adj* looking and feeling happy.
cheese *n* a solid food made from milk.
cheetah *n* a wild cat with a spotted coat found in Africa and Asia. Cheetahs can run very fast.

cheetah

chef *(sheff)* *n* a head cook in a restaurant or hotel.
chemical¹ *n* a substance used in chemistry.
chemical² *adj* to do with chemistry, made by chemistry.
chemist *n* **1** a person who makes and sells medicines. **2** a scientist who studies or works in chemistry.
chemistry *n* a branch of science that is about what substances are made of and how they work together.
cheque *(check)* *n* a piece of paper which, when filled in and signed, tells a bank to pay money to somebody.
cherish *v* to value highly, to care for lovingly.
cherry *n* a small, round, usually red fruit with a stone.
chess *n* a game for two people, each with 16 pieces, called chesspieces, played on a board with black and white squares.

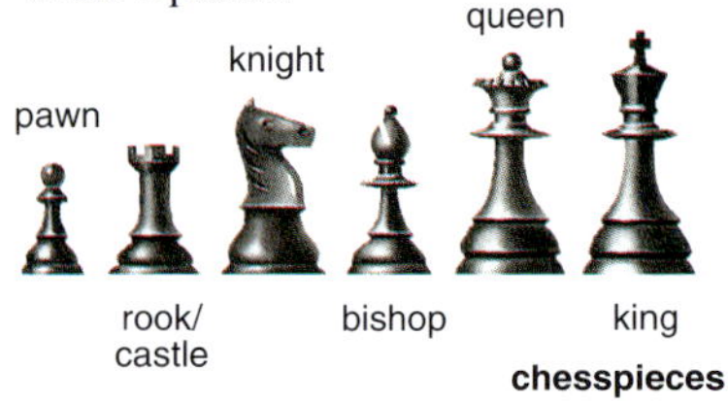

chesspieces

chest *n* **1** the top part of the front of your body. **2** a large, strong box with a lid. **chest of drawers** a piece of furniture with drawers.
chestnut *n* **1** a large tree with prickly fruits containing shiny, red-brown nuts. **2** this edible nut. See **nut**.
chew *v* to break up food in your mouth with your teeth.
chewing-gum *n* a type of sweet that you chew for a long time but do not swallow.
chick *n* a very young bird.
chicken *n* **1** a young hen. **2** the meat from a hen. **3** a coward.
chickenpox *n* a disease that causes red, itchy spots on your skin.
chief¹ *n* a ruler or leader.
chief² *adj* most important, main.
child *n* (*pl* children) **1** a young boy or girl. **2** somebody's son or daughter.
childhood *n* the time when you are a child.
childish *adj* like a child, silly, immature. **childishness** *n*.
child minder *n* a person who looks after children when their parents are at work.
children *plural of* child.
chill¹ *v* to make something cold.
chill² *n* **1** a feeling of coldness. **2** a slight cold or fever.
chilly *adj* (chillier, chilliest) rather cold.
chime *v* to make a ringing sound, like a bell. **chime** *n*.
chimney *n* (*pl* chimneys) a kind of pipe in a building that allows the smoke from a fire to escape.
chimpanzee *n* an African ape.

chin *n* the part of your face below your mouth.
china *n* **1** very thin, fine pottery. **2** cups, plates, etc made from this.
chink *n* **1** a narrow opening, a gap. **2** a light, ringing sound like that of glasses hitting together.
chip[1] *n* **1** a piece of fried potato. **2** a tiny electronic device made of silicon, which can hold a lot of information and is used in computers. **3** a small piece broken off something.
chip[2] *v* (chips, chipping, chipped) to break a small piece off something.
chipmunk *n* a small member of the squirrel family.
chiropodist *(ki-**rop**-o-dist)* *n* a person who treats people's feet.
chirp *v* to make short, high sounds like a bird. **chirp** *n*.
chisel *n* a sharp tool used for shaping wood or stone. **chisel** *v*.
chivalry *(**shiv**-ul-ree)* *n* **1** polite and helpful behaviour. **2** the rules of behaviour which knights in the Middle Ages were expected to follow.
chive *n* a herb related to the onion.
chlorine *n* a strong-smelling gas that is used to kill germs in water and to make cleaning products.
chlorophyll *n* the green colouring in plants' cells which allows them to absorb energy from sunlight. See **cell**.
chocolate *n* a brown sweet or drink made from the ground, roasted seeds of the cacao tree.
choice *n* **1** choosing. **2** a thing or person that is chosen. *a good choice.* **3** all the things that you can choose from. *a wide choice of colours.*
choir *(kwire)* *n* a group of people trained to sing together.
choke[1] *v* **1** to be unable to breathe because something is blocking your throat or lungs. **2** to kill somebody by squeezing their neck.
choke[2] *n* a control in a vehicle that helps it start when the engine is cold.
choose *v* (choosing, chose, chosen) **1** to make a choice between two or more possibilities. **2** to decide.
chop[1] *v* (chops, chopping, chopped) to cut into pieces with an axe or a knife.
chop[2] *n* a thick slice of lamb or pork with a piece of bone in it.
chopsticks *n pl* a pair of sticks for eating with, used especially in China and Japan.

chopsticks

choral *(**kor**-al)* *adj* sung by a choir. *choral music.*
chord *(kord)* *n* **1** a group of musical notes sounded together. **2** a straight line joining any two points on a curve. See **circle**.
chore *n* a boring task.
choreography *(kor-ee-**og**-ra-fee)* *n* the art of arranging the steps and movements of a dance. **choreographer** *n*
chorus *(**kawr**-us)* *n* **1** the part of a song that is repeated after each verse. **2** a choir. **3** music for a choir.
christen *v* to give a name to a baby and accept them into the Christian Church in a special ceremony.
christening *n* a ceremony in which a child is given a name and accepted into the Christian Church.
Christian *n* a person who believes in and follows the teachings of Jesus Christ. **Christian** *adj*.
Christianity *n* the religion based on the teachings of Jesus Christ.
Christmas *n* 25 December, when Christians celebrate the birth of Jesus.
chrome, chromium *n* a hard silver-coloured metal.
chromosome *n* a part of a cell in an animal or a plant, containing parts called genes which determine the animal or plant's characteristics.
chronic *adj* **1** (of an illness) lasting for a long time. *chronic asthma.* **2** *(informal)* very bad. **chronically** *adv*.

chronicle *(kron-ik-ul) n* a record of events in the order in which they happened. **chronicle** *v*.
chronological *adj* in the order in which events happened. **chronologically** *adv*.
chrysalis *n* a stage between caterpillar and adult in the development of a moth or butterfly.
chrysanthemum *n* a garden flower.
chubby *adj* (chubbier, chubbiest) rather fat.
chuck *v (informal)* to throw something in a careless way.
chuckle *v* to laugh quietly.
chunk *n* a thick piece of something. *chunks of meat.*
church *n* a building where Christians go to pray.
churchyard *n* the land around a church, often where people are buried.
churn *n* a container in which cream is shaken about to make butter.
chutney *n* a food made from fruit or vegetables with vinegar, sugar and spices. It is eaten cold with meat, cheese, etc.
cider *n* an alcoholic drink made from apples.
cigar *n* tobacco rolled in a tobacco leaf for smoking.
cigarette *n* tobacco rolled in thin paper for smoking.
cinder *n* a piece of partly burned coal or wood.
cinema *n* a place where people go to watch films.
cinnamon *n* a spice obtained from the bark of an Asian tree. See **spice**.
cipher *n* a secret code.
circa *prep* the Latin word for "about", used with dates. You can also write circa as "c". *He died circa 1782.*
circle[1] *n* **1** a perfectly round, flat shape, or a curved line around this shape. **2** anything in the shape of a circle. **3** the upper floor of seats in a theatre.
circle[2] *v* to make a circle around something.
circuit *n* **1** a circular racecourse. **2** the complete path of an electric current.

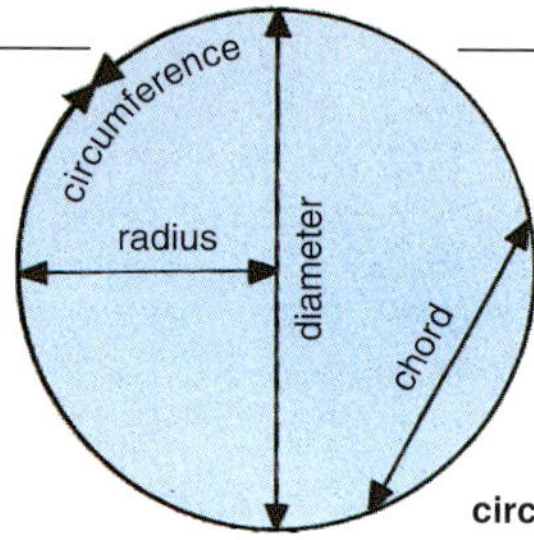

circle

circular *adj* **1** in the shape of a circle, round. **2** beginning and ending at the same point. *a circular walk.*
circulate *v* to move or send round. *Blood circulates through your body.*
circulation *n* **1** the movement of blood around the body. **2** the number of copies of a newspaper or magazine sold.
circumcision *n* the cutting away of the loose skin at the end of a boy's or a man's penis for religious or medical reasons.
circumference *n* the distance around the outside of a circle.
circumstance *n* a fact or condition connected with something. *He died in mysterious circumstances.*
circus *n* a travelling show with clowns, acrobats, animals and other acts, usually performed in a tent.
cistern *n* a water tank.
citadel *n* a fortress protecting a city.
citizen *n* **1** a person who has the legal right to live in a particular country. *She is an American citizen.* **2** a person who lives in a town or city.
citrus fruit *n* a fruit such as an orange, lemon or lime.
city *n* a large or important town.
civil *adj* **1** to do with the citizens of a country, etc. **2** to do with ordinary people, not the armed forces. **3** polite.
civilian *n* a person who is not in the armed forces. **civilian** *adj*.
civilization *n* a human society that is highly developed and organized.
civilized *adj* living in a highly developed, well-organized society.
civil servant *n* a person who works for any of the government departments (the **civil service**).

civil war *n* a war between groups of people within the same country.
claim *v* **1** to say that something is yours. *You should claim your prize.* **2** to say that something is true. *He claims he's a millionaire.* **claim** *n.*
clamber *v* to climb using your hands and feet.
clammy *adj* (clammier, clammiest) damp and sticky.
clamp *n* a metal object for holding things in place. **clamp** *v.*
clan *n* a large group of related families, especially in Scotland.
clap[1] *v* (claps, clapping, clapped) to hit the palms of your hands together to make a noise, especially to show appreciation.
clap[2] *n* **1** an act of clapping. **2** the sudden loud noise made by thunder.
clarify *v* (clarifies, clarifying, clarified) to make something easier to understand. **clarification** *n.*
clarinet *n* a woodwind instrument with a single reed.
clarity *n* clearness.
clash *v* **1** to fight or disagree violently. **2** to make a loud, crashing sound like metal objects being hit together. **3** (of colours) to not go well together. **4** (of two events) to happen at the same time, so that you cannot attend both. *The party clashes with my violin lesson.* **clash** *n.*
clasp[1] *v* to hold something tightly.
clasp[2] *n* a small device for fastening jewellery, a bag, etc.
class *n* **1** a group of pupils or students who are taught together. **2** a school lesson. **3** a group of people or things that are alike in some way.
classic[1] *adj* generally considered to be very good and important. *classic novels.*
classic[2] *n* a book, film, etc that is generally considered to be very good and important.
classical music *n* serious music that people listen to over a long period.
clatter *v* to bang together noisily, making a lot of short, loud sounds.
clause *(klawz)* *n* **1** a part of a sentence containing a verb. **2** one section in a legal document.
claustrophobia *(klos-tro-**foh**-bee-yuh)* *n* the fear of being in enclosed spaces. **claustrophobic** *adj.*
claw *n* a curved, pointed nail on an animal's foot.
clay *n* a soft, sticky earth that becomes hard when baked.
clean *adj* free from dirt and unwanted marks. **clean** *v.*
clear[1] *adj* **1** easy to see, hear or understand. *a clear message.* **2** easy to see through. *clear glass.* **3** free from obstacles or dangers. *Make sure the road is clear before you cross.* **4** not cloudy. *a clear sky.*
clear[2] *v* to make or become clear.
clearing *n* a small area in a forest where there are no trees growing.
clergy *n* the people who conduct religious services.
clerk *(rhymes with* dark*)* *n* a worker in an office or bank who looks after the accounts, records, etc.
clever *adj* (cleverer, cleverest) **1** quick to learn, intelligent, skilful. **2** skilfully made. *a clever plan.*
cliché *(**klee**-shay)* *n* a phrase that has been used so much that it is no longer effective or interesting.
client *n* a customer.
cliff *n* a very steep, high rock, especially by the sea.
climate *n* the usual weather that a particular place has. *a warm climate.*
climax *n* the most exciting and important part of something.
climb *v* to go up, sometimes using both hands and feet to hold on. **climb** *n,* **climber** *n.*
cling *v* (clinging, clung) to hold tightly to something.
clinic *n* a place where you can go for medical advice or treatment.
clip[1] *n* **1** a small device for holding things together. *a paper-clip.* **2** a short piece from a film or TV programme.
clip[2] *v* (clips, clipping, clipped) **1** to fasten something to something else. **2** to cut with scissors or shears.

clipboard *n* a board with a clip at the top, for holding papers.
clipper *n* a fast sailing ship.
cloak *n* a loose coat with no sleeves.
cloakroom *n* **1** a place to leave your coat. **2** a toilet.
clock *n* an instrument which shows the time.
clockwise *adj, adv* going round in the same direction as the hands of a clock.
clockwork *n* a mechanism in some clocks, toys, etc, which makes them work when wound up with a key.
clod *n* a lump of earth.
clog[1] *v* (clogs, clogging, clogged) to block up.
clog[2] *n* a heavy, wooden shoe, originally from the Netherlands.
cloister *n* a covered passageway around a quadrangle in a monastery or other building.
clone *n* an animal or a plant produced in a laboratory from the cells of another animal or plant, so that it is identical to the original. **clone** *v.*
close[1] *(rhymes with* dose*) adj, adv* **1** near. *We stood close together.* **2** having a good relationship. *I am close to my sister.* **3** with not much difference between the winner and loser. *It was a close contest.* **4** careful and thorough. *Have a closer look.* **5** uncomfortably warm, stuffy.
close[2] *(rhymes with* doze*) v* **1** to shut. **2** to bring or come to an end. **close down** to close for good.
closure *n* the closing of something.
cloth *n* **1** a material woven or knitted from wool, cotton, etc. **2** a piece of cloth used for cleaning.
clothes *n pl* things to wear.
clothing *n* clothes.
cloud *n* a grey or white mass floating in the sky, made of tiny drops of water.
cloudy *adj* (cloudier, cloudiest) **1** covered with clouds. **2** (of a liquid) not clear.
clout *v* to hit something hard. **clout** *n.*
clover *n* a small plant with leaves divided into three parts and with pink or white flowers.
clown *n* a person in a circus who performs funny tricks.
club *n* **1** a heavy stick with one thicker end, used as a weapon. **2** a stick used for hitting the ball in golf. **3** a group that people join to do things together. **4 clubs** one of the four suits in a pack of cards, with the symbol ♣ on them.
cluck *v* to make a noise like a hen.
clue *n* something that helps to solve a puzzle or crime.
clump *n* a group of things growing close together.
clumsy *adj* (clumsier, clumsiest) awkward, lacking skill. **clumsily** *adv,* **clumsiness** *n.*
clung *past of* cling.
cluster *n* a group of people or things close together, a bunch. **cluster** *v.*
clutch[1] *v* to seize or hold tightly.
clutch[2] *n* **1** a firm hold. **2** the control in a car that you press with your foot when you change gear. **3** a group of eggs in a nest.
Co *short for* company.
co- *prefix* together, working with. *cooperate, co-author.*
coach[1] *n* **1** a bus used for long journeys. **2** a part of a train, which carries passengers. **3** a carriage pulled by horses. **4** a sports instructor.
coach[2] *v* to teach somebody something, especially a sport.
coal *n* a black mineral that burns slowly and gives out heat.
coalition *(koh-a-**lish**-un) n* the joining together of political parties for a period of time.
coarse *adj* **1** rough in texture, not fine. **2** rude, not refined. *coarse language.*
coast *n* the land beside the sea.
coastguard *n* a person who watches the sea for ships in danger.
coat[1] *n* **1** a piece of outdoor clothing with sleeves that you wear over your other clothes. **2** a covering. *a coat of paint.* **3** an animal's fur.
coat[2] *v* to cover with a thin layer of something. *raisins coated with chocolate.* **coating** *n.*
coax *v* to persuade gently. *She coaxed him into giving her the gun.*

cobblestones *n pl* rounded stones used in the past for making road surfaces.

cobra *n* a poisonous, hooded snake.

cobra

cobweb *n* a fine net made by a spider to catch insects for food.

cocaine *n* an illegal drug which is addictive.

cock *n* **1** a fully grown male chicken. **2** any male bird.

cockatoo *n* a parrot with a crest on its head.

cockerel *n* a young cock.

cockle *n* a type of shellfish.

cockney *n* (*pl* cockneys) a person from the East End of London.

cockpit *n* **1** the part of a small plane where the pilot sits. **2** the part of a racing car where the driver sits.

cockroach *n* a large, black beetle found in dirty places.

cocoa *n* chocolate powder made from the seeds of the cacao tree.

coconut *n* the very large, oval nut of a tree called the coco palm. Coconuts are hairy on the outside and have sweet, white flesh and juice inside.

cocoon *n* a silky case made by a caterpillar to protect itself while it turns into a moth or butterfly.

cod *n* a large, edible sea fish.

code *n* **1** a way of sending secret messages. **2** a set of rules. *the Highway Code.*

coeducation *n* the education of boys and girls together.

coffee *n* a hot, brown drink made from the roasted and ground beans of the coffee plant.

coffee berries

coffee beans (roasted berries)

coffee plant

coffin *n* a box in which a dead person is buried or cremated.

cog *n* **1** a wheel with sharp teeth around the rim, used in machinery to turn another wheel. **2** one of the teeth around the rim of such a wheel.

coil *v* to wind something round and round to form loops or spirals. **coil** *n.*

coin *n* a piece of metal money.

coincide *v* to happen at the same time.

coincidence *n* when two or more things happen at the same time by chance. *It was a coincidence that Bob and Jim were wearing the same tie.*

coke *n* a solid, black substance made from coal and burnt as fuel.

cold[1] *adj* **1** having a low temperature. **2** unfriendly. **cold** *n*, **coldness** *n.*

cold[2] *n* an illness which makes you sneeze and gives you a sore throat, a cough, etc.

cold-blooded *adj* **1** cruel and unfeeling. **2** (of fish or reptiles) having a body temperature that changes according to the surroundings.

collaborate *v* to work together with somebody. **collaboration** *n.*

collage *n* a picture made by sticking down small pieces of paper or other materials onto a surface.

collapse *v* **1** to fall down or inwards. **2** to fail completely. *The business has collapsed.* **collapse** *n.*

collapsible *adj* folding.

collar *n* **1** the part of a shirt or other clothing that goes around your neck. **2** a band of leather, metal, etc put around an animal's neck.

collect *v* **1** to gather or bring together. *The teacher collected our books.* **2** to bring a number of things together because you are interested in them. *to collect stamps.* **3** to fetch. *Mum usually collects me from school.* **collection** *n*, **collector** *n.*

college *n* a place where people can go to study after they have left school.
collide *v* to crash together. *The two lorries collided.*
collie *n* a breed of sheepdog.
colliery *n* a coalmine.
collision *n* a crash.
colon *n* the punctuation mark (:).
colonel ***(kern**-ul)* *n* a senior officer in the army.
colony *n* **1** country that has been settled in by people from a foreign country, and which is still governed by that country. **2** a group of insects or animals that live together. *a colony of ants.* **colonial** *adj,* **colonize** *v.*
colossal *adj* huge, vast.
colour[1] *n* red, blue, yellow, green, etc.
colour[2] *v* to put colour on something.
colt *n* a young male horse.
column *n* **1** a tall, round pillar. **2** a long, narrow piece of writing running down a page.
coma *n* a state of deep unconsciousness.
comb[1] *n* a small object with a row of teeth, used for making hair tidy.
comb[2] *v* **1** to make hair tidy with a comb. **2** to search a place thoroughly.
combat *n* fighting, a battle.
combine *v* to join or mix together. *Combine the eggs and butter in a large bowl.* **combination** *n.*
combine harvester *n* a farm machine that cuts and threshes grain.

combine harvester

combustion *n* burning.
come *v* (coming, came, come) **1** to move towards a place. *Come here!* **2** to arrive. *A letter came for you today.* **3** to happen. *Friday comes before Saturday.* **4** to become. *His wish came true.* **5** to go with somebody. *I'm going out. Do you want to come?* **6** to add up to something. *The bill came to £12.*
comedian *n* an entertainer who makes people laugh.
comedy *n* a funny play or film.
comet *n* an object with a tail-like trail of light, which moves around the Sun.
comfort[1] *v* to make somebody less worried or upset.
comfort[2] *n* **1** a pleasant condition of being relaxed, happy, warm, etc. **2** a person or thing that gives you comfort.
comfortable *adj* **1** pleasant to sit in, to wear, etc. *a comfortable chair.* **2** at ease, free from pain or worry. *Sit down and make yourself comfortable.*
comic[1] *adj* funny.
comic[2] *n* a children's paper with stories told in pictures.
comical *adj* funny.
comma *n* the punctuation mark (,) used in writing to show a pause.
command *v* **1** to order somebody to do something. **2** to be in charge of something. *He commanded a large regiment.* **command** *n.*
commence *v* to begin.
comment *n* a remark about somebody or something. **comment** *v.*
commentary *n* a description of something, especially a sports event, as it is happening.
commentator *n* a person giving a commentary.
commerce *n* buying and selling, trade.
commercial[1] *adj* to do with trade.
commercial[2] *n* an advertisement on television or radio.
commit *v* (commits, committing, committed) to do, to carry out. *She committed a crime.*
committee *n* a group of people who are chosen by a larger group to plan and organize things on its behalf. *Our club's committee meets once a month.*
common[1] *adj* **1** found in large numbers. **2** happening often. **3** shared by two or more people or things. *characteristics common to apes and humans.* **4** ordinary, not special.

common[2] *n* an area of grassy land where anyone can go.
common sense *n* sensible thinking.
communicate *v* to pass on information, ideas or feelings to other people.
communication *n* the passing of information from one person to another.
Communion *n* a ceremony in the Christian Church at which people eat blessed bread and drink wine in memory of the death of Christ.
communism *n* the political belief that there should be no private property and that everything should be owned by the people. **communist** *n.*
community *n* all the people who live in a place.
commuter *n* a person who travels some distance every day to and from work. **commute** *v.*
compact *adj* small, taking up little space.
compact disc *n* a plastic disc containing digitally stored information or music, played on a compact disc player.
companion *n* a person who you spend time with.
company *n* **1** a business organization that makes or sells things. **2** being together with somebody. *She has a dog for company.* **3** a gathering of people, especially guests.
compare *v* to look at things to see how alike or different they are. *We compared the two shirts and decided to buy the red one.* **comparison** *n,* **comparative** *adj.*
compartment *n* a section separated off inside something. *The drawer has a secret compartment.*
compass *n* an instrument that shows direction, used for finding the way.

compass

compasses *n pl* an instrument for drawing circles.
compassion *n* a feeling of pity or sympathy for somebody who is suffering. **compassionate** *adj.*
compel *v* (compels, compelling, compelled) to force somebody to do something. *I felt compelled to tell the truth.* **compulsion** *n.*
compensate *v* to make up for loss or injury. **compensation** *n.*
compete *v* to take part in a contest. *to compete in a race.*
competent *adj* able to do things efficiently and effectively. **competence** *n.*
competition *n* a game or contest in which a number of people take part to see who is the best.
competitive *adj* **1** liking to compete with others. **2** organized as a competition. *competitive sports.*
competitor *n* a person who takes part in a competition.
complain *v* **1** to say that you are not pleased with something. *We complained that the food was cold.* **2** to say that you are ill or in pain. *He complained of a headache.*
complaint *n* **1** saying you are not pleased with something. **2** an illness.
complete[1] *adj* **1** finished. **2** whole, with no parts missing. **3** total, perfect. *I felt a complete fool.*
complete[2] *v* to finish something. **completion** *n.*
complex[1] *adj* complicated, made up of many different parts. **complexity** *n.*
complex[2] *n* a group of buildings, or one building with several different parts. *a sports complex.*
complexion *n* the natural colour and appearance of the skin of a person's face.
complicated *adj* made up of many different parts or aspects, difficult to understand. **complication** *n.*
compliment *n* a remark that expresses admiration. **compliment** *v.*
complimentary *adj* **1** showing admiration. **2** given free. *complimentary tickets to the theatre.*

component *n* one of the parts that make up something. *car components.*
compose *v* to write a piece of music, poem, story, etc. **composed of** made up of. *Water is composed of hydrogen and oxygen.* **composition** *n.*
composer *n* a person who writes music.
compound *n* something made up of separate parts or elements.
comprehend *v* to understand.
comprehensible *adj* easy to understand.
comprehension *n* understanding.
comprehensive *adj* including everything that is needed.
comprehensive school *n* a school where children of all abilities are taught together.
compress *v* to press or squeeze something into a small space. **compression** *n.*
compromise *n* an agreement between two people or groups, each giving up part of what they originally wanted. **compromise** *v.*
compulsive *adj* unable to stop yourself. *a compulsive gambler.*
compulsory *adj* having to be done, obligatory. *English lessons are compulsory in all schools.*
computer *n* an electronic machine that stores and organizes information, solves problems, or controls other machines. **computing** *n.*
con *v* (cons, conning, conned) to trick somebody. **con** *n.*
concave *adj* curving inwards, like the inside of a saucer.
conceal *v* to hide something.
conceited *adj* too proud of yourself.
conceive *v* to become pregnant.
concentrate *v* **1** to give all your attention to something. **2** to make a liquid thicker or stronger by removing water from it. **concentration** *n*
concept *n* an idea.
conception *n* becoming pregnant.
concern[1] *n* **1** worry. **2** something of interest to or affecting you. *That's not my concern.*
concern[2] *v* **1** to have to do with, to affect. *This news doesn't concern us.* **2** to worry. *His attitude concerns me.*
concerning *prep* about.
concert *n* a musical performance.
concise *adj* saying everything that is necessary in few words.
conclude *v* **1** to come to an opinion, after looking at the facts. *He concluded that she was the thief.* **2** to finish. **conclusion** *n.*
concrete *n* a hard building material made by mixing cement, sand, small stones and water.
condemn *v* **1** to say very strongly that somebody or something is wrong or very bad. **2** to sentence somebody to a punishment. **condemnation** *n.*
condense *v* **1** to make something shorter. *She condensed the story into five lines.* **2** to change from a gas into a liquid. **condensation** *n.*
condition *n* **1** the general state that somebody or something is in. *My bike is in good condition.* **2** something that must be agreed to. *You can go on condition that you are back for lunch.*
condom *n* a thin, rubber covering that a man wears on his penis as a contraceptive.
conduct[1] *(kon-**dukt**)* *v* **1** to carry out. *to conduct a survey.* **2** to direct an orchestra or a choir during a performance. **3** to allow heat or electricity to pass through.
conduct[2] *(**kon**-dukt)* *n* behaviour. *good conduct.*
conductor *n* **1** a person who directs an orchestra or choir. **2** a person who sells tickets on a bus. **3** something which conducts electricity or heat.
cone *n* **1** a shape or object with a circular base and a point at the top. **2** the fruit of a fir or pine tree.

pine cone

confectionary *n* sweets.
conference *n* a meeting for discussion.
confess *v* to admit to doing wrong. **confession** *n.*
confetti *n pl* tiny pieces of coloured paper thrown over a couple after their wedding.
confide *v* to tell your secrets to somebody. *She confided in her sister.*
confidence *n* trust or belief, especially in your own abilities.
confident *adj* having confidence. *I'm confident that I can win.*
confidential *adj* private, secret. **confidentially** *adv.*
confine *v* **1** to limit, to restrict. *They confined the fire to a small area.* **2** to imprison. **confinement** *n.*
confirm *v* to say that something is definite. *We confirmed the date of our holiday.* **be confirmed** to be fully accepted as a member of some Christian churches. **confirmation** *n.*
confiscate *v* to take something away from somebody as a punishment. **confiscation** *n.*
conflict[1] *(**kon**-flikt) n* a fight, war or serious disagreement.
conflict[2] *(kon-**flikt**) v* to be so different from something else that the two things cannot both exist or be true. *Joe and I had conflicting plans.*
conform *v* to follow the accepted customs and rules.
confront *v* to meet somebody face-to-face to fight or accuse them. **confrontation** *n.*
confuse *v* **1** to mix up somebody's ideas so they cannot think clearly or understand. **2** to mistake one person or thing for another. *I always confuse Hannah with her twin sister.* **confusion** *n.*
congested *adj* **1** blocked up. **2** crowded with traffic. **congestion** *n.*
congratulate *v* to tell somebody you are glad they have succeeded or had good luck. **congratulation** *n.*
congregate *v* to come together in a crowd.
congregation *n* a group of people at a church service.
Congress *n* the parliament of the USA.
conical *adj* cone-shaped.
conifer *n* an tree with needle-like leaves which produces cones.
conjunction *n* a word which joins two parts of a sentence or phrase. *And* and *but* are conjunctions.
conjure *v* to do clever tricks that seem like magic. **conjuror** *n.*
conker *n* the hard, shiny nut of the horse-chestnut tree.
connect *v* to join or fasten together. **connection** *n.*
conquer *v* to defeat an enemy, to overcome. **conquest** *n.*
conscience *(**kon**-shuns) n* your sense of what is right and wrong.
conscientious *adj* careful and hard-working.
conscious *(**kon**-shus) adj* awake, aware of what is happening. **consciousness** *n.*
consecutive *adj* following one after the other.
consent *v* to agree to, to give permission. **consent** *n.*
consequence *n* the result of something.
conservation *n* looking after nature, wildlife, old buildings, etc so that they are not spoiled. **conservationist** *n.*
conservative *adj* not liking great change or new ideas.
Conservative Party *n* one of the main political parties in Britain.
conserve *v* **1** to keep something as it is without changing it. **2** to avoid wasting something. *conserve energy.*
consider *v* to think about something.
considerable *adj* great.
considerate *adj* kind and thoughtful.
consideration *n* **1** careful thought. **2** something that must be thought about carefully. **3** thoughtfulness towards other people.
consist *v* to be made up of something.
consistent *adj* not changing.
console[1] *(kon-**sole**) v* to comfort or cheer somebody up. **consolation** *n.*
console[2] *(**kon**-sole) n* a control panel for operating an electronic machine.

consonant *n* any letter of the alphabet except a, e, i, o and u.
conspicuous *adj* very noticeable.
conspire *v* to plan in secret to do something illegal or wrong. **conspiracy** *n*, **conspirator** *n*.
constable *n* a police officer.
constant *adj* all the time.
constellation *n* a group of stars forming a certain shape in the sky.
constipated *adj* finding it difficult to empty your bowels. **constipation** *n*.
constituency *n* a district with its own member of parliament.
constitution *n* **1** the laws or rules by which a country, etc is governed. **2** your general health.
construct *v* to build. **construction** *n*.
constructive *adj* helpful.
consult *v* to try to get advice or help from somebody or from a book. **consultant** *n*, **consultation** *n*.
consume *v* **1** to eat or drink. **2** to use up. *The car consumes a lot of fuel.* **3** to destroy. *Fire consumed the building.* **consumption** *n*.
contact[1] *n* **1** touching. **2** communication. *I've lost contact with my old school friends.*
contact[2] *v* to get in touch with somebody.
contact lens *n* a small, plastic lens worn on the eye to help you see better.
contagious *adj* caught by touching infected people. *a contagious disease.*
contain *v* to have something inside. *This jar contains jam.*
container *n* a box, jar, pot or tin in which you put things.
contaminate *v* to make something dirty or impure. **contamination** *n*.
contemplate *v* to think about or look at something for a long time. **contemplation** *n*.
contemporary *adj* of the present time, modern.
contempt *n* a total lack of respect.
content, contented *adj* happy, satisfied.
contents *n pl* the things that are in something.
contest *n* a competition.
continent *n* one of the seven main land masses of the world: North America, South America, Asia, Africa, Europe, Australia and Antarctica. **the Continent** the mainland of Europe. **continental** *adj*.

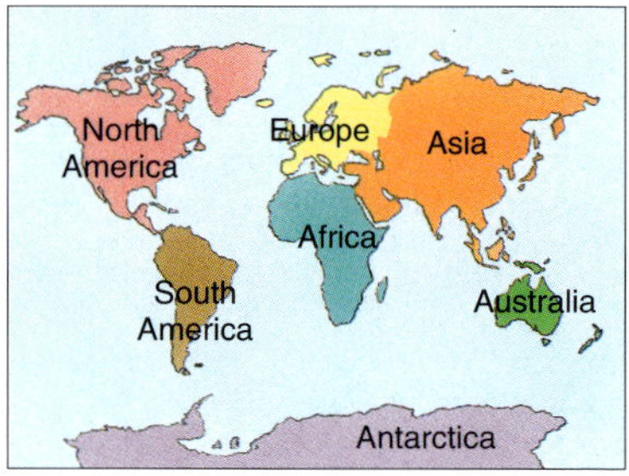

continents

continual *adj* happening again and again. *continual warnings.* **continually** *adv*.
continue *v* to go on, to keep on. **continuation** *n*.
continuous *adj* going on all the time, never stopping. *a continuous noise.*
contour *n* **1** an outline. **2** a line on a map joining points of equal height.
contra- *prefix* against, opposite. *contraflow* (= traffic travelling in the opposite direction to normal).
contraception *n* the prevention of pregnancy.
contraceptive *n* a device or drug which prevents pregnancy.
contract[1] *(kon-**trakt**)* *v* to get smaller.
contract[2] *(**kon**-trakt)* *n* a written agreement.
contradict *v* to say the opposite of what somebody else has said. **contradiction** *n*.
contrary *adj* opposite.
contrast *(kon-**trast**)* *v* to compare different things and notice the differences. **contrast** *(**kon**-trast)* *n*.
contribute *v* to give money, help, etc. **contribution** *n*.
control[1] *v* (controls, controlling, controlled) to make somebody or something do what you want.

control[2] *n* **1** controlling something. **2 controls** the levers, buttons, etc that you use to control a machine.
controversial *adj* causing a lot of argument.
controversy *n* a long argument.
convalescence *n* a time when somebody is recovering from an illness. **convalescent** *adj*.
convenient *adj* **1** easy to use or reach. *Our house is very convenient for the station.* **2** suitable. *When would be a convenient time to meet?* **convenience** *n*.
convent *n* a place where nuns live, pray and work.
conventional *adj* normal, not unusual. **conventionally** adv.
converge *v* to come together from different directions.
conversation *n* talk.
convert *v* to change from one thing to another. **conversion** *n*.
convex *adj* curved outwards, like the surface of your eye.
convey *v* **1** to carry from one place to another. **2** to communicate.
convict[1] *(**kon**-vikt) n* a person who is in prison for committing a crime.
convict[2] *(kon-**vikt**) v* to find somebody guilty of a crime. **conviction** *n*.
convince *v* to make somebody believe that something is true.
convoy *n* (*pl* convoys) a group of vehicles or ships travelling together.
cook[1] *v* to make food ready to eat by heating. **cooking** *n*, **cookery** *n*.
cook[2] *n* a person who cooks.
cooker *n* an apparatus for cooking food.
cookie *n* a biscuit.
cool[1] *adj* **1** rather cold. **2** calm. *Keep cool!* **3** rather unfriendly.
cool[2] *v* to make or become cool.
cooperate *(koh-**op**-er-ate) v* to work together to do something. *If we co-operate we will finish the job sooner.* **cooperation** *n*, **cooperative** *adj*.
cope *v* to deal with problems, etc successfully.
copper *n* a reddish-brown metal.
copy[1] *n* something made to be exactly like something else.
copy[2] *v* (copies, copying, copied) **1** to make a copy of something. **2** to do the same as another person.
coral *n* a hard material found on the sea bed, made from the skeletons of tiny sea creatures.
cord *n* a thin rope.
core *n* the centre part of something. *an apple core.*
cork *n* **1** the light, tough outer bark of the cork oak tree. **2** a piece of cork used as a stopper for a bottle.
corkscrew *n* a tool for taking corks out of bottles.

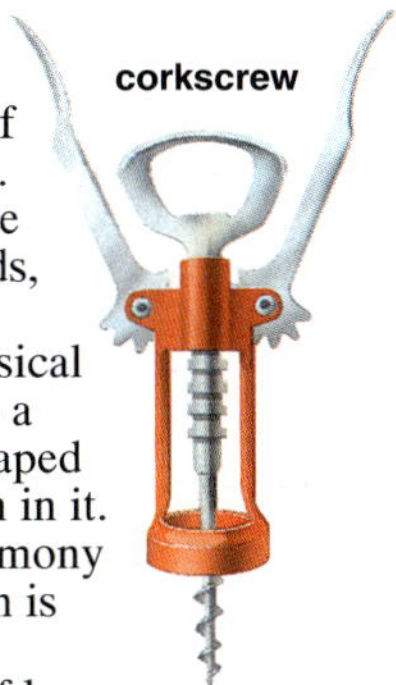

corkscrew

corn *n* **1** the seeds of wheat, oats, maize, etc. **2** a small lump of hard skin on the foot.
corner *n* a place where two lines, walls, roads, etc meet.
cornet *n* **1** a brass musical instrument similar to a trumpet. **2** a cone-shaped wafer with ice-cream in it.
coronation *n* the ceremony when a king or queen is crowned.
corporal *n* a soldier of low rank in the army.
corporal punishment *n* punishment by beating or whipping.
corps *(kor) n* (*pl* corps) a part of an army.
corpse *n* a dead human body.
correct[1] *adj* right or true, with no mistakes. *All my sums were correct.*
correct[2] *v* to make something right. **correction** *n*.
correspond *v* **1** to be similar to or the same as. **2** to exchange letters.
correspondence *n* letters.
corridor *n* a long passage in a building, with rooms leading off it.
corrode *v* to wear away by the action of rust, etc. **corrosion** *n*.
corrugated *adj* shaped into regular, narrow ridges. *corrugated iron.*
corrupt[1] *adj* **1** morally wrong, doing illegal things in return for money. **2** (of computer data) containing errors and so useless. **corrupt** *v*, **corruption** *n*.

cosmetics *n pl* beauty products such as lipstick, eye-shadow, etc.
cosmic *adj* to do with the universe.
cosmos *n* the universe.
cost *v* (costing, cost) **1** to have a certain price. **2** to cause the loss of something. **cost** *n.*
costume *n* **1** clothes. *eighteenth-century costume.* **2** clothes worn by an actor in a play or film.
cosy *adj* (cosier, cosiest) warm and comfortable. **cosily** *adv,* **cosiness** *n.*
cot *n* a small bed with high sides, for a baby.
cottage *n* a small house, usually in the country.
cotton *n* the soft material covering the seeds of the cotton plant. Cotton is made into cloth and thread.
cotton wool *n* soft, fluffy cotton used for wiping the skin or applying lotion.
couch *n* a long, soft seat.
cough *(koff) v* to suddenly force air out of your throat and lungs with a loud sound. **cough** *n.*
council *n* a group of people who are chosen to run a town, city, etc.
councillor *n* a member of a council.
count[1] *v* **1** to say numbers in order. *Count to ten.* **2** to add up. *Count the number of people in the room.* **3** to include. *There are six people in the room, counting me.*
count[2] *n* a European nobleman.
counter *n* **1** a table or flat surface in a shop. **2** a small, flat disc used in some board games.
counter- *prefix* against, opposing. *counteract* (= to act in opposition to), *counter-attack* (= to attack somebody who has attacked you).
counterfeit *adj* not real, fake. *counterfeit money.* **counterfeit** *n,* **counterfeit** *v.*
countess *n* **1** a woman with the same rank as a count. **2** the wife of an earl or a count.
countless *adj* too many to count.
country *n* **1** a land with its own people and government. France and Chile are countries. **2** (*also* **countryside**) land away from towns and cities.
county *n* a part of a country with its own local government.
couple *n* **1** two, a pair. **2** two people who have a romantic relationship.
coupon *n* a ticket which allows you to pay less for something, or that you fill in to apply for something.
courage *n* bravery.
courageous *adj* brave.
courgette *(kor-**jhet**) n* a long vegetable like a small marrow.
courier *(**koo**-ree-er) n* **1** a messenger. **2** a person who looks after groups of people on holiday.
course *n* **1** a series of lessons. **2** one part of a meal. *the main course.* **3** a piece of ground for some kinds of sport. *a racecourse.* **4** the direction which something follows. *the course of the river.*
court *n* **1** a place where trials are held, a law court. **2** a place where games such as tennis and squash are played. **3** the place where a king or queen receives visitors
courteous *(**kur**-tee-us) adj* polite. **courtesy** *n.*
courtyard *n* a space without a roof, enclosed by walls or buildings.
cousin *n* the child of your aunt or uncle.
cove *n* a small bay.
cover *v* to put something over another thing. **cover** *n.*
covering *n* a layer that covers something. *a covering of snow on the ground.*
cow *n* a farm animal kept for its milk.
coward *n* a person who is easily frightened and cannot hide fear. **cowardice** *n,* **cowardly** *adj.*
cowboy, cowgirl *n* a person who looks after cattle, especially in the USA.

cowgirl

cox *n* a person who steers a rowing boat.
crab *n* a sea creature with a hard shell and ten legs, two of which have large claws, called pincers.
crack[1] *v* to break without falling into pieces. *I dropped the plate and it cracked.*
crack[2] *n* **1** a thin line on something that is nearly broken. *There's a crack in the cup.* **2** a sharp noise. **3** *(slang)* a form of cocaine.
cracker *n* **1** a thin, crisp biscuit. **2** a paper tube that bangs when you pull it apart and that contains a small present.
crackle *v* to make a lot of short, sharp sounds. *The dry branches crackled under my feet.*
cradle *n* a bed for a small baby.
craft *n* **1** skilled work with the hands. **2** a boat, spaceship or aircraft.
craftsman, craftswoman *n* a person who is skilled at making something.
crafty *adj* (craftier, craftiest) cunning and sly.
cram *v* (crams, cramming, crammed) to push something into a small space.
cramp *n* a sudden, painful contraction of the muscles.
cramped *adj* too small for all the people or things that have to fit into it.
crane *n* **1** a machine that lifts and moves heavy things. **2** a large water bird with long legs.

crane

crash[1] *v* to hit something violently and noisily. *The car crashed into a tree.*
crash[2] *n* **1** an accident in which a vehicle hits something. **2** a sudden, loud noise. *a crash of thunder.*
crate *n* a large wooden box.
crater *n* **1** the mouth of a volcano. **2** a hole in the ground caused by an explosion.
crave *v* to have a great desire for something.
crawl[1] *v* to move on your hands and knees.
crawl[2] *n* a style of swimming in which you bring your hands over your head in turn, while kicking your legs.
crayon *n* a coloured wax stick for drawing and colouring.
craze *n* a fashion which does not last very long.
crazy *adj* (crazier, craziest) foolish or mad. **crazily** *adv*.
creak *v* to make a harsh, squeaky sound. *The stairs creak when you walk on them.* **creak** *n*, **creaky** *adj*.
cream *n* **1** the thick, fatty part of milk. **2** a thick, smooth liquid that you put on your skin. *face cream.* **3** the yellowish-white colour of cream.
crease *n* a line in paper or cloth made by folding. **crease** *v*.
create *v* to make, to bring something into existence. *Authors create characters for their stories.* **creation** *n*.
creative *adj* good at making or thinking of original things.
creator *n* a person who has created something. **the Creator** God.
creature *n* any living thing that is not a plant.
crèche *n* a nursery for young children.
credit *n* **1** praise or acknowledgement. *She did the work but her brother got all the credit.* **2** a person or thing that brings honour. *He's a credit to his parents.* **3** being allowed to pay for something later. *They got the TV on credit.*
credit card *n* a plastic card used to obtain things and pay for them later.
creek *n* **1** a small inlet in the coastline. **2** a small stream.
creep *v* (creeping, crept) to move slowly and quietly.
cremate *v* to burn a dead body. **cremation** *n*.

crematorium *n* a place where bodies are cremated.
crept *past of* creep.
crescent *n* **1** a curved shape like the new Moon. **2** a row of houses shaped like a crescent.
cress *n* a green plant used in salads.
crest *n* **1** a tuft of feathers, fur, etc on the head of a bird or other creature. **2** the highest point. *the crest of a wave.* **3** a badge on a coat of arms.

crest

crew *n* the team of people who work on a ship or an aircraft.
crib *n* a baby's cot.
cricket[1] *n* **1** an outdoor game played with bats and a ball by two teams of eleven players. **cricketer** *n.*
cricket[2] *n* a small insect similar to a grasshopper.
crime *n* something that is against the law.
criminal *n* a person who has committed a crime.
crimson *n, adj* deep red.
cringe *v* to back away or shrink in fear.
cripple *n* a disabled person. **crippled** *adj.*
crisis *n* **1** a deciding moment or a worst point. **2** a difficult or dangerous time.
crisp[1] *adj* dry, hard and easy to break.
crisp[2] *n* a thin, crisp slice of fried potato.
critical *adj* **1** very serious or dangerous. *He is in hospital and his condition is critical.* **2** criticizing. **critically** *adv.*
criticize *v* to say what you think is wrong with somebody or something. **criticism** *n.*
croak *v* to make a low, hoarse sound like a frog makes. **croak** *n.*
crochet *(**kro**-shay) n* a kind of knitting done with a hooked needle. **crochet** *v.*
crockery *n* plates, cups, saucers, etc that you use at mealtimes.
crocodile *n* a large, long-tailed tropical reptile that lives in rivers.
crocus *n* a small spring flower.
crook *n* **1** a dishonest person. **2** a stick with a hooked end, used by shepherds.
crooked *adj* **1** not straight, bent. **2** dishonest.
crop[1] *n* **1** a plant grown for food, such as wheat or rice. **2** the plants that are gathered at harvest time.
crop[2] *v* (crops, cropping, cropped) to cut. **crop up** to happen unexpectedly.
croquet *(**krow**-kay) n* an outdoor game in which balls are hit through hoops with a wooden hammer.
cross[1] *n* **1** the mark X or +. **2** the sign † used in the Christian religion. **3** a mixture of two things. *a cross between a spaniel and a poodle.*
cross[2] *adj* angry.
cross[3] *v* **1** to go from one side to the other. *We crossed the road.* **2** to place two things across each other. *She crossed her legs.* **3** to pass each other. *Our letters must have crossed in the post.* **cross out** to put a line through something.
crossbow *n* an ancient weapon for firing arrows.
crossing *n* a place where people can go across a street or river.
crossroads *n* a place where two roads meet each other and cross.
cross-section *n* the flat part that you see when you cut straight through an object. *a cross-section of an apple.*
crossword *n* a word puzzle where small squares have to be filled with letters to make words.
crotchet *n* a note in music equal to two quavers in length. See **note**.
crouch *v* to bend your knees and back so your body is close to the ground.
crow[1] *n* a large, black bird.
crow[2] *v* to make the sound that a cock makes.

crowd *n* a large group of people together in one place.
crowded *adj* containing too many people or things.
crown *n* a circular ornament worn by kings and queens on their heads.
crucial *adj* very important.
crucifix *n* a model of Christ on the cross.
crucify *v* (crucifies, crucifying, crucified) to kill somebody by fixing their hands and feet to a cross.
crude *adj* **1** in its natural, unrefined state. *crude oil.* **2** rude and vulgar. *a crude joke.* **crudity** *n.*
cruel *adj* (crueller, cruellest) deliberately causing pain to others. **cruelly** *adv*, **cruelty** *n.*
cruise[1] *n* a holiday on a ship, stopping at different ports along the way.
cruise[2] *v* **1** to go on a cruise. **2** to travel at a steady speed.
crumb *n* a tiny piece of bread, cake or biscuit.
crumble *v* to break into small pieces. **crumbly** *adj.*
crumple *v* to make or become creased. *a crumpled piece of paper.*
crunch *v* to crush noisily, especially with your teeth. **crunchy** *adj.*
crusade *n* a campaign in support of a cause. **crusader** *n.*
crush[1] *v* to press something under a heavy weight.
crush[2] *n* a strong liking for somebody that usually lasts only a short time.
crust *n* **1** the hard, outer part of bread or pastry. **2** any hard, outer covering.
crustacean *n* one of a group of animals most of which have a hard shell and live in water.
crutch *n* one of a pair of sticks which people who have an injured leg can use to help them walk.
cry[1] *v* (cries, crying, cried) **1** to have tears coming from your eyes. **2** to shout.
cry[2] *n* **1** a shout. *a cry of pain.* **2** the sound made by some animals. *the cry of the seagulls.* **3** crying.
crypt *n* an underground room beneath a church.

crystal *n* **1** a rock that is clear like glass. **2** a small, symmetrically shaped piece of a substance, such as salt or ice. **3** very clear glass of a good quality.

snowflake crystals

cub *n* **1** the young of a bear, lion, fox, tiger, or some other animal. **2** a junior Boy Scout.
cube *n* a solid object with six square sides. **cubic** *adj.*
cubicle *n* a small room where you can get changed.
cuckoo *n* a grey bird that lays its eggs in the nests of other birds.
cucumber *n* a long, green vegetable eaten in salads.
cud *n* food that cows, sheep, etc bring up from their stomach to chew again.
cuddle *v* to hug. **cuddle** *n*
cuddly *adj* (cuddlier, cuddliest) pleasant to cuddle.
cue *n* **1** a signal for an actor to say or do something. **2** a long rod for playing snooker, pool or billiards.
cuff *n* the end part of a sleeve.
culprit *n* a person who has done wrong.
cultivate *v* to prepare land for growing crops. **cultivation** *n.*
culture *n* **1** the customs and ways of life of a particular society. **2** music, literature, painting, etc.
cultured *adj* well-educated.
cunning *adj* good at deceiving, sly.
cup *n* a small bowl with a handle, that you drink from.
cupboard ***(kub-ud)*** *n* a piece of furniture where you store things.
curb *v* to keep something under control. *We must curb our spending.*
cure *v* **1** to make better. **2** to preserve some substances such as leather, tobacco and meat by drying, smoking or salting them. **cure** *n.*
curious *adj* **1** wanting to find out about something. **2** odd, strange. **curiosity** *n.*
curl *n* a curved length, especially of hair. **curl** *v*, **curly** *adj.*
currant *n* a small dried grape.

currency *n* the money used in a country.
current[1] *adj* happening now.
current[2] *n* **1** a flow of air or water. **2** a flow of electricity through a wire.
curriculum *n* (*pl* curricula) a programme of study.
curry *n* a hot-tasting, spicy food, often served with rice.
curse[1] *n* a spell intended to bring harm or bad luck to somebody.
curse[2] *v* to swear, to complain angrily about somebody.
cursor *n* an indicator showing your position on a computer screen.
curtain *n* a piece of material that is pulled across a window or the front of a theatre stage to cover it.
curtsy *n* a gesture of respect sometimes made by women, for example when meeting an important person, by bending the knees slightly. **curtsy** *v*.
curve[1] *v* to bend.
curve[2] *n* a rounded line.
cushion *n* a soft object, used for making a chair more comfortable.
custard *n* a sweet, yellow sauce made with milk, sugar, eggs, etc.
custody *n* the legal right to look after a child. **in custody** arrested and waiting for trial.
custom *n* the usual way of doing something.
customary *adj* usual.
customer *n* a person who buys things from a shop or business,
customs *n pl* the place at an airport or port where officials check to make sure you are not carrying anything illegal.
cut *v* (cuts, cutting, cut) **1** to use a sharp object such as a knife, scissors or an axe on something. **2** to reduce. *The shop has cut its prices.* **cut** *n*.
cutlery *n* knives, forks and spoons.
cute *adj* attractive.
cycle[1] *n* a bicycle. **cycle** *v*, **cyclist** *n*.
cycle[2] *n* a series of events happening repeatedly.
cyclone *n* a violent storm with strong winds.
cygnet *n* a young swan.
cylinder *n* **1** an object with round ends and straight sides. **2** a piece of machinery with this shape, especially in an engine. **cylindrical** *adj*.
cymbal *n* a musical instrument like a brass plate that you hit with another cymbal or with a stick to make a clashing sound.
cynic *n* a person who thinks the worst about everybody. **cynical** *adj*.

cymbals

Dd

dab *v* (dabs, dabbing, dabbed) to touch something lightly and quickly. *Jenny dabbed the cut with cotton wool.* **dab** *n*.
dabble *v* **1** to put hands, feet, etc in water and move them about. **2** to be involved in something, but not in a serious way. *She dabbles in politics.*
dad, daddy *n* informal words for "father".
daffodil *n* a yellow spring flower.
daft *adj* silly, foolish.
dagger *n* a short, two-edged knife used as a weapon.
dahlia *n (day-lee-uh)* a garden flower.
daily *adj, adv* happening or coming every day. *a daily newspaper.*
dainty *adj* (daintier, daintiest) small, delicate and pretty. **daintily** *adv*, **daintiness** *n*.
dairy *n* a place where milk is kept and butter and cheese are made.
daisy *n* a small wild flower with a yellow centre and white petals.
dale *n* a valley.
Dalmatian *n* a large, spotted dog.

dam *n* a thick wall built across a river to hold back the water.

dam

damage *v* to do harm to something. **damage** *n*.
damn a word used to express anger.
damp *adj* slightly wet. **dampness** *n*.
dance[1] *v* to move about to the rhythm of music. **dancer** *n*.
dance[2] *n* **1** a series of steps and movements that you do in time to music. **2** a party where people dance.
dandelion *n* a yellow wild flower.
dandruff *n* small, white pieces of dead skin in a person's hair.
danger *n* **1** something that may cause harm or injury. **2** a situation that is not safe. **dangerous** *adj*.
dangle *v* to hang or swing loosely.

dandelion

dank *adj* unpleasantly damp and cold.
dappled *adj* with patches of dark and light.
dare *v* **1** to be brave enough to do something. **2** to challenge somebody to show you how brave they are. **daring** *adj*.
dark *adj* **1** without light. *a dark night.* **2** not light in colour, nearer to black than white. *dark blue.* **3** (of hair or skin) brown or black. **the dark** darkness. **darkness** *n*.
darken *v* to make or become dark.
darn *v* to mend a hole in cloth by sewing threads across it.
dart[1] *n* **1** a small arrow that you throw in the game of darts. **2 darts** a game in which players score points by throwing small arrows at a round target with numbers on it.
dart[2] *v* to move forward suddenly. *Jane darted across the road.*
dash[1] *v* to rush, to run quickly.
dash[2] *n* **1** the mark (—) used in writing. **2** a small quantity. *a dash of sauce.*
data *(day-tuh) n pl* facts or information.
database *n* a large amount of information stored on a computer.
date *n* **1** a particular day, month, or year. **2** an appointment to meet somebody, especially a boyfriend or girlfriend. **3** the sweet, sticky fruit that grows on the date-palm tree.
daughter *n* somebody's female child.
daunt *v* to discourage or frighten somebody. *She was daunted by the amount of work to be done.*
dawdle *v* to waste time by moving slowly.
dawn[1] *n* sunrise.
dawn[2] *v* to begin to get light.
day *n* (*pl* days) **1** a time of 24 hours, from midnight to the next midnight. **2** the part of the day when it is light. **3** a particular time. *In my granddad's day, not everyone had a television.*
daydream *n* pleasant thoughts that take your mind away from what you are doing. **daydream** *v*.
daytime *n* the time when it is light.
daze[1] *v* to make somebody confused and unable to think clearly. *The blow to my head dazed me for a moment.*
daze[2] *n* a state of stunned confusion.
dazzle *v* **1** to blind somebody for a short time with a very bright light. *She was dazzled by the car's headlights.* **2** to impress somebody greatly with beauty, charm, etc.
de- *prefix* opposite or negative of. *defrost* (= to remove ice from something), *derail* (= to make a train go off the rails).

dead *adj* no longer alive.
dead-end *n* a road closed off at one end.
deadline *n* a time by which something must be finished.
deadly *adj* (deadlier, deadliest) causing or likely to cause death.
deaf *adj* not able to hear properly.
deafen *v* to make so much noise that nothing else can be heard.
deal[1] *n* a bargain or agreement.
deal[2] *v* (dealing, dealt) **1** to do business. *He deals in stocks and shares.* **2** to give out playing-cards. **deal with 1** to take action on something. *You tidy this room and I'll deal with the kitchen.* **2** to be concerned with something. *The book deals with some interesting subjects.* **dealer** *n.*
dear *adj* **1** costing a lost of money, expensive. **2** much loved or valued. *a dear friend.* **3** a word that you use to start a letter. *Dear Tom...*
death *n* the end of life.
deathly *adj* like death.
debate *v* to discuss or argue about something in a formal way, often in public. **debate** *n.*
debris *(**deb**-ree)* *n* the remains of something broken or destroyed.
debt *(rhymes with* yet*)* *n* what one person owes to another.
début *(**day**-byoo)* *n* a first public appearance. *She made her début on the stage at the age of fourteen.*
decade *n* a period of ten years.
decapitate *v* to cut off somebody's head. **decapitation** *n.*
decathlon *n* a sporting competition made up of ten athletic events.
decay *v* to rot, to go bad. **decay** *n.*
deceased *adj* dead.
deceive *v* to make somebody believe something that is not true. **deceit** *n,* **deceitful** *adj,* **deception** *n.*
December *n* the twelfth month of the year.
decent *adj* **1** satisfactory, good. *decent quality.* **2** respectable, proper. *a decent way to behave.* **decency** *n.*
deceptive *adj* making somebody believe something that is not true.
decibel *n* a unit for measuring how loud a sound is.
decide *v* to make up your mind about something.
deciduous *adj* losing all its leaves in winter. *a deciduous tree.*
decimal[1] *adj* using units of ten. *decimal currency.*
decimal[2] *n* a fraction written as a number, with amounts less than 1 placed after a dot (a **decimal point**).
decipher *(di-**sigh**-fer)* *v* to work out the meaning of something that is written in code or that is difficult to read.
decision *n* **1** deciding something. **2** something that is decided.
decisive *adj* **1** final, putting an end to a contest, etc. *a decisive battle.* **2** able to decide things quickly and easily.
deck *n* the floor of a ship or bus.
declare *v* **1** to announce something publicly. *War was declared in 1939.* **2** to say very firmly. **3** in cricket, to end an innings before all the team has batted. **declaration** *n.*
decline *v* **1** to become less strong or less good. *Her health is declining.* **2** to refuse something, to turn down. *I declined his offer.* **decline** *n.*
decompose *v* to rot.
decorate *v* **1** to make something more beautiful. **2** to paint or put up wallpaper in a room. **decoration** *n,* **decorative** *adj.*
decrease *v* to make or become smaller or less. **decrease** *n.*
decree *n* an official order. **decree** *v.*
dedicate *v* **1** to give all your time and energy to something. *She dedicated her life to helping the poor.* **2** to say that a book, etc is written in honour of somebody. **dedication** *n.*
deduce *v* to work out something from the facts given. **deduction** *n.*
deduct *v* to take away something, to subtract. *£50 was deducted from her wages.* **deduction** *n.*
deed *n* something that is done.
deep *adj* **1** going down a long way. *a deep hole.* **2** going back a long way from the front. *The shelf was not deep*

enough. **3** strong and dark. *deep red.* **4** low. *a deep voice.* **5** intense. *deep sadness.*

deepen *v* to make or become deeper.

deer *n* (*pl* deer) a wild animal that can run fast. Male deer have antlers.

Sika deer

deface *v* to spoil the appearance of something, eg by writing on it.

defeat *v* to beat somebody in a competition, war, etc. **defeat** *n.*

defect[1] *n (**dee**-fekt)* a fault.

defect[2] *v (di-**fekt**)* to leave your country or political party and go to join another. **defection** *n*, **defector** *n.*

defective *adj* faulty.

defend *v* **1** to protect from harm or attack. *The soldiers defended the castle.* **2** to speak in support of somebody or something. **defence** *n,* **defender** *n,* **defensive** *adj.*

defendant *n* a person being accused of a crime in a court of law.

defer *v* (defers, deferring, deferred) to put something off until later.

defiant *adj* standing up to somebody and openly refusing to obey them. **defiance** *n.*

deficient *adj* lacking in something. **deficiency** *n.*

define *v* to explain the meaning of a word. **definition** *n.*

definite *adj* certain, without doubt.

deformed *adj* with an unnatural shape. *a deformed foot.*

defrost *v* to thaw, to remove ice from something.

defuse *(dee-**fyooz**) v* **1** to make a bomb safe so that it does not explode. **2** to make a situation less dangerous.

defy *v* (defies, defying, defied) to disobey somebody openly. *She defied her parents and went out.*

degree *n* **1** a unit for measuring temperature or angles. *ninety degrees* (often written *90°*). **2** a qualification given by a university or college.

dehydrated *adj* **1** dried out, with the water removed. *dehydrated food.* **2** having lost too much water from your body. **dehydration** *n.*

dejected *adj* sad or disappointed.

delay *v* **1** to make somebody late. *The bus was delayed because there was a lot of traffic.* **2** to put off something until later. **delay** *n.*

delete *v* to cross out or remove words from writing. **deletion** *n.*

deliberate *adj* done on purpose.

delicacy *n* something that is considered especially delicious to eat.

delicate *adj* **1** easily damaged or broken, fragile. *delicate china.* **2** finely made. *delicate lace.* **3** sensitive. *a delicate instrument.* **4** not very strong, easily becoming ill. *a delicate child.*

delicatessen *n* a shop selling unusual foods.

delicious *adj* very good to eat.

delight[1] *n* great pleasure.

delight[2] *v* to give great pleasure to somebody. **delighted** *adj.*

delightful *adj* very pleasant.

delinquent *n* a person who breaks the law.

deliver *v* **1** to take things to a place where they are needed. *The postman delivered two letters.* **2** to help at the birth of a baby. *The doctor arrived in time to deliver the baby.* **delivery** *n.*

delta *n* **1** a triangular area of land at the mouth of a river where its main stream divides into several smaller streams. **2** the fourth letter of the Greek alphabet (Δ).

demand *v* to ask for something very firmly. *She demanded an explanation.* **demand** *n.*

democracy *n* **1** a system of government in which the people of a country elect their own leaders. **2** a country governed in this way. **democrat** *n,* **democratic** *adj.*

demolish *v* to knock something down. *They demolished the tower block at the end of our street.* **demolition** *n.*
demon *n* a devil or an evil spirit.
demonstrate *v* **1** to show or explain something. **2** to take part in a protest march or similar gathering. **demonstration** *n.*
den *n* **1** the home of a wild animal. **2** a private or secret place.
denial *n* denying something.
denim *n* strong, cotton fabric used for making jeans.
denounce *v* to say in public that somebody has done wrong.
dense *adj* **1** closely packed together. *a dense forest.* **2** thick. *dense fog.* **3** *(informal)* stupid. **density** *n.*
dent *n* a hollow part in the surface of something, made by hitting or pressing it. **dent** *v.*
dental *adj* to do with teeth.
dentist *n* a person who takes care of and treats teeth.
dentures *n pl* a set of false teeth.
deny *v* (denies, denying, denied) to say that something is not true.
deodorant *n* a substance put on the body to prevent or cover up smells.
depart *v* to leave, to go away. **departure** *n.*
department *n* one of the parts of a big organization, such as a government, a university or a business.
depend *v* **1** to rely. *I'm depending on you to help me.* **2** to be controlled or decided by. *It all depends on the weather.* **dependent** *adj,* **dependence** *n.*
depict *v* to paint, draw or describe somebody or something.
deport *v* to send somebody out of a country. **deportation** *n.*
deposit[1] *v* **1** to put something somewhere. **2** to put money in a bank.
deposit[2] *n* **1** a sum of money given as the first part of a payment. **2** an amount of money paid into a bank.
depot *(dep-oh) n* **1** a warehouse. **2** a bus station.
depressed *adj* sad and gloomy.
depression *n* **1** sadness and hopelessness. **2** a hollow. **3** a time when businesses are doing badly and there is a lot of unemployment.
deprive *v* to take something away from somebody. **deprivation** *n.*
depth *n* how deep something is. **in depth** thoroughly.
deputy *n* a person who helps somebody in their job and who takes over when that person is ill or away.
descant *n* a tune that is sung or played above the main tune.
descend *(di-send) v* to go down. **descended from** related to somebody who lived a long time ago.
descendant *n* a person related to somebody who lived a long time ago.
describe *v* to say what somebody or something is like. **description** *n,* **descriptive** *adj.*
desert[1] *(**dez**-ert) n* a large area of land where there is little water or rain.

desert

desert[2] *(di-**zert**) v* to abandon somebody or something.
deserve *v* to have earned something by what you have done. *You deserve the prize for all your hard work.*
design[1] *v* to prepare a plan or drawing to show how something will be made. **designer** *n.*
design[2] *n* **1** a plan or drawing of how something will be made. **2** a style or pattern. *The building is very modern in design.*
desire[1] *v* to want something very much.
desire[2] *n* a strong wish or need.
desk *n* a piece of furniture similar to a table, for writing at.
desktop publishing *n* the preparation of a book or magazine for printing using a computer.
despair[1] *v* to lose all hope.
despair[2] *n* a feeling of hopelessness.
desperate *adj* **1** willing to do anything

to get what you want. *She was so desperate for money that she began to steal.* **2** very serious. *a desperate situation.* **desperation** *n.*
despicable *adj* very unpleasant or evil.
despise *v* to dislike and have a very low opinion of somebody.
despite *prep* in spite of.
dessert *(di-**zert**) n* the sweet course at the end of a meal, a pudding.
destination *n* where you are going to.
destiny *n* fate.
destitute *adj* extremely poor.
destroy *v* to damage something so it cannot be repaired. **destruction** *n,* **destructive** *adj.*
detach *v* to remove something that was attached to something else.
detached *adj* standing by itself. *a detached house.*
detail *n* a small part of something.
detailed *adj* having many details.
detain *n* to keep somebody somewhere against their will. **detention** *n.*
detect *v* to discover or notice something. **detection** *n.*
detective *n* a person, especially a police officer, who follows clues to find a criminal.
deter *(di-**ter**) v* (deters, deterring, deterred) to discourage or prevent somebody from doing something.
detergent *n* a liquid or powder used for cleaning.
deteriorate *v* to become worse. **deterioration** *n.*
determined *v* having firmly made up your mind. **determination** *n.*
deterrent *n* something that deters.
detest *v* to hate something.
detonate *v* to set off an explosion. **detonator** *n.*
detour *n* a route away from and longer than the planned route, especially to avoid something such as an obstacle.
devastate *v* to destroy a place completely. **devastation** *n.*
develop *v* **1** to grow bigger or better. *A tadpole develops into a frog.* **2** to make the pictures on a photographic film visible by using chemicals. **3** to get, have or show something. *He developed a fever.* **development** *n.*
device *n* something, such as a tool or an instrument, made to do a particular thing.
devil *n* **1** in Christianity, the supreme evil spirit. **2** any evil spirit.
devious *adj* doing things in a complicated, dishonest way.
devise *v* to invent something.
devoted *adj* loyal and loving. *He is a devoted father.*
devour *v* to eat something up greedily.
devout *adj* deeply religious.
dew *n* tiny drops of water that form on the ground and other surfaces outside overnight.
diabetes *(die-a-**bee**-teez) n* a disease in which there is too much sugar in the blood. **diabetic** *adj, n.*
diagnose *v* to decide what illness a patient has. **diagnosis** *n.*
diagonal *n* a straight line across a square or rectangle from one corner to the opposite corner. **diagonal** *adj,* **diagonally** *adv.*
diagram *n* a drawing that explains something.
dial[1] *n* the face of a clock, watch or other instrument.
dial[2] *v* (dials, dialling, dialled) to make a telephone call by pressing buttons or turning a dial.
dialect *n* a form of a language spoken in a particular region.
dialogue *n* conversation.
diameter *n* a line right across a circle passing through the centre.
diamond *n* **1** a very hard, colourless precious stone. **2** a four-sided figure with equal sides but no right angles. **3 diamonds** one of the four suits in a pack of cards with the symbol ♦ on them.

diamond
(uncut, *top*, and cut, *bottom*)

diarrhoea *(die-uh-**ree**-uh)* *n* a stomach illness which makes you need to go to the toilet often and that makes your faeces runny.
diary *n* a book in which you write down what happens each day.
dice, die *n* (*pl* dice) a small cube with one to six dots on its sides, used in games.
dictate *v* to speak or read aloud so that somebody can write down what you say. **dictation** *n*.
dictator *n* a ruler who has complete control of a country.
dictionary *n* an alphabetical book that explains the meanings of words and shows you how to spell them.
did *past of* do.
die *v* (dies, dying, died) **1** to stop living. **2** to come to an end. **die down** to lose strength or power. *The wind has died down.* **die out** to no longer exist anywhere.
diesel engine *n* a type of engine that burns a special type of oil (**diesel**) to supply power.
diet *(**dye**-ut)* *n* **1** the food you usually eat. *a healthy diet.* **2** a controlled eating plan to help you lose weight or stay healthy.
differ *v* **1** to be different. **2** to disagree.
difference *n* **1** the way that one thing is not the same as another. **2** the amount by which one number is bigger than another. **3** a disagreement.
different *adj* not the same.
difficult *adj* **1** hard, not easy. **2** not easy to please. *a difficult child.*
difficulty *n* a problem.
dig *v* (digs, digging, dug) **1** to use a spade, etc to move earth or make a hole. **2** to poke something.
digest *v* to break up food in your stomach and turn it into a form that your body can use. **digestion** *n*, **digestive** *adj*.
digit *n* **1** any of the figures 0 to 9. *The number 100 has 3 digits.* **2** a finger or toe.
digital *adj* showing the time, speed, etc in numbers rather than by hands on a dial. *a digital watch.*
dignity *n* a serious, calm manner.
dike *n* a wall to stop the sea or a river flooding the land.
dilapidated *adj* falling to pieces.
dilemma *n* a difficult situation in which you must choose between two or more courses of action.
dilute *v* to reduce the strength of a liquid by adding water. **dilution** *n*.
dim *adj* (dimmer, dimmest) not bright. **dimness** *n*.
dimension *n* a measurement of length, width, height, etc.
diminish *v* to make or become less.
din *n* a loud, unpleasant noise.
dine *v* to have dinner.
dinghy *n* a small, open boat.
dingy *adj* (dingier, dingiest) dull and gloomy. *a dark, dingy room.*
dinner *n* the main meal of the day, usually eaten in the evening.
dinosaur *n* one of a large number of prehistoric reptiles that became extinct millions of years ago.
dip[1] *v* (dips, dipping, dipped) **1** to put something into a liquid for a moment. **2** to go downwards. *The road dips just ahead.*
dip[2] *n* **1** a hollow. **2** a soft, savoury mixture in which you dip crackers, crisps and vegetables. **3** a short swim.
diplomacy *n* **1** the management of friendly relations between countries. **2** tact.

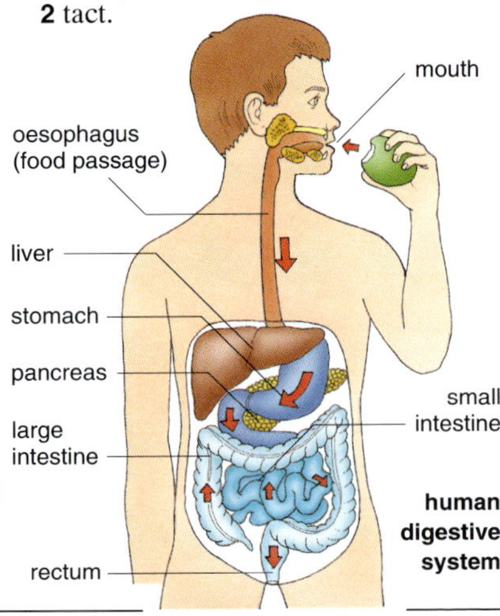

human digestive system

diplomat *n* a person who works for his or her country in diplomacy. *She is a diplomat in the French Embassy.*
diplomatic *adj* **1** to do with diplomats. **2** tactful. **diplomatically** *adv*.
dire *adj* terrible, urgent.
direct[1] *adj* **1** straight, shortest. *the most direct route.* **2** saying exactly what you think. **direct** *adv*, **directly** *adv*.
direct[2] *v* **1** to tell somebody the way to go. **2** to organize people and tell them what to do, especially in a play or film.
direction *n* **1** the place or point to which you are moving or facing. **2 directions** instructions on how to do something.
director *n* **1** a senior manager of a business. **2** a person who directs a play or film.
directory *n* a list of names, addresses, telephone numbers, etc.
dirt *n* dust, mud or any other unclean substance.
dirty *adj* (dirtier, dirtiest) not clean, covered in dirt. **dirtiness** *n*.
dis- *prefix* the opposite or negative of. *disappear, disapprove.*
disable *v* to harm or injure somebody in a way that seriously affects their life. **disability** *n*, **disabled** *adj*.
disadvantage *n* something that is not helpful, a drawback.
disagree *v* (disagreeing, disagreed) **1** to have different ideas about something. **2** to have a bad effect on somebody. *Onions disagree with me.* **disagreement** *n*.
disagreeable *adj* unpleasant.
disappear *v* to go out of sight, to vanish. **disappearance** *n*.
disappoint *v* to make someone sad by not being or doing what they had hoped for. **disappointment** *n*.
disapprove *n* to think that something is bad, wrong, etc. **disapproval** *n*.
disaster *n* an event that causes great damage or suffering. **disastrous** *adj*.
disc *n* **1** any flat, circular object. **2** a compact disc. **3** a gramophone record. **4** *another spelling of* disk.
discard *v* to throw something away.
disciple *(di-**sigh**-pul)* *n* a follower.
discipline *n* punishment or training that makes people obey rules.
disc jockey *n* a person who introduces and plays recorded music on radio, etc.
disco *n* (*short for* discotheque) a place where people dance to pop music.
discomfort *n* lack of comfort, slight pain or worry.
discount *n* a reduction in the price of something.
discover *v* to find out something new. **discovery** *n*.
discriminate *v* **1** to see the differences between things. **2** to treat one person or group differently from another, often unfairly. **discrimination** *n*.
discus *n* a heavy disc used in a throwing competition.

discus thrower

discuss *v* to talk about something. **discussion** *n*.
disease *n* an illness.
disgrace *n* **1** shame. **2** something to be ashamed of. *Your clothes are a disgrace!* **in disgrace** out of favour.
disguise *v* to change somebody's appearance so they will not be recognized. *He was disguised as a police officer.* **disguise** *n*.
disgust *n* a feeling of strong dislike. *He looked away in disgust.* **disgust** *v*, **disgusted** *adj*, **disgusting** *adj*.
dish *n* **1** a plate or bowl for cooking or serving food. **2** one course of a meal.
dishonest *adj* not honest. **dishonesty** *n*.
disinfect *v* to make something free from germs. **disinfectant** *n*.
disintegrate *v* to break into many small pieces. **disintegration** *n*.
disk *n* in computing, a flat plastic case that stores information.
dislike *v* to not like something. **dislike** *n*.
dismal *adj* gloomy and sad. *a dismal, grey day.* **dismally** *adv*.
dismantle *v* to take something to bits.

dismay *n* a strong feeling of disappointment, shock or worry. *She reacted to the bad news with dismay.* **dismay** *v*.
dismiss *v* **1** to send somebody away. **2** to order somebody to leave their job. **3** to refuse to consider something. **dismissal** *n*.
disobey *v* to refuse to obey somebody. **disobedience** *n*, **disobedient** *adj*.
disorder *n* **1** confusion, lack of order. **2** rioting. **3** an illness.
display[1] *v* to put something where people can look at it.
display[2] *n* (*pl* displays) an exhibition or show.
disposable *adj* intended to be thrown away after use.
dispose *v* to get rid of something. **disposal** *n*.
dispute[1] *(di-**spyoot**)* *v* to argue about something.
dispute[2] *(**dis**-pyoot)* *n* an argument.
disregard *v* to pay no attention to something.
disrespect *n* a lack of respect.
disrupt *v* to stop something progressing normally. **disruption** *n*, **disruptive** *adj*.
dissect *v* to cut something into pieces to examine it. **dissection** *n*.
dissolve *v* to mix something with a liquid so that it becomes part of the liquid. *Salt dissolves easily in water.*
distance *n* the amount of space between two places. **in the distance** far away.
distant *adj* far away.
distil *v* (distils, distilling, distilled) to purify a liquid by turning it into steam and then cooling it until it becomes liquid again. **distillation** *n*.
distinct *adj* **1** easily seen or heard. **2** clearly different.
distinction *n* **1** a difference. **2** excellence. *a man of distinction.*
distinguish *v* **1** to tell the difference between things. *Can you distinguish between a butterfly and a moth?* **2** to see or hear something clearly, to identify. *I could barely distinguish the figure in the distance.*
distinguished *adj* famous and well respected. *a distinguished novelist.*
distract *v* to take somebody's attention away from what they were doing. **distraction** *n*.
distress *n* great pain, sorrow or trouble. **distress** *v*.
distribute *v* to share something out. **distribution** *n*, **distributor** *n*.
district *n* a part of a country or city.
disturb *v* **1** to interrupt somebody when they are doing something. **2** to upset or worry somebody. **3** to move something from its usual position. **disturbance** *n*.
ditch *n* a long, narrow channel for draining away water.
dive *v* **1** to plunge headfirst into water. **2** to drop down suddenly. **dive** *n*.
diver *n* a person who works or explores underwater using special breathing equipment.
diverse *adj* varied, assorted.
diversion *n* **1** a route different from the planned or usual one, that must be taken when the usual road is closed. **2** something that takes your attention away from something else.
divert *v* **1** to change the direction of something. **2** to take somebody's attention away from something.
divide *v* **1** to separate into parts, to share. **2** to find out how many times one number goes into another. *If you divide eight by two, you get four.* **divisible** *adj*, **division** *n*.
divine *adj* of or like God or a god.
divorce *n* the legal ending of a marriage. **divorce** *v*.
Diwali *n* a Hindu and Sikh festival of lights in October or November.
dizzy *adj* (dizzier, dizziest) feeling that everything is spinning and that you are going to fall. **dizziness** *n*.
do *v* (does, doing, did, done) **1** to carry out an action. **2** to finish or deal with something. **3** to be acceptable. *Will soup do for lunch?* **4** a word used in questions and negative statements. *Do you like it?*
docile *adj* easily controlled, obedient.
dock *n* **1** a place in a harbour where

ships are loaded and unloaded. **2** the place in a law court where the accused person stands or sits.
doctor *n* a person who treats sick people.
document *n* a piece of paper with official or important information.
documentary *n* a film about real situations and people.
dodge *v* to get quickly out of the way.
doe *n* a female deer or rabbit. See **deer**.
dog *n* a four-legged mammal often kept as a pet.
dole *(informal) n* money paid by the government to unemployed people.
doll *n* a toy in the shape of a small person or baby.
dollar *n* the unit of money in many countries, including Australia, Canada and the USA.
dolphin *n* an intelligent sea mammal with a long snout.
dome *n* a rounded roof.
domestic *adj* **1** to do with the home. **2** kept as pets. *domestic animals.*
dominate *v* **1** to control powerfully. **2** to be the most important or noticeable feature. *The castle dominates the town.* **dominant** *adj*, **domination** *n*.
dominoes *n pl* small, rectangular tiles marked with dots, used for playing a game.
donate *v* to give something, especially to a charity. **donation** *n*, **donor** *n*.
done *past participle of* do.
donkey *n* (*pl* donkeys) an animal of the horse family, with long ears.
doodle *v* to draw without concentrating. **doodle** *n*.
doom *n* a terrible fate which cannot be prevented.
door *n* a flat piece of wood or glass which opens and closes the entrance to a building, room, cupboard, etc.
dormant *adj* not active, sleeping.
dormitory *n* a bedroom for several people.
dose *n* an amount of medicine to be taken at one time.
dot *n* small spot.
dotted *adj* made of dots. *a dotted line.*
double[1] *adj* **1** twice as much or as many **2** made up of two parts. **double** *v*.
double[2] *n* a person who looks exactly like somebody else.
double bass *n* a large stringed instrument that you play standing up.
double-cross *v* to betray somebody.
doubt[1] *(rhymes with* out*) v* to feel uncertain about something.
doubt[2] *n* a feeling of uncertainty. **doubtful** *adj*.
dough *(rhymes with* go*) n* a mixture of flour, water and other ingredients for making bread or cakes.
doughnut *n* a small, fried cake coated in sugar.
dove *n* a bird related to the pigeon.
down[1] *prep, adv* **1** from a higher to a lower level, amount, etc. **2** from standing to sitting or lying. *Lie down.*
down[2] *n* very soft feathers.
down[3] *adj* sad, depressed.
downward, downwards *adv* towards a lower place.
doze *v* to sleep lightly. **doze** *n*.
dozen *n* twelve.
Dr *a short way of writing* Doctor.
drab *adj* dull, not colourful.
drag *v* (drags, dragging, dragged) **1** to pull something roughly along the ground. *She dragged the heavy sack into the garden.* **2** to pass very slowly. *The lesson really dragged.*
dragon *n* a fierce, fire-breathing creature in stories and legends.

Chinese New year dragon

dragonfly *n* a large, often brightly coloured insect with long wings.

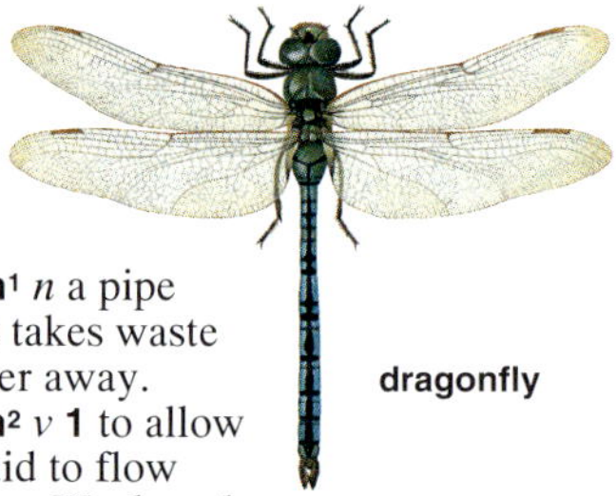

dragonfly

drain[1] *n* a pipe that takes waste water away.

drain[2] *v* **1** to allow liquid to flow away. *Wash and drain the lettuce.* **2** to flow away.

drained *adj* exhausted, lacking energy.

drake *n* a male duck.

drama *n* **1** a play. **2** acting and the theatre. **3** exciting events.

dramatic *adj* **1** to do with acting and the theatre. **2** noticeable, striking. *a dramatic improvement.* **3** exciting, impressive. *dramatic events.* **dramatically** *adv.*

drank *past of* drink.

drastic *adj* extreme, severe.

draught *(rhymes with* raft*) n* a flow of cold air indoors. **draughty** *adj.*

draughts *(rhymes with* rafts*) n* a game played with counters on a board that has black and white squares.

draw[1] *v* (drawing, drew, drawn) **1** to make a picture with a pencil, crayon, etc. **2** to pull something. *a horse-drawn carriage.* **3** to attract something. *The show drew a large crowd.*

draw[2] *n* **1** a game which neither side has won. **2** the selecting of winning tickets in a lottery, etc. *a prize draw.*

drawback *n* a disadvantage.

drawbridge *n* a bridge across a moat that could be pulled up when a castle was being attacked.

drawer *n* a box-shaped part of a chest or cupboard that can be pulled open.

drawing *n* a picture made with a pen, pencil, crayon, etc.

drawing-pin *n* a pin with a large, flat head for fastening paper to a surface.

drawn *past participle of* draw.

dread *v* to be very afraid of something. **dread** *n.*

dreadful *adj* terrible, unpleasant. **dreadfully** *adv.*

dreadlocks *n pl* hair twisted into long, thin ringlets.

dream *n* **1** things that seem to happen to you when you are asleep. **2** a hope or ambition. **dream** *v.*

dreary *adj* (drearier, dreariest) dull, gloomy.

dredge *v* to clear away sand and mud from a river bed or harbour.

drench *v* to make something completely wet.

dress[1] *n* **1** a piece of clothing worn by women and girls, that covers the body from the shoulders to the legs. **2** clothing. *men in evening dress.*

dress[2] *v* to put on clothes.

dresser *n* a piece of furniture like a cupboard with shelves above.

dressing *n* **1** a covering for a wound. **2** a sauce for salads.

dressing gown *n* a loose robe that you wear over your nightclothes.

drew *past of* draw.

dribble *v* **1** to let saliva fall from your mouth. **2** in football, to move the ball along with short kicks.

drift *v* to be carried slowly along by wind or water.

drill *n* **1** a pointed tool that is used for making holes. **2** exercises that are part of a soldier's training. **3** an exercise intended to train people in what to do in a dangerous situation. **drill** *v.*

drink[1] *v* (drinking, drank, drunk) to swallow a liquid.

drink[2] *n* **1** any liquid that you swallow. **2** an alcoholic drink.

drip *v* (drips, dripping, dripped) to fall in drops. **drip** *n.*

drive[1] *v* (driving, drove, driven) **1** to be in control of a vehicle. **2** to take somebody somewhere in a car. **3** to force something along. *They drove the herd of cattle across the road.* **4** to make something work. *The engine was driven by steam.* **driver** *n.*

drive[2] *n* **1** a journey in a car. **2** a road from the street to the front of a house.

drizzle *n* light rain. **drizzle** *v.*

dromedary *n* a camel with one hump.

dromedary

drone[1] *v* to make a low, steady, humming noise.
drone[2] *n* a male bee or ant that does no work.
drool *v* **1** to dribble. **2** to show in an obvious way that you want something.
droop *v* to hang down limply.
drop[1] *n* a small amount of a liquid.
drop[2] *v* (drops, dropping, dropped) to fall or let something fall. **drop in** to visit somebody casually.
drought *(rhymes with* out*)* *n* a long period of dry weather.
drove *past of* drive.
drown *v* to die or to kill somebody by suffocation in water.
drowsy *adj* (drowsier, drowsiest) sleepy. **drowsily** *adv*.
drug *n* **1** a medicine. **2** a substance swallowed, smoked or injected by people to produce an effect such as happiness or excitement. **drug** *v*.
drum[1] *n* a round, hollow musical instrument with a skin stretched over a frame, which you beat.
drum[2] *v* (drums, drumming, drummed) **1** to play a drum. **2** to beat on a surface with your fingers, etc. **drummer** *n*.
drunk[1] *adj* having drunk too much alcohol.
drunk[2] *past participle of* drink.
dry[1] *adj* (drier, driest) not wet, without water. **dryness** *n*.
dry[2] *v* (dries, drying, dried) to make or become dry.
dry-clean *v* to clean clothes using special chemicals instead of water.
DTP *short for* desktop publishing.
dual *adj* double.
dual carriageway *n* a wide road with a strip of concrete or grass down the middle.
dubious *(dyoo-bee-us) adj* doubtful.
duchess *n* **1** a woman with the same rank as a duke. **2** the wife of a duke.
duck[1] *n* a common water bird with a broad beak and webbed feet.
duck[2] *v* to bend down quickly to get out of the way of something.
duckling *n* a young duck.
due *adj* **1** expected to arrive or happen. *What time is the train due?* **2** owing, to be paid. *The payment is now due.* **3** suitable. *After due consideration she decided to take the job.* **due to** caused by something.
duel *n* a fight between two people.
duet *(dyoo-et) n* a piece of music for two performers.
dug *past of* dig.
duke *n* a nobleman of the highest rank.
dull *adj* **1** not bright. *a dull, grey day.* **2** not interesting. *a dull book.* **3** not sharp. *a dull ache.*
dumb *adj* **1** not able to speak. **2** *(slang)* stupid.
dummy *n* **1** a model of a human figure. **2** a rubber teat for a baby to suck.
dump[1] *n* a place where rubbish is left.
dump[2] *v* **1** to put something on a dump. **2** to put something down carelessly. *She dumped her bag on the floor.*

drummer playing the bongos

dune *n* a low hill of sand.
dung *n* faeces from large animals.
dungarees *n pl* trousers with a top part that covers your chest, and with straps that go over your shoulders.
dungeon *(**dun**-jun) n* an underground prison in a castle.
duplicate *(**dyoo**-plee-kate) v* to make an exact copy of something. **duplicate** *(**dyoo**-pli-kut) n.*
durable *adj* lasting a long time.
during *prep* **1** throughout. *Hedgehogs hibernate during the winter.* **2** at some time in. *They arrived during the afternoon.*
dusk *n* the time of evening when it is starting to get dark.
dust[1] *n* tiny particles of dirt. **dusty** *adj.*
dust[2] *v* to remove dust with a cloth.
dustbin *n* a container for rubbish that you keep outside your house.
duster *n* a soft cloth that you use for dusting furniture.
duty *n* **1** something that you must do. **2** tax on goods that you buy. **on duty** working. **off duty** not working.
duvet *(**doo**-vay) n* a thick bed cover filled with feathers or other soft material.
dwarf *n* (*pl* dwarfs *or* dwarves) a very small person, animal or plant.
dwell *v* (dwelling, dwelt) to live somewhere.
dwelling *n* a place to live in.
dwindle *v* to become smaller or less.
dye[1] *n* a substance used to change the colour of something.
dye[2] *v* (dyeing, dyed) to change the colour of something by soaking it in a dye.
dyke *another spelling of* dike.
dynamic *adj* full of energy.
dynamite *n* an explosive.
dynamo *n* (*pl* dynamos) a machine that uses movement to make electricity. *The light on my bike is powered by a dynamo.*
dynasty *n* a series of kings and queens belonging to the same family.
dyslexia *(dis-**lek**-see-a) n* a special difficulty with reading and spelling. **dyslexic** *adj.*

Ee

each *adj* every person or thing. **each** *pron.*
eager *adj* keen, enthusiastic. **eagerness** *n.*
eagle *n* a large bird of prey.
ear *n* the part of the body used for hearing.
earache *n* a pain the ear.
earl *n* a British nobleman.
early *adj, adv* **1** near the beginning of a period of time. *early morning.* **2** before the expected or usual time. *We went to bed early.* **earliness** *n.*

bald eagle

earn *v* **1** to get something by working for it. **2** to deserve something.
earnest *adj* serious, sincere.
earnings *n pl* money that is earned.
earring *n* a piece of jewellery that you wear on your ear.
earth *n* **1** **Earth** the planet on which we live. **2** soil. **3** the hole where a fox lives.

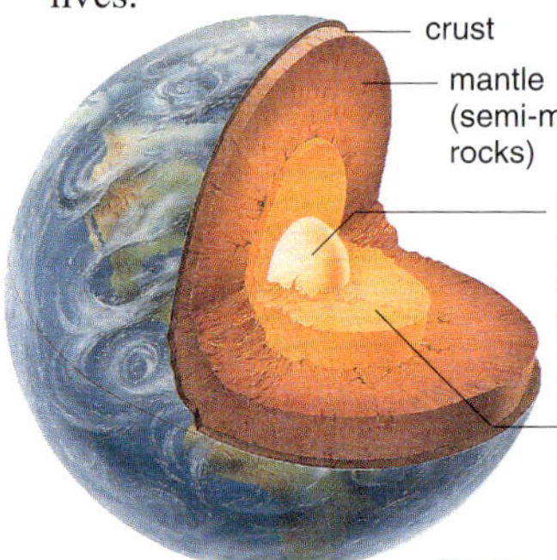

Earth

earthquake *n* a violent shaking of the surface of the Earth.
earthwork *n* a mound of earth used as a fortification.
earwig *n* an insect with pincers at the end of its abdomen.
ease[1] *n* comfort, freedom from pain.
ease[2] *v* **1** to make or become less difficult or unpleasant. *The drugs eased the pain.* **2** to move something gently and carefully. *We eased the lid off the box.*
easel *n* a stand for supporting a picture or blackboard.
east *n* **1** the direction from which the Sun rises. **2 the East** the countries of Asia, such as Japan and China. **east** *adj, adv.*
Easter *n* the day on which Christians remember the resurrection of Jesus Christ.
eastern *adj* in or of the east part of a place. *eastern England.*
easy *adj* (easier, easiest) **1** able to be done without much effort or ability. **2** free from pain, trouble or worry. *an easy life.* **easily** *adv.*
easy-going *adj* not easily upset or worried.
eat *v* (eating, ate, eaten) **1** to take in food through your mouth. **2** to destroy something by chemical action. *Acid eats into metal.*
ebb *v* **1** (of the tide) to move away from the land. **2** to become less.
ebony *n* a hard, black wood.
eccentric *(ek-**sen**-trik) adj* odd, strange.
echo *(**ek**-oh) n* (*pl* echoes) a sound that is heard again when it bounces back off something. **echo** *v.*
eclipse *n* **1** a time when the Sun's light is blocked because the Moon passes between the Earth and the Sun. **2** a time when the Moon's light is blocked because the Earth passes between the Sun and the Moon. **eclipse** *v.*
ecology *n* the study of living things, the places where they live and how they depend on each other. **ecological** *adj,* **ecologist** *n.*
economical *adj* not wasteful. *This car is very economical to run.*
economize *v* to save money by being careful.
economy *n* the management of a country's money. **make economies** to save money by being careful.
ecu *n* (*short for* European currency unit) a unit of money in the EU.
eczema *(**ex**-ma) n* a disease of the skin that makes it rough and dry.
edge *n* the part along the side or end of something. **on edge** nervous.
edible *adj* fit to be eaten.
edifice *n* a large, impressive building.
edit *v* **1** to prepare a piece of writing or a film by changing, shortening and arranging it. **2** to get a newspaper or magazine ready for publication.
edition *n* all the copies of a book or newspaper printed at one time.
editor *n* a person who edits.
educate *v* to teach or train somebody. **education** *n,* **educational** *adj.*
eel *n* a long, snake-like fish.

common eel

effect *n* **1** a result. **2** an impression made by something.
effective *adj* doing a job very well.
efficient *adj* doing a job well, without wasting time or effort. **efficiency** *n.*
effort *n* **1** trying hard. **2** hard work. **effortless** *adj.*
eg *short for* for example. *Please wear comfortable shoes, eg trainers.*
egg *n* **1** one of the oval or rounded objects that young birds, insects, fish and reptiles live inside before they are born. **2** a hen's egg used as food. **3** in a female animal, the cell from which a baby is formed.
either[1] *conj, pron, adj* **1** one or the other, one of two. *You can have either milk or lemonade.* **2** each. *a street with trees along either side.*
either[2] *adv* also. *If you don't go, I won't go either.*
eject *v* to push or send something out with force. **ejection** *n,* **ejector** *n.*

elaborate *adj* very detailed or complicated. *an elaborate design.*
elastic *n* a material that stretches and then goes back to the same size. **elastic** *adj.*
elated *adj* extremely happy. **elation** *n.*
elbow *n* the joint where your arm bends.
elder *adj* older.
elderly *adj* rather old.
eldest *adj* oldest.
elect *v* to choose somebody by voting.
election *n* a time when people vote to choose the people who will lead their town, country, club, etc.
elector *n* a person who can vote.
electric *adj* worked by electricity.
electrical *adj* **1** to do with electricity. **2** worked by electricity.
electrician *n* a person who works with electrical equipment.
electricity *n* energy that is used to make heat and light and to work machines.
electrocute *v* to kill or badly injure somebody by contact with an electrical current. **electrocution** *n.*
electrode *n* a conductor through which an electrical current enters or leaves a battery, etc.
electron *n* a very small particle within an atom, carrying an electric charge. See **atom**.
electronic *adj* operated by silicon chips or transistors which carry and control electrical currents. Many pieces of equipment, such as computers and televisions, contain electronic devices. **electronically** *adv.*
electronics *n pl* the science or technology that deals with electronic devices.
elegant *n* graceful and stylish. **elegance** *n.*
element *n* **1** in chemistry, a substance that cannot be divided into simpler substances. **2** a single part of something. **3 the elements** the weather.
elementary *adj* simple, basic.
elephant *n* a very large mammal with thick skin, a trunk and tusks.
elf *n* (*pl* elves) a mischievous fairy.
eligible *adj* qualified. *You are not eligible to vote until you are 18.* **eligibility** *n.*
eliminate *v* to remove somebody or something. **elimination** *n.*
elm *n* a tall tree with broad leaves.
elongated *adj* long and thin.
elope *v* to run away with a lover. **elopement** *n.*
eloquent *adj* able to express your ideas well. **eloquence** *n.*
else *adv* **1** more, extra. *Would you like anything else to eat?* **2** other, different. *He took someone else's book.* **or else** otherwise.
E-mail *n* (*short for* electronic mail) messages sent and received by computer.
embankment *n* a wall of earth built to carry a railway or to hold back water.
embark *v* to go on board a ship.
embarrass *v* to make somebody feel uncomfortable or ashamed. **embarrassment** *n.*
embassy *n* the building used by an ambassador and his or her staff.
emblem *n* a badge or symbol.
embrace *v* to put your arms around somebody. **embrace** *n.*

Asiatic elephant

African elephant

embroider *v* to sew pictures or designs onto cloth. **embroidery** *n.*

embryo *(em-bree-oh) n* (*pl* embryos) an unborn animal or human in the early stages of development.
emerald *n* a green precious stone.
emerge *v* to come out, to appear.
emergency *n* a sudden, dangerous situation needing quick action.
emigrate *v* to leave your own country and go to live in another. **emigrant** *n,* **emigration** *n.*
eminent *adj* well-known and highly respected. *an eminent lawyer.*
emit *v* (emits, emitting, emitted) to send out something. **emission** *n.*
emotion *n* a strong feeling, such as love, joy or grief. **emotional** *adj,* **emotionally** *adv.*
emperor *n* a man who rules an empire.
emphasis *(em-fa-sis) n* stress, eg on words, to show special importance.
emphasize *v* to stress something to show it is especially important.
empire *n* a group of countries under one ruler. *the Roman Empire.*
employ *v* **1** to pay somebody to work. **2** to use something. **employment** *n.*
employee *n* a person who works for an employer, a worker.
employer *n* a person or company that employs others.
empress *n* a woman who rules an empire, or the wife of an emperor.
empty[1] *adj* (emptier, emptiest) with nothing inside.
empty[2] *v* (empties, emptying, emptied) to make or become empty. **emptiness** *n.*
emu *n* (*pl* emus) a large Australian bird that cannot fly.
enable *v* to make something possible for somebody.
enamel *n* **1** a very hard, shiny coating on things such as metal saucepans, pottery and glass. **2** the hard, white surface of your teeth.
enchant *v* **1** to delight somebody. **2** to put a spell on somebody or something. **enchantment** *n.*
enclose *v* **1** to surround something on all sides. **2** to put something inside a letter or envelope. *I enclose a cheque for £10.*
enclosure *n* an area with a fence or wall around it.
encounter *n* **1** an unexpected meeting. **2** a fight or contest. **encounter** *v.*
encourage *v* to give somebody the confidence to do something. **encouragement** *n.*
encyclopedia *(en-sye-klo-**pee**-dee-uh) n* a book or set of books containing information on many different topics, usually arranged in alphabetical order.
end[1] *n* the last or furthest part of something. *the end of the road.*
end[2] *v* to bring or come to an end.
endanger *v* to put something in danger.
endangered species *n* a species of animal in danger of becoming extinct.
endeavour *v* to try to do something.
endless *adj* without an end.
endure *v* **1** to suffer something. **2** to last, to continue. **endurance** *n.*
enemy *n* **1** the people that you are fighting against in a war. **2** a person who hates you and wants to harm you.
energetic *adj* strong and active. **energetically** *adv.*
energy *n* the strength or power to do work.
engage *v* **1** to employ somebody. **2** to involve or occupy somebody. *She engaged him in conversation.*
engaged *adj* busy. **get engaged** to agree to marry.
engine *n* a machine which changes energy into movement.
engineer *n* **1** a person who designs and builds things such as bridges, roads or machines. **2** a person who repairs or looks after machinery.
engineering *n* the work of an engineer.
engrave *v* to cut a picture or writing into metal or glass. **engraving** *n.*
enigma *n* a mystery or puzzle.
enjoy *v* to get pleasure from something. **enjoyable** *adj,* **enjoyment** *n.*
enlarge *v* to make or become bigger. **enlargement** *n.*
enormous *adj* very big.
enough *adj, adv, n* as much as you need. *Have you had enough to eat?*
enquire *v* to ask. **enquiry** *n.*

enrol *v* (enrols, enrolling, enrolled) to put your name on a list to join something. **enrolment** *n*.
ensure *v* to make certain.
enter *v* **1** to go into a place. **2** to type something into a computer or write something down in a book, etc. **3** to take part in a competition.
enterprise *n* something you try to do that is new and challenging. *We wish you success in your enterprise.*
entertain *v* **1** to amuse and interest people. **2** to have people as guests in your home. **entertainment** *n*.
enthusiasm *n* a keen and lively interest. **enthusiastic** *adj*, **enthusiastically** *adv*.
entire *adj* whole, complete.
entrance[1] *(en-truns) n* **1** entering. **2** the place where you enter.
entrance[2] *(en-**traans**) v* to delight somebody very much.
entry *n* **1** a way in, an entrance. **2** something that you enter for a competition. *a winning entry.*
envelope *n* a paper cover for a letter.
envious *adj* feeling envy. *He was envious of his friend's happiness.*
environment *n* **1** the surroundings and conditions in which a person or an animal lives. **2** the natural world. **environmental** *adj*.
envy *n* a feeling of wanting what somebody else has. **envy** *v*.
epic *n* a long story, poem or film that tells about great adventures and heroic deeds.
epidemic *n* an outbreak of a disease affecting a large number of people at the same time.
epilepsy *n* a brain condition causing unconsciousness and often fits. **epileptic** *adj*.
episode *n* **1** one programme in a television or radio series. **2** one in a series of events.
epitaph *n* words written on a tomb.
equal[1] *adj, n* the same in size, number or value. **equality** *n*, **equally** *adv*.
equal[2] *v* (equals, equalling, equalled) to be the same in size, number or quality.
equation *n* a mathematical formula stating that two values are equal.
equator *n* an imaginary line around the Earth, exactly half-way between the North and South Poles. **equatorial** *adj*.
equilateral *adj* with all sides of equal length. *an equilateral triangle.* See **triangle**.
equinox *n* one of the two days of the year, in spring and autumn, when day and night are of equal length all over the world.
equip *v* (equips, equipping, equipped) to provide somebody or something with everything needed.
equipment *n* the things needed for a particular purpose.
equivalent *adj* equal in value, size or meaning. **equivalent** *n*.
era *n* a period of history.
eradicate *v* to get rid of something completely. **eradication** *n*.
erase *v* to rub something out. **eraser** *n*.
erect[1] *v* to put up or build something. *They erected a war memorial in the square.* **erection** *n*.
erect[2] *adj* standing upright.
erode *v* to gradually wear away.
erosion *n* the slow wearing away of soil or rock by wind, water or ice.
erotic *adj* to do with sexual desire.
err *v* to make a mistake.
errand *n* a small job that somebody is sent away to do.
erratic *adj* irregular, not having a fixed pattern.
error *n* a mistake.
erupt *v* **1** (of a volcano) to burst out violently and shoot out lava, etc. **2** to break out suddenly and violently. *The demonstration started quietly, but violence suddenly erupted.* **eruption** *n*.

volcano erupting

escalator *n* a moving staircase.
escape *v* to get away from somebody or something, to get free. **escape** *n*.
escort[1] *(es-**kort**)* *v* to go with somebody, especially to protect or guard them.
escort[2] *(es-kort)* *n* a person who escorts somebody.
especially *adj* specially, particularly.
espionage *n* spying.
essay *n* (*pl* essays) a piece of writing on a particular subject.
essence *n* **1** the most important part or quality. **2** a concentrated liquid from a plant, used to flavour food.
essential[1] *adj* absolutely necessary.
essential[2] *n* something that is essential. **essentially** *adv*.
establish *v* **1** to set something up. *The firm was established in 1902.* **2** to show that something is true. *They established the cause of death.* **establishment** *n*.
estate *n* **1** an area of land on which houses or factories have been built. **2** an area of land owned by one person. **3** all the money and property left by somebody when they die.
estate agent *n* a person whose job is selling houses and land for people.
estate car *n* a long car with a door at the back and space behind the back seats for carrying things.
estimate *(es-tim-ate)* *v* to guess something, to calculate roughly. **estimate** *(es-tim-ut)* *n*.
estuary *n* the wide part of a river, where it flows into the sea.

estuary

et cetera (*shortened to* etc) and so on, and other things. *We need basic foodstuffs – milk, bread, rice, etc.*
eternal *adj* without end, lasting forever. **eternally** *adv*.
eternity *n* time without end.
ethnic *adj* to do with a particular race of people.
EU *n* (*short for* European Union) a group of countries in Europe.
euthanasia *(yooth-an-**ay**-zee-uh)* *n* the painless killing of somebody who is suffering from an illness that cannot be cured.
evacuate *v* to move somebody away from an area for a time because it is dangerous. *They were evacuated to the countryside during the war.* **evacuation** *n*.
evade *v* to avoid something. *She evaded the question.* **evasion** *n*, **evasive** *adj*.
evaporate *v* to turn from a liquid into a gas, usually because of heat. **evaporation** *n*.
eve *n* the day before an event or special day. *New Year's Eve.*
even[1] *adv* a word that you use to point out the unexpected in what you are saying. *He's not my friend – I don't even know him!* **even if** no matter that.
even[2] *adj* **1** smooth and level. *an even surface.* **2** equal. *The scores are even.* **3** that can be divided exactly by two. *2, 4, 6 and 8 are even numbers.*
evening *n* the time between afternoon and night.
event *n* a happening.
eventually *adv* in the end, at last.
ever *adv* at any time, at all times.
evergreen *n* a tree that has green leaves all the year round.
every *adj* all of the people or things mentioned.
everybody, everyone *pron* every person.
everything *pron* all things, each thing.
everywhere *adv* in every place.
evict *v* to force somebody to move out of their home. **eviction** *n*.
evidence *n* information that makes somebody believe something is true.

evident *adj* clear and obvious.
evil *adj* very bad, wicked. **evil** *n*.
evolution *n* the process by which animals and plants develop and change over thousands of years.
evolve *v* to develop gradually over a period of time.
ewe *n* a female sheep.
ex- *prefix* former. *ex-president.*
exact *adj* just right, perfectly correct.
exaggerate *v* to make something sound bigger or more impressive than it really is. **exaggeration** *n*.
examination *n* **1** (*also* **exam**) an important test to find out how much you know. **2** a close look at something. *The doctor gave her a thorough examination.*
examine *v* to look at something very closely.
example *n* **1** something that shows what other things of the same kind are like. *This poem is a fine example of the poet's work.* **2** a model for other people to copy. *You should set an example to the younger children.*
exasperate *v* to irritate and frustrate somebody. **exasperation** *n*.
excavate *v* to uncover something by digging. **excavation** *n*.
exceed *v* to go beyond or be greater than something. *You must not exceed the speed limit.*
excel *v* (excels, excelling, excelled) to be very good at something.
excellent *adj* extremely good.
except *prep* not including.
exception *n* somebody or something that is not included.
exceptional *adj* unusual, remarkable.
excerpt *n* a short piece taken from a book, play, film, etc.
excess *n* a larger amount than is needed or usual. **excessive** *adj*.
exchange *v* to give one thing and get another for it. **exchange** *n*.
excite *v* to make somebody have strong feelings of happiness about something they are looking forward to. **excitement** *n*.
exclaim *v* to say something suddenly and loudly. **exclamation** *n*.
exclamation mark *n* the punctuation mark (!).
exclude *v* **1** to stop somebody taking part or joining in. **2** to not include. **exclusion** *n*.
excruciating *adj* very painful.
excursion *n* an outing.
excuse[1] *(ex-**kyoos**)* *n* a reason that you give for doing something wrong.
excuse[2] *(ex-**kyooz**)* *v* **1** to allow somebody not to do something. **2** to forgive somebody.
execute *v* to kill somebody legally as a punishment. **execution** *n*.
executive *n* a senior employee of a company.
exercise[1] *n* **1** physical activity that you do to keep strong and healthy. **2** a piece of work that you do to practise a skill.
exercise[2] *v* **1** to do physical exercises. **2** to use something. *exercise one's judgement.*
exhale *v* to breathe out. **exhalation** *n*.
exhaust[1] *(ig-**zawst**)* *v* **1** to make somebody very tired. **2** to use something up completely. **exhaustion** *n*.
exhaust[2] *n* a pipe through which waste gases from an engine are sent out.
exhibit[1] *v* to show something in public.
exhibit[2] *n* something that is shown, especially in an exhibition.
exhibition *n* a public display, especially of works of art.
exhilarating *adj* very exciting.
exile *v* to send somebody away from their own country, often as a punishment. **exile** *n*.
exist *v* to be real, to live. **existence** *n*.
exit *n* **1** a way out of a place. **2** going out. *He made a quick exit.* **exit** *v*.
exotic *adj* strange and interesting because of coming from a distant place. *exotic plants.*
expand *v* to make or become larger. **expansion** *n*.
expanse *n* a wide area. *a vast expanse of sky.*
expect *v* **1** to think that something will happen or that somebody or something will come. *I'm expecting a*

letter today. **2** to require something. *Mum expects us to tidy our own rooms.* **be expecting** to be pregnant.

expedition *n* a long journey for a special reason, such as climbing a mountain.

expel *v* (expels, expelling, expelled) to force somebody or something out. *She was expelled from school for stealing.*

expensive *adj* costing a lot of money.

experience[1] *n* **1** something that happens to you or something that you do. *Getting lost was a frightening experience.* **2** knowledge and skill gained by doing something. *She has a lot of teaching experience.*

experience[2] *v* **1** to have experience of something. **2** to feel something.

experiment *n* a test done in order to find out something. **experiment** *v.*

expert *n* a person who knows a lot about a subject.

expire *v* **1** to come to an end. *My membership expires at the end of this month.* **2** to die. **expiry** *n.*

explain *v* to make the meaning of something clear. **explanation** *n.*

explode *v* to burst with a loud bang. **explosion** *n*

exploit[1] *(ex-**ployt**)* *v* **1** to use somebody unfairly for your own advantage. **2** to use something fully.

exploit[2] *(**ex**-ployt)* *n* a daring action.

explore *v* to look carefully around a place. **exploration** *n,* **explorer** *n.*

explosive[1] *n* a substance that can explode.

explosive[2] *adj* likely to explode.

export *(ex-**port**)* *v* to sell goods to another country. **export** *(**ex**-port)* *n.* something that is exported.

expose *v* **1** to uncover or leave something unprotected. **2** to reveal the truth about somebody. **3** to allow light to fall on a film as you take a photograph. **exposure** *n.*

express[1] *v* to show something by words or actions. **expressive** *adj.*

express[2] *adj* fast. *an express train.*

expression *n* **1** the look on a person's face. **2** expressing something. **3** a phrase that has a special meaning.

extend *v* **1** to make something longer or larger. **2** to stretch out. **extension** *n.*

extensive *adj* covering a large area.

extent *n* the size or level of something.

exterior *n* the outside of something.

exterminate *v* to kill large numbers of people or animals. **extermination** *n.*

external *adj* outside. **externally** *adv.*

extinct *adj* **1** no longer in existence. *The dodo is an extinct bird.* **2** no longer active. *an extinct volcano.*

extinguish *v* to put out a fire.

extra *adj* more than is usual.

extra- *prefix* **1** beyond, outside. *extraordinary.* **2** very. *extra-special.*

extract[1] *(ik-**strakt**)* *v* to pull something out, especially by force.

extract[2] *(**ek**-strakt)* *n* a short piece taken from a book, film, etc.

extraordinary *adj* very unusual. **extraordinarily** *adv.*

extravagant *adj* spending or costing too much. **extravagance** *n.*

extreme *adj* **1** very great or strong. *extreme cold.* **2** furthest. *the extreme south-western tip of England.*

extremely *adv* very.

eye *n* **1** the part of the body that we use for seeing. **2** the small hole of a needle.

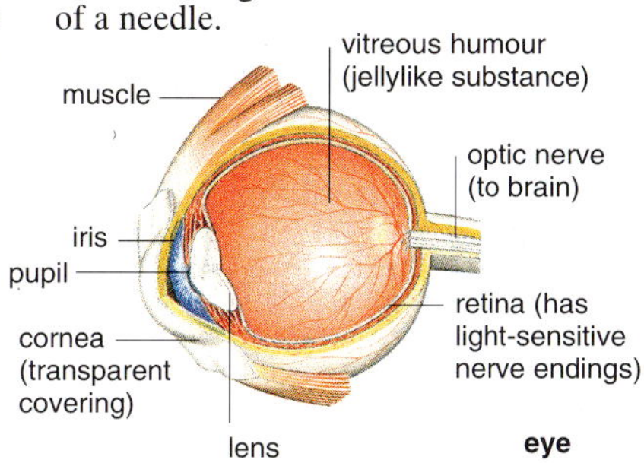

eye

eyebrow *n* the curve of hair above the eye.

eyelash *n* one of the short, curved hairs that grow on your eyelids.

eyelid *n* the flap of skin that covers your eye when it is closed.

eyesight *n* the ability to see.

eye-witness *n* a person who saw an event happen and so can describe it.

Ff

fable *n* a story that teaches a lesson, usually with animals as characters.

fabric *n* cloth.

fabulous *adj* **1** wonderful, marvellous. **2** occurring only in stories and legends. *fabulous creatures.*

face[1] *n* **1** the front part of your head. **2** the front surface of something. *a mountain face.*

face[2] *v* **1** to look towards something, to be opposite. *Our house faces north.* **2** to deal with or accept something bravely. *We have to face the truth.*

facial *adj* of your face.

facility *n* a building, service or piece of equipment for a particular purpose. *Our school has very good sports facilities.*

fact *n* something that is known to have happened or to be true. **in fact** actually.

factor *n* **1** one of the things that affect an outcome. **2** a number which divides exactly into another. *Three and two are factors of six.*

factory *n* a building where machines are used to make things.

factual *adj* containing facts.

fad *n* a fashion that does not last long.

fade *v* **1** to become gradually paler. *Our curtains have faded in the sun.* **2** to become gradually weaker or fainter.

faeces *(fee-seez)* *n* the solid waste matter that people and animals get rid of from their bodies.

Fahrenheit *(fa-ren-hite) adj* measured on the temperature scale where water freezes at 32° and boils at 212°.

fail *v* **1** not to pass something. *She failed her driving test again.* **2** not to succeed in doing something. *John failed to convince me.*

failing *n* a weakness or fault.

failure *n* **1** a lack of success. **2** an unsuccessful person or thing. **3** the fact of not doing something. *I was surprised by his failure to reply to my letter.*

faint[1] *adj* weak, not clear. *We could hear a faint sound when we listened carefully.*

faint[2] *v* to lose consciousness for a short time.

fair[1] *adj* **1** reasonable and just. **2** (of hair or skin) light-coloured. **3** quite good or quite large. **4** fine, without rain or clouds. *fair weather.*

fair[2] *n* a group of outdoor amusements, with rides, games and stalls.

fairly *adv* quite. *I know him fairly well.*

fairy *n* an imaginary magical creature like a very small person with wings.

fairy story, fairy tale *n* a traditional story for children, involving fairies, giants, magic, etc.

faith *n* **1** trust. *I have complete faith in you.* **2** a religion.

faithful *adj* loyal and true. **faithfully** *adv*, **faithfulness** *n*.

fake *n* a copy of something that is made to fool people. **fake** *adj, v*.

falcon *n* a bird of prey.

Eleanora's falcon

fall[1] *v* (falling, fell, fallen) **1** to drop to the ground. **2** to become lower or less. *The temperature falls at night.* **3** to happen. *My birthday falls on a Tuesday this year.* **fall out** to quarrel. **fall through** to fail to happen as expected.

fall[2] *n* **1** dropping or falling down. **2** American English for "autumn". **3 falls** a waterfall.

fall-out *n* radioactive dust settling after a nuclear explosion.

false *adj* **1** not true, wrong. **2** artificial, not real.

falsehood *n* a lie.

falter *v* to move or speak in an unsteady, hesitant way.

fame *n* being famous.

familiar *adj* already well-known. *Her face was familiar to me.* **be familiar with** to know about something. **familiarity** *n.*
family *n* **1** a group of people who are all related to each other. **2** a group of related animals or plants.
family tree *n* a chart showing a person's ancestors and relations.
famine *n* a serious shortage of food.
famous *adj* known to a lot of people.
fan[1] *n* an enthusiastic supporter.
fan[2] *n* a machine or object that moves the air to make you cooler. **fan** *v.*
fanatic *n* a person who is too enthusiastic about something.
fancy[1] *adj* (fancier, fanciest) elaborate and highly decorated. *a fancy hat.*
fancy[2] *v* (fancies, fancying, fancied) to be attracted to somebody or something.
fancy dress *n* unusual clothes that you wear, for example to a party, so that you look like another person or a thing. *She went to the fancy-dress party as a mermaid.*
fanfare *n* a short tune played loudly on trumpets.
fang *n* a long, sharp tooth.
fantastic *adj* **1** wonderful. **2** strange, like a fantasy. *a fantastic story.*
fantasy *n* something, usually pleasant, that you imagine or dream about, but that is not real.
far[1] *adv* (farther *or* further, farthest *or* furthest) **1** a long way away. *Our flat isn't far from the station.* **2** very much. *It's far colder than yesterday.*
far[2] *adj* distant, opposite. *They live on the far side of the lake.*
farce *n* a funny play, full of ridiculous events. **farcical** *adj.*
fare *n* the price of travelling on a bus, train, etc.
Far East *n* China, Japan and other countries in eastern Asia.
farewell goodbye. *a farewell speech.*
farm[1] *n* land and buildings where crops are grown and animals raised.
farm[2] *v* to manage a farm. **farmer** *n.*
fascinate *v* to interest and attract somebody strongly. **fascination** *n.*
fashion *n* **1** a way of dressing or doing things that is very popular for a time. **2** a way of doing things. **fashionable** *adj,* **fashionably** *adv.*
fast[1] *adj* **1** quick. **2** showing a time later than the right time. *My watch is fast.*
fast[2] *adv* **1** quickly. **2** thoroughly. *Lucy is fast asleep.* **3** firmly fixed. *My boot was stuck fast in the mud.*
fast[3] *v* to give up food for a time. *He fasted for four days.* **fast** *n.*
fasten *v* to tie or fix something firmly. **fastener** *n,* **fastening** *n.*
fat[1] *n* **1** the soft, oily substance found in animals and some plants. **2** an oily substance used in cooking, such as butter or margarine. **fatty** *adj.*
fat[2] *adj* (fatter, fattest) **1** having too much flesh on the body. **2** thick.
fatal *adj* **1** causing death. *a fatal accident.* **2** causing disaster. *a fatal decision.* **fatally** *adv.*
fate *n* **1** a power that some people believe controls events. **2** what will happen to somebody or something. *A terrible fate awaited her.*
father *n* a male parent.
fathom *n* a unit for measuring the depth of water, equal to 1.8 metres.
fatigue *(fat-eeg) n* tiredness, weakness.
fault *n* a mistake, something wrong. **faulty** *adj.*
fauna *n* the animal life of an area.
favour[1] *n* **1** a helpful or kind action. **2** approval or preference. **be in favour of** to like or support something.
favour[2] *v* to show a preference for something.
favourite *adj* liked more than any other. **favourite** *n.*
fawn *n* **1** a young deer. **2** a light yellowish-brown colour.
fax *n* **1** a machine that sends a copy of a document along telephone lines and then allows it to be printed at the other end. **2** a document sent in this way. **fax** *v.*
fear[1] *n* the feeling of being afraid.
fear[2] *v* to feel afraid of something.
fearful *adj* **1** afraid. **2** awful.
fearless *adj* brave, without fear.

fearsome *adj* frightening, terrible.
feast *n* a large and special meal. *a wedding feast.*
feat *n* a difficult and impressive achievement.
feather *n* one of the light coverings that grow on a bird's body.
feature *n* **1** one of the parts of the face, such as the nose or the mouth. **2** an important part of something. **3** a newspaper article or part of a television programme about a particular subject.
February *n* the second month of the year.
fed *past of* feed.
fed up *adj* unhappy or bored.
fee *n* a payment made to somebody for a service.
feeble *adj* weak.
feed *v* (feeding, fed) **1** to give food to a person or an animal. **2** to eat. **3** to put something into a machine. *The information is fed into a computer.*
feel *v* (feeling, felt) **1** be aware of something by touch. *She felt his hand on her shoulder.* **2** to experience an emotion or sensation. *I felt angry.* **feeling** *n.*
feeler *n* one of the two long, thin parts on the heads of insects and some other creatures, used for feeling with.
feet *plural of* foot.
feline *(fee-line) adj* to do with cats.
fell *v* **1** *past of* fall. **2** to cut or knock something down. *They felled the tree.*
fellow[1] *n* a man or boy.
fellow[2] *adj* belonging to the same group. *He doesn't know many of his fellow students.*
felt[1] *past of* feel.
felt[2] *n* thick cloth made from bits of wool that are pressed together rather than woven.
female *adj* of the sex that gives birth to children or produces eggs. **female** *n.*
feminine *adj* to do with or typical of women.
feminist *n* a supporter of women's rights. **feminism** *n.*
fen *n* low, marshy land.
fence[1] *n* a wooden or wire barrier.
fence[2] *v* to fight with special swords, called foils. **fencing** *n.*

fencing

fend *v* **fend for yourself** to take care of yourself. **fend off** to defend yourself against attack.
ferment *v* to change chemically, as bread dough does when yeast is added and as grape juice does when it turns into wine. **fermentation** *n.*
fern *n* a plant with feathery leaves.
ferocious *adj* fierce, savage. *a ferocious beast.* **ferocity** *n.*
ferret *n* a small mammal that can be trained to hunt rabbits and rats.
ferry *n* a boat that carries people and often cars for short distances.
fertile *adj* **1** able to produce babies. **2** able to produce a lot of good crops. **fertility** *n.*
fertilize *v* to make fertile. *Fertilize the soil with manure.* **fertilization** *n.*
fervent *adj* extremely keen.
fervour *n* strong enthusiasm for something. *religious fervour.*
festival *n* **1** a time when people celebrate something, especially a religious day. **2** an organized series of events, such as concerts or films.
fetch *v* to go to get somebody or something.
fetching *adj* attractive, pretty.
fête *(rhymes with* late*) n* an outdoor event with games, stalls and things to buy. A fête is usually held to collect money for charity.
feud *(fyood) n* a long-lasting, bitter quarrel between people or groups.
feudal system *n* the social system of Europe in the Middle Ages, by which people served a nobleman in return for land and protection.

fever *n* a much higher body temperature than normal, due to illness. **feverish** *adj.*

few *adj* not many, a small number. **few** *n.*

fiancé *(fee-**on**-say) n* a man that a woman is engaged to marry.

fiancée *(fee-**on**-say) n* a woman that a man is engaged to marry.

fiasco *n* (*pl* fiascos) a complete failure.

fib *n* a small lie. **fib** *v*, **fibber** *n.*

fibre *n* **1** a fine thread. **2** the substances in plants which cannot be digested by our bodies when we eat them, but which help our digestive system to work properly.

fickle *adj* changing your mind often.

fiction *n* stories about imaginary people and events. **fictional** *adj.*

fictitious *adj* not true or real. *a fictitious account of events.*

fiddle[1] *n* a violin.

fiddle[2] *v* **1** to keep touching or playing about with something. **2** to cheat.

fiddly *adj* difficult to do because it is small or complicated.

fidget *v* to move about restlessly.

field[1] *n* **1** a piece of land used for growing crops or keeping animals, often with a fence or hedge around it. **2** a piece of land used for something particular. *a sports field.* **3** an area of study or interest.

field[2] *v* to catch or stop the ball in games such as cricket. **fielder** *n.*

fiend *(feend) n* a devil or an evil person.

fierce *adj* violent and aggressive.

fiery *adj* **1** like fire. **2** easily made angry. *a fiery temper.*

fig *n* a sweet fruit full of small seeds.

fig

fight *v* (fighting, fought) **1** to try to hurt somebody using your hands or a weapon. **2** to try hard to do or get something. *We must fight for our freedom.* **3** to argue. **fight** *n.*

fighter *n* **1** a person who fights. **2** a small warplane.

figure *n* **1** a sign that we use to show a number, such as 1, 2 or 6. **2** the shape of a person's body. **3** a well-known person. *a public figure.* **4** a diagram or picture in a book.

file[1] *n* **1** a box or folder for keeping papers tidy. **2** in computing, a collection of data. **3** a metal tool with a rough surface for making things smooth. **4** a line of people walking one behind the other.

file[2] *v* **1** to put papers in a file. **2** to use a file to make something smooth. **3** to walk in a line.

fill *v* to make or become full.

fillet *n* a piece of meat or fish with the bones removed.

filling *n* **1** a substance that a dentist uses to fill a hole in a tooth. **2** the mixture inside a cake or sandwich.

film[1] *n* **1** moving pictures shown at a cinema or on television. **2** a roll of material used in a camera to make photographs. **3** a thin coating of something. *a film of oil on the water.*

film[2] *v* to make a film or television programme.

filter *n* a device that cleans liquids or gases which pass through it. **filter** *v.*

filthy *adj* (filthier, filthiest) very dirty.

fin *n* one of the parts on the outside of a fish's body that help it to swim and balance. See **fish**.

final[1] *adj* last. **finally** *adv.*

final[2] *n* the last game, match, etc of a competition. **finalist** *n.*

finance[1] *n* money affairs. **financial** *adj*, **financially** *adv.*

finance[2] *v* to provide money for something.

find *v* (finding, found) **1** to discover or come across something. **2** to know something by experience, or have an opinion about something. *I found that film funny.* **find out** to discover something.

fine[1] *adj* **1** very good. *a fine view.* **2** (of weather) good and clear. *a fine day.* **3** very thin or delicate. *fine wire.* **4** in very small pieces. *fine sand.*
fine[2] *n* an amount of money that has to be paid as a punishment.
fine[3] *v* to make somebody pay a fine. *She was fined for parking on the pavement.*
finger *n* one of the long, thin end parts of the hand.
fingernail *n* one of the nails at the end of your fingers.
fingerprint *n* the mark left on something by the tip of your finger.
finicky *adj* fussy. *He's really finicky about his food.*
finish[1] *v* to bring or come to an end.
finish[2] *n* the end, the last part.
fiord *(fee-ord) n* a long, narrow inlet in a high, rocky coast.
fir *n* an evergreen tree with cones and needle-like leaves.
fire[1] *n* **1** the light and heat that is produced when something is burning. **2** a device for heating. *an electric fire.* **3** shooting. *enemy fire.*
fire[2] *v* **1** to shoot a gun or other weapon. **2** to dismiss somebody from their job.
fire engine *n* a vehicle that carries fire-fighters and their equipment.
fire extinguisher *n* a container full of chemicals for putting out a fire.
fire-fighter *n* a person whose job is to put out fires.
fireplace *n* a space in the wall of a room for a fire.
fire station *n* a place where fire engines are kept.
fireworks *n pl* small, exploding devices that make coloured sparks or a loud noise when they are lit.
firm[1] *adj* **1** strong and steady. *The castle was built on firm ground.* **2** not changing your mind. *a firm decision.*
firm[2] *n* a business company.
first *adj*, *adv* number one in order, before all others. **first** *n*, **firstly** *adv*.
first aid *n* emergency medical treatment given to an ill or injured person before a doctor arrives.
fish[1] *n* (*pl* fish *or* fishes) a water animal with gills, fins and scales.
fish[2] *v* to try to catch fish.

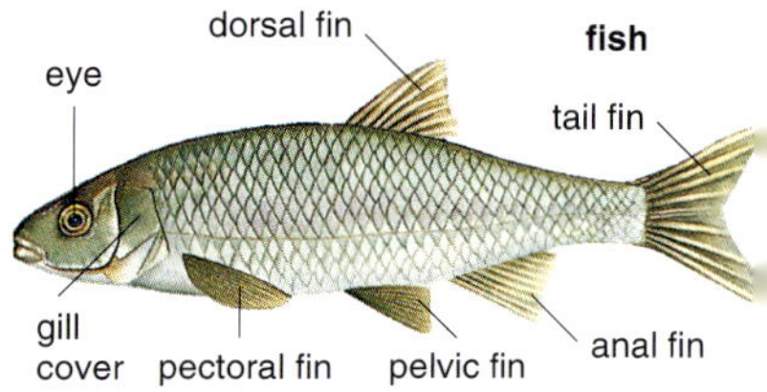

fishmonger *n* a person who sells fish to eat.
fist *n* a tightly closed hand.
fit[1] *adj* (fitter, fittest) **1** healthy and strong. **2** suitable.
fit[2] *v* (fits, fitting, fitted) **1** to be the right size and shape. *These shoes don't fit me.* **2** to put something in place. *She fitted a new lock on the door.*
fit[3] *n* **1** a sudden loss of consciousness with uncontrolled movements of the body. **2** a sudden, uncontrolled outburst. *a coughing fit.*
fitness *n* being healthy and strong.
fix[1] *v* **1** to mend something. **2** to attach or make something firm. **3** to decide something.
fix[2] *n* a difficult situation. *We're in a fix – can you help?*
fixture *n* **1** a sports event that has been arranged. **2** an object in a building that has been fixed in position, such as a cupboard or a basin.
fizz *v* to produce a lot of small bubbles. **fizzy** *adj*.
fjord *another spelling of* **fiord**.
flabby *adj* (flabbier, flabbiest) having loose, soft flesh.
flag[1] *n* a piece of coloured cloth with a pattern on it, often representing a country or an organization.
flag[2] *v* (flags, flagging, flagged) to become tired.
flair *n* a natural ability. *She has a flair for writing.*
flake *n* a small, thin, light piece of something, such as snow. **flaky** *adj*.
flamboyant *adj* bold and showy.

flamingo

flame *n* the burning gas from a fire.
flamingo *n* (*pl* flamingoes) a large, long-legged bird with pink feathers.
flammable *adj* able to burn easily.
flan *n* a flat, open pie.
flank *n* the side of an animal's body.
flannel *n* **1** a piece of cloth used for washing yourself. **2** light, woollen cloth.
flap[1] *n* a piece of material that hangs down over an opening. *a tent flap.*
flap[2] *v* (flaps, flapping, flapped) to move up and down. *The bird flapped its wings.*
flare[1] *v* **flare up** to suddenly become stronger, brighter or more violent. *The fire flared up when the oil dripped onto it.*
flare[2] *n* a flame or light used as a signal.
flash[1] *n* a sudden burst of light. **in a flash** very quickly, suddenly.
flash[2] *v* **1** to shine brightly and quickly. **2** to move quickly. *A car flashed past.*
flask *n* a bottle, especially one for keeping liquids hot or cold.
flat[1] *adj* (flatter, flattest) **1** level and smooth. **2** (of a tyre) having lost most of its air. **3** (of a drink) no longer fizzy.
flat[2] *n* **1** a set of rooms for living in, especially on one floor of a building. **2** a sign (♭) in music which indicates that a note should be played lower by half a tone.
flatten *v* to make something flat.
flatter *v* to praise somebody more than they deserve. **flattery** *n*.
flavour *n* the taste of something. **flavour** *v*.
flaw *n* a fault or weakness.
flea *n* a small, jumping insect that feeds on blood.
fledgling *n* a young bird that is just ready to fly.
flee *v* (fleeing, fled) to run away.
fleece *n* a sheep's woolly coat.
fleet *n* a group of ships or trucks.
flesh *n* **1** the soft part of humans and animals, between the bones and the skin. **2** the soft part of fruit.
flew *past of* fly.
flex *n* covered wire for carrying electricity.
flexible *adj* bending or changing easily.
flick *v* to make a quick, sharp movement. **flick** *n*.
flicker *v* to shine unsteadily. *The candle flickered.* **flicker** *n*.
flight *n* **1** flying. **2** a journey in an aircraft. **3** running away from danger. **4** a set of steps.
flimsy *adj* (flimsier, flimsiest) thin or easily broken.
fling *v* (flinging, flung) to throw something with great force.
flint *n* a very hard type of stone.
flip *v* (flips, flipping, flipped) to toss or turn something over quickly.
flipper *n* **1** an arm-like limb used by seals, walruses, etc for swimming. **2** a type of large, flat, rubber shoe that helps you swim underwater.
flirt *v* to talk to somebody to show that you are sexually attracted to them, but not in a serious way. **flirt** *n*.
float[1] *v* to be held up in water or air.
float[2] *n* a light object attached near to the end of a fishing line.
flock[1] *n* a large group of animals, particularly sheep or birds.
flock[2] *v* to move in a large group.
flog *v* (flogs, flogging, flogged) **1** to beat or whip a person or an animal. **2** *(slang)* to sell something.
flood[1] *n* a lot of water that spreads over land that is usually dry.
flood[2] *v* **1** to cover something with a flood. **2** to overflow.
floor *n* **1** the part of a room that you walk on. **2** one level or storey of a building. *We live on the second floor.*
flop[1] *v* (flops, flopping, flopped) to fall limply. **floppy** *adj*.
flop[2] *n* a complete failure.
floppy disk *n* a magnetic disk for storing data for a computer.

florist *n* a person who sells flowers.
flour *n* a powder made from grain, used for baking.
flourish *(**fluh**-rish)* *v* to grow well, to be successful.
flow *v* to move along smoothly, as water does in a river. **flow** *n.*
flower[1] *n* the coloured part of a plant that produces seeds.

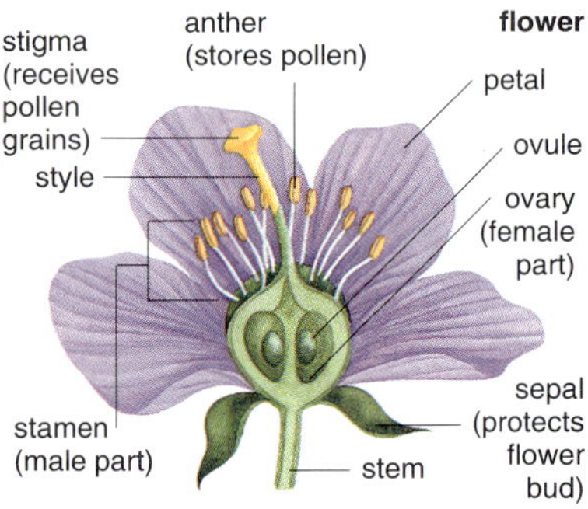

flower[2] *v* to produce flowers.
flown *past participle of* fly.
flu *n* (*short for* influenza) an illness that gives you a high temperature, a headache and aching muscles.
fluctuate *v* to change all the time. *Her mood fluctuates between delight and despair.* **fluctuation** *n.*
fluent *adj* able to speak or write easily and well.
fluff *n* small pieces of soft, woolly material from blankets or clothes.
fluffy *adj* (fluffier, fluffiest) soft and furry. *a fluffy kitten.*
fluid *n* a liquid or gas.
flung *past of* fling.
fluorescent *adj* so bright that it seems to give out light. *fluorescent colours.*
fluoride *n* a mixture of chemicals added to water and toothpaste to prevent tooth decay.
flush *v* **1** to blush. **2** to clean something by a rush of water. **flush** *n.*
flustered *adj* nervous and confused.
flute *n* a wind instrument in the shape of a long tube with holes in it.
flutter *v* to move up and down or from side to side with small, quick movements.
fly[1] *v* (flies, flying, flew, flown) **1** to move through the air. **2** to travel in or pilot an aircraft. **3** to move very quickly.
fly[2] *n* a flying insect.
flyover *n* a bridge carrying one road over another.
foal *n* a young horse.
foam *n* a mass of small bubbles. **foam** *v.*
focus *v* (focuses, focusing, focused) **1** to adjust the lens of a camera, etc, in order to get a clear picture. **2** to concentrate on something. **focus** *n.*
fodder *n* food for cows or horses.
foe *n* an enemy.
foetus *(**feet**-us)* *n* an unborn animal or human in its mother's womb.
fog *n* a thick mist that is difficult to see through. **foggy** *adj.*
foil[1] *n* **1** metal in the form of very thin sheets. **2** a sword used in fencing.
foil[2] *v* to prevent somebody from succeeding.
fold[1] *v* to bend part of a thing back over itself.
fold[2] *n* **1** a folded part of something. **2** an enclosure for sheep.
folder *n* a cover for keeping papers in.
foliage *n* the leaves of plants.
folk *n pl* people.
follow *v* **1** to go along behind somebody or something. **2** to go along a road or path. **3** to understand something.
folly *n* **1** a foolish act. **2** a building that has no real purpose.
fond *adj* **be fond of** to like something. **fondly** *adv*, **fondness** *n.*
fondle *v* to touch or stroke a person or an animal gently.
font *n* a stone basin in a church which holds water for baptism.
food *n* anything that is eaten.
fool[1] *n* a silly person.
fool[2] *v* to trick somebody.
foolish *adj* stupid, silly.
foot *n* (*pl* feet) **1** the part of the leg which you stand on. **2** the lower part of something. *the foot of the page.* **3** an old measure of length, equal to 12 inches or 30.48 centimetres.

football *n* **1** a game played by two teams who try to score goals with a large ball. **2** this ball. **footballer** *n*.

American football

footnote *n* a note at the bottom of a printed page.

footprint *n* the mark left by a foot in the ground.

footsteps *n pl* the sound of somebody walking.

forbid *v* (forbids, forbidding, forbade, forbidden) to tell somebody that they must not do something.

force[1] *v* **1** to make somebody do something against their will. **2** to push something with violence.

force[2] *n* **1** power, strength. **2** a group of people who work together, such as the police force.

ford *n* a shallow place where a river can be crossed.

forecast *v* to say what is likely to happen in the future. **forecast** *n*.

forehead *n* the part of your face above your eyebrows.

foreign *adj* from or of another country. **foreigner** *n*.

forest *n* a large area of land thickly covered with trees.

forfeit *v* to lose the right to something because of something you have done wrong. **forfeit** *n*.

forge[1] *v* to make a copy of something in order to trick people. *forged banknotes.* **forgery** *n*.

forge[2] *n* a furnace used by a blacksmith to heat metal for shaping.

forget *v* (forgets, forgetting, forgot, forgotten) not to remember.

forgive *v* (forgiving, forgave, forgiven) to stop being angry with somebody for something they have done wrong. **forgiveness** *n*.

fork *n* **1** a tool with prongs for eating with or for digging earth. **2** a place where something divides. *a fork in the road.* **fork** *v*.

forlorn *adj* lonely and unhappy.

form[1] *n* **1** the shape of something. **2** a printed paper with spaces where answers have to be filled in. **3** all the people in one year of a school.

form[2] *v* **1** to make. *Would you all stand up and form a circle.* **2** to take shape.

formal *adj* **1** following the accepted rules, official. **2** suitable for important and serious occasions. **formally** *adv*.

format[1] *v* (formats, formatting, formatted) to prepare a computer disk for use.

format[2] *n* the size, form or shape of something.

former *adj* previous, earlier. **the former** the first of two things just mentioned. *We visited France and Italy, spending longer in the former.*

formerly *adv* in past times.

formula *n* (*pl* formulae *or* formulas) a rule or fact in science or maths, written in signs or numbers.

fort *n* a building that is strongly defended against attack.

forthcoming *adj* coming soon.

fortify *v* to make a place stronger against attack. **fortification** *n*.

fortnight *n* a period of two weeks.

fortress *n* a castle or fortified town.

fortunate *adj* lucky.

fortune *n* **1** luck. **2** a lot of money.

forward, forwards *adv* towards the front.

fossil *n* the remains of a prehistoric animal or plant that are preserved as rock.

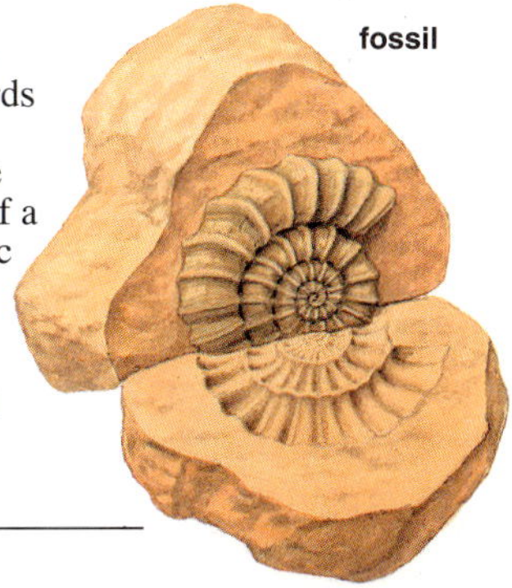

fossil

foster *v* **1** to bring up a child who is not your own, without becoming his or her legal parent. **2** to encourage something.
foster-parent *n* a person who fosters a child.
fought *past of* fight.
foul[1] *adj* dirty, disgusting, bad.
foul[2] *n* an action that breaks the rules of a sport. **foul** *v*.
found *v* **1** *past of* find. **2** to establish something. *The school was founded in 1898.* **foundation** *n*, **founder** *n*.
foundations *n pl* the strong base of a building below the ground.
foundry *n* a place where metals or glass are melted and moulded.
fountain *n* a structure producing a jet of water that rises into the air.
fountain pen *n* a pen with a nib and a supply of ink inside.
fowl *n* (*pl* fowl *or* fowls) a bird, eg a chicken, kept for its eggs or meat.
fox *n* a wild animal with red-brown fur and a bushy tail.

red fox

foyer *(foy-ay)* *n* the entrance hall of a theatre or other large building.
fraction *n* **1** a part of a whole number. ½ (one half) and ¼ (one quarter) are fractions. **2** a small amount.
fracture *v* to break or crack something, especially a bone. **fracture** *n*.
fragile *adj* delicate, easily damaged.
fragment *n* a small, broken piece.
fragrance *n* a nice smell. **fragrant** *adj*.
frail *adj* weak, feeble. **frailty** *n*.
frame *n* **1** the main, hard structure around which something is built. *The aircraft has a steel frame.* **2** the border around the edge of a picture.
framework *n* the basic supporting structure of something.
frank *adj* open and honest. **frankness** *n*.
frantic *adj* very upset or excited because of worry, fear, etc. **frantically** *adv*.
fraud *n* **1** the crime of taking money by deceit. **2** a person who pretends to be something they are not.
freckle *n* a small, brown mark on the skin. **freckly** *adj*.
free[1] *adj* **1** costing no money. **2** not tied up or shut in. **3** able to do what you want. **4** available. **freedom** *n*.
free[2] *v* (freeing, freed) to set a person or an animal free.
freeze *v* (freezing, froze, frozen) **1** to change into ice, to become solid because of cold. **2** to make food very cold so it can be kept for a long time. **3** to stand completely still.
freezer *n* a large, metal box where you can store food below freezing-point.
freezing-point *n* the temperature at which a liquid freezes.
freight *(frate)* *n* cargo.
frenzy *n* wild excitement or anger.
frequency *n* **1** the number of times that something happens. **2** the rate at which a radio wave vibrates.
frequent *adj* happening often.
fresh *adj* **1** recently made or picked. *fresh bread, fresh flowers.* **2** not tinned or preserved. *fresh fruit.* **3** cool and clean. *fresh air.*
freshwater *adj* (of a fish) living in rivers and lakes, not in the sea.
fret *v* (frets, fretting, fretted) to worry.
friction *n* the resistance an object meets with when it rubs against something else.
Friday *n* the sixth day of the week.
fridge *short for* refrigerator.
friend *n* a person that you know well and that you like. **friendship** *n*.
friendly *adj* (friendlier, friendliest) kind and helpful.
frieze *n* a decorated strip, often around the top of a wall.
frigate *n* a small, fast warship.
fright *n* a sudden feeling of fear.
frighten *v* to make somebody afraid.
frill *n* a strip of cloth or other material with many small folds, attached to something as decoration.

fringe *n* **1** hair that is cut so that it hangs down over your forehead. **2** a border of hanging threads, for example on a carpet or shawl.
frisk *v* **1** to search somebody for something illegal. **2** to jump about playfully.
frisky *adj* playful.
frivolous *adj* silly, not serious.
frock *n* a girl's or woman's dress.
frog *n* a small amphibian with long back legs and webbed feet.

front *n* **1** the part of something that faces forward. **2** in a war, the place where the fighting is. **front** *adj*.
frontier *n* a border between countries.
frost *n* powdery ice that forms on the ground when it gets very cold. **frosty** *adj*.
froth *n* a mass of small bubbles on top of a liquid.
frown *v* to pull your eyebrows together and wrinkle your forehead when you are cross or thinking hard.
froze *past of* freeze.
frozen *past participle of* freeze.
fruit *n* **1** the part of a plant with seeds inside, often used as food. **2** the result of something. *the fruit of all your hard work.*
frustrate *v* **1** to make somebody feel disappointed or angry because they cannot do what they wanted to. **2** to prevent something. **frustration** *n*.
fry *v* (fries, frying, fried) to cook food in hot oil.
fudge *n* a soft, brown sweet.
fuel *n* anything that is burned to make heat or energy, such as coal, oil, wood or gas.
fulfil *v* (fulfils, fulfilling, fulfilled) to carry out a task or promise.
full *adj* **1** with no room left inside. **2** complete. *a full explanation.*
fumble *v* to use your hands clumsily.
fumes *n pl* strong-smelling or poisonous smoke or gases.
fun *n* amusement, a good time.
function[1] *n* the special work of a person or thing.
function[2] *v* to work.
fund *n* a sum of money for a charity or other purpose.
fundamental *adj* basic and important. **fundamentally** *adv*.
funeral *n* the ceremony at which somebody who has died is buried.
fungus *n* (*pl* fungi *or* funguses) a soft, spongy plant-like growth, such as a mushroom or toadstool.
funnel *n* **1** a cone-shaped object, used to pour liquid into a narrow container. **2** a chimney on a ship.
funny *adj* (funnier, funniest) **1** amusing. **2** strange, odd. *a funny noise.* **funnily** *adv*.
fur *n* the soft, hairy covering on some animals. **furry** *adj*.
furious *adj* extremely angry.
furnace *n* a very hot oven.
furnish *v* to equip a room or building with furniture.
furniture *n* chairs, tables, beds, desks and other similar things.
furrow *n* a straight, narrow cut made in the ground by a plough.
further *adj, adv* **1** more far. **2** more, extra. *I have one further question.*
furthermore *adv* in addition.
furthest *adj, adv* most far.
fury *n* violent anger.
fuse[1] *n* **1** a safety device in an electrical circuit. **2** a string attached to a bomb, which is lit to set off the bomb.
fuse[2] *v* **1** to join together by heat. **2** to stop working because a fuse has melted. **fusion** *n*.
fuselage *n* the body of an aircraft.
fuss *n* unnecessary excitement or worry. **fuss** *v*.
fussy *adj* (fussier, fussiest) difficult to please, too concerned with detail.
future *n* the time to come.
fuzzy *adj* (fuzzier, fuzziest) **1** having a soft, hairy texture. *a fuzzy jumper.* **2** not clear. *fuzzy photographs.*

Gg

gabble *v* to talk very quickly and not very clearly.

gadget *n* a small device or tool. *A can opener is a gadget.*

gag[1] *n* **1** a piece of cloth tied over somebody's mouth to stop them speaking. **2** a joke.

gag[2] *v* (gags, gagging, gagged) to tie a piece of cloth over somebody's mouth to stop them speaking.

gain *v* to get something, to get more of something. *The baby has gained weight.* **gain** *n.*

galaxy *n* a very large group of stars and planets. **galactic** *adj.*

gale *n* a very strong wind.

gallant *adj* **1** brave and daring. **2** courteous, especially to women.

gall bladder *n* the organ in your body next to your liver, containing a greenish liquid, called bile, that helps with digestion.

galleon *n* in earlier times, a large Spanish sailing ship.

galleon

gallery *n* **1** a building where pictures or other works of art are displayed. **2** the highest part in a theatre where people sit.

galley *n* (*pl* galleys) **1** the kitchen on a ship or aircraft. **2** a long ship with one deck, moved along by oars and sails.

gallon *n* an old measure for liquids equal to 8 pints or 4.55 litres.

gallop *n* the fastest pace of a horse. **gallop** *v.*

gallows *n* a wooden frame on which criminals used to be hanged.

galore *adv* in large quantities. *At the party there was food galore.*

gamble *v* **1** to bet money on the result of a game or race. **2** to take a risk. **gambler** *n,* **gambling** *n.*

game *n* **1** an activity with rules, for one or more players. Tennis and draughts are both games. **2** wild animals and birds that are hunted for food or for sport.

gammon *n* a type of ham or bacon.

gander *n* a male goose.

gang[1] *n* a group of people who do things together.

gang[2] *v* **gang up on** to join with others against somebody.

gangster *n* a member of a gang of violent criminals.

gangway *n* (*pl* gangways) **1** a passage between rows of seats. **2** a movable bridge between a ship and the shore.

gaol *another spelling of* jail.

gap *n* a space between things.

gape *v* **1** to stare in surprise at something, with your mouth open. **2** to be wide open. *a gaping hole.*

garage *n* **1** a building where vehicles are kept. **2** a place where vehicles are repaired.

garbage *n* rubbish.

garden *n* a piece of land where flowers, vegetables, etc are grown. **gardener** *n,* **gardening** *n.*

gargle *v* to wash your throat with a liquid without swallowing it.

gargoyle *n* an ugly stone carving of a human's or animal's head for carrying water away from the roof of a building.

garish *(gair-ish) adj* too brightly coloured.

garland *n* a ring of leaves or flowers.

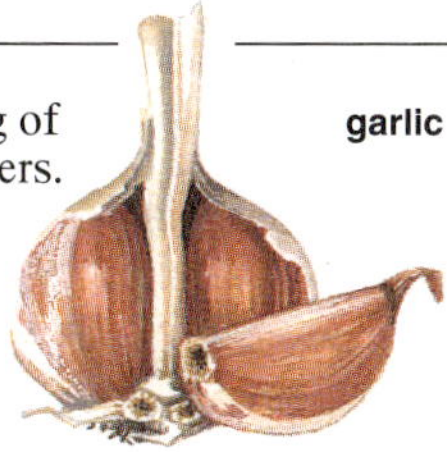

garlic

garlic *n* a plant with a strong-tasting bulb used in cooking.

garment *n* a piece of clothing.

garnish *v* to decorate food with small amounts of another food. *Garnish the dish with sprigs of parsley.*

garter *n* a band used to hold up a sock or stocking.

gas *n* **1** any substance like air. Oxygen and helium are gases. **2** the gas used for heating and cooking in our homes. **3** American English for "petrol".

gash *n* a long, deep cut.

gasp *v* **1** to take a sudden, sharp breath. **2** to breathe with difficulty. **gasp** *n.*

gastric *adj* to do with the stomach.

gate *n* a kind of door in a wall, fence or hedge.

gateau *(**ga**-toe)* *n* (*pl* gateaus *or* gateaux) a rich cream cake.

gatecrash *v* to go to a party that you have not been invited to.

gateway *n* (*pl* gateways) an opening that contains a gate, an entrance.

gather *v* **1** to collect or pick something. **2** to bring or come together. **3** to discover something. *I gather it's your birthday.*

gathering *n* a meeting of people.

gaudy *(**gor**-dee)* *adj* (gaudier, gaudiest) too brightly coloured.

gauge[1] *(rhymes with* rage*)* *v* **1** to measure something accurately. **2** to estimate something.

gauge[2] *n* **1** an instrument for measuring something. *a petrol gauge.* **2** the distance between the two rails of a railway track.

gauntlet *n* a long, thick, protective glove.

gauze *(gorz)* *n* thin, woven cloth used as a bandage.

gave *past of* give.

gay *adj* **1** homosexual. **2** cheerful, happy.

gaze *v* to look at something for a long time. **gaze** *n.*

gazelle *n* a type of small antelope found in parts of Africa and Asia.

gear *n* **1** one of a set of toothed wheels working together to send power to the wheels of a car, bicycle, etc. **2** equipment or clothes. *sports gear.*

geese *plural of* goose.

gel *n* a thick substance like jelly.

gem *n* a precious stone.

gender *n* the sex of a person or an animal.

gene *n* a tiny part of the cells of all living things. Genes are responsible for the way living things look and develop, and are passed on from parents to their children.

general[1] *adj* **1** to do with most people or things. *The general feeling is that the prime minister should resign.* **2** not detailed or specific. *a general description of events.*

general[2] *n* a senior officer in the army.

generally *adv* usually, mostly.

generate *v* to produce something, especially electricity.

generation *n* **1** all the people of about the same age. *People of my generation listen to different music from our parents.* **2** the generating of something. *the generation of electricity.*

generator *n* a machine that produces electricity.

generous *adj* ready to give money, help, etc freely and happily. **generosity** *n.*

genetic *adj* to do with genes.

genetics *n* the study of the way that characteristics are passed on from one generation to the next through genes.

genitals *n pl* the sex organs on the outside of the body.

genius *(**jeen**-yus)* *n* an extremely clever person.

gentle *adj* **1** quiet and kind, not rough. *Be gentle with the kitten.* **2** not harsh or strong, soft. *a gentle breeze.* **3** rising gradually. *a gentle slope.* **gentleness** *n,* **gently** *adv.*

gentleman *n* (*pl* gentlemen) **1** a polite word for a man. **2** a man with good manners.
genuine *adj* real and true, not fake.
geography *n* the study of the Earth and its countries, physical features, weather and people. **geographer** *n*, **geographical** *adj*.
geology *n* the study of the Earth's rocks and soil and how they were formed. **geological** *adj*, **geologist** *n*.
geometric, geometrical *adj* **1** to do with geometry. **2** consisting of regular lines or shapes. *a geometric design.*
geometry *n* the study in mathematics of lines, angles and shapes.
geranium *n* a garden plant with red, pink, white or purple flowers.
gerbil *n* a small rodent often kept as a pet.
geriatric *adj* to do with older people. *The hospital has a geriatric ward.*
germ *n* a very small living thing that can cause disease.
germinate *v* (of a seed) to begin to develop into a plant. **germination** *n*.
gesture *n* **1** a movement of your hands or head to express a feeling or idea. **2** something that you do to express your feelings. *She sent him some flowers as a gesture of friendship.*
get *v* (getting, got) **1** to receive or obtain. *I got a bike for my birthday.* **2** to buy or bring. *Will you get me some fruit from the shop?* **3** to go somewhere, to arrive. *How do we get across the river?* **4** to become. *He's getting fat.* **5** to persuade. *Can you get him to agree?* **6** to catch an illness. *I'm getting a cold.* **7** to understand. *She didn't get the joke.* **get away with** to do something bad but not be punished for it. **get by** to manage. *She gets by on a very small salary.* **get on** to make progress. **get on with** to have a friendly relationship with somebody. **get out of** to avoid doing something. **get over** to recover from something. *She's getting over her cold.* **get through 1** to pass an exam or test. **2** to contact somebody on the telephone.

gibbon

geyser *(gee-zer) n* a natural hot spring from which hot water and steam shoot out.
ghastly *adj* horrible, terrible.
ghost *n* the spirit of a dead person that appears to somebody who is still living. **ghostly** *adj*.
giant[1] *n* a huge, usually frightening, person in fairy stories.
giant[2] *adj* unusually large. *a giant fish.*
gibberish *n* nonsense.
gibbon *n* an ape with long arms and no tail.
giddy *adj* (giddier, giddiest) dizzy. **giddiness** *n*.
gift *n* **1** a present, something that is given. **2** a natural ability. *He has a gift for music.*
gifted *adj* with great natural ability.
gig *n* a performance by a musician or band.
gigantic *(jy-**gan**-tik) adj* very large.
giggle *v* to laugh in a silly way. **giggle** *n*, **giggly** *adj*.
gill *n* one of the parts of a fish's body through which it breathes. See **fish**.
gilt *adj* covered thinly with gold.
gimmick *n* something unusual used as a way of attracting attention. *an advertising gimmick.*
gin *n* a colourless, alcoholic drink made from grain.
ginger *n* **1** a hot-tasting root of a plant, used as a flavouring. See **spice**. **2** a reddish-brown colour. **ginger** *adj*.
gingerbread *n* a cake flavoured with ginger.
gingham *n* checked cotton cloth.
gipsy *another spelling of* gypsy.
giraffe *n* an African mammal with a long neck and very long legs.

girder *n* a large iron or steel bar supporting a floor or wall.
girl *n* a female child or a young woman.
gist *(jist) n* the main points. *Just give me the gist of what she said.*
give *v* (giving, gave, given) **1** to hand something over to somebody else. *She gave me a present for my birthday.* **2** to let somebody have something. *Can you give me some advice?* **3** to make a sound, movement, etc. *He gave a shout.* **4** to bend or break. *We pushed hard against the door and at last the lock gave.* **give in** to finally agree to something that you do not want to do. *Her dad finally gave in and said she could have an ice-cream.* **give out** to distribute. *Can you give out these books to the class?* **give up** to stop doing or using something. *My uncle is trying to give up smoking.* **give way 1** to let other people go in front of you. **2** to break or collapse.
glacier *(**glas**-ee-er) n* a huge mass of ice that moves slowly down a mountain valley.
glad *adj* (gladder, gladdest) pleased.
gladiator *n* in ancient Rome, a man trained to fight for the entertainment of spectators.
glamour *n* attractiveness and excitement. *the glamour of Hollywood.* **glamorous** *adj.*
glance *v* to look quickly at something. **glance** *n.*
gland *n* an organ in the body that stores substances for the body to use or get rid of.
glare *v* **1** to look angrily at somebody. **2** to shine with an unpleasantly bright light. **glare** *n.*
glass *n* **1** a hard, transparent material used to make windows and bottles. **2** a container made of glass, used for drinking out of. **3** a mirror.
glasses *n pl* lenses in a frame that you wear over your eyes to help you see better.
glaze[1] *v* **1** to fit glass into a window. **2** to cover something with a shiny coating. *The potter glazed the vase.*
glaze[2] *n* a shiny coating painted onto pottery before it is fired.
glazier *n* a person who fits glass into windows.
gleam *v* to shine brightly. **gleam** *n.*
glee *n* great joy. **gleeful** *adj.*
glen *n* a narrow valley.
glide *v* to move smoothly and easily.
glider *n* a small, light aircraft without an engine.
glimmer *n* to shine faintly. **glimmer** *n.*
glimpse *v* to see something for only a moment. **glimpse** *n.*
glisten *v* to shine like a wet surface.
glitter[1] *v* to shine with a lot of tiny, bright flashes of light, to sparkle.
glitter[2] *n* tiny, sparkly pieces used for decoration.
global *adj* concerning the whole world. **globally** *adv.*
globe *n* an object shaped like a ball, especially a map of the Earth shaped like this.
gloomy *adj* (gloomier, gloomiest) **1** dark and dull. **2** sad. *Don't look so gloomy.* **gloom** *n*, **gloomily** *adv.*
glorious *adj* magnificent, beautiful.
glory *n* **1** fame, honour. **2** beauty, splendour.
gloss *n* a shine on a surface. *Her hair has a lovely gloss.* **glossy** *adj.*
glossary *n* a list of special words and their meanings.
glove *n* a covering for your hand.
glow *v* to send out a steady heat or light without flames. *The barbecue is ready to use when the coals are glowing.* **glow** *n.*
glow-worm *n* a beetle whose tail glows green in the dark.
glucose *n* a natural sugar found in plant and animal tissue.
glue *n* a sticky substance used for joining things together. **glue** *v.*
glum *adj* (glummer, glummest) sad and gloomy.
glut *n* too large a supply of something. *a glut of apples.*
gnat *(nat) n* a small flying insect that bites.
gnaw *(naw) v* to keep chewing or biting at something.

gnome *(nome)* *n* a small creature in fairy stories that lives underground.
go[1] (goes, going, went, gone) **1** to walk, travel or move somewhere. *We went to the cinema.* **2** to lead somewhere. *Where does this road go?* **3** to become. *This apple has gone bad.* **4** to work properly. *My watch doesn't go.* **5** to disappear. *Your bike has gone!* **going to** intending to, about to. *I'm going to phone Sam later.* **go off** **1** to explode. *A bomb has gone off.* **2** to become rotten. *This meat has gone off.* **3** to stop liking somebody or something. **go on** to continue.
go[2] *n* (*pl* goes) a turn or attempt.
goal *n* **1** the space into which a ball must go to score in games such as football and hockey. **2** the point scored by doing this. **3** something you are trying to achieve. *Her goal in life is to become a ballet dancer.*
goat *n* a farm animal with horns and a beard.
gobble *v* to eat quickly and greedily.
goblin *n* a small, ugly and usually evil creature in fairy stories.
god *n* **1** a supernatural being that is worshipped because people believe that it has control over their lives. **2 God** in the Christian, Jewish and Muslim religions, the creator and ruler of the universe.
goddess *n* a female god.
godparent, godfather, godmother *n* a person who promises at a child's baptism to make sure that the **godchild** (**goddaughter** or **godson**) is brought up in the Christian way.
goggles *n pl* large glasses that protect your eyes from water, dust, etc.
gold *n* **1** a precious, shiny, yellow metal used for making jewellery. **2** a yellow colour. **gold** *adj*.
golden *adj* **1** made of gold. **2** with the colour of gold.
goldfish *n* (*pl* goldfish *or* goldfishes) an orange fish often kept as a pet.
golf *n* a game in which a small ball is hit across open ground and into small holes with a stick (called a **golf club**). **golfer** *n*.

gondola *n* a long, narrow boat used on the canals in Venice.
gondolier *n* a person who moves a gondola through the water.
gone *past participle of* go.
gong *n* a metal disc that makes a ringing note when it is hit with a hammer.
good *adj* (better, best) **1** of a high quality or standard. *a good book.* **2** well-behaved. *Be a good dog.* **3** pleasant. *I'm in a good mood today.* **4** kind, virtuous. *You've been very good to me.* **5** suitable. *She's a good person for the job.* **6** skilful. *a good swimmer.* **7** healthy, beneficial. *Fresh fruit is good for you.* **goodness** *n*.
goodbye a word that you say when leaving somebody.
Good Friday *n* the Friday before Easter.
goods *n pl* **1** things that are bought and sold. **2** things that are carried on trains or lorries.
goose *n* (*pl* geese) a large water bird with webbed feet.
gooseberry *n* a sour-tasting green berry with a hairy skin.
goose-pimples *n pl* small bumps that sometimes appear on your skin when you are cold or afraid.
gore *n* blood from a wound.
gorge[1] *n* a steep, narrow valley.
gorge[2] *v* **gorge yourself** to eat greedily.
gorgeous *adj* extremely beautiful or attractive.

gorilla *n* the largest type of ape, found in Africa.
gory *adj* (gorier, goriest) full of violence and blood. *a gory film.*
gosling *n* a young goose.
gospel *n* one of the four books of the New Testament, containing accounts of the life and teachings of Jesus.
gossip *n* talk about other people that is often unkind or untrue. **gossip** *v.*
got *past of* get.
govern *v* to rule or control, especially a country. **governor** *n.*
government *n* the people who govern a country.
gown *n* **1** a woman's dress. **2** a loose robe worn by lawyers, judges, etc.
GP *n* (*short for* general practitioner) a family doctor who treats all kinds of minor illnesses.
grab *v* (grabs, grabbing, grabbed) to take something quickly and roughly.
grace *n* **1** beauty of movement. *The dancer moved with incredible grace.* **2** mercy. *the grace of God.* **3** decency, politeness. *He didn't even have the grace to apologize.* **4** a short prayer said before a meal.
graceful *adj* moving beautifully. **gracefully** *adv.*
gracious *adj* polite and kind.
grade *n* **1** one level in a scale of qualities or sizes. *Grade 1 eggs are the biggest.* **2** a mark for an exam or a piece of school work.
gradient *n* the steepness of a slope.
gradual *adj* happening slowly, little by little. **gradually** *adv.*
graduate[1] *(**graj**-yoo-ate)* *v* to successfully complete a course of study, especially at a university. **graduation** *n.*
graduate[2] *(**graj**-yoo-ut)* *n* a person who has graduated.
graffiti *n pl* words or drawings scribbled on a wall.
graft *v* **1** to cut part of one plant and join it to another so that it grows. **2** to remove skin or bone from one part of the body to help repair a damaged part. **graft** *n.*
grain *n* **1** the seeds of plants such as wheat, rice and oats. **2** a very small, hard piece of something. *a grain of sand.* **3** the natural pattern in wood.
grammar *n* the rules for using words and putting them together. **grammatical** *adj.*
gramme, gram *n* a measure of weight. There are 1,000 grammes in a kilogramme.
gramophone *n (old-fashioned)* a record-player.
granary *n* a building where grain is stored.
grand *adj* **1** important, splendid, impressive. **2** very pleasant.
grandchild, granddaughter, grandson *n* the child of your daughter or son.
grandparent, grandfather, grandmother *n* the parent of one of your parents.
grandstand *n* a covered stand with rows of seats at a sports ground.
granite *(**gran**-it)* *n* a hard, grey or reddish rock often used in building.
grant[1] *v* to allow or give something. *He was granted permission to stay in the country.* **take something for granted** **1** to assume that something is true without checking. **2** to have something without appreciating it.
grant[2] *n* a sum of money awarded for a particular purpose.
grape *n* a green or purple berry that grows in bunches on a vine and from which wine is made.
grapefruit *n* (*pl* grapefruit *or* grapefruits) a large, yellow fruit similar to an orange.
graph *n* a diagram used to show changes in a quantity or value.
graphic *adj* **1** clear and detailed. *a graphic description.* **2** to do with drawing and designing. *a graphic artist.*
graphics *n pl* drawings, pictures or designs.
grasp *v* **1** to take hold of something firmly. **2** to understand something. **grasp** *n.*
grass *n* a plant with thin, green leaves that grows on lawns and in fields.

grasshopper *n* a small, jumping insect which makes a noise by rubbing its wings together.

grasshopper

grate[1] *v* to shred food into small, thin pieces by rubbing it against a metal tool (a **grater**) that has a rough surface full of small holes.
grate[2] *n* a framework of metal bars in a fireplace, for holding coal or wood.
grateful *adj* feeling thankful. **gratefully** *adv*.
gratitude *n* being grateful.
grave[1] *n* a hole in the ground in which a dead body is buried.
grave[2] *adj* serious, solemn.
gravel *n* small stones used in the making of roads and paths.
graveyard *n* a place, often near a church, where dead people are buried.
gravity *n* **1** the natural force that attracts things towards the Earth. **2** being grave, seriousness.
gravy *n* a hot sauce, usually made with meat juices.
graze *v* **1** to eat grass that is growing. **2** to scrape your skin. **graze** *n*.
grease *n* any thick, oily substance. **greasy** *adj*.
great *adj* **1** very large. **2** important and famous. **3** very good, wonderful.
greedy *adj* (greedier, greediest) wanting more of something than you need. **greed** *n*, **greedily** *adv*.
green[1] *n* **1** the colour of grass or leaves. **2** an open, grassy area.
green[2] *adj* **1** having the colour green. **2** to do with the care and protection of the environment.
greengrocer *n* a shopkeeper who sells fresh fruit and vegetables.
greenhouse *n* a glass building where plants are grown.
greenhouse effect *n* the warming up of the Earth's surface, due to gases such as carbon dioxide in the atmosphere trapping the Sun's heat.
greet *v* to welcome somebody. *She greeted me with a kiss.* **greeting** *n*.
grenade *n* a small bomb thrown by hand.
grew *past of* grow.
grey *n* a colour half-way between black and white. **grey** *adj*.
grid *n* a set of straight lines which cross each other to make squares.
grief *n* great sadness.
grieve *v* to feel grief, especially because somebody has died.
grill[1] *v* to cook something under or over direct heat.
grill[2] *n* a part of a cooker used for grilling food.
grim *adj* (grimmer, grimmest) **1** serious, stern. **2** very unpleasant.
grime *n* dirt. **grimy** *adj*.
grin *n* a broad smile. **grin** *v*.
grind *v* (grinding, ground) to crush something into a powder.
grip *v* (grips, gripping, gripped) to hold something firmly. **grip** *n*.
gripping *adj* keeping your attention because it is so exciting.
gristle *n* a tough, rubbery substance found in meat.
grit *n* tiny pieces of stone.
groan *v* to make a long, deep sound showing pain or sorrow. **groan** *n*.
grocer *n* a shopkeeper who sells food and household supplies.
groceries *n pl* things bought in a grocer's shop.
groom[1] *n* **1** a person who looks after a horse. **2** a bridegroom.
groom[2] *v* to brush and clean an animal's coat.
groove *n* a long, thin cut in a surface.
grope *v* to feel your way by touch.
gross[1] *(grohs) adj* **1** unpleasantly fat or large. **2** very bad indeed. *a gross error*. **3** rude, coarse. **4** total, with nothing taken away. *gross salary* (= before tax and other deductions).
gross[2] *n* 12 dozen, 144.
grotesque *(grow-**tesk**) adj* very unnatural or strange-looking.
grotto *n* (*pl* grottoes) a small cave.
grotty *adj* (grottier, grottiest) unpleasant, in bad condition.

ground[1] *n* **1** the surface of the Earth. **2** a sports field.

ground[2] *past of* grind.

grounds *n pl* **1** the land around a large building. *the castle grounds.* **2** good reasons. *What grounds do you have for calling him a liar?*

group *n* **1** a number of people or things gathered together or belonging together. **2** a number of musicians who play or sing together. **group** *v.*

grove *n* a group of trees.

grovel *v* (grovels, grovelling, grovelled) to behave too humbly towards somebody.

grow *v* (growing, grew, grown) **1** to develop, to get bigger or taller. **2** to plant something in the ground and look after it. **3** to become. *She grew tired.* **grow up** to become an adult.

growl *v* to make a low, rough sound in the throat. **growl** *n.*

grown-up *n* an adult person. **grown-up** *adj.*

growth *n* **1** growing. **2** a lump growing on or inside a living thing.

grub *n* **1** the young of some insects after they hatch. **2** *(slang)* food.

grubby *adj* (grubbier, grubbiest) dirty. **grubbiness** *n.*

grudge[1] *n* a feeling of anger or resentment towards somebody because of an event in the past.

grudge[2] *v* to be unhappy that somebody has something.

gruelling *adj* difficult and exhausting.

gruesome *adj* horrible.

grumble *v* to complain in a cross way.

grumpy *adj* (grumpier, grumpiest) bad-tempered. **grumpily** *adv.*

grunt *v* to make a low, rough noise, like a pig. **grunt** *n.*

guarantee *n* a promise, especially to mend or replace an item that goes wrong after it is bought. **guarantee** *v.*

guard[1] *v* **1** to protect something from being attacked or stolen. **2** to watch somebody to stop them escaping.

guard[2] *n* **1** a person who guards. **2** a railway employee in charge of a train. **3** the duty of guarding. **4** an object that protects. *a fire-guard.*

guardian *n* a person who is legally responsible for looking after a child but who is not the child's parent.

guerrilla *(guh-**ril**-uh) n* a member of a small, unofficial army that makes surprise attacks, especially against official government troops.

guess *v* to give an answer or opinion without knowing if it is exactly right. **guess** *n.*

guest *n* a person who is visiting another person's house or who is staying in a hotel.

guide[1] *v* to show somebody the way, to lead.

guide[2] *n* a person or thing that guides.

guidebook *n* a book of information for tourists.

guide dog *n* a dog specially trained to guide blind people safely.

guillotine *(gil-uh-teen) n* **1** an instrument for cutting off people's heads. **2** an instrument with a large blade for cutting paper.

guilty *adj* having done something wrong. **guilt** *n,* **guiltily** *adv.*

guinea-pig *n* **1** a small, furry rodent without a tail, often kept as a pet. **2** a person who is used in an experiment.

guitar *n* a musical instrument with strings which you pluck. **guitarist** *n.*

gulf *n* a large bay.

gull *n* a large sea bird.

gulp *v* to swallow noisily and quickly.

gum *n* **1** the pink flesh in which your teeth are set. See **tooth**. **2** glue. **3** chewing-gum.

gun *n* a weapon that fires bullets from a long tube that is open at one end.

gunfire *n* the firing of guns.

gurgle *v* to make a bubbling sound.

gush *v* to flow out suddenly. *Blood gushed from the wound.*

gust *n* a sudden blast of wind.

guts *n pl* **1** the intestines. **2** courage.

gutter *n* a small channel for carrying away rainwater.

guy *n* (*pl* guys) **1** a man or boy. **2** a dummy of Guy Fawkes, burnt on 5 November.

gym *short for* gymnasium *and* gymnastics.

gymkhana *n* a competition for horses or ponies and their riders.
gymnasium *n* a room or building with equipment for physical exercise.
gymnast *n* a person who does gymnastics.
gymnastics *n pl* exercises to strengthen your body and make you more agile, often using equipment such as bars and ropes.

gymnastics

gypsy *n* a member of a race of people who live and travel around in caravans.

Hh

habit *n* **1** something that you do so often that you do not think about it. **2** a monk's or nun's robe. **habitual** *adj*, **habitually** *adv*.
habitable *adj* fit to be lived in.
habitat *n* the natural home of an animal or plant.
hack *v* **1** to chop something roughly. **2** to get into a computer system illegally in order to get information from it. **hacker** *n*.
had *past of* have.
haddock *n* an edible sea fish.
haggard *adj* looking tired and ill because of pain or worry.
hail[1] *n* frozen rain falling as small balls of ice. **hail** *v*.
hail[2] *v* to call or wave to somebody or something. *We hailed a taxi.*
hair *n* **1** one of the thread-like growths on the skin of mammals. **2** a mass of these on a person's head.
haircut *n* the cutting of somebody's hair, or the style in which it is cut.
hairdresser *n* a person who cuts and styles people's hair.
hair-raising *adj* very frightening.
hairy *adj* (hairier, hairiest) **1** covered in hair. **2** *(informal)* frightening.
halal *n* meat from animals that have been killed according to Muslim law.
half[1] *n* (*pl* halves) one of the two equal parts of something.
half[2] *adv* partly, not completely. *She left her dinner half-eaten.*
half-hearted *adj* not eager.
half term *n* a short holiday in the middle of a school term.
hall *n* **1** the entrance room of a house. **2** a large public room for meetings, concerts or other events.
Hallowe'en *n* the evening of 31 October when, in the past, people believed that witches and ghosts roamed about.
hallucinate *v* to see something in your mind that does not really exist. **hallucination** *n*.
halo *n* (*pl* haloes *or* halos) a circle of light around something.
halt *v* to stop. **halt** *n*.
halve *v* **1** to divide into two equal parts. **2** to reduce something by half.
halves *plural of* half.
ham *n* salted or smoked meat from a pig's leg.
hamburger *n* a round, flat cake of minced beef inside a roll, eaten hot.
hamlet *n* a very small village.
hammer[1] *n* a tool with a heavy metal head used for hitting nails into things.
hammer[2] *v* **1** to hit with a hammer. **2** to hit loudly and repeatedly. *He hammered on the door.*
hammock *n* a long piece of cloth hung up at the corners and used as a bed.
hamper[1] *n* a large basket with a lid.
hamper[2] *v* to make it difficult to do something. *She tried to run, but was hampered by her high heels.*

common hamster

hamster *n* a small rodent with a short tail and pouches in its mouth for storing food, often kept as a pet.

hand[1] *n* **1** the part at the end of your arm, with four fingers and a thumb. **2** a pointer on a clock. **3** the set of playing-cards that you hold in your hand during a card game. **give somebody a hand** to help somebody.

hand[2] *v* to pass something with your hand. *Please hand me the salt.*

handbag *n* a small bag for carrying your personal belongings.

handcuffs *n pl* steel rings joined by a short chain, used for locking a prisoner's hands together.

handful *n* **1** as much of something as you can hold in your hand. **2** a small number or amount. **3** *(informal)* a person who is difficult to control. *Her youngest son is quite a handful!*

handicap *n* **1** anything that makes it more difficult to do things, a disadvantage. **2** a physical or mental disability. **handicapped** *adj*.

handicraft *n* an activity which needs skilful use of your hands, such as pottery or embroidery.

handkerchief *(hang-ker-chief)* *n* a piece of cloth or paper used for wiping your nose.

handle[1] *n* the part of an object that you can hold it by.

handle[2] *v* **1** to touch something with your hands. **2** to deal with something. *You handled the situation very well.*

handlebars *n pl* the bar at the front of a bicycle or motorcycle that the rider holds and uses to steer.

handsome *adj* good-looking.

handwriting *n* writing done by hand.

handy *adj* (handier, handiest) **1** easy to reach, in a convenient place. *The house is handy for the shops.* **2** easy to use. *a handy tool.* **3** clever with your hands. *She's handy with a screwdriver.*

hang *v* **1** (hanging, hung) to fix or be fixed from above so that the lower part is free. **2** (hanging, hanged) to kill somebody by hanging them by a rope around their neck. **hang around** to wait in a place without having anything special to do there. **hang on** **1** to wait. **2** to hold on to something firmly. **hang up** to end a telephone call by putting down the receiver.

hangar *n* a large building where aircraft are kept.

hanger *n* a shaped wooden, metal or plastic object with a hook, for hanging clothes on.

hang-glider *n* a type of very large kite to which you can strap yourself and use to fly from the top of a cliff, hill, etc in the sport of **hang-gliding**.

Hanukka *n* the Jewish festival of lights in December.

happen *v* to take place, to occur. **happen to** to do something by chance. *My friend and I happen to have the same birthday.*

happening *n* an event.

happy *adj* (happier, happiest) **1** feeling or showing pleasure. **2** willing. *I'd be happy to help you.* **happily** *adv*, **happiness** *n*.

harass *v* to annoy or trouble somebody constantly. **harassment** *n*.

harbour[1] *n* a place where ships shelter, or unload their cargoes.

harbour[2] *v* to give shelter or a hiding-place to somebody.

hard[1] *adj* **1** solid or firm, not soft. *The ground was too hard to dig.* **2** difficult. *Yesterday's homework was really hard.* **3** harsh, tough, not kind or gentle. *Don't be too hard on the children.* **harden** *v*, **hardness** *n*.

hard[2] *adv* **1** with great effort. **2** with great force.

hard copy *n* information from a computer printed on paper.

hard disk *n* a part inside a computer that holds large amounts of data.

hardly *adv* only just, almost not. *There's hardly any money left.*

hardware *n* **1** computer equipment. **2** household tools and equipment.

hare *n* an animal like a large rabbit with long ears and a short tail.
harm *v* to hurt or damage somebody or something. **harm** *n.*
harmful *adj* causing harm.
harmless *adj* safe, not dangerous.
harmonica *n* a mouth-organ.
harmony *n* **1** a pleasant combination of musical notes played at the same time. **2** peaceful agreement. *The two organizations work together in harmony.* **harmonize** *v.*
harness *n* the leather straps by which a horse is attached to the cart that it is pulling. **harness** *v.*
harp *n* a large musical instrument played by plucking strings with your fingers. **harpist** *n.*

harp

harpoon *n* a spear used for hunting whales.
harpsichord *n* a stringed instrument with a keyboard, similar to a piano.
harsh *adj* **1** cruel, stern. **2** rough and unpleasant to see or hear. *a harsh voice.*
harvest *n* **1** the time for cutting and bringing in grain and other crops. **2** the crops brought in. **harvest** *v.*
has *form of* have.
hassle[1] *n* **1** something that is a nuisance and difficult to do. *It was a real hassle finding someone to mend our car.* **2** a disagreement.
hassle[2] *v* to bother somebody all the time. *Stop hassling me!*
haste *n* doing things quickly.
hasten *v* to hurry.
hasty *adj* (hastier, hastiest) **1** done in a hurry. **2** done without thinking carefully. **hastily** *adv.*
hat *n* a covering for the head.
hatch[1] *n* an opening in a wall, floor, etc, often covered by a small door.
hatch[2] *v* **1** to break out of an egg. **2** to plan something in secret.
hatchback *n* car with a back door that opens upwards.
hatchet *n* a small axe.
hate[1] *v* to dislike something very much.
hate[2], **hatred** *n* a strong dislike.
haughty *adj* (haughtier, haughtiest) too proud and thinking that you are better than other people.
haul *v* to pull a heavy load.
haunt *v* (of a ghost) to visit a place often. **haunted** *adj.*
have *v* (has, having, had) **1** to own or possess. *Katie has a new bike.* **2** to feel or experience. *I have a bad cold.* **3** to get or take. *We had hamburgers for lunch.* **4** to cause to be done. *Have you had your hair cut?* **have to** must. *I have to go out now.*
haven *n* a safe place.
havoc *n* destruction, great disorder.
hawk *n* a bird of prey.
hay *n* grass that has been cut and dried, used as food for animals.
hay fever *n* an allergy to pollen which affects some people in summer. It causes sneezing and sore eyes.
haystack *n* a large pile of hay.
hazard *n* a danger or risk. *the hazards of mountain-climbing.* **hazardous** *adj.*
haze *n* a thin mist. **hazy** *adj.*
hazel *n* **1** a small tree that produces hazelnuts. **2** the brownish-green colour of some people's eyes.
head[1] *n* **1** the top part of your body, containing your eyes, mouth, brain, etc. **2** the chief person, the person in charge. **3** the top or front part of something. *the head of a queue.*
head[2] *v* **1** to lead something. *He heads a team of scientists.* **2** to move in a certain direction. *We're heading home.* **3** to hit a ball with your head.
headache *n* a pain in your head.
headdress *n* a covering for the head.
heading *n* words written above a piece of writing, a title.
headlight *n* one of the main lights on the front of a vehicle.
headline *n* **1** words in larger print at the top of a story in a newspaper. **2 the headlines** the most important items of news, on TV or radio.

headphones *n pl* a pair of small speakers that you wear over your ears, for listening to music, etc.
headquarters *n* the main office of an organization, from which the whole organization is controlled.
headteacher *n* a person who is in charge of a school.
headway *n* progress.
heal *v* to make or become well or healthy again. *The cut on my arm healed quickly.*
health *n* how well or ill you are. *The old man is in poor health.*
healthy *adj* (healthier, healthiest) **1** well and strong. **2** good for your health. *healthy food.* **healthily** *adv.*
heap *n* a pile of things. **heap** *v.*
hear *v* (hearing, heard) **1** to take in sounds through your ears. *Can you hear that funny noise?* **2** to receive information. *Have you heard the good news?*
hearing *n* the ability to hear.
hearing aid *n* a small device worn by a person with poor hearing to make sounds louder.
hearse *(rhymes with* nurse*) n* a car that carries a coffin to a funeral.
heart *n* **1** the organ that pumps blood around your body.

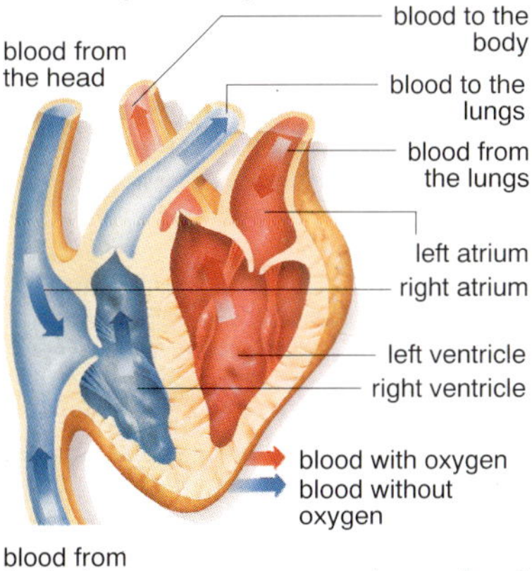

human heart

2 the central or most important part. **3** feelings, emotions. **4** courage. **5** a shape like this ♥. **6 hearts** one of the four suits in a pack of cards.
heart attack *n* a sudden failure of the heart to work properly, sometimes causing death.
heartbreak *n* great sadness. **heartbreaking** *adj,* **heartbroken** *adj.*
hearth *n* the floor of a fireplace.
heartless *adj* without feeling or pity.
hearty *adj* (heartier, heartiest) **1** cheerful and enthusiastic. *a hearty welcome.* **2** large and strong. *a hearty appetite.* **heartily** *adv.*
heat[1] *n* **1** how hot something is. **2** the warmth from something hot. **3** one of the stages in a competition, to decide who will take place in the final.
heat[2] *v* to make or become hot. *We heated up the soup.*
heater *n* something that produces heat.
heath *n* an area of unused land, usually covered with grass and shrubs.
heather *n* a low-growing shrub that grows on moors and hills.
heat wave *n* a period of very hot weather.
heave *v* to lift, push or throw something with effort. *They heaved the wardrobe up into the van.*
heaven *n* the home of God, where good people are believed to go when they die.
heavy *adj* (heavier, heaviest) **1** weighing a lot. *a heavy parcel.* **2** having a particular weight. *How heavy is that box?* **3** great in amount or force. *heavy rain.* **heavily** *adv,* **heaviness** *n.*
heavy metal *n* a type of very loud rock music played especially on electric guitars and drums.
hectare *n* a measure of area equal to 10,000 square metres.
hectic *adj* very busy, rushed.
hedge *n* a row of bushes making a boundary around a field or garden.
hedgehog *n* a small animal that is covered in prickles. It defends itself by rolling up into a ball.
heel *n* **1** the back part of your foot. **2** the part of a sock or shoe under your heel.

hefty *adj* (heftier, heftiest) big and strong.
heifer *(**hef**-er)* *n* a young cow that has not had a calf.
height *n* **1** the measurement of how high something is. **2** the highest, greatest or strongest point. *The storm was at its height.*
heir *(air)* *n* the person who will inherit somebody's property or position.
heiress *(**air**-ess)* *n* a female heir.
held *past of* hold.
helicopter *n* an aircraft with a horizontal rotor which acts as both propeller and wings.

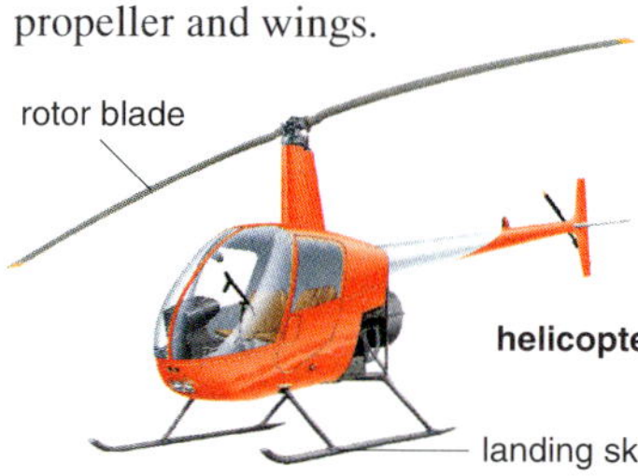

helicopter

helium *n* a very light gas, used in balloons and airships.
hell *n* the place where the Devil is believed to live and where evil people are believed to be punished when they die.
helm *n* the wheel or handle used to steer a ship.
helmet *n* a hard protective hat.
help *v* **1** to do something useful for somebody. *He helped me to carry the heavy bags.* **2** to improve something. *Good exam results will help her chances of getting a job.* **3** to prevent something happening. *I couldn't help laughing.* **help** *n*, **helper** *n.*
helpful *adj* useful, giving help. **helpfully** *adv*, **helpfulness** *n.*
helping *n* a share of food at a meal.
helpless *adj* not able to look after yourself. **helplessness** *n.*
hem *n* the edge of a piece of cloth that is turned over and sewn.
hemisphere *n* one half of the Earth. *France is in the northern hemisphere.*
hen *n* **1** a female chicken, kept for its eggs and meat. **2** any female bird.
hence *adv* **1** for this reason. *She has just lost her job, hence her lack of money.* **2** from this time. *a few days hence.*
herald *v* to be a sign that something is about to happen. *Dark clouds in the sky heralded a storm.*
herb *n* a plant used for flavouring food or for making medicines. **herbal** *adj.*
herbivore *n* an animal that eats only plants. **herbivorous** *adj.*
herd[1] *n* a group of animals grazing or moving together. *a herd of cattle.*
herd[2] *v* to gather together in a group. *The dogs herded the sheep together.*
here *adv* in, at or to this place.
hereditary *adj* capable of being passed on from parents to their children. *hereditary diseases.*
heritage *n* things which are passed on from one generation to another.
hermit *n* a person who chooses to live completely alone.
hero *n* (*pl* heroes) **1** a person admired for their bravery. **2** the most important male character in a play, film or story. **heroic** *adj*, **heroism** *n.*
heroin *n* a very powerful, addictive drug.
heroine *n* **1** a woman admired for her bravery. **2** the most important female character in a play, film or story.
heron *n* a long-legged wading bird.
herring *n* a small sea fish.
hesitate *v* to stop briefly before you do something, because of uncertainty. **hesitant** *adj*, **hesitation** *n.*
hexagon *n* a shape with six sides. **hexagonal** *adj.*
heyday *n* the time when a person or thing is most successful or popular.
hibernate *v* to spend the winter in a kind of deep sleep. *Hedgehogs hibernate.* **hibernation** *n.*
hiccup, hiccough *(**hik**-up)* *n* a sudden and repeated jumping feeling in your throat that makes you let out a sharp noise. **hiccup, hiccough** *v.*
hide[1] *v* (hiding, hid, hidden) **1** to put something where others cannot find it. **2** to go somewhere where you cannot be seen.

hide[2] *n* the skin of an animal.
hideous *adj* very ugly.
hieroglyphics *(hy-er-uh-**glif**-iks) n pl* ancient Egyptian writing using little pictures instead of words or letters. *The hieroglyphics shown represent the name CLEOPATRA.*

hieroglyphics

high *adj* **1** rising a long way above the ground. *high mountains.* **2** having a particular height. *The wall is two metres high.* **3** more than the normal amount, level or strength. *high speed, high winds.* **4** very important. *high rank.* **5** not deep in sound. *a high voice.* **high, highly** *adv.*
highlight[1] *v* **1** to draw special attention to something. **2** to mark important parts of a piece of writing with a brightly coloured pen.
highlight[2] *n* the best part of something. *The highlight of our holiday was a trip in a helicopter.*
highway *n* (*pl* highways) a main road.
highwayman *n* (*pl* highwaymen) in earlier times, a robber on horseback.
hijack *v* to take control of a plane, car, etc and force the pilot or driver to take you somewhere. *Terrorists have hijacked a plane in Japan.* **hijack** *n,* **hijacker** *n.*
hike *n* a long walk in the country. **hike** *v,* **hiker** *n.*
hill *n* an area of high land, smaller than a mountain. **hilly** *adj.*
hilt *n* the handle of a sword.
hind *adj* at the back. *hind legs.*
hinder *v* to delay or prevent the progress of something. **hindrance** *n.*
Hinduism *n* the main religion of India which involves the worship of many gods and the belief that people return to life in a different form after death. **Hindu** *adj, n.*
hinge *n* a moving joint by which a door is fixed to a doorway or a lid is fixed to a box.
hint *v* to suggest something without really saying it. *Ben hinted that he wanted a new bike.* **hint** *n.*
hip *n* one of the two parts at the sides of your body between the tops of your legs and your waist.
hip-hop *n* a type of rap music.
hippopotamus *n* (*pl* hippopotami *or* hippopotamuses) a large, thick-skinned African animal that lives near rivers.
hire *v* to pay for the use of something. *We hired a car for a week when we went to Florida.* **hire** *n.*
hiss *v* to make a sound like a long letter *s.* **hiss** *n.*
historian *n* a person who studies history.
historic *adj* famous in history. *a historic battle.*
historical *adj* of or about people and events from history. *a historical novel.* **historically** *adv.*
history *n* the study of things that happened in the past.
hit[1] *v* (hits, hitting, hit) to strike or knock something.
hit[2] *n* **1** the action of hitting. **2** a thing that is popular or successful. *The song was a big hit.*
hitch[1] *v* **1** to fasten something to something else. *He hitched his horse to the post.* **2** to hitch-hike. **hitch up** to pull up. *He hitched up his trousers.*
hitch[2] *n* a small, temporary problem.
hitch-hike *v* to travel by getting a free ride in somebody else's car.
HIV *n* (*short for* human immunodeficiency virus) a virus which can cause AIDS.
hive *n* a beehive.
hoard *n* a secret store of treasure, food, etc. **hoard** *v.*
hoarse *adj* (of the voice) rough, harsh and croaking, especially because of a sore throat or too much shouting.
hoax *n* a trick. *There wasn't really a bomb – it was just a hoax.* **hoax** *v.*
hob *n* the surface on top of a cooker.
hobble *v* to walk with difficulty, taking small, unsteady steps, for example because your feet are hurt.

hobby *n* something that you enjoy doing in your spare time.
hockey *n* a game played by two teams of eleven players with curved wooden sticks and a ball.
hoe *n* a gardening tool used for digging out weeds.
hog[1] *n* a castrated male pig.
hog[2] *v* (hogs, hogging, hogged) to use more than your fair share of something.
Hogmanay *n* in Scotland, New Year's Eve.
hold[1] *v* (holding, held) **1** to have in your hand. **2** to support or keep firmly in one position. *The shelf was held up by a pile of bricks.* **3** to contain. *How much does this bottle hold?* **4** to make something take place. *We are holding a party.* **5** to keep somebody prisoner. *The police are holding a man for questioning.* **6** to have or possess. *She holds the world record.* **hold on** to wait. **hold up** to delay.
hold[2] *n* the part of a ship or aircraft where cargo is stored.
hole *n* **1** an opening or gap. *a hole in my sock.* **2** an animal's burrow.
holiday *n* (*pl* holidays) **1** a day off work or school. **2** a time when you are staying away from home for enjoyment and relaxation. *We're going to France on holiday this year.*
hollow[1] *adj* having an empty space inside, not solid. *a hollow tree.*
hollow[2] *n* **1** a hollow place. **2** a small valley.
hollow[3] *v* to make something hollow.
holly *n* an evergreen tree with shiny, prickly leaves and red berries.
hologram *n* an image created by lasers which appears to be three-dimensional.
holster *n* a leather case for carrying a pistol, worn on a belt.
holy *adj* to do with God or a god. **holiness** *n.*
home *n* the place where you live.
homeless *adj* having nowhere to live.
homeopathy *(ho-mee-**op**-ath-ee)* *n* a way of treating an illness by giving tiny quantities of medicines which cause symptoms similar to those of the illness itself. **homeopathic** *adj.*
homesick *adj* sad because you are away from your home.
homework *n* school work that you have to do at home.
homosexual *adj* sexually attracted to people of your own sex. **homosexual** *n,* **homosexuality** *n.*
honest *(**on**-ist)* *adj* truthful, not likely to cheat or steal. **honesty** *n.*
honey *n* a sweet, sticky food made by bees.
honeycomb *n* a wax structure made by bees. It has many six-sided holes in which the bees store their honey and eggs.

honeycomb

honeymoon *n* a holiday for a couple who have just got married.
honeysuckle *n* a climbing plant with sweet-smelling flowers.
honour[1] *(**on**-er)* *n* **1** great respect or public regard. **2** a privilege. *It would be an honour to accompany you.*
honour[2] *v* **1** to respect somebody greatly. **2** to give an award or praise to somebody or something.
honourable *adj* good, deserving respect. *She behaved in an honourable way by refusing to betray her friend.* **honourably** *adv.*
hood *n* **1** a part of a coat or jacket that goes over your head. **2** the folding cover of a pram or car.
hoodwink *v* to trick somebody.
hoof *n* (*pl* hoofs *or* hooves) the hard part of the foot of a horse, cow, etc.
hook *n* a curved piece of metal, plastic or wood, used for catching or holding

things. *Hang your coat on the hook.* **hooked** *adj.*

hooligan *n* a person who behaves violently and noisily. *football hooligans.* **hooliganism** *n.*

hoop *n* a large wooden or metal ring.

hoot *v* to make a sound like a car horn or the cry of an owl. **hoot** *n.*

hooves *plural of* hoof.

hop[1] *v* (hops, hopping, hopped) **1** to jump on one leg. **2** (of an animal, bird, insect, etc) to jump with both or all feet together.

hop[2] *n* a plant used in making beer.

hope[1] *v* to want something that may happen. *I hope you can come.*

hope[2] *n* **1** the feeling that what you want may happen. **2** a person or thing that you are relying on for help. *She's my last hope – there's nobody else I can ask.*

hopeful *adj* full of hope. **hopefully** *adv,* **hopefulness** *n.*

hopeless *adj* without hope.

horizon *n* the line where the land and the sky seem to meet.

horizontal *adj* lying level or flat, parallel to the horizon. *a horizontal line.* **horizontally** *adv.*

hormone *n* a chemical produced in your body which has a specific effect on the way your body works.

horn *n* **1** a hard, bony growth on the head of some animals. **2** a brass musical instrument that you blow. **3** the device in a vehicle for making warning sounds.

horn 1

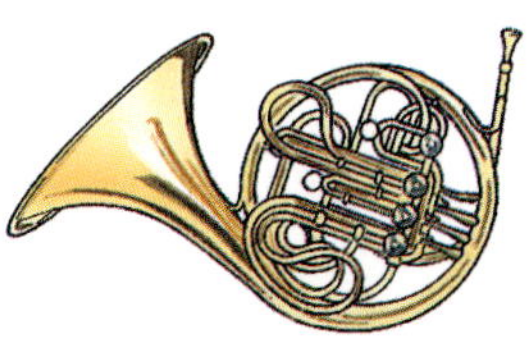

horn 2

hornet *n* a type of large wasp.

horoscope *n* a prediction about somebody's future, based on the position of the stars and planets at the time of their birth.

horrible *adj* very unpleasant. *a horrible smell.* **horribly** *adv.*

horrid *adj* horrible.

horrific *adj* terrifying or shocking.

horrify *v* (horrifies, horrifying, horrified) to shock somebody greatly. **horrifying** *adj.*

horror *n* **1** great fear or shock. **2** something which causes great fear or shock.

horse *n* **1** a four-legged animal with hooves, a long mane and a tail. **2** an object in a gym which you use for jumping over.

horse-chestnut *n* the tree on which conkers grow.

horsepower *n* a unit for measuring the power of engines.

horseshoe *n* a U-shaped piece of iron nailed to a horse's hoof to protect it.

horticulture *n* the growing of flowers, fruit and vegetables. **horticultural** *adj.*

hose *n* a long, flexible tube through which water can pass.

hospitable *adj* showing kindness to guests or strangers. **hospitality** *n.*

hospital *n* a building where people who are ill or injured are looked after.

host *n* **1** a person or organization that receives and entertains guests. **2** the person who introduces the performers on a TV or radio show. **3** a large number of something.

hostage *n* a person who is held captive by people who will not let him or her go until they have what they want.

hostel *n* a building where people can stay cheaply for a short time.

hostile *adj* unfriendly, behaving like an enemy. **hostility** *n.*

hot *adj* (hotter, hottest) **1** having a high temperature. **2** having a sharp, burning taste. *hot curry.*

hot dog *n* a hot sausage in a soft bread roll.

hotel *n* a building where you pay to stay the night and have meals.

hound[1] *n* a dog often used in hunting.
hound[2] *v* to chase somebody. *The actor is being hounded by journalists.*
hour *n* a period of 60 minutes. *There are 24 hours in a day.*
hourly *adj, adv* happening or coming every hour. *an hourly bus to London.*
house[1] *(rhymes with* mouse*) n* **1** a building where people, especially a single family, live. **2** a building used for a particular purpose. *the Houses of Parliament.*
house[2] *(rhymes with* cows*) v* to provide a place for somebody to live or for something to be.
household *n* all the people who live together in a house.
housekeeper *n* a person who is paid to look after a house.
housework *n* the work of keeping a house clean and tidy.
hovel *n* a small, dirty house or hut.
hover *n* **1** to stay in the air in one place. *A dragonfly hovered above the boat.* **2** to move around while staying near a person or thing. *Julie hovered by the phone, waiting for it to ring.*
hovercraft *n* a vehicle which can move over land or water, supported by a cushion of air.

hovercraft

however *adv* **1** but, nevertheless. *I'd like to go – however I can't afford it.* **2** no matter how. *I can't do it, however hard I try.* **3** how. *However did you manage to find me?*
howl *v* to make a long, sad noise like a dog makes when it is hurt. **howl** *n.*
hub *n* the centre of a wheel.
hue *n* a colour or shade.
huff *n* **in a huff** in a bad mood.
hug *v* (hugs, hugging, hugged) to hold somebody tightly in your arms. **hug** *n.*
huge *adj* extremely large, enormous.
hull *n* the body of a ship.
hum *v* (hums, humming, hummed) **1** to sing with your lips closed. **2** to make a low, buzzing noise. **hum** *n.*
human, human being *n* a person. **human** *adj.*
humane *adj* kind, not cruel.
humanity *n* **1** all human beings. **2** being humane.
humble *adj* modest and not proud. **humbly** *adv.*
humid *adj* damp and warm. *a humid climate.* **humidity** *n.*
humiliate *v* to make a person look ridiculous or feel ashamed. **humiliation** *n.*
humming-bird *n* a small, brightly coloured bird that makes a humming sound by beating its wings very fast.

humming-bird

humorous *adj* funny.
humour[1] *n* the ability to make people laugh or smile or to see when something is funny. *She has a really good sense of humour.*
humour[2] *v* to try to keep somebody happy by agreeing with them or doing what they want. *Don't tell him he's wrong – just humour him.*
hump *n* **1** a small hill. **2** a rounded lump, for example on a camel's back.
hunch[1] *n* an idea about something, based on a feeling rather than fact. *I have a hunch that something is wrong.*
hunch[2] *v* to sit with your shoulders bent forward and your head down.
hung *past of* hang.
hunger *n* the feeling of wanting food.
hungry *adj* (hungrier, hungriest) feeling that you want food. **hungrily** *adv.*
hunk *n* **1** a large, thick piece. *a hunk of bread.* **2** *(slang)* a good-looking man.
hunt[1] *v* **1** to chase and kill wild animals as a sport or for food. **2** to search for something. **hunter** *n.*
hunt[2] *n* **1** the act of hunting animals. **2** a group of hunters. **3** a search.

hurdle *n* **1** a small fence that you jump over in a running race. **2** an obstacle, a difficulty.
hurl *v* to throw something with great force.
hurricane *n* a violent, windy storm.
hurry *v* (hurries, hurrying, hurried) **1** to move or do something quickly. **2** to make somebody hurry. **hurry** *n.*
hurt *v* (hurting, hurt) **1** to cause pain or unhappiness. *He's hurt his leg.* **2** to be painful. *My tooth hurts.*
hurtle *v* to move along very fast.
husband *n* the man that a woman is married to. *Her husband is a doctor.*
hush[1] a warning to be quiet.
hush[2] *n* a sudden silence.
husky[1] *adj* (huskier, huskiest) low and rough in sound. *a husky voice.* **huskily** *adv.*
husky[2] *n* a dog that is used to pull sledges in arctic regions.
hut *n* a small house or shelter, often made of wood.
hutch *n* a wooden box with a wire front for rabbits or other small pets.
hybrid *n* plant or animal produced from two different species.
hydrant *n* an outdoor water tap.
hydraulic *adj* using the power produced by water or some other liquid being forced along pipes. *hydraulic brakes.*
hydroelectricity *n* electricity produced from the power of running water.
hydrofoil *n* a fast, light boat that rests on special supports and skims the surface of the water.
hydrogen *n* a very light, colourless gas that burns easily. Hydrogen and oxygen together make water.
hyena *n* a dog-like animal found in Africa and Asia, with a howl that sounds like human laughter.
hygiene *(**high**-jeen)* *n* cleanliness and healthiness. **hygienic** *adj.*
hymn *(rhymes with* him*)* *n* a religious song praising God.
hype *n* excessive publicity about something in order to sell it. *There has been a lot of hype on TV about the band's new album.* **hype** *v.*
hyphen *n* a mark (-) used in writing to separate parts of a word, as in *grown-up*, or to show that a word continues on the next line.
hypnosis *n* a state like deep sleep in which somebody's actions can be controlled by another person.
hypnotize *v* to put somebody into hypnosis. **hypnotic** *adj*, **hypnotism** *n.*
hypocrite *(**hip**-a-krit)* *n* a person who pretends to believe or feel something that is different from their actual feelings or beliefs. **hypocrisy** *(hip-**ok**-ra-see)* *n*, **hypocritical** *adj.*
hypodermic syringe *n* a medical instrument with a hollow needle for injecting drugs under the skin.
hypotenuse *(high-**pot**-uh-nyooz)* *n* the side of a right-angled triangle opposite the right angle. See **triangle**.
hypothermia *n* a dangerous medical condition caused by exposure to cold.
hysterical *adj* in a state of uncontrolled excitement, grief, panic or other strong emotion. **hysteria** *n,* **hysterically** *adv.*

Ii

ice[1] *n* **1** frozen water. **2** an ice-cream.
ice[2] *v* to cover a cake with icing.
iceberg *n* a huge mass of ice floating in the sea.
ice-cream *n* a soft, very cold, sweet food.
ice cube *n* a small cube of ice used for cooling drinks.
iced *adj* **1** very cold. **2** covered with icing.
ice hockey *n* a form of hockey played on ice by skaters, using a rubber disc, called a puck.
ice rink *n* a building with a floor of ice for skating on.

ice skate *n* a boot with a blade underneath for moving on ice. **ice skate** *v*, **ice skating** *n*.
icicle *n* a hanging, pointed piece of ice, made of dripping water that has frozen.
icing *n* a sweet covering for cakes.
icon *n* **1** a small picture on a computer screen representing a program. **2** a picture of Christ or a saint, often painted on wood, found in churches.
icy *adj* (icier, iciest) like or covered with ice, very cold.
idea *n* a thought, a plan in your mind.
ideal[1] *adj* perfect, just what you want. *This box is ideal for storing your toys.* **ideally** *adv*.
ideal[2] *n* the person, thing or situation that is the best possible.
identical *adj* exactly the same.
identify *v* (identifies, identifying, identified) to recognize or name somebody or something. **identification** *n*.
identity *n* who somebody is. *The police do not know the dead man's identity.*
idiom *n* a group of words that, when used together, have a meaning other than the one they appear to have.
idiot *n* a silly or foolish person.
idiotic *adj* foolish. **idiotically** *adv*.
idle *adj* **1** lazy. **2** not being used. *Ships were lying idle in the harbour.* **3** not really meant. *idle threats.* **idleness** *n*, **idly** *adv*.
idol *n* **1** somebody or something that people worship as a god. **2** somebody who is greatly admired. *a pop idol.*
idolize *v* to admire or love somebody very much.
ie *short for* that is, that is to say. *Young children, ie those under 5 years of age, travel free on many buses.*
igloo *n* a dome-shaped hut made of blocks of snow or ice, traditionally built by the Inuit people in the Arctic.
ignite *v* **1** to set something on fire. **2** to catch fire.
ignition *n* the device in a car which ignites the fuel and starts the engine.
ignorant *adj* not knowing about something. **ignorance** *n*.

igloo

ignore *v* to take no notice of something. *The man ignored us and walked straight past.*
iguana *(ig-**wah**-na) n* a large tropical lizard that lives in trees.
il- *prefix* not. *illegal, illogical.*
ill *adj* **1** not well, not in good health. **2** bad or harmful. *ill effects.*
illegal *adj* against the law.
illegible *adj* impossible to read. *Your writing is illegible.*
illegitimate *adj* **1** born to parents who are not married to each other. **2** against the law. **illegitimacy** *n*.
illiterate *adj* not able to read and write. **illiteracy** *n*.
illuminate *v* to light something up. *The gardens were illuminated by rows of lamps.* **illumination** *n*.
illusion *n* something that seems to be real or true, but is not. **illusory** *adj*.
illustrate *v* to add pictures to help to explain something in a book, etc.
illustration *n* a picture in a book, magazine, etc.
im- *prefix* not. *immoral, impatient.*
image *n* **1** a picture or statue. **2** a picture in your mind. **3** the way you appear to other people.
imaginary *adj* not real, existing only in your mind. *an imaginary friend.*
imagination *n* the ability to imagine things.
imaginative *adj* using imagination.
imagine *v* to create a picture in your mind.
imitate *v* to copy somebody or something. **imitation** *n*.
immature *adj* **1** not fully grown or

developed. **2** acting in a childish way. **immaturity** *n*.
immediately *adv* now, at once. **immediate** *adj*.
immense *adj* very large. **immensely** *adv*, **immensity** *n*.
immerse *v* to put something in a liquid, so that it is completely covered. **immersion** *n*.
immigrant *n* a person who comes to live permanently in a country.
immigrate *v* to come to live permanently in a country. **immigration** *n*.
imminent *adj* about to happen.
immobile *adj* not able to move or be moved. *After he broke his ankle he was immobile for several weeks.*
immune *adj* safe from the danger of catching a disease. *She has had measles so she is now immune to it.* **immunity** *n*.
immunize *v* to make somebody safe from the danger of catching a disease, especially by giving them an injection. **immunization** *n*.
impact *n* **1** the force of an object hitting another. **2** a strong effect. *The film had a huge impact on me.*
impatient *adj* not patient, not wanting to wait. **impatience** *n*.
imperfect *adj* not perfect. **imperfection** *n*.
imperial *adj* to do with an empire or with an emperor or empress.
impersonate *v* to pretend to be somebody else. **impersonation** *n*.
impertinent *adj* cheeky, rude, not showing respect. **impertinence** *n*.
impetuous *adj* tending to act without thinking first.
implement *n* a tool or an instrument. *Chopsticks are eating implements.*
imply *v* (implies, implying, implied) to suggest something without really saying it. *She implied that I was lying.* **implication** *n*.
impolite *adj* not polite, rude.
import *(im-**port**)* *v* to bring goods from abroad to sell in your own country. **import** *(**im**-port)* *n*.
important *adj* **1** mattering a lot, to be taken seriously. *It is important that you all know the rules.* **2** having great power or influence. *The Queen is a very important woman.* **importance** *n*.
impose *v* to force somebody to accept something. *Don't impose your ideas on other people.* **imposition** *n*.
impossible *adj* not possible. **impossibility** *n*, **impossibly** *adv*.
impostor *n* a person pretending to be somebody else.
impress *v* to make somebody think well of you. *I was impressed by the clear way he spoke.* **impressive** *adj*.
impression *n* **1** the effect that something has on you. *That book made a deep impression on me.* **2** an idea or feeling. *I got the impression that he was bored.* **3** a hollow mark made by pressing. *an impression of the dog's paw in the cement.* **4** an impersonation.
imprison *v* to put somebody in prison. **imprisonment** *n*.
improve *v* to make or become better. *My teacher says my work has improved a lot this term.* **improvement** *n*.
improvise *v* **1** to do the best you can with what you have. *We didn't have any shelves, so we improvised with bricks and planks of wood.* **2** to make something up as you go along. *She improvised a tune on the piano.* **improvisation** *n*.
impudent *adj* rude, cheeky. **impudence** *n*.
impulse *n* a sudden desire to do something. **impulsive** *adj*.
in- *prefix* not. *insensitive, informal, incorrect.*
inborn *adj* natural. *an inborn ability.*
incense *n* a substance that gives off a sweet smell when burned.
incentive *n* a thing that encourages you to do something. *They offered huge prizes as an incentive to enter the competition.*
inch *n* an old measure of length equal to 2.54 centimetres. There are 12 inches in one foot.
incident *n* something that happens.

incidentally *adv* by the way. *Incidentally, when's your birthday?*
incinerator *n* a container in which rubbish is burnt.
incision *n* a cut.
incite *v* to provoke or urge somebody to do something bad.
inclination *n* a tendency, a slight desire or preference.
incline *v* to lean or slope towards something. **be inclined** to be likely to behave in a certain way. *She is inclined to be lazy.*
include *v* to contain or count something as part of the whole. *Does the price of the hotel room include breakfast?* **inclusion** *n.*
incognito *adj, adv* in disguise, so that people do not know who you are.
income *n* the money that somebody earns or receives regularly.
income tax *n* money paid regularly to the government from a person's earnings.
incongruous *adj* seeming out of place.
incorporate *v* to include something so that it is part of the whole.
increase[1] *(in-**krees**)* *v* to make or become greater in size or amount.
increase[2] *(**in**-krees)* *n* growth.
incredible *adj* hard to believe, amazing. **incredibly** *adv.*
incriminate *v* to suggest that somebody is responsible for a crime or fault.
incubate *v* to hatch eggs by keeping them warm. **incubation** *n.*
incubator *n* a piece of hospital equipment in which babies who are born too early are kept warm and safe until they are strong and well.
incurable *adj* not able to be cured. *incurable diseases.*
indecent *adj* rude or shocking, not decent. *an indecent joke.*
indeed *adv* **1** really, certainly. *"She's very clever." "She is indeed!"* **2** used for emphasis. *Thanks very much indeed.*
indefinite *adj* not clear, not fixed. *The workers have gone on strike for an indefinite period.*
indelible *adj* not easily rubbed out.
independent *adj* not controlled by or needing help from others. **independence** *n.*
indestructible *adj* not able to be destroyed.
index *n* an alphabetical list at the end of a book, giving all the subjects in the book and the pages where they are mentioned.
index finger *n* the finger next to your thumb.
indicate *v* **1** to point out or show something. *There is an arrow painted on the tree to indicate the right path.* **2** to signal. *Drivers must always indicate before turning.* **indication** *n,* **indicator** *n.*
indifferent *adj* **1** not caring or not interested. *He was indifferent to the feelings of others.* **2** not very good. **indifference** *n.*
indigestion *n* pain caused by difficulty in digesting food.
indignant *adj* angry, especially at something wrong that has been done to you. **indignation** *n.*
indigo *n* a deep colour between blue and purple.
indispensable *adj* essential, not easy to replace.
individual[1] *adj* **1** to do with, or for, one person only. *Each of the children had an individual lunch box.* **2** single, separate. *Put price labels on each individual item.* **individually** *adv.*
individual[2] *n* a person.
indoors *adv* inside a building. *Let's go indoors.* **indoor** *adj.*
indulge *v* to let somebody have what they want. **indulgence** *n,* **indulgent** *adj.*
industrial *adj* to do with industries.
industrious *adj* working hard. *an industrious pupil.*
industry *n* **1** the work of making things in factories. **2** a trade or business.
inevitable *adj* certain to happen.
inexplicable *adj* impossible to explain.
infamous *(**in**-fuh-mus)* *adj* well-known for being bad or evil. *an infamous murderer.*

infancy *n* the time when you are a very young child.
infant *n* a very young child or baby.
infantry *n* soldiers who fight on foot.
infect *v* to give a disease to somebody.
infection *n* an illness caused by germs.
infectious *adj* (of a disease or illness) easily passed on from one person to another.
inferior *adj* lower in rank or quality.
infested *adj* full of insects, rats or other pests.
infinite *(**in**-fin-it) adj* without end or limits. *We believe that the universe is infinite.* **infinitely** *adv*.
infinitive *n* a basic form of a verb, for example, *to be*, *to live* and *to find*.
infinity *n* space, time or an amount that is without end or limits.
infirmary *n* a hospital.
inflammable *adj* easily set on fire.
inflate *v* to fill something with air. **inflatable** *adj*.
inflation *n* a general rise in prices.
inflict *v* to make somebody suffer something.
influence *v* to have an effect on somebody or something. *The weather seems to influence her moods.* **influence** *n*.
inform *v* to tell somebody. *Please inform us of your decision.*
informal *adj* friendly and relaxed, not formal. **informality** *n*, **informally** *adv*.
information *n* facts or knowledge.
information technology *n* the use of computers to store and send out information.
informative *adj* providing useful information.
infuriate *v* to make somebody very angry.
ingredient *n* one of several things that go into a mixture, especially in cooking.
inhabit *v* to live in a place.
inhabitant *n* a person who lives in a place.
inhale *v* to breathe in. **inhalation** *n*.
inherit *v* **1** to receive money or property from somebody who has died. **2** to have qualities the same as your parents. *She has inherited her mother's intelligence.* **inheritance** *n*.
inhuman *adj* extremely cruel and brutal. **inhumanity** *n*.
initial[1] *adj* at the beginning. **initially** *adv*.
initial[2] *n* the letter that begins a word, especially a name. *John Paton's initials are J.P.*
initiative *n* the ability to lead the way and make decisions for yourself.
inject *v* to use a needle and syringe to force medicine into somebody's body. **injection** *n*.
injure *v* to hurt somebody. *Two people were injured in the accident.*
injury *n* damage done to a person's body.
injustice *n* unfairness, lack of justice.
ink *n* a coloured liquid used for writing, drawing or printing.
inland *adj* away from the coast. *Chicago is an inland city.*
inlet *n* a small bay.
inmate *n* a person who lives in an institution, especially a prison.
inn *n* a public house or a small hotel.
inner *adj* inside.
innings *n* (*pl* innings) a team's turn at batting in cricket.
innocent *adj* not guilty of a crime or of doing anything wrong. **innocence** *n*.
inoculate *v* to protect somebody from a disease by giving them an injection. **inoculation** *n*.
input *n* **1** what you put into something. **2** the information that is fed into a computer.
inquest *n* an official investigation to find out why somebody died.
inquire *v* to ask about something. *Helen inquired about the times of trains to Leeds.*
inquiry *n* **1** a question or a request for information. **2** an official investigation.
inquisitive *adj* keen to find out about things, curious. **inquisitiveness** *n*.
insane *adj* mad, not sane. **insanity** *n*.
inscribe *v* to carve or write words on an object. *The ring was inscribed with his initials.* **inscription** *n*.

insect *n* a small creature with six legs and no backbone.

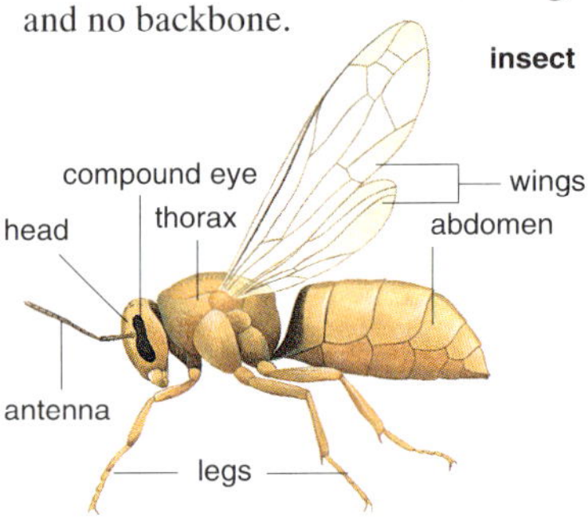

insecticide *n* a chemical used to kill insects.
insert *v* to put something inside something else. *She inserted a coin into the slot.* **insertion** *n.*
inside[1] *n* the inner part of something.
inside[2] *adj* in or near the inner part.
inside[3] *prep, adv* in or to the inside. *It's raining – let's go inside.*
insist *v* to say very firmly that you must do or have something. *Paul insisted on paying for the ice-creams.* **insistence** *n,* **insistent** *adj.*
insomnia *v* an inability to sleep.
inspect *v* to examine something carefully. **inspection** *n.*
inspector *n* **1** a person whose job is to inspect something. *a school inspector.* **2** a senior police officer.
inspire *v* to encourage somebody by filling them with enthusiasm or confidence. *The exhibition inspired me to paint a picture.* **inspiration** *n.*
install *v* to put equipment, etc in a place ready for use. *The engineer installed a new telephone line.*
instalment *n* **1** one of a series of payments. *We are paying for our new car in instalments.* **2** an episode of a story.
instance *n* an example. **for instance** for example.
instant *n* a moment, a very short time.
instantly *adv* immediately.
instead *adv* in place of something. *I don't like ice-cream – can I have fruit instead?*
instinct *n* a natural habit that does not need to be learnt. *Birds build nests by instinct.* **instinctive** *adj.*
institute *n* an organization set up for a special purpose, especially teaching or research.
institution *n* **1** a large organization where people can live or work together. **2** a custom or tradition.
instruct *v* to teach or direct somebody. **instruction** *n,* **instructor** *n.*
instrument *n* **1** a delicate tool for doing a specific job. *medical instruments.* **2** an object used for making music.
insulate *v* to cover something with a material so that heat or electricity cannot pass through it. *Rubber and plastic are used for insulating electric cables.* **insulation** *n.*
insult[1] *(in-**sult**)* *v* to uspet somebody by being rude to them.
insult[2] *(**in**-sult)* *n* a remark or action that insults somebody.
insurance *n* an agreement with a company that if you pay them a regular sum, they will give you money if something of yours is lost or damaged or if you become ill. **insure** *v.*
intact *adj* whole, not damaged.
integrate *v* to combine several people or things into one whole. **integration** *n.*
integrity *n* honesty.
intellectual *adj* involving your mind and thoughts. *an intellectual problem.*
intelligent *adj* clever and able to understand easily. **intelligence** *n.*
intend *v* to mean to do something.
intense *adj* very strong. *intense heat.* **intensity** *n.*
intensive *adj* very thorough. *The police began an intensive search for the killer.*
intention *n* what you mean to do.
intentional *adj* done on purpose.
inter- *prefix* among or between. *intercontinental* (= between or connecting different continents).
interactive *adj* allowing two-way

communication, eg between a computer programme and its user.

intercept *v* to stop somebody or something that is moving from one place to another.

intercom *n* a system that people use for communicating with one another when they are in different rooms.

interest[1] *n* **1** wanting to know or learn about something. **2** something that you like doing or learning about. **3** extra money that you pay back to somebody who has lent you money.

interest[2] *v* to make somebody want to know more about something, to keep somebody's attention. **interested** *adj,* **interesting** *adj.*

interfere *v* **1** to involve yourself in something that does not concern you. **2** to get in the way of something.

interference *n* **1** interfering in something. **2** the interruption of a radio signal so that it cannot be received properly.

interior *n* the inside of something. **interior** *adj.*

intermediate *adj* in the middle, between two stages or levels.

internal *adj* on the inside of something. **internally** *adv.*

international *adj* involving different countries. *The United Nations is an international organization.*

interpret *v* **1** to translate a speaker's words from one language to another. **2** to decide what something means. *She interpreted his smile as a sign of approval.* **interpretation** *n.*

interrogate *v* to question somebody thoroughly. **interrogation** *n.*

interrupt *v* **1** to disturb somebody who is in the middle of speaking or doing something. **2** to stop something for a time. **interruption** *n.*

interval *n* a time between two events or between parts of a play or concert.

intervene *v* to interrupt a quarrel or fight and try to stop it. **intervention** *n.*

interview *n* a meeting at which somebody is asked questions. *She has an interview for a job.* **interview** *v.*

intestines *n pl* the long tubes through which food passes after it leaves your stomach. See **digestion**.

intimate *adj* close, very friendly.

intimidate *v* to frighten somebody so that they will do what you want. **intimidation** *n.*

into *prep* **1** to the inside of something. *Come into my room.* **2** against. *The car drove into a wall.* **change into, turn into** to become. *A tadpole turns into a frog.*

intrepid *adj* brave, fearless.

intricate *adj* complicated and detailed.

intrigue[1] *(**in**-treeg) n* a secret plan.

intrigue[2] *(in-**treeg**) v* to make somebody curious. *The story intrigued me.*

introduce *v* **1** to make people known to each other. *Ben introduced me to his sister.* **2** to bring in something new. **3** to say a few words at the beginning of a TV or radio show, explaining what it is about.

introduction *n* **1** introducing somebody or something. **2** words at the beginning of a book telling you what it is about.

intrude *v* to enter somewhere where you are not wanted or invited. **intrusion** *n.*

intuition *n* the power of understanding or realizing something without thinking it out. **intuitive** *adj.*

invade *v* to go into another country or place to fight against the people who live there. **invasion** *n.*

invalid[1] *(**in**-va-lid) n* a person who is ill or disabled.

invalid[2] *(in-**val**-id) adj* not able to be used legally, not valid.

invaluable *adj* extremely useful.

invent *v* **1** to think of or make something for the first time. **2** to make up a story. **invention** *n*

inventor *n* a person who invents things.

invertebrate *n* an animal with no backbone, eg an insect, worm or snail.

inverted commas *n pl* the marks " and ", or ' and ' used in writing before and after speech.

invest *v* to put money into something in order to make a profit. **investment** *n.*

investigate *v* to try to find out all about something. *The police are investigating the robbery.* **investigation** *n.*
invisible *adj* not able to be seen. **invisibility** *n.*
invite *v* to ask somebody to come somewhere. **invitation** *n.*
invoice *n* a document showing the goods or services you have received and asking for payment.
involve *v* **1** to require something as a necessary part. *Her job involves a lot of travelling.* **2** to interest or concern somebody. *I don't want to get involved in your argument.* **involvement** *n.*
ir- *prefix* not. *irregular, irrelevent.*
irate *(eye-**rate**)* *adj* very angry.
iris *n* **1** a tall, flowering plant. **2** the coloured part of your eye. See **eye**.
iron[1] *n* **1** a heavy, grey metal. **2** a piece of electrical equipment with a flat bottom that heats up, for making clothes smooth.
iron[2] *v* to make something smooth with an iron.
irregular *adj* **1** not regular. **2** not even.
irresistible *adj* too tempting to resist.
irrigate *v* to supply water to land by canals or other means. **irrigation** *n.*
irritable *adj* bad-tempered.
irritate *v* to make somebody annoyed. **irritation** *n.*
Islam *n* the Muslim religion. **Islamic** *adj.*
island *n* land surrounded by water.
isle *n* an island.
isosceles *(eye-**sos**-il-eez)* *n* a triangle with two sides of equal length. See **triangle**.
isolate *v* to separate somebody or something from others. **isolation** *n.*
issue[1] *v* to send out or give out something.
issue[2] *n* **1** one edition of a newspaper or magazine. **2** a subject for discussion.
IT *short for* information technology.
italics *n pl* letters printed so that they slope to the right.
itch *n* a feeling in your skin, that makes you want to scratch. **itchy** *adj.*
item *n* one of a number of things. *He ticked each item on the list.*
itinerary *n* a detailed plan of a journey.
its *adj* belonging to it. *The cat has hurt its paw.*
it's it is.
ivory *n* the hard, creamy-white substance that elephants' tusks are made of.
ivy *n* a climbing evergreen plant with shiny, pointed leaves.

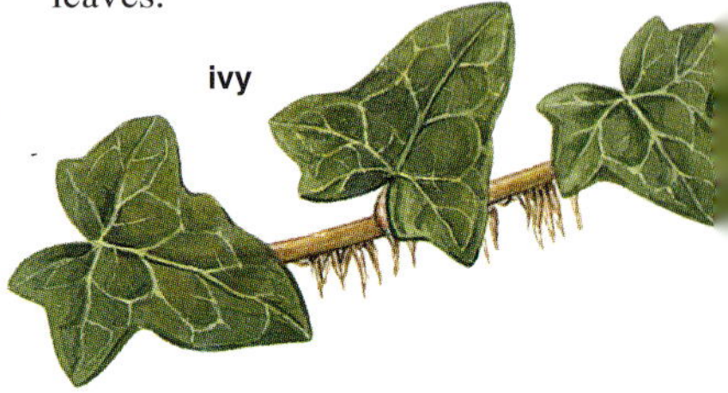
ivy

Jj

jab *v* (jabs, jabbing, jabbed) to poke with something sharp. *He jabbed me with the end of his umbrella.*
jack *n* **1** a device for raising part of a vehicle off the ground so it can be repaired. **2** the playing-card between the ten and the queen.
jackal *n* a type of wild dog.
jacket *n* **1** a short coat. **2** an outer covering. *a book jacket.*
jackpot *n* the top prize in a game or lottery.
jade *n* a precious, usually green, stone used for making jewellery and ornaments.
jagged *adj* having sharp, uneven edges.
jaguar *n* a large wild cat, similar to a leopard, found in South America.

jail *n* a prison.

jam[1] *n* a sweet, sticky food made from fruit boiled with sugar.

jam[2] *v* (jams, jamming, jammed) **1** to squeeze into place. *He jammed his belongings into a suitcase.* **2** to get stuck or make something get stuck. *My key got jammed in the lock.*

jam[3] *n* **1** a situation in which vehicles cannot move. *a traffic jam.* **2** a difficult situation.

jangle *v* to make a loud, ringing sound.

January *n* the first month of the year.

jar[1] *n* a glass container with a lid, used for storing food.

jar[2] *v* (jars, jarring, jarred) **1** to have a harsh, unpleasant effect on somebody. *Her voice jarred on my ears.* **2** to jolt.

jargon *n* the special or technical language of a group of people.

jaunt *n* a short pleasure trip.

javelin *n* a short, light spear, thrown in an athletics competition.

jaw *n* **1** one of the two bones that hold your teeth. **2** the lower part of your face.

jazz *n* a type of lively music with a strong rhythm, first played and sung by black Americans.

jealous *adj* **1** wanting what somebody else has. **2** angry because the person you love seems to love, or be loved by, somebody else. **jealousy** *n.*

jeans *n pl* trousers made of denim.

jeep *n* a motor vehicle used for travelling over rough ground.

jeer *v* to laugh unkindly at somebody.

jelly *n* **1** a soft, wobbly food flavoured with fruit juice. **2** a substance like this.

jellyfish *n* (*pl* jellyfish *or* jellyfishes) a sea creature with tentacles and a jelly-like body.

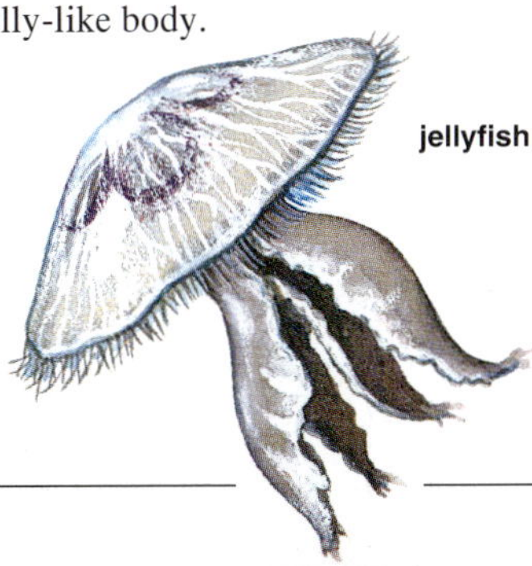

jellyfish

jeopardy *(jep-er-dee) n* **in jeopardy** in danger, under threat. *Her job is in jeopardy.* **jeopardize** *v.*

jerk[1] *n* a short, sudden movement. *We felt a jerk as the train started to move.*

jerk[2] *v* to move with a jerk.

jersey *n* (*pl* jerseys) a sweater.

jest *n* a joke. **jest** *v.*

jester *n* in the Middle Ages, an entertainer in the courts of kings.

jet *n* **1** a strong, fast stream of liquid or gas. **2** an aircraft with an engine that sucks in air and pushes it out at the back, so pushing the aircraft forward.

jetlag *n* a feeling of extreme tiredness caused by a long plane journey.

jetty *n* a small pier.

Jew *n* **1** a person of the Hebrew race. **2** a person who practises the religion of Judaism. **Jewish** *adj.*

jewel *n* a precious stone, such as a diamond, ruby or emerald.

jeweller *n* a person who makes or sells jewellery.

jewellery *n* ornaments that you wear, such as rings, necklaces and bracelets.

jig *n* a fast, lively dance.

jigsaw *n* a puzzle made up of wooden or cardboard pieces of various shapes that fit together to make a picture.

jingle[1] *v* to make a short, sharp ringing sound like small bells or keys.

jingle[2] *n* **1** the sound of something jingling. **2** a simple song or tune, used in TV and radio advertising.

jinx *n* something that brings bad luck.

job *n* **1** the work that somebody does for money. **2** a task.

jockey *n* (*pl* jockeys) a person who rides horses in races.

jodhpurs *(jod-purs) n pl* trousers that fit tightly from your knee to your ankle, worn for horse-riding.

jog *v* (jogs, jogging, jogged) **1** to run at a slow, steady pace. **2** to knock gently. *She jogged my arm and I spilt my drink.* **jog somebody's memory** to remind somebody of something.

join[1] *v* **1** to put things together, to connect or unite. *Join the two pieces of the model with glue.* **2** to become a member of a group or club. *She wants to join the army.* **3** to come together with somebody. *Will you join us for dinner?*

join[2] *n* a place where something is joined.

joiner *n* a person who makes things from wood, a carpenter. **joinery** *n.*

joint[1] *n* **1** a point where two parts join. *The knee is the joint between the upper and lower bones of the leg.* **2** a big piece of meat.

joint[2] *adj* shared. *a joint bank account.*

joke *n* something that you do or say to make people laugh. **joke** *v.*

joker *n* **1** a person who jokes. **2** in a pack of playing-cards, an extra card with a picture of a jester on it.

jolly[1] *adj* (jollier, jolliest) happy and cheerful.

jolly[2] *adv* very. *jolly good!*

jolt *v* to move or shake with sudden jerks. **jolt** *n.*

jostle *v* to push somebody roughly. *He was jostled by the crowd.*

jot *v* (jots, jotting, jotted) to write something quickly. *Let me jot down your phone number.*

journal *n* **1** a diary where you write what you do each day. **2** a magazine, especially one on a particular subject.

journalist *n* a writer for a newspaper, magazine, etc. **journalism** *n.*

journey *n* (*pl* journeys) travelling from one place to another.

joust *n* a contest between two knights on horses, armed with lances. **joust** *v.*

joust

joy *n* great happiness.

joyful *adj* filled with joy. *joyful celebrations.* **joyfully** *adv.*

joy-ride *v* to ride in a stolen car, just for fun. **joy-ride** *n,* **joy-rider** *n.*

joy-stick *n* a control lever that can be moved in different directions.

jubilee *n* a celebration of a special anniversary, for example the start of a king's or queen's reign.

Judaism *n* the religion of the Jewish people.

judge[1] *n* **1** a person who hears and decides cases in a law court. **2** a person who decides on the winner of a competition.

judge[2] *v* **1** to act as a judge. **2** to make a guess about something. *It's difficult to judge her age.* **judgement** *n.*

judo *n* a form of Japanese wrestling in which two people fight and try to throw each other to the ground.

jug *n* a container for liquids, with a handle and a lip for pouring.

juggernaut *n* a huge lorry.

juggle *n* to keep throwing a number of balls or other objects up into the air and catching them. **juggler** *n.*

juice *n* liquid from fruit, vegetables or other food. **juicy** *adj.*

juke-box *n* a machine that plays music when you put coins into it.

July *n* the seventh month of the year.

jumble[1] *v* to mix things up so that they are untidy or in the wrong order.

jumble[2] *n* a confused or untidy collection of things.

jumble sale *n* a sale of second-hand clothes, etc, usually to raise money for charity.

jumbo *adj* very large.

jumbo jet *n* a very large jet aircraft.

jump *v* **1** to spring off the ground, to leap. **2** to get over something by leaping. **3** to move suddenly and quickly. **jump** *n.*

jumper *n* a knitted piece of clothing with sleeves, that you wear on the top part of your body.

junction *n* a place where roads or railway lines meet.

June *n* the sixth month of the year.

jungle *n* a thick forest in a hot country.

junior *adj* **1** less important in rank. *a junior officer in the navy.* **2** younger.

junior school *n* a school for pupils between the ages of about seven and eleven.

junk *n* **1** things that are worthless or useless. **2** a Chinese sailing boat.

junk food *n* food that is not good for you, but that is easy and quick to get or prepare.

jury *n* people who are chosen to decide whether an accused person is guilty or not guilty in a law court.

just[1] *adv* **1** exactly. *That's just what I wanted.* **2** very recently. *I have just arrived.* **3** almost not. *There is only just enough.* **4** only. *She wrote just a brief note.* **5** at this moment. *I'm just going out.*

just[2] *adj* fair, right. *a just law.*

justice *n* **1** fairness and rightness. *a sense of justice.* **2** the law.

justify *v* (justifies, justifying, justified) to prove or show that something is just or right. **justification** *n.*

jut *v* (juts, jutting, jutted) to stick out.

juvenile *adj* **1** to do with young people. **2** childish. **juvenile** *n.*

Kk

kaleidoscope *n* a tube that you look through and turn to see changing patterns of colours.

kangaroo *n* an Australian marsupial with strong back legs for jumping.

karaoke *(ka-ree-**oh**-kee)* *n* a form of entertainment, originally from Japan, in which people sing along to recorded music.

karate *(ka-**rah**-tee)* *n* a Japanese form of fighting, using blows and kicks.

kayak *(**kye**-ak)* *n* a covered canoe.

kebab *n* small pieces of meat or vegetables cooked on a stick called a skewer.

keel *n* the long piece of a ship's frame that lies along the bottom.

keen *adj* **1** eager, enthusiastic. **2** strong, sharp. *Many animals have a keen sense of smell.* **keen on** very fond of. *She's keen on dancing.*

keep[1] *v* (keeping, kept) **1** to have something and not give it away. **2** to stay the same, to remain. *Please keep still!* **3** to go on doing something. *He keeps interrupting me.* **4** to make somebody or something stay the same. *This coat should keep you warm.* **5** to have something in a particular place. *Where do you keep your bike?* **6** to provide a home, food, etc for people or animals.

keep[2] *n* a strong tower in a castle.

keeper *n* a person who looks after something, such as animals in a zoo.

keg *n* a small barrel.

kennel *n* **1** a small hut for a dog. **2 kennels** a place where dogs can stay to be looked after while their owners are away.

kept *past of* keep.

kerb *n* the edge of a pavement.

kernel *n* the inner part of a nut.

kestrel *n* a small type of falcon.

ketchup *n* a thick tomato sauce.

kettle *n* a container with a lid, handle and spout, used for boiling water in.

key *n* (*pl* keys) **1** a metal object for opening a lock. **2** one of the small parts of a musical instrument, computer keyboard, etc that you press with your fingers. **3** something that helps solve a code or explain a mystery. **4** a scale of musical notes that starts on a particular note.

keyboard *n* **1** the keys of a piano, computer, etc. **2** an electronic musical instrument like a small piano.

khaki *(kah-**kee**)* *n* a brownish-green colour.

kick *v* to hit something with your foot. **kick off** to start a football match by kicking the ball. **kick** *n.*

kid[1] *n* **1** a young goat. **2** a child.

kid[2] *v* (kids, kidding, kidded) to fool somebody for fun. *I'm just kidding.*

kidnap *v* (kidnaps, kidnapping, kidnapped) to capture somebody and often to demand money for their release. **kidnapper** *n,* **kidnapping** *n.*

kidney *n* (*pl* kidneys) one of the two organs inside your body that clean your blood and produce urine.

kill *v* to end the life of a person or animal.

kiln *n* an oven for baking bricks or pottery to make them hard.

kilo *n* (*pl* kilos) a kilogramme.

kilogramme, kilogram *n* a measure of weight, equal to 1,000 grammes.

kilometre *n* a measure of length, equal to 1,000 metres.

kilowatt *n* a measure of electrical power, equal to 1,000 watts.

kilt *n* a type of skirt often made of tartan cloth, traditionally worn by Scottish men.

kimono *n* (*pl* kimonos) a loose gown with wide sleeves, traditionally worn by Japanese women.

kimono

kin *n* relatives. **next of kin** your closest relative.

kind[1] *adj* friendly and good to people. **kindness** *n.*

kind[2] *n* a type or sort.

kindergarten *n* a school for very young children.

king *n* **1** a male ruler who has inherited the position. **2** the playing-card with a picture of a king on it. **3** the important chesspiece that must avoid capture. See **chess**.

kingdom *n* a country ruled by a king or queen.

kingfisher *n* a small bird with bright blue and orange feathers, that lives near rivers and feeds on fish.

kiosk *(**kee**-osk)* *n* a small hut where you can buy things such as newspapers and sweets.

kiss *v* to touch somebody with your lips to show love or friendship. **kiss** *n.*

kit *n* **1** a set of clothes, equipment or tools that you need to do something. *Have you seen my football kit?* **2** a set of all the things that you need to make something. *a model-aeroplane kit.*

kitchen *n* a room in a house where you prepare and cook food.

kite *n* a toy made of a light frame covered with cloth or paper, that is flown in the wind.

kitten *n* a young cat.

kiwi *(**kee**-wee)* *n* (*pl* kiwis) a New Zealand bird that cannot fly.

knack *n* the ability to do something easily.

knave *n* the jack in a pack of playing-cards.

knead *v* to press and squeeze dough with your hands to make it ready for baking.

knee *n* the joint in the middle of your leg.

knee-cap *n* the bone at the front of your knee.

kneel *v* (kneeling, knelt) to go down on your knees.

knew *past of* know.

knickers *n pl* a woman's or girl's underpants.

knife *n* (*pl* knives) a tool with a blade and a handle, used for cutting.

knight *n* **1** in the Middle Ages, a nobleman who fought on horseback to serve a king or lord. **2** a man with the title "Sir". **3** a chesspiece shaped like a horse's head. See **chess**.

knit *v* (knits, knitting, knitted) to make clothes or other things out of woollen thread, using two long needles or a machine.

knob *n* a round handle.

knock *v* **1** to hit something to make a noise. *He knocked on the door.* **2** to hit somebody or something, making them fall. *I knocked the vase off the table.* **knock out** to hit somebody hard enough to make them unconscious. **knock** *n.*

knocker *n* a metal object fixed to a door, used for knocking.

knot[1] *n* **1** a join made in string or rope by tying and pulling tight. **2** a hard lump in wood, where a branch joined the tree trunk. **3** a measure of the speed of ships or aircraft, equal to 1.85 kilometres per hour.

knot[2] *v* (knots, knotting, knotted) to tie something in a knot.

know *v* (knowing, knew, known) **1** to be aware of or have something correctly in your mind. *Do you know what the time is?* **2** to be familiar with or able to recognize something.

knowledge *n* what you know and understand. **knowledgeable** *adj.*

knuckle *n* one of the joints of your fingers.

koala *n* a furry Australian mammal that lives in trees.

Koran *(ko-**rahn**)* *n* the holy book of Islam.

kosher *(**koh**-sher)* *adj* prepared in the way required by Jewish law.

Ll

label *n* a piece of paper, card or cloth with writing on it, attached to something to give information about it. **label** *v.*

laboratory *n* a room or building used for scientific experiments.

labour[1] *n* **1** work, especially physical work. **2** giving birth to a baby.

labour[2] *v* to work hard.

labourer *n* a person who does hard physical work.

Labour Party *n* one of the main political parties in Britain.

Labrador *n* a large black or golden-coloured dog.

lace[1] *n* **1** a thin, delicate material with a pattern of small holes. *The picture shows a lace-maker from Brittany, France.* **2** a shoelace.

lace

lace[2] *v* to fasten with laces.

lack *v* to be without something. *We lacked the strength to go on.* **lack** *n.*

lacquer *n* a shiny paint.

lad *n* a boy.

ladder *n* **1** a set of steps between two long pieces of wood, metal or rope. **2** a long tear in tights or stockings.

laden *adj* carrying a lot of heavy things. *He returned from shopping laden with bags.*

ladle *n* a large, deep spoon.

lady *n* **1** a polite word for a woman. **2** a special title given to some women. *Lady Eleanor Wilson.*

ladybird *n* a small, flying beetle, usually red with black spots.

lag *v* (lags, lagging, lagged) to move too slowly and get left behind.

lager *n* a light-coloured beer.

lagoon *n* a shallow salt-water lake separated from the sea by a long bank of sand.

laid *past of* lay[2].

lain *past participle of* lie[2].

lair *n* a wild animal's den.

lake *n* a large area of water surrounded by land.

lamb *n* **1** a young sheep. **2** the meat from a young sheep.

lame *adj* **1** not able to walk properly. **2** not good enough, weak. *That's a lame excuse.* **lameness** *n.*

lamp *n* an object that produces light by using electricity or burning oil or gas.
lance *n* a type of spear with a long handle and sharp point, used in the past by soldiers on horseback.
land[1] *n* **1** the parts of the Earth's surface that are not covered by water. **2** a country. *foreign lands.* **3** a piece of ground owned by somebody.
land[2] *v* to come on to land from the sea or the air. *Our plane landed on time.* **landing** *n.*
landing *n* a flat area of floor at the top of a flight of stairs.
landlady, landlord *n* **1** a person who owns a house or flat and rents it to others. **2** a person who owns or runs a pub.
landmark *n* a clearly visible building or object that helps you find the way.
landscape *n* **1** everything you can see when you look across an area of land. *a beautiful landscape.* **2** a picture of an area of countryside.
landslide *n* a fall of rock or earth down the side of a hill or cliff.
lane *n* **1** a narrow road, usually in the country. **2** one of the strips that a wide road, a racetrack or a swimming-pool is divided into.
language *n* **1** the words that we use to talk or write to each other. *Many different languages are spoken in Africa.* **2** any other way of communicating. *sign language.*
lantern *n* a box with glass sides for holding a candle or oil lamp so that it does not blow out.
lap[1] *n* **1** the tops of your legs when you are sitting. **2** the distance around a racetrack.
lap[2] *v* (laps, lapping, lapped) **1** to drink by licking with the tongue, as a cat does. **2** (of a liquid) to move gently against something. *Waves lapped against the rocks.*
lapel *n* the part of a coat or jacket that is joined to the collar and folded back across your chest.
lapse *n* **1** a small mistake. **2** a length of time that has passed. *a lapse of ten years.*
laptop *n* a small, light, portable computer.
lard *n* the fat of a pig, melted and then solidified, used in cooking.
larder *n* a small room or cupboard where food is kept cool.
large *adj* big. **largeness** *n.*
lark *n* a small, brown bird that sings beautifully.
larva *n* (*pl* larvae) an insect in the first stage after coming out of the egg.
laser *n* an instrument that produces a very narrow and powerful beam of light, called a **laser beam**.
lash[1] *v* **1** to strike a person or an animal with a whip. **2** to make sudden, violent movements like a whip. *The shark's tail lashed from side to side.* **3** to fasten tightly with a rope.
lash[2] *n* an eyelash.
lass *n* a girl.
lasso *(la-soo) n* (*pl* lassos) a long rope with a loop that tightens when the rope is pulled, used for catching animals. **lasso** *v.*

lasso

last[1] *adj, adv* **1** at the end, after all the others. **2** most recent. *last week.* **last** *n.*
last[2] *v* **1** to go on for a length of time. *How long does this film last?* **2** to be enough or to remain in good condition for a certain length of time.
latch *n* a fastening for a gate or door.
late *adj, adv* **1** coming after the usual

or right time. *They were late for school.* **2** near the end of a time. *the late afternoon.* **3** no longer alive. *the late prime minister.*

lately *adv* recently, not long ago.

lather *n* a mass of small soap bubbles.

Latin *n* the language of ancient Rome.

latitude *n* the distance, measured in degrees on a map, that a place is north or south of the equator.

latter *adj* towards the end. *the latter part of the year.* **the latter** the second of two things just mentioned.

laugh *v* to make a sound to show that you think something is funny. **laugh** *n*, **laughter** *n*.

launch[1] *v* **1** to put a boat into water for the first time. **2** to send a rocket up into space. **3** to start something new.

launch[2] *n* **1** launching something. **2** a large boat with a motor.

launderette *n* a shop with machines where people can do their washing.

laundry *n* **1** a place where you send clothes to be washed. **2** clothes that are waiting to be washed.

lava *n* hot, liquid rock that flows from an active volcano.

lavatory *n* a toilet.

lavender *n* **1** a small shrub with purple flowers that have a pleasant smell. **2** a pale bluish-purple colour.

law *n* **1** a set of rules in a society, that people must obey. **2** one of these rules. **3** a rule in science. *the law of gravity.*

law court *n* a place where it is decided whether somebody is guilty of a crime, and where disagreements between people are judged.

lawful *adj* allowed by law. **lawfully** *adv*.

lawn *n* an area of short, cut grass.

lawnmower *n* a machine that you use for cutting grass.

lawyer *n* a person who gives advice about the law and speaks for people in a law court.

lax *adj* careless, not strict.

lay[1] *past of* lie[2].

lay[2] *v* (lays, laying, laid) **1** (of a bird) to produce an egg. **2** to put something down carefully.

layby *n (pl* laybys) a place at the side of a road where vehicles can park for a while.

layer *n* a thickness of something spread over the surface of something else. *The ground was covered with a layer of snow.*

lazy *adj* (lazier, laziest) not wanting to do work or take exercise. **lazily** *adv*, **laziness** *n*.

lead[1] *(rhymes with* bed*) n* **1** a soft, heavy, grey metal. **2** the part of a pencil that makes a mark.

lead[2] *(rhymes with* reed*) v* (leading, led) **1** to go in front, especially to show others the way. *She led me to the door.* **2** to be in first place. **3** to be in charge. **4** to go to a place. *Where does this road lead?* **leader** *n*, **leadership** *n*.

lead[3] *(rhymes with* reed*) n* **1** leading. **2** a long strap that you attach to a dog's collar so you can take it for walks. **3** a cable that carries electricity to an appliance. **4** a clue. *Do the police have any leads yet?*

leaf *n (pl* leaves) **1** one of the flat, usually green, parts of a plant or tree. **2** a page of a book.

leaflet *n* a printed paper giving information about something.

league *(leeg) n* **1** a group of sports clubs that play matches against each other. **2** a group of people or countries that work together to help each other.

leak[1] *n* a hole through which liquid or gas escapes. *a leak in the water-pipe.*

leak[2] *v* **1** to pass through a leak. *Gas was leaking from the cracked pipe.* **2** to have a leak. *This bucket leaks.*

lean[1] *v* (leaning, leant *or* leaned) **1** to slope to one side, to not be upright. **2** to rest against or on something.

lean[2] *adj* **1** slim. **2** having little fat. *lean meat.*

leap *v* (leaping, leapt *or* leaped) to jump. **leap** *n*.

learn *v* (learning, learnt *or* learned) **1** to get knowledge or skill. *Are you learning French at school?* **2** to get to know. *We learnt that Julie was ill.*

learned *(ler-nid) adj* knowing a lot.

lease *n* a legal document giving use of a building, etc in exchange for rent.

least *adj* smallest in size or amount. **least** *adv, pron.*

leather *n* the skin of an animal used to make things like shoes and clothes.

leave[1] *v* (leaving, left) **1** to go away. **2** to let something or somebody stay or remain. *I left my books on the bus.* **leave out** not to include.

leave[2] *n* time away from work, a holiday. *He is on leave this week.*

leaves *plural of* leaf.

lecture[1] *n* a formal talk given to a group of people to teach them something.

lecture[2] *v* to give a lecture. **lecturer** *n.*

led *past of* lead.

ledge *n* a narrow shelf on a wall or cliff.

leek *n* a long, white vegetable with thick, green leaves at one end.

left[1] *past of* leave.

left[2] *adj* of, on or towards the side opposite to the right. *Raise your left hand.* **left** *adv, n.*

left-handed *adj* using your left hand more easily than your right.

leftovers *n pl* food that remains after a meal is finished.

left-wing *adj* in politics, supporting the idea that all people are equal and that the government should look after people.

leg *n* **1** one of the parts of your body that you use for standing and walking. **2** one of the supports of a chair or table.

legal *adj* **1** allowed by the law. **2** to do with the law. **legally** *adv.*

legend *n* an old, traditional story.

legendary *adj* **1** told about in old stories. **2** very famous.

leggings *n pl* close-fitting trousers made from a stretchy material.

legible *adj* able to be read easily. *Your handwriting is barely legible!* **legibility** *n*, **legibly** *adv.*

legion *n* **1** a division of the Roman army. **2** a large group of soldiers.

legislation *n* laws.

leisure *n* free time.

leisurely *adj* not hurrying.

lemon *n* a fruit with a thick, yellow skin and very sour juice.

lemonade *n* **1** a sweet, fizzy drink. **2** a cold drink flavoured with lemons.

lend *v* (lending, lent) to give somebody the use of something for a time. *She had forgotten to bring her coat, so I lent her mine.*

length *n* **1** the distance from one end of something to the other. **2** the time that something lasts.

lengthen *v* to make or become longer.

lengthy *adj* (lengthier, lengthiest) long.

lenient *adj* not strict.

lens *n* **1** a piece of curved glass for focusing or magnifying, used in cameras, spectacles, etc. **2** the part of your eye that focuses light. See **eye**.

Lent *n* in the Christian religion, the 40 days before Easter.

lent *past of* lend.

lentil *n* a small, dried seed that can be cooked and eaten.

leopard *(lep-erd) n* a large wild cat with black spots on a yellowish coat, found in Africa and Asia.

leopard

leotard *(lee-a-tard) n* a tight, one-piece garment worn for dancing, gymnastics, etc.

less *adj* smaller in size or amount. **less** *adv, pron.*

lessen *v* to make or become less or smaller.

lesson *n* **1** a time during which something is taught and learnt. *I am having guitar lessons after school.* **2** something learnt by experience. **3** a piece from the Bible, read in church.

let *v* (lets, letting, let) **1** to allow somebody to do something. *Billy let* *me ride his bike.* **2** used for giving orders or making suggestions. *Let us pray.* **3** to rent property to somebody. **let down** to disappoint somebody. **let off** to allow somebody to go without being punished, etc.

lethal *adj* causing death. **lethally** *adv.*

letter *n* **1** one of the signs that we use in writing to make up words. **2** a written message, usually sent by post in an envelope.

lettuce *n* a salad vegetable with large, green leaves.

leukaemia *(loo-**kee**-mee-a)* *n* a very serious blood disease.

level[1] *adj* **1** flat and even, horizontal. *a level surface.* **2** of the same height, standard, amount, etc. *The scores of the two teams are level.*

level[2] *n* **1** a height. *sea level.* **2** a standard. *advanced level students.*

level[3] *v* (levels, levelling, levelled) to make something level.

level crossing *n* a place where a road crosses a railway line without using a bridge or tunnel.

lever *n* **1** a bar used for lifting something heavy or for forcing something open. **2** a handle that you use to make a machine work. **lever** *v.*

liable *adj* responsible for something by law. **liable to** likely to. *She's liable to make careless mistakes.*

liar *n* a person who tells lies.

liberal *adj* **1** tolerant of other people and their ideas, not strict. **2** generous. **liberally** *adv.*

liberate *v* to set a person or an animal free, to release. **liberation** *n.*

liberty *n* freedom.

librarian *n* a person who works in a library.

library *n* a place where you can go to read or borrow books, tapes, etc.

lice *plural of* louse.

licence *n* an official document giving you permission to do something. *a driving licence.*

license *v* to give a licence to somebody. *Pubs are licensed to sell alcohol.*

lichen *(**lie**-ken* or ***litch**-en)* *n* a tiny plant that grows in patches on rocks and trees.

lick *v* to pass your tongue over something. **lick** *n.*

licorice *another spelling of* liquorice.

lid *n* **1** a cover for a pot, box, etc. **2** an eyelid.

lie[1] *v* (lies, lying, lied) to say something that you know is not true. **lie** *n.*

lie[2] *v* (lies, lying, lay, lain) **1** to be in, or get into, a flat position. *She lay down and went to sleep.* **2** to be situated somewhere. *The island lies just off the coast.*

lieutenant *(lef-**ten**-ent)* *n* an officer in the army or navy.

life *n* (*pl* lives) **1** the state of being able to grow, develop and change, that makes plants and animals different from stones, water, minerals, etc. *The doctor saved the man's life.* **2** the time between birth and death. **3** liveliness, energy.

lifeboat *n* a boat for rescuing people at sea.

life-jacket *n* a jacket that will keep you afloat in water.

lift[1] *v* **1** to raise something. *The box was so heavy that I couldn't lift it.* **2** to rise. *The fog lifted.*

lift[2] *n* **1** a machine like a large, moving box for carrying people or goods up and down in a building. **2** a ride in somebody else's car or another vehicle. *Our neighbour gave me a lift to school this morning.*

light[1] *n* **1** the brightness that comes from the Sun, a flame or a lamp, that makes it possible for us to see things. **2** an object that gives out light, for example an electric lamp. **3** a flame from a match or cigarette lighter.

light[2] *v* (lighting, lit *or* lighted) **1** to start something burning. **2** to give light to something. *The room was lit by several lamps.*

light[3] *adj* **1** with a lot of light, not dark. **2** with a pale colour. *light green.* **3** weighing little, not heavy. **4** gentle. *light rain.* **lighten** *v,* **lightness** *n.*

lighter *n* a device for lighting cigarettes.

light-hearted *adj* happy, not sad or serious.
lighthouse *n* a tower by or in the sea, with a flashing light to guide or warn ships.

lighthouse

lightning *n* a flash of light in the sky during a thunderstorm.
like¹ *v* to enjoy something, to find somebody or something pleasant. **likeable** *adj*.
like² *prep* **1** the same as or similar to. *She looks like her sister.* **2** in the same or a similar way to. *She sang like a bird.* **3** typical of. *It's not like Dan to be late.* **like** *conj*.
likely *adv* (likelier, likeliest) expected to happen. *They said on the weather forecast that it is likely to rain today.* **likelihood** *n*.
likewise *adv* the same, in the same way.
lilac *n* a shrub with sweet-smelling, pale-purple or white flowers.
lily *n* a tall plant with white or coloured flowers, grown from a bulb.
limb *n* **1** a leg or an arm. **2** the branch of a tree.
lime *n* a green fruit similar to a lemon. **2** a white substance left after heating limestone, used in making cement.
limerick *n* a funny five-line poem.
limestone *n* a type of rock containing calcium carbonate.
limit¹ *n* a line or point that you cannot or should not go beyond. *The speed limit in the town is 30 miles an hour.*
limit² *v* to keep something from going beyond a certain point or amount. **limitation** *n*.
limp¹ *adj* not stiff. *a limp lettuce.*
limp² *v* to walk unevenly, usually because you have hurt your foot or leg.
limpet *n* a small, cone-shaped shellfish that clings to rocks.
line¹ *n* **1** a long, thin mark. **2** a piece of rope, string or wire. **3** a row of people, things or words. **4** a railway or a railway track. **5 lines** the words spoken in a play.
line² *v* to cover something on the inside.
linen *n* a type of cloth that is heavier than cotton, used to make things such as sheets and clothing.
liner *n* a big passenger ship.
linesman *n* a person who decides if the ball has gone over the line in games such as football and tennis.
linger *v* to wait around, to stay.
linguist *n* a person who studies language or is good at languages.
lining *n* a layer of material inside something. *Her coat has a silk lining.*
link¹ *n* **1** one loop of a chain. **2** a connection.
link² *v* to join things together.
lino *n* (*short for* linoleum) a shiny floor covering.
lion *n* a large wild cat, found in Africa and Asia. The male has a thick mane.
lioness *n* a female lion.
lip *n* **1** one of the edges of the mouth. **2** the specially shaped part of a jug from which liquid is poured.
lipstick *n* make-up for colouring your lips.
liquid *n* a substance that flows, such as water or oil. **liquid** *adj*.
liquor *n* any strong, alcoholic drink.
liquorice *(lik-er-iss) n* a strong-tasting, black sweet made from a plant root.
lisp *v* to speak using a *th* sound instead of *s*.
list¹ *n* a number of names or things written down or said one after the other. *Did you put bread on the shopping list?* **list** *v*.
list² *v* (of a ship) to lean to one side.
listen *v* to pay attention so that you hear something. **listener** *n*.
lit *past of* light.
literacy *n* the ability to read and write.
literally *adv* exactly as stated. *She was literally too tired to walk any further.*

literate *adj* able to read and write.
literature *n* **1** novels, poetry and plays. **2** any written material. **literary** *adj*.
litre *n* a measure for liquids, equal to 1,000 millilitres.
litter *n* **1** an untidy mess of rubbish, paper, etc that is left around. **2** all the animals born at one time to the same mother. *Our cat had a litter of four kittens.*
little *adj* **1** small in size. **2** not much. **little** *adv, pron.*
live[1] *(rhymes with* give*)* *v* **1** to have life, to be alive. **2** to have your home somewhere. *They live in Glasgow.*
live[2] *(rhymes with* hive*)* *adj* **1** living, not dead. *They found a live mouse in the biscuit tin.* **2** heard or seen on the radio or television as it is actually happening. **3** carrying an electrical current. *a live wire.*
lively *adj* (livelier, liveliest) full of life and energy. **liveliness** *n*.
liver *n* an organ in your body that does several important jobs, including cleaning the blood. See **digestion**.
lives *plural of* life.
livestock *n* farm animals, such as cattle, sheep and pigs.
living[1] *adj* having life, alive.
living[2] *n* the money that you need in order to live. *She earns her living as a taxi-driver.*
living-room *n* a sitting-room.
lizard *n* a small, four-legged reptile with a tail.
llama *(**lah**-ma)* *n* a South American mammal like a small camel with no hump.
load[1] *n* something that is carried, especially something heavy. **a load of, loads of** *(informal)* a lot of.
load[2] *v* **1** to put a load onto or into the thing that will carry it. *We loaded the boxes into the van.* **2** to put bullets in a gun or film in a camera. **3** to put data or a program onto a computer.
loaf *n* (*pl* loaves) a large piece of bread baked in one piece.
loan[1] *n* something that has been lent, especially a sum of money.
loan[2] *v* to lend something.
loathe *v* to hate something.
loaves *plural of* loaf.
lob *v* (lobs, lobbing, lobbed) to throw or hit a ball high into the air. **lob** *n*.
lobby *n* an entrance hall.
lobster *n* a shellfish with a hard shell and large claws, used as food.

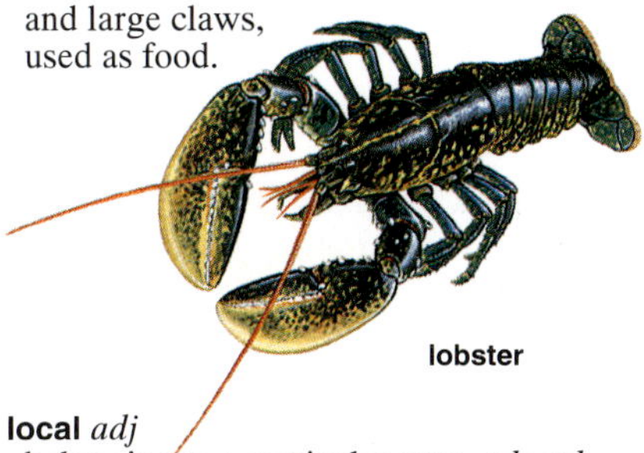

lobster

local *adj* belonging to a particular area. *a local newspaper.* **locally** *adv*.
locality *n* an area, a neighbourhood.
locate *v* to find the position of something. *Can you locate your street on this map?* **be located** be in a particular place. *The kitchen is located in the basement.*
location *n* a place, a position.
loch *(lockh)* *n* a Scottish lake.
lock[1] *n* **1** a device for fastening a door, box, etc so that it cannot be opened without a key. **2** a section of a canal where the water levels can be changed by opening and shutting large gates.
lock[2] *v* to fasten with a lock.
locker *n* a small cupboard that can be locked.
locket *n* a small case worn on a chain around the neck, sometimes containing a photograph.
locks *n pl* hair.
locomotive *n* a railway engine.
locust *n* an insect like a large grasshopper, that destroys crops by eating them.
lodge[1] *n* **1** a small house, often at the entrance to a larger building. **2** a beaver's home.
lodge[2] *v* **1** to live in a room in somebody's house, usually paying them money to do so. **2** to get stuck. *The bullet lodged in his brain.*

lodger *n* a person who pays to live in a room in somebody's house.
loft *n* a room or space just under the roof of a building.
log *n* **1** a length of wood cut from a tree that has been felled. **2** a written record, especially of a ship's or an aeroplane's journey.
logic *n* correct reasoning. **logical** *adj*, **logically** *adv*.
logo *n* (*pl* logos) a symbol representing a company or other organization.
loiter *v* to stand around doing nothing in particular. *They were loitering outside the shop.*
lollipop *n* a sweet on a stick.
lolly *n* a lollipop.
lonely *adj* (lonelier, loneliest) **1** sad because you are alone. **2** far away from busy places. *a lonely island off the coast of Scotland.* **loneliness** *n*.
long[1] *adj* **1** not short, measuring a lot from end to end. **2** measuring a certain amount. *Make a cut 2 cm long.* **3** taking a lot of time. *a long film.* **long** *adv*.
long[2] *v* to wish for something very much. *She longed to go home.*
longitude *n* the distance measured in degrees east or west of a line that runs through Greenwich in London and the North and South Poles.
loo *n (informal)* a toilet.
look *v* **1** to use your eyes to see. **2** to appear or seem. *You look tired.* **look after** to take care of somebody or something. **look for** to search for something. **look forward to** to wait with pleasure for something. **look out!** be careful! **look up** to search for something in a book.
lookout *n* a person who keeps watch for something.
loom[1] *n* a machine for weaving cloth.
loom[2] *v* to appear as a large, frightening shape. *A tall figure loomed out of the darkness.*
loop *n* a shape formed by a curve that bends right round and crosses over itself. **loop** *v*.
loose *adj* **1** not tight. *loose trousers.* **2** not firm. *One of my teeth is loose.* **3** not tied up. *The horses are loose in the field.* **4** not in a packet or fastened together. *loose sweets.*
loosen *v* to make or become loose.
loot[1] *n* stolen money or goods.
loot[2] *v* to steal goods in a riot or war.
lop *v* (lops, lopping, lopped) to cut something off.
lop-sided *adj* with one side higher than the other, crooked.
lord *n* **1** a nobleman. **2** a title for a male member of the aristocracy or a bishop, judge, etc. **3 Lord** a title for God or Christ.
lorry *n* a big motor vehicle that carries heavy loads.
lose *v* (losing, lost) **1** to no longer have something. **2** to be beaten in a game, argument, fight, etc. **loser** *n*.
loss *n* **1** losing something. **2** something that is lost.
lost *adj* **1** not able to be found. **2** puzzled or confused. **3** not knowing where you are or in which direction you should go.
lot *pron* a large number or amount. **draw lots** to decide who will do something by pulling names out of a hat, etc.
lotion *n* a liquid that you rub on your skin to clean or heal it.
lottery *n* an event in which people buy tickets to try to win prizes.
loud *adj* making a lot of sound, noisy. **loudness** *n*.
loudspeaker *n* a part of a radio, stereo system, etc that turns electrical waves into sound.
lounge[1] *n* a sitting-room.
lounge[2] *v* to sit about lazily.
louse *n* (*pl* lice) a small insect that lives on the bodies of animals or humans.
love[1] *v* to like somebody or something very much. **lovable** *adj*, **lover** *n*.
love[2] *n* a strong feeling of liking somebody or something very much.
love[3] *n* in tennis, no score.
lovely *adj* (lovelier, loveliest) **1** attractive, beautiful. *Those flowers are lovely!* **2** pleasant, enjoyable. *We had a lovely holiday.*

low[1] *adj* not high. **low** *adv*.
low[2] *v* to make a sound like a cow.
lower *v* to move something down.
loyal *adj* faithful, not betraying your friends, country, etc.
lubricate *v* to put oil or grease on something to make it move more easily or smoothly. **lubrication** *n*.
luck *n* **1** things that happen by chance, that you cannot control. *There is no skill involved in this game – it's just luck whether you win or not.* **2** something good that happens by chance.
lucky *adj* (luckier, luckiest) **1** having good luck. **2** bringing good luck. **luckily** *adv*.
luggage *n* the cases and bags that you take with you when you travel.
lukewarm *adj* slightly warm.
lull[1] *v* to make somebody calm or quiet. *The music lulled him to sleep.*
lull[2] *n* a short period of calm.
lullaby *n* a song that is sung to send a baby to sleep.
lumberjack *n* a person who cuts down, saws up and moves trees.
luminous *adj* shining in the dark.
lump *n* **1** a small, solid mass. **2** a swelling.
lunacy *n* insanity, madness.
lunar *adj* to do with the Moon.
lunatic *n* a person who is insane.
lunch *n* a meal that you eat in the middle of the day.
lung *n* one of the two organs inside your chest that you use for breathing. See **respiration**.
lunge *v* to move forwards quickly and suddenly. **lunge** *n*.
lurch *v* to make a sudden, jerky movement, often to one side. *The drunken man lurched towards the bar.*
lurk *v* to wait in hiding. *Somebody was lurking in the shadows.*
lush *adj* growing thickly and strongly.
lust *n* a strong desire.
luxury *n* **1** something that is pleasant to have but that you do not really need. **2** the enjoyment of luxuries. **luxurious** *adj*.
lyrics *n pl* the words of a song.

Mm

machine *n* a piece of equipment with moving parts that work together to do something.
machinegun *n* a gun that can fire bullets very quickly without being reloaded.
machinery *n* **1** machines. **2** the working parts of machines.
mackerel *n* an edible sea fish.
mackintosh *n* a waterproof coat.
mad *adj* (madder, maddest) **1** mentally ill, insane. **2** very angry. **mad about** liking somebody or something very much. **madness** *n*.
madam *n* a polite way of speaking to a woman, instead of using her name.
made *past of* make.
magazine *n* **1** a thin book that is published regularly, containing pictures, stories, etc. **2** the part of a gun that holds the bullets.
maggot *n* the larva of some types of fly, similar to a small worm.
magic *n* **1** in stories, the power of supernatural forces to do amazing things that cannot be explained. **2** clever tricks that seem like magic. **magical** *adj*.
magician *(ma-ji-shun)* *n* a person who does magic tricks.
magistrate *n* a person who acts as a judge in dealing with less serious crimes.
magnet *n* a piece of metal that has the power to attract iron or steel. **magnetic** *adj*, **magnetism** *n*.

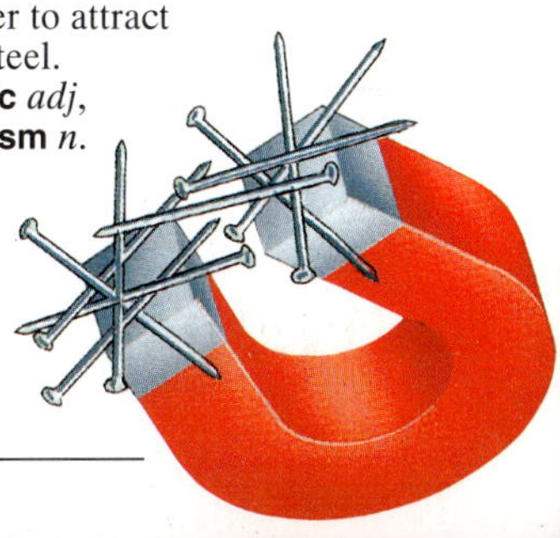
magnet

magnificent *adj* extremely impressive, splendid. **magnificence** *n.*
magnify *v* (magnifies, magnifying, magnified) to make something appear bigger by using special lenses. **magnification** *n.*
magpie *n* a large, long-tailed, black and white bird that likes to collect shiny objects.
mahogany *n* a hard, reddish-brown wood.
maid *n* **1** a female servant in a hotel or private home. **2** *(old-fashioned)* a girl.
mail[1] *n* letters and parcels sent by post. **mail** *v.*
mail[2] *n* armour made of metal rings.
maim *v* to injure somebody badly, so that they are permanently disabled.
main *adj* most important or largest.
mainland *n* a large piece of land, not the islands nearby.
mainly *adv* mostly.
mains *n pl* the pipes or cables bringing gas, water or electricity to a building.
maintain *v* **1** to keep something in good working order. *The machinery is maintained regularly.* **2** to continue something. *We must maintain high standards.* **3** to give money to support something. *He has a family to maintain.* **4** to say firmly. *He maintains he is innocent.* **maintenance** *n.*
maize *n* a plant that produces sweetcorn.
majesty *n* impressive dignity, splendour. **Your Majesty** the polite way of speaking to a king or queen. **majestic** *adj,* **majestically** *adv.*
major[1] *adj* great in size or importance.
major[2] *n* a senior army officer.
majority *n* the greater part or number.
make[1] *v* (making, made) **1** to create or produce something. **2** to force or cause something to happen. *She made me go first.* **3** to do something. *May I make a phone call?* **4** to add up to. *Two and six make eight.*
make[2] *n* a brand or type.
makeshift *adj* built or made very quickly and only intended to last for a short time. *We built a makeshift shelter out of old planks of wood.*
make-up *n* coloured powders and creams that women and actors put on their faces.
mal- *prefix* bad or badly. *malformed, malfunction, maltreat.*
malaria *n* a tropical disease that you can get from mosquito bites.
male *adj* of the sex that does not give birth to children or produce eggs. **male** *n.*
malicious *adj* hurting people on purpose, spiteful. *a malicious remark.*
mall *n* a shopping centre.
mallard *n* a wild duck, the male of which has a green head.
mallet *n* a wooden hammer.
malnutrition *n* a disease caused by not getting enough nutritious food.
malt *n* barley or other grain that has been prepared, by soaking and drying, for making beer or whisky.
mammal *n* any animal of which the female gives birth to live young and feeds them with milk from her body.
mammoth *n* a very large animal like a hairy elephant, that is now extinct.

mammoth

man *n* (*pl* men) **1** a fully grown male human. **2** human beings in general.
manage *v* **1** to succeed in doing something even if it is difficult. *I just managed to finish the work on time.* **2** to have control or charge of something. *She manages the local football team.* **management** *n,* **manager** *n.*

mane *n* the long hair on the head and neck of a horse or lion.
manger *n* a box for horses or cattle to eat from.
mangle *v* to crush or damage something badly. *The car was mangled in the accident.*
mango *n* (*pl* mangoes) a tropical fruit with juicy, orange-coloured flesh.
maniac *n* a mad or dangerous person.
manic *adj* very energetic or excited.
manicure *n* care of the hands and nails.
manipulate *v* **1** to use or control something skilfully. **2** to influence somebody in a clever and cunning way, so that they do what you want.
mankind *n* all people.
man-made *adj* artificial.
manner *n* **1** the way in which you do something. *He greeted me in a friendly manner.* **2** the way in which you behave. *I don't like her manner.* **3 manners** polite behaviour.
manoeuvre *(man-oo-ver)* *n* **1** a movement performed with care and skill. **2 manoeuvres** training exercises for large numbers of troops. **manoeuvre** *v*.
manor *n* a large, old country house surrounded by land.
mansion *n* a large, grand house.
manslaughter *n* killing a person without planning to do it.
mantelpiece *n* a shelf over a fireplace.
manual[1] *adj* done or worked with your hands. *manual controls.* **manually** *adv*.
manual[2] *n* a book that gives you instructions on how to do something.
manufacture *v* to make things by machine in a factory.
manure *n* dung from animals, spread on soil to help produce better crops.
many *adj* a great number. **many** *pron*.
map *n* a drawing of part of the Earth's surface, showing rivers, mountains, countries, towns, roads, etc.
maple *n* a tree with large, five-pointed leaves.
mar *v* (mars, marring, marred) to spoil something.
marathon *n* a race for runners covering approximately 26 miles.
marble *n* **1** hard stone that can be carved and polished. **2** a small glass ball used in children's games.
march[1] *v* to walk with regular steps.
march[2] *n* **1** a distance marched. **2** a piece of music for marching to. **3** an organized walk by a group of people to protest against, or show their support for, something.
March *n* the third month of the year.
mare *n* a female horse.
margarine *n* a yellow substance like butter, made from vegetable fats.
margin *n* the blank space around the edge of a page of writing or print.
marigold *n* a garden plant with bright yellow or orange flowers.
marijuana *(ma-ra-**wah**-nuh)* *n* a drug that people smoke.
marina *n* a harbour where yachts and other boats can moor.
marine[1] *adj* to do with the sea.
marine[2] *n* a soldier who serves on board a ship.
marionette *n* a puppet that is moved by pulling strings.
mark[1] *n* **1** a stain, spot or scratch on something. **2** a number or letter put on a piece of school work to show how good it is. **3** a shape or special sign on something.
mark[2] *v* **1** to put a mark on something. **2** to give marks to a piece of school work. **3** to keep close to an opposing player in a game.
market *n* a place where things are bought and sold, usually in the open air. *a fruit and vegetable market.*
marmalade *n* a jam made from oranges or other citrus fruits.
maroon[1] *n* a brownish-red colour. **maroon** *adj*.
maroon[2] *v* to leave somebody in a lonely place from which they cannot escape. *marooned on a desert island.*
marquee *n* a large tent.
marriage *n* **1** the relationship between a husband and wife. **2** a wedding ceremony.
marrow *n* **1** the soft substance in the hollow part of bones. See **bone**. **2** a large, long, green vegetable.

marry *v* (marries, marrying, married) **1** to become husband and wife. **2** to perform a marriage ceremony.
marsh *n* an area of low, wet land. **marshy** *adj*.
marsupial *n* an animal such as a kangaroo that carries its young in a pouch on the female's stomach.
martial *adj* to do with war or battle.
martial arts *n pl* the self-defence techniques, such as judo and karate, which come from the Far East.
martyr *(**mar**-ter) n* a person who suffers or dies for their beliefs. **martyrdom** *n*.
marvel *n* an astonishing or wonderful thing.
marvellous *adj* wonderful, excellent.
marzipan *n* a sweet paste made from ground almonds and sugar.
mascot *n* a person, animal or thing that is supposed to bring good luck.
masculine *adj* to do with men, or typical of men.
mash *v* to crush food until it becomes a soft mass.
mask[1] *n* a covering for the face, that hides or protects it.
mask[2] *v* to cover up or disguise something.
mason *n* a person who carves stone.
mass *n* a large quantity or a lump.
massacre *n* the killing of a very large number of people. **massacre** *v*.

ancient masks from North Africa

massage *n* the rubbing of parts of the body to remove pain or to help relaxation. **massage** *v*.
massive *adj* huge or heavy.
mast *n* the pole that holds a ship's sails.
master[1] *n* **1** a person who controls others. **2** a male teacher. **3** a person who is very skilled at something. **4** the male owner of a dog, horse, etc.
master[2] *v* **1** to become skilled at something. **2** to control something.
masterpiece *n* a work of art done with great skill.
mat *n* a flat piece of material for wiping shoes on, covering a floor, putting dishes on, etc.
match[1] *n* **1** a game or contest between two players or teams. *a football match.* **2** a thing that is similar to or the same as another. **3** a small, thin piece of wood used for lighting fires.
match[2] *v* to be similar to something, to go well with something. *Does this scarf match my gloves?*
mate[1] *v* (of animals) to come together to breed.
mate[2] *n* **1** a friend or companion. **2** the sexual partner of an animal or bird.
material *n* **1** any substance from which something is made. *Bricks, wood and cement are all building materials.* **2** cloth.
maternal *adj* of or like a mother.
maternity *adj* for or to do with a woman who is having, or about to have, a baby. *maternity clothes.*
mathematics *n* the study of measurements, numbers and quantities. **mathematical** *adj*.
maths *short for* mathematics.
matinée *(**ma**-tin-ay) n* an afternoon performance of a play, film or show.
matrimony *n* marriage. **matrimonial** *adj*.
matron *n (old-fashioned)* a senior nurse in a hospital.
matt *adj* not shiny, dull. *a matt surface.*
matter[1] *n* **1** any substance or material that takes up space. **2** a subject.
matter[2] *v* to be important.
mattress *n* a soft, thick layer of padding on a bed for sleeping on.
mature *adj* **1** fully grown or developed. *She is mature for her age.* **2** ripe. *mature cheese.* **maturity** *n*.
maul *v* to severely injure somebody by treating them roughly or savagely.
mauve *(rhymes with* drove*) n* a purple colour. **mauve** *adj*.
maxi- *prefix* very large or very long.
maximum *n* (*pl* maxima) the greatest

possible number or amount, or the highest point. *The temperature reached its maximum at midday.* **maximum** *adj.*

may *v* (might) **1** used to show possibility. *I may see you tomorrow.* **2** used to ask or give permission. *May I go now?* **3** used to express a wish. *May you live a long and happy life.*

May *n* the fifth month of the year.

maybe *adv* perhaps.

mayonnaise *n* a thick sauce for salads, made from eggs, oil and vinegar.

mayor *(rhymes with* hair*) n* the leader of a town or district council.

maze *n* a confusing network of paths in a park, etc designed as a puzzle for you to find your way through.

meadow *n* a field of grass.

meal *n* the food eaten at one time.

mean[1] *v* (meaning, meant) **1** to intend to do something. *I didn't mean to upset you.* **2** to express something. *"Begin" means the same as "start".*

mean[2] *adj* **1** not generous. **2** not kind, nasty. **meanness** *n.*

meaning *n* what something means.

meantime *n* the time between two events.

meanwhile *adv* during this time.

measles *n* an infectious disease causing red spots on the skin.

measure[1] *v* to find out the size, amount, etc of something. **measurement** *n.*

measure[2] *n* **1** a unit used for measuring. *A metre is a measure of length.* **2** an instrument or container used for measuring. **3** an action that is intended to achieve something. *measures to prevent drug abuse.*

meat *n* the flesh of an animal used as food.

mechanic *n* a person who is skilled at repairing or operating machinery.

mechanical *adj* **1** to do with machinery. **2** worked by machinery. **3** done without thinking. *a mechanical action.* **mechanically** *adv.*

mechanism *n* a set of working parts in a machine.

medal *n* a piece of metal, usually similar to a large coin, given as a reward, eg for bravery in war or for sporting achievements. **medallist** *n.*

media *n pl* the ways of communicating with the public, especially radio, television and newspapers.

medical[1] *adj* to do with doctors or medicine. **medically** *adv.*

medical[2] *n* an examination by a doctor or nurse.

medicine *n* **1** a substance, usually a liquid, that you swallow to treat an illness. **2** the treatment of illnesses. **medicinal** *adj.*

medieval *adj* to do with the Middle Ages.

mediocre *(mee-dee-**oh**-ker) n* not very good, of average quality. **mediocrity** *n.*

meditate *v* to think deeply in silence, in order to relax or for spiritual reasons. **meditation** *n.*

medium[1] *adj* average or middle in size, quality, etc. *The packets came in three sizes – small, medium and large.*

medium[2] *n* **1** (*pl* media) a way of communicating something or producing an effect. **2** (*pl* mediums) a person who claims to be able to communicate with the spirits of dead people.

meek *adj* quiet, gentle and obedient.

meet *v* (meeting, met) **1** to come face to face with somebody. *We met Lucy on the way home.* **2** to come together, to join. *Where do the two roads meet?* **3** to be introduced to somebody. *Have you met Tom?*

meeting *n* a time when people come together to discuss something.

mega *adj (slang)* **1** huge. **2** excellent.

megabyte *n* a unit of computer memory (about 1 million bytes).

melancholy *adj* sad.

mellow *adj* **1** (of colours and sounds) soft, not strong or unpleasant. **2** (of food) ripe and pleasant to taste.

melody *n* a tune.

melon *n* a large, juicy fruit containing a lot of seeds.

melt *v* **1** to become liquid by heating. **2** to make something liquid by heating. *The ice melted in the sun.*

member *n* a person who belongs to a club or group. **membership** *n.*
Member of Parliament *n* a person who is elected by people to represent them in Parliament.
memorable *adj* easy to remember, or worth remembering.
memorial *n* a monument that is built to remind people of a historical event or a person who has died.
memorize *v* to learn something by heart.
memory *n* **1** the power to remember. *You've got a good memory!* **2** a thing that you remember. *happy memories of childhood.* **3** the part of a computer that stores and retrieves information.
men *plural of* man.
menace *n* a person or thing that is likely to cause injury or damage. **menace** *v*, **menacing** *adj.*
mend *v* **1** to repair something that is broken. **2** to heal. *Her broken leg is mending well.*
mental *adj* to do with the mind. **mentally** *adv.*
mention *v* to speak or write briefly about something.
menu *n* (*pl* menus) **1** a list of food that you can choose from at a restaurant, etc. **2** a list of choices shown on a computer screen.
mercenary *n* a soldier paid by a foreign country to fight in its army.
merchant *n* a person whose job is buying and selling things.
mercury *n* a poisonous, silver-coloured, liquid metal, used in thermometers.
mercy *n* kindness and forgiveness towards somebody that you have the power to punish. **merciful** *adj*, **mercifully** *adv.*
merely *adv* only, simply. *I am merely telling you what I saw.*
merge *v* to combine or join together.
merit *n* a good point or quality.
mermaid *n* in stories, a sea creature with the upper body of a woman and the tail of a fish.
merry *adj* (merrier, merriest) happy and cheerful, full of fun. **merrily** *adv.*
merry-go-round *n* a roundabout at a fair.
mesh *n* a net.
mess[1] *n* an untidy or unpleasant state.
mess[2] *v* **mess up** to make untidy or muddled.
mess[3] *n* a room where soldiers, sailors or airmen eat their meals.
message *n* a piece of information sent from one person to another.
messenger *n* a person who carries a message.
met *past of* meet.
metal *n* any one of a group of substances, such as gold, iron or copper, that conduct heat and are usually shiny. **metallic** *adj.*
meteor *n* a small piece of rock moving rapidly through space and burning up as it enters the Earth's atmosphere.
meteorite *n* a meteor that falls to Earth as a piece of rock.
meteorologist *n* a person who studies or forecasts the weather. **meteorological** *adj*, **meteorology** *n.*
meter *n* an instrument for measuring amounts, speeds, etc. *a gas meter.*
method *n* a way of doing something.
methodical *adj* careful and well-organized.
metre *n* a measure of length, equal to 100 centimetres.
metric system *n* the system of weights and measures based on units of ten. Metres, kilogrammes and litres are all units in the metric system.
miaow *n* the sound that a cat makes. **miaow** *v.*
mice *plural of* mouse.
micro- *prefix* very small.
microbe *n* a tiny living thing that cannot be seen without a microscope.
microchip *n* a tiny piece of silicon that has an electronic circuit printed on it, used in electronic equipment.
microcomputer *n* a small computer that is not part of a larger system.
microlight *n* a type of very small, light aircraft.
microphone *n* an instrument that picks up sound waves so they can be broadcast, recorded or made louder.

microscope *n* an instrument with lenses, that makes very small objects look much larger so that they can be studied.

microscope

microscopic *adj* too small to be seen without a microscope.
microwave *n* an oven that cooks food very quickly.
mid- *prefix* in the middle of. *mid-morning.*
midday *n* 12 o'clock in the middle of the day, noon.
middle *n* the part of something that is half-way between its ends or edges, the centre. **middle** *adj.*
middle-aged *adj* (of a person) between the ages of about 45 and 60.
Middle Ages *n pl* the period in history between about AD1100 and AD1500.
Middle East *n* the region east of the Mediterranean sea, including Iran, Egypt and the countries in between.
midge *n* a small, biting insect.
midget *n* an extremely small person.
midnight *n* 12 o'clock at night.
midwife *n* (*pl* midwives) a person who is trained to help when a baby is born.
might *n* power, strength.
mighty *adj* (mightier, mightiest) very powerful. **mightily** *adv.*
migraine *(mee-grain) n* a very bad headache that makes you feel sick.
migrate *v* to move from one place to another to live, as birds do at a particular time of year. **migrant** *n*, **migration** *n*, **migratory** *adj.*
mild *adj* **1** (of a person) gentle, not aggressive. *a mild-mannered man.* **2** not harsh or severe. *She got a mild telling-off.* **3** (of weather) not cold. **4** (of food or drink) not strong or spicy. *a mild curry.* **mildness** *n.*
mildew *n* a tiny, white fungus that grows in warm, damp conditions.
mile *n* a measure of distance, equal to 1,760 yards or 1.621 kilometres.
militant *adj* ready to fight.
military *adj* to do with soldiers and war.
milk[1] *n* a white liquid produced by female mammals as food for their young.
milk[2] *v* to take milk from a cow or other animal.
mill *n* **1** a building with machinery for grinding grain into flour. **2** a factory. *a paper-mill.* **3** a device for grinding something. *a pepper-mill.*
millennium *n* (*pl* millennia) a period of one thousand years.
millet *n* a grain used as food in some parts of Africa and Asia.
milli- *prefix* one thousandth part of. *millimetre, millisecond.*
million *n* one thousand thousand (1,000,000). **millionth** *adj.*
millionaire *n* a rich person who has at least a million pounds or dollars.
millipede *n* a small creature with many legs and a long body.
mime *n* a form of acting in which you use actions and facial expressions instead of words. **mime** *v.*
mimic *v* (mimics, mimicking, mimicked) to copy somebody's speech or actions. **mimic** *n.*
minaret *n* a tall, thin tower on a mosque.
mince[1] *v* to chop food into very small pieces.
mince[2] *n* meat that has been chopped into very small pieces.
mincemeat *n* a sweet mixture of dried fruits, spices, etc used in pies.
mind[1] *n* the part of you that thinks, understands and remembers. **make up your mind** to decide.
mind[2] *v* **1** to look after something. *Mind my bag for a moment, will you?* **2** to be careful of something. *Mind the step.* **3** to be bothered about something. *I don't mind what film we go to see.*
mine[1] *n* a deep hole in the ground from which coal, metals, etc are dug. **mine** *v.*

mine[2] *n* a bomb hidden under the ground or at sea.
mineral *n* a substance found in the earth, such as coal, salt and diamonds.
mineral water *n* water from a spring in the ground, containing mineral salts and gases.
mingle *v* to mix.
mini- *prefix* smaller than average. *minibus* (= a small bus).
miniature *adj* very small.
minibeast *n* an insect or other small creature.
minim *n* a note in music equal to two crotchets in length. See **note**.
minimum *n* (*pl* minima) the smallest possible number or amount, or the lowest point. *Tickets will cost a minimum of £10 each.* **minimum** *adj.*
minister *n* **1** a member of the clergy. **2** the person in charge of a government department.
ministry *n* **1** a government department. **2** the work of a member of the clergy.
minor *adj* small in size or importance. *a minor operation.*
minority *n* the smaller part or number.
minstrel *n* a travelling musician in medieval times.
mint *n* **1** a plant with strong-smelling leaves used as a flavouring. **2** a sweet flavoured with these leaves.
minus *prep* used in maths to show subtraction. *Six minus two is four* (6 – 2 = 4).
minute[1] *(**min**-it) n* **1** a unit of time. There are 60 minutes in an hour. **2** a very short time. *See you in a minute.*
minute[2] *(my-**nyoot**) adj* very small.
miracle *(**mir**-ik-ul) n* an amazing event that cannot be explained. **miraculous** *adj.*
mirage *n* something that you think you see but that is not really there, such as a pool of water in the road, caused by hot weather conditions.
mirror *n* a piece of special glass which reflects what is in front of it.
mis- *prefix* wrong or bad, wrongly or badly. *misbehave* (= to behave badly), *miscalculate* (= to work something out wrongly).
miscarriage *n* the loss of a foetus from its mother's womb before it is able to survive in the outside world.
miscellaneous *(mis-uh-**lay**-nee-us) adj* made up of several kinds, mixed.
mischief *n* naughty behaviour. **mischievous** *(**mis**-chiv-os) adj.*
miser *(**my**-zer) n* a very mean person. **miserly** *adj.*
miserable *adj* very unhappy. **miserably** *adv.*
misery *n* great unhappiness.
misfortune *n* **1** bad luck. **2** an unlucky event.
mishap *n* an unlucky accident.
mislay *v* (mislays, mislaying, mislaid) to lose something for a short time by putting it somewhere where you cannot find it.
mislead *v* (misleading, misled) to give somebody the wrong idea.
miss *v* **1** to fail to hit, catch, etc something. *The arrow missed the target.* **2** to fail to see, hear, etc something. *The bank is at the end of the road – you can't miss it.* **3** to feel sad because you are not with somebody. *I'll miss you!*
Miss *n* a title put before the name of a girl or an unmarried woman.
missile *n* an object or weapon that is thrown or fired through the air.
missing *adj* **1** lost. **2** not present.
mission *n* a task that somebody is sent to do.
missionary *n* a person sent to another country to teach and spread a religion.
mist *n* a cloud of water in the air, a thin fog. **misty** *adj.*
mistake[1] *n* a wrong action or statement.
mistake[2] *v* (mistaking, mistook, mistaken) **1** to think that one person or thing is another. *I mistook you for my sister.* **2** to be wrong about something. *She mistook what I said.*
mistletoe *n* an evergreen plant with white berries, often used as a decoration at Christmas.
mistreat *v* to treat somebody wrongly or badly.
mistress *n* a female teacher.
mistrust *v* not to trust somebody.

misunderstand *v* (misunderstanding, misunderstood) to understand something wrongly.

mitten *n* a kind of glove without separate parts for the four fingers.

mix *v* **1** to put things together to form one mass. **2** to come together to form one mass. **mix up** to confuse.

mixture *n* something made by mixing things together.

moan *v* **1** to make a long, deep sound showing pain or sadness. **2** to complain. **moan** *n.*

moat *n* a deep ditch around a castle.

mob *n* a noisy or violent crowd.

mobile[1] *adj* able to move or be moved easily. *a mobile phone.* **mobility** *n.*

mobile[2] *n* a hanging decoration with parts that move in currents of air.

mock[1] *v* to make fun of somebody or something in an unkind way. **mockery** *n.*

mock[2] *adj* false, not real. *a mock battle.*

model *n* **1** a copy of something that is much smaller than the real-life object. **2** a person whose job is to wear clothes to show to possible buyers. *a fashion model.* **3** a person who poses for an artist or photographer. **4** a particular type of product. *Our car is the latest model.* **model** *v.*

modem *n* a device which sends information from one computer to another along telephone lines.

moderate *adj* not extreme, average. **moderation** *n.*

modern *adj* not old or old-fashioned.

modernize *v* to make something more modern.

modest *adj* **1** not boastful. **2** not excessive, moderate. *She earns a modest salary.* **modesty** *v.*

module *n* a section that can be joined together with other sections to form something, such as a spacecraft or a building. *a lunar module.*

moist *adj* slightly wet. **moisten** *v*, **moisture** *n.*

mole *n* **1** a small, furry animal that digs and lives in tunnels underground. **2** a small, dark mark on the skin.

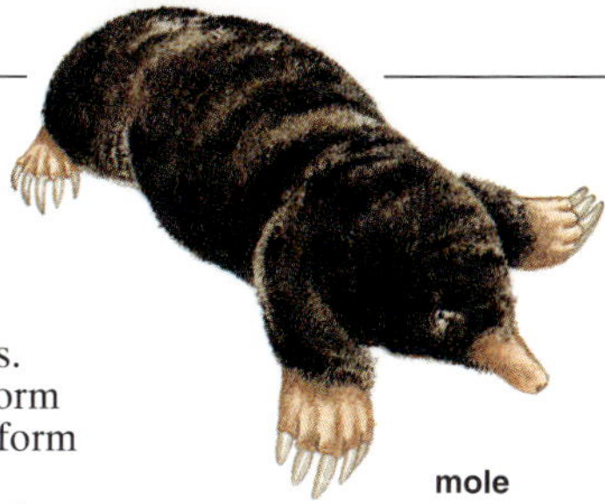

mole

molecule *n* the smallest part that a substance can be divided into without changing its basic nature.

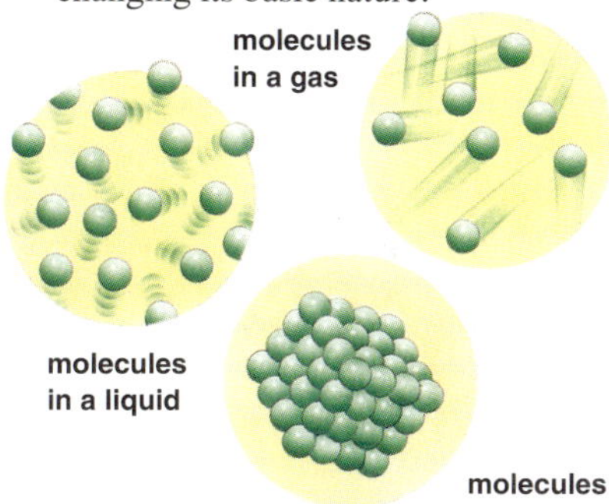

mollusc *n* a creature with a soft body, no backbone, and usually a hard shell. Snails and oysters are molluscs.

mollycoddle *v* to look after and protect somebody too much.

molten *adj* melted. *molten rock.*

moment *n* a very brief period of time. *Wait a moment.* **momentary** *adj*, **momentarily** *adv.*

monarch *(mon-ark)* *n* a king, queen, emperor or empress. **monarchy** *n.*

monastery *n* a place where monks live and work. **monastic** *adj.*

Monday *n* the second day of the week.

money *n* the coins and notes that people use to buy things.

mongrel *n* a dog of mixed breeds.

monitor[1] *n* **1** the screen of a computer. **2** an instrument, usually with a screen, that is used for keeping a check on something. *a heart monitor.*

monitor[2] *v* to keep a check on something over a period of time. *The radar monitors the plane's progress.*

monk *n* a member of a religious group of men who live, work and pray together in a monastery.
monkey *n* (*pl* monkeys) a small, long-tailed mammal that climbs trees and walks on four legs.
mono- *prefix* one, single.
monopoly *n* the right to be the only person or company to sell or supply a product or service.
monotonous *adj* going on and on in the same dull way. *That song was so monotonous!* **monotony** *n*.
monsoon *n* **1** a wind that blows in the Indian Ocean. **2** a season of heavy rain caused by the summer monsoon.
monster *n* **1** a huge, frightening creature. **2** an evil person.
month *n* one of the twelve parts of the year.
monthly *adj*, *adv* happening or coming once a month or every month.
monument *n* a building, statue, etc built to remind people of a person or an event.
mood *n* the way that you are feeling. *I'm in a really good mood today.*
moody *adj* (moodier, moodiest) **1** often bad-tempered. **2** having moods that change often. **moodily** *adv*, **moodiness** *n*.
moon *n* **1** a natural satellite of a planet. **2 Moon** the natural satellite that travels around the Earth once every month.
moonlight *n* the light reflected by the Moon.
moor[1] *n* a large area of open land, often covered with heather.
moor[2] *v* to tie up a boat.
moose *n* (*pl* moose) a large, brown deer with large antlers, found in Alaska and Canada.
mop[1] *n* a sponge pad or a bunch of thick strings or cloths on a long handle, used for cleaning floors.
mop[2] *v* (mops, mopping, mopped) to wipe a surface with a mop or cloth.
mope *v* to be sad and depressed.
moped *(**moh**-ped)* *n* a type of small motorbike with pedals.
moral[1] *adj* **1** to do with right and wrong behaviour. **2** good, behaving in the right way. **3 morals** rules or standards of behaviour. **morality** *n*, **morally** *adv*.
moral[2] *n* the point taught by a story.
morale *(mor-**ahl**)* *n* confidence and enthusiasm. *The win was good for the team's morale.*
more *adj* larger in size or amount. **more** *adv, pron.*
morning *n* the early part of the day, before noon.
Morse code *n* a way of sending messages using long and short sounds or flashes of light to represent letters.
mortal[1] *adj* **1** unable to live for ever. **2** causing death. *a mortal injury.* **mortality** *n*, **mortally** *adv*.
mortal[2] *n* a human being.
mortar *n* a mixture of cement, lime, sand and water, used to hold bricks together.
mortgage *(**mor**-gij)* *n* a loan from a bank or building society in order to buy a house or flat.
mortuary *n* a room where dead bodies are kept before burial or cremation.
mosaic *n* a picture or design made up of small pieces of coloured stone or glass.

mosaic

Moslem *another spelling of* Muslim.
mosque *(mosk)* *n* a building where Muslims worship.
mosquito *(mos-**kee**-toe)* *n* (*pl* mosquitoes *or* mosquitos) a small insect that sucks blood.
moss *n* a very small plant that grows in damp places, forming a soft, green covering. **mossy** *adj*.
most *adj* largest in size or amount. **most** *adv, pron.*
mostly *adv* mainly, generally.

motel *n* a hotel for motorists, with parking spaces near the rooms.
moth *n* a winged insect, like a butterfly, usually seen at night.
mother *n* a female parent.
motion *n* movement.
motive *n* a reason for doing something.
motor *n* an engine that uses electricity, petrol, etc to produce movement.
motorbike, motorcycle *n* a two-wheeled vehicle with a petrol engine.
motorist *n* a car driver.
motorway *n* (*pl* motorways) a wide road with several lanes for fast traffic.
mottled *adj* marked with spots of different colours.
mould[1] *n* **1** a hollow container that you can pour a liquid into, so that the liquid takes on the shape of the mould when it hardens. **2** a fungus that grows on damp things or stale food.
mould[2] *v* to shape something with your hands.
moult *v* (of an animal or bird) to lose hair or feathers. *Our cat is moulting.*
mound *n* a small hill or pile.
mount[1] *v* **1** to climb up on to something. *She mounted her horse and rode off.* **2** to rise or increase. *Excitement is mounting.* **3** to put something into a frame or stick it on card to display it.
mount[2] *n* a mountain.
mountain *n* a very high hill.
mountain bike *n* a bicycle with a strong frame and many gears, for riding on rough ground.
mountaineer *n* a person who climbs mountains. **mountaineering** *n*.
mourn *v* to feel great sadness because somebody has died. **mourning** *n*.
mouse *n* (*pl* mice) **1** a small, furry animal with a long tail. **2** a device that you move with your hand to control the movement of the cursor on a computer screen.
mousse *(mooss)* *n* a cold food, usually sweet, made with cream and eggs.
moustache *n* the unshaved hair above a man's upper lip.
mouth *n* **1** the opening in your face into which you put food and through which you make sounds. **2** the part of a river where it flows into the sea.
mouth-organ *n* a small musical instrument played by blowing and sucking, a harmonica.
move *v* **1** to change place or position. **2** to change houses. **3** to affect the feelings of somebody. *I was moved by the film.* **moving** *adj*.
movement *n* **1** moving. **2** a section of a piece of classical music. **3** a group of people united for a purpose. *the peace movement.*
movie *n* a film.
mow *(rhymes with* toe*)* *v* (mowing, mowed, mown) to cut grass. **mower** *n*.
MP *short for* Member of Parliament.
Mr *(**mis**-tur)* a title put before a man's name.
Mrs *(**mis**-iz)* a title put before the name of a married woman.
Ms *(miz)* a title put before the name of a woman, that does not show whether or not she is married.
much *adj* a great amount of. **much** *adv, pron.*
muck *n* dirt or dung. **mucky** *adj*.
mud *n* soft, wet earth. **muddy** *adj*.
muddle[1] *n* an untidy mess.
muddle[2] *v* to confuse or mix things up.
muesli *(**myooz**-lee)* *n* a mixture of grain, dried fruit, etc eaten with milk.
mug[1] *n* a large, straight-sided cup.
mug[2] *v* (mugs, mugging, mugged) to attack and rob somebody in the street. **mugger** *n*.
muggy *adj* (muggier, muggiest) (of the weather) warm and damp.
mule *n* an animal whose parents are a horse and a donkey.
multi- *prefix* many. *multi-coloured.*
multimedia *adj* involving different forms of communication, such as sound, pictures and video.
multiple *adj* involving many parts or items. *multiple injuries.*
multiply *v* (multiplies, multiplying, multiplied) to add a number to itself a given number of times. *Two multiplied by three is six* (2 x 3 = 6). **multiplication** *n*.
mum *n* an informal word for "mother".

mumble *v* to speak so that the words are difficult to hear.
mummy *n* **1** an informal word for "mother". **2** a dead body preserved by wrapping it in bandages and treating it with special oils and spices.

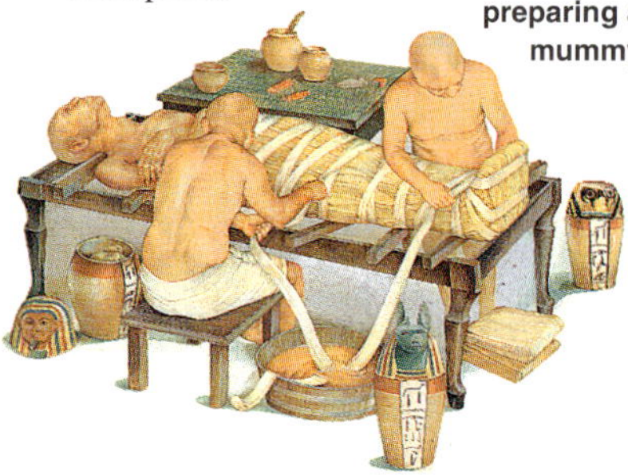

ancient Egyptians preparing a mummy

mumps *n* an infectious disease that makes your neck and face swell up.
munch *v* to chew noisily.
mural *n* a picture painted on a wall.
murder *v* to kill somebody on purpose. **murder** *n*, **murderer** *n*.
murmur *n* a low, quiet sound, especially of voices. **murmur** *v*.
muscle *(mus-ul) n* one of the parts of your body that tighten and relax to make you move. **muscular** *adj.*
museum *(myoo-zee-um) n* a building where interesting objects are kept and shown to the public.
mushroom *n* a type of fungus. Many mushrooms are edible.
music *n* an arrangement of sounds, played on an instrument, or sung.
musical[1] *adj* to do with music.
musical[2] *n* a play or film with a lot of singing and dancing.
musician *n* a person who plays music.
musket *n* a gun once used by soldiers.
Muslim *n* a follower of the Islamic religion which was founded by the prophet Mohammed. **Muslim** *adj.*
mussel *n* an edible shellfish with a black shell.
must *v* **1** used to express need. *We must go.* **2** used to express a rule, duty or order. *You must not walk on the grass.* **3** used to express what is definite or likely. *You must be tired.*
mustard *n* a hot-tasting, yellow paste eaten with food, especially meats.
mutilate *v* to injure or damage somebody or something badly. **mutilation** *n*.
mutiny *n* a refusal to obey the people in charge, especially in the armed forces. **mutineer** *n*, **mutinous** *adj.*
mutter *v* to speak in a low voice so that people cannot hear you properly.
mutton *n* the meat from a sheep.
muzzle *n* **1** an animal's nose and mouth. **2** a cover for an animal's mouth, to stop it biting. **3** the open end of a gun barrel.
mystery *n* something that is hard to explain or understand. **mysterious** *adj.*
myth *n* a story from ancient times about gods, heroes, etc. **mythical** *adj.*

Nn

nag *v* (nags, nagging, nagged) to talk to somebody constantly in a complaining or criticizing way.
nail[1] *n* **1** a thin, pointed piece of metal for hammering into wood. **2** the hard covering at the tip of a finger or toe.
nail[2] *v* to fasten something with nails.
naked *adj* without clothes on, bare.
name *n* what a person, place or thing is called. **name** *v*.
nanny *n* **1** a person who looks after children in their own home. **2** an informal word for "grandmother".
nanny-goat *n* a female goat.
nap *v* (naps, napping, napped) to sleep for a short time. **nap** *n*.
napkin *n* a piece of cloth or paper for wiping your lips and hands at meals.
nappy *n* a piece of thick padding worn around a baby's bottom.
narrate *v* to tell a story. **narrator** *n*.

narrow *adj* **1** not far from side to side, not wide. **2** only just managed. *I had a narrow escape.*
nasal *adj* to do with the nose.
nasty *adj* (nastier, nastiest) unpleasant, not nice. **nastily** *adv*, **nastiness** *n*.
nation *n* a country and the people who live in it. **national** *adj*, **nationally** *adv*.
nationalist *n* a person who wants their country or province to become independent. **nationalism** *n*.
nationality *n* membership of a particular nation. *He is of French nationality.*
native *n* a person born in a particular place. **native** *adj*.
Nativity *n* the birth of Jesus Christ.
natural[1] *adj* **1** found in nature, not caused or made by people. **2** ordinary, normal. *It's natural to feel afraid of going to the dentist's.* **naturally** *adv*.
natural[2] *n* a sign (♮) in music indicating that a note should be played neither as a sharp nor a flat.
nature *n* **1** all the things that make up the world, such as trees, animals, rivers, etc, but not the things made by people. **2** what a person or thing is like. *She has a kind nature.*
naughty *adj* (naughtier, naughtiest) badly-behaved. **naughtily** *adv*, **naughtiness** *n*.
nausea *(naw-zee-uh) n* a feeling of sickness. **nauseous** *adj*.
nautical *adj* to do with ships or sailors.
navel *n* the small hollow in your stomach, just below your waist.
navigate *v* to work out the way that a ship, plane, car, etc should go, using maps or instruments to guide you. **navigation** *n*, **navigator** *n*.
navy *n* a country's warships and sailors. **naval** *adj*.
navy blue *n* a very dark blue.
near *prep* at a very short distance from. **near** *adj, adv*.
nearby *adj, adv* near.
nearly *adv* almost, not quite.
neat *adj* tidy, having everything in the right place. **neatness** *n*.
necessary *adj* needed, essential. **necessarily** *adv*.
necessity *n* something that is necessary.
neck *n* **1** the narrow part between your head and shoulders. **2** a narrow part of something. *the neck of a bottle.*
necklace *n* a piece of jewellery worn around your neck.
nectar *n* a sweet liquid in flowers, collected by bees to make honey.
nectarine *n* a type of peach with a smooth skin.
need *v* **1** to have to have something. *I need a drink!* **2** to have to do something. *You need to clean your bike.* **need** *n*.
needle *n* **1** a small, pointed piece of steel used for sewing. **2** a long, thin stick used for knitting. **3** the moving pointer of a meter or compass. **4** a long, thin, pointed leaf of a pine tree. **5** the sharp metal part that is attached to a syringe for giving injections.
needlework *n* sewing or embroidery.
negative[1] *adj* **1** meaning or saying "no", not positive. **2** less than zero.
negative[2] *n* a photographic film showing light areas as dark and dark areas as light.
neglect *v* not to look after something. *The new owners have neglected the garden.* **neglect** *n*, **neglectful** *adj*.
negotiate *v* to discuss something to try to reach an agreement. **negotiation** *n*.
neigh *v* to make the sound that a horse makes. **neigh** *n*.
neighbour *n* a person living near you.
neighbourhood *n* the area you live in.
neither *adj, pron* not one and not the other.
neon light *n* a light containing neon gas which shines when electricity is passed through it.
nephew *n* the son of your brother or sister.
nerve *n* **1** one of the fibres that carry feelings and messages between your body and your brain. **2** courage and calmness. *You need a lot of nerve to be a racing driver.* **3** cheek, rudeness. *He's got a nerve, asking me for £100!*
nervous *adj* **1** to do with the nerves. *the nervous system.* **2** anxious or easily frightened. **nervousness** *n*.

nest[1] *n* a home built by birds and some animals and insects, in which they hatch or give birth to their young and bring them up.
nest[2] *v* to build a nest and live in it.

weaver birds building a nest

net *n* **1** a material made of loosely woven thread, string or rope, with holes between the threads. **2** a piece of net used for catching fish.
netball *n* a team game in which a ball is thrown into a high net.
nettle *n* a weed with stinging hairs on its leaves.
network *n* **1** an arrangement of lines crossing one another. **2** a system with lots of lines or connections.
neuter *v* to remove part of the sex organs of an animal, so that it cannot produce young.
neutral *adj* **1** not taking sides in a war or argument. **2** (of colours) not strong or bright, like grey and beige.
neutron *n* one of the parts that make up the nucleus of an atom, carrying no electrical charge. See **atom**.
never *adv* not ever, at no time.
nevertheless *adv* in spite of that. *The team played well but they lost nevertheless.*
new *adj* **1** not used or worn. *new trainers.* **2** not seen or done before. *new ideas.* **3** different, changed. *I'm starting at a new school in September.*
news *n* recent or up-to-date information about events.
newsagent *n* a shopkeeper who sells newspapers and other goods.
newspaper *n* printed sheets of paper containing news, published daily or weekly.
newt *n* a small lizard-like animal that lives on land and in water.
next *adj* **1** immediately following. **2** nearest. **next** *adv*.
nib *n* the metal point of a pen.
nibble *v* to eat in very small bites.
nice *adj* good or pleasant.
nickname *n* a name that you call somebody instead of their real name.
nicotine *n* a poisonous substance found in tobacco.
niece *n* the daughter of your brother or sister.
night *n* the time between sunset and sunrise, when it is dark.
nightingale *n* a small bird that sings beautifully.
nightmare *n* **1** a frightening dream. **2** a very frightening or unpleasant situation.
nil *n* nothing, zero.
nimble *adj* quick and light in movement. **nimbly** *adv*.
nip *v* (nips, nipping, nipped) **1** to pinch or bite something. *A crab nipped her toe.* **2** to go quickly. *He's just nipped out to buy some milk.*
nipple *n* the round, pink part in the middle of a breast.
nitrogen *n* a colourless gas that makes up four-fifths of the air we breathe.
no. *a short way of writing* number.
noble *adj* **1** aristocratic, of high social rank. *a noble family.* **2** acting in a good, unselfish way. **nobility** *n*, **nobleman** *n*, **noblewoman** *n*, **nobly** *adv*.
nobody *pron* not a single person.
nocturnal *adj* happening or active at night. *Owls are nocturnal birds.*
nod *v* (nods, nodding, nodded) to move your head quickly forward and down, as a way of saying yes. **nod** *n*.
noise *n* a sound, especially a loud, unpleasant one.
noisy *adj* making a lot of noise, full of noise. **noisily** *adv*.
nomad *n* a member of a tribe of people who wander from place to place. **nomadic** *adj*.
non- *prefix* not. *non-smoker* (= a person who does not smoke).
none *pron* not one, not any.
nonsense *n* **1** words that do not mean anything. **2** silly talk or behaviour.
noodles *n pl* long, thin strips of pasta.
noon *n* midday.

no one *pron* nobody.
noose *n* a loop of rope that gets tighter when one end is pulled.
nor *conj* and not. *neither young nor old.*
normal *adj* usual or ordinary. **normality** *n*, **normally** *adv.*
north *n* one of the points of the compass. When you face the rising Sun, north is on your left. **north** *adj, adv.*
northern *adj* in or of the north part of a place. *northern Europe.*
nose *n* the part of your face that you use for smelling and breathing.
nostril *n* one of the two openings in your nose.
nosy *adj* (nosier, nosiest) too interested in things that do not concern you. **nosily** *adv.*
notch *n* a small, V-shaped cut.
note[1] *n* **1** words written down to help you remember something. **2** a short letter or message. **3** a piece of paper used as money. **4** a musical sound or the sign that represents it.

musical notes (symbols showing length)

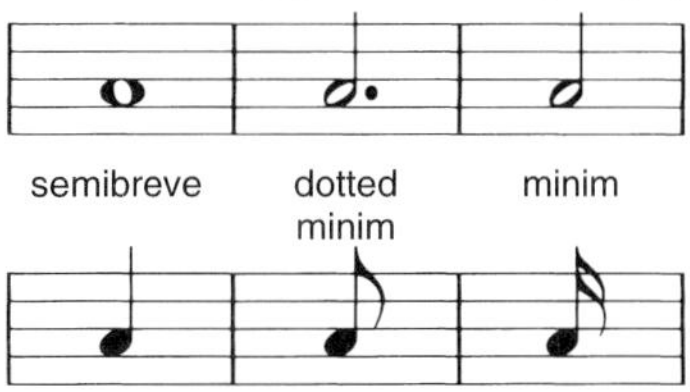

note[2] *v* **1** to write something down. *I noted his phone number.* **2** to notice something.
notebook *n* a small book for making notes in.
nothing *pron* not anything.
notice[1] *n* **1** a written message where people can read it. *The notice on the door said "KEEP OUT".* **2** attention. *The colour attracted my notice.* **3** a statement that you are going to leave a job at a particular time. *John has handed in his notice.*
notice[2] *v* to see something. *I noticed that Ella had a new coat.*
notify *v* (notifies, notifying, notified) to tell somebody about something formally. **notification** *n.*
notorious *n* well-known for bad reasons. *a notorious criminal.*
nought *n* nothing, zero, the figure 0.
noun *n* a word used as the name of a person, place or thing. *Tim, card* and *laughter* are all nouns.
nourish *v* to give a person, an animal or a plant the food needed for health and growth. **nourishment** *n.*
novel[1] *n* a book that tells a story.
novel[2] *adj* new and unusual.
novelist *n* a writer of novels.
novelty *n* **1** newness. **2** something new and unusual.
November *n* the eleventh month of the year.
novice *(nov-iss) n* a beginner.
nowadays *adv* at the present time.
nowhere *adv* not anywhere.
nuclear *adj* **1** to do with a nucleus. **2** using the power produced by the splitting of the nuclei of atoms. *nuclear weapons.*
nucleus *n* (*pl* nuclei) **1** the central part of an atom. See **atom**. **2** the part of a plant or animal cell that controls growth and development. See **cell**.
nude *adj* naked, without clothes. **nudity** *n.*
nudge *v* to push something gently with your elbow. **nudge** *n.*
nugget *n* a lump, especially of gold.
nuisance *n* a person or thing that annoys you or causes you trouble.
numb *(num) adj* not able to feel anything. *Her fingers were numb with cold.* **numbness** *n.*
number *n* **1** a word or figure showing how many. **2** a quantity. *A large number of people disagreed.*
numeral *n* a figure, for example 1, 2, 3, etc, used to express a number.
numerous *adj* many.
nun *n* a member of a religious group of women who live, work and pray together in a convent.
nurse *n* a person who is trained to look after people who are ill or hurt, especially in a hospital. **nurse** *v.*

nursery *n* **1** a place where young children are looked after while their parents are at work. **2** a room where a young child sleeps and plays. **3** a place where plants are grown for sale.
nursery rhyme *n* a short poem or song for young children.
nursery school *n* a school for very young children.
nut *n* **1** a type of fruit with a hard shell and a softer part inside. *a hazelnut.*

2 a piece of metal with a hole in it, that screws on to a bolt to fasten it.
nutritious *adj* (of food) good for you.
nylon *n* an artificial fibre used for making clothes, brushes, ropes, etc.

Oo

oak *n* a large tree that produces acorns.
OAP *n* (*short for* Old Age Pensioner) an old person who receives a pension.
oar *n* a pole with a flat end used for moving a rowing boat through water.
oasis *(oh-**ay**-sis) n (pl* oases) a place in the desert where water is found and trees grow.
oath *n* a serious promise.
oats *n pl* grain from a type of cereal plant, used as food. Oats are used to make porridge.
obedient *adj* doing what you are told to do. **obedience** *n.*
obelisk *n* a tall pillar with four sides and a pointed top.
obese *(oh-**bees**) adj* very fat. **obesity** *n.*
obey *v* to do what you are told to do.
obituary *n* an announcement of a person's death in a newspaper, etc.
object[1] *(**ob**-jekt) n* **1** anything that can be touched or seen, but that is not a living thing. **2** a purpose or aim.
object[2] *(ob-**jekt**) v* to say that you dislike or do not agree with something. *She objects to people smoking in her house.* **objection** *n.*
objective *n* something that you are trying to achieve.
obligation *n* a duty.
obligatory *adj* compulsory.
oblige *v* **1** to make somebody do something. **2** to do something to help somebody.
obliged *adj* **1** having to do something. **2** feeling grateful. *I am much obliged to you for your help.*
oblong *n* a shape with four sides and four right angles, with two opposite sides longer than the other two.
obnoxious *adj* very unpleasant or offensive.
oboe *n* a woodwind instrument.
obscene *(ob-**seen**) adj* shocking, sexually indecent. **obscenity** *n.*
obscure *adj* **1** not easy to understand or see. **2** not famous. *an obscure painter.* **obscurity** *n.*
observatory *n* a building with large telescopes for watching the stars, etc.

observe *v* **1** to watch something carefully. **2** to notice something. **3** to obey something. *We must observe the rules.* **4** to make a remark. **observation** *n.*
obsolete *adj* no longer used, out-of-date. *Gas lamps are obsolete now that we have electricity.*
obstacle *n* something that gets in the way and prevents you going forwards.
obstinate *adj* refusing to give in or change your mind. **obstinacy** *n.*
obstruct *v* to block something. **obstruction** *n.*
obtain *v* to get something. *Tickets can be obtained from the box office.*
obtuse angle *n* an angle of more than 90°. See **triangle**.
obvious *adj* easy to see or understand.
occasion *n* a particular time or event.
occasional *adj* happening or appearing now and then. **occasionally** *adv.*
occupant *n* a person who lives in or uses a building, room, etc.
occupation *n* **1** a job. **2** a way of spending time. **3** the capturing of a town or country by an army.
occupy *v* (occupies, occupying, occupied) **1** to live in or use a room, etc. **2** to fill somebody's time. **3** to capture a town or country.
occur *v* (occurs, occurring, occurred) to happen, to take place. **occur to** to come into somebody's mind. **occurrence** *n.*
ocean *n* one of the large seas that surround the continents.
o'clock *adv* used with numbers to show an exact hour on the clock. *9 o'clock.*
octagon *n* a flat shape with eight straight sides. **octagonal** *adj.*
octave *n* in music, a range of eight notes, for example from one C to the next C above or below it.
October *n* the tenth month of the year.
octopus *n* (*pl* octopuses) a sea creature with a soft body and eight tentacles.
odd *adj* **1** strange, unusual. **2** (of a number) not able to be divided exactly by two. **3** not one of a pair. *odd socks.*
odds *n pl* chances, probability. *The odds are that they will lose again.*
odour *n* a smell.
offend *v* **1** to hurt somebody's feelings. **2** to break a law. **offence** *n,* **offensive** *adj.*
offer *v* **1** to ask somebody if they would like something. *Sean offered me a sweet.* **2** to say that you are willing to do something for somebody. *She offered to drive us to the airport.* **offer** *n.*
office *n* a place where work is done, usually containing desks, telephones, computers, etc.
officer *n* **1** a senior person in the army, air force or navy. **2** a person in some other job who has the power to tell others what to do. *a police-officer.*
official *adj* done or given out by people in authority. *The Prime Minister will make an official announcement today.* **officially** *adv.*
off-licence *n* a shop that is allowed to sell alcoholic drinks.
offside *adj* in football and some other games, in a position in front of the ball where, according to the rules, it may not be played. **offside** *adv.*
offspring *n* (*pl* offspring) an animal's young, or a human's children.
often *adv* many times, frequently.
ogre *(oh-ger) n* a cruel giant in stories.
oil *n* a greasy liquid that does not mix with water, used for many different purposes, such as cooking, and helping machines run smoothly.
oilrig *n* a structure used to drill wells from which oil is obtained.
ointment *n* a substance that you rub on your skin to heal sores and cuts.
old *adj* **1** having lived for a long time. *an old man.* **2** having a certain age. *I'm 12 years old.* **3** having existed for a long time. *an old building.* **4** not recent, belonging to the past. *In the old days, things were different.*
old-fashioned *adj* out-of-date, in a style not worn or used nowadays.
olive *n* a small, black or green, oval fruit with a hard stone. Olives can be eaten or crushed to make cooking oil.
omelette *n* a food made from eggs beaten and fried.

omen *n* a sign or warning of something that is going to happen.
ominous *adj* giving a sign or warning that something bad is going to happen.
omit *v* (omits, omitting, omitted) to leave something out. *You can omit the last chapter of the book.* **omission** *n.*
omnibus *n* a radio or television programme made up of several programmes that were previously shown separately.
omnivore *n* an animal that feeds on plants and meat. **omnivorous** *adj.*
once[1] *adv* **1** a single time. *I have met him once.* **2** at a time in the past. *She once lived here.* **at once** immediately.
once[2] *conj* as soon as, when. *Once you've finished, you can go.*
onion *n* a strong-tasting bulb eaten as a vegetable.
on-line *adj* connected to a computer. *an on-line database.*
only[1] *adv* **1** no more than, just. *There is only one cake left.* **2** alone. *Only you can do it!*
only[2] *adj* without any others of the same type.
only child *n* a child who has no brothers or sisters.
onward, onwards *adv* forward.
ooze *v* to flow slowly. *The glue oozed out of the tube.*
opaque *(oh-**pake**)* *adj* not able to be seen through. *an opaque liquid.*
open[1] *adj* **1** not closed, so that people and things can pass in and out. *an open window.* **2** allowing the inside to be seen. *an open book.* **3** not enclosed or covered. *open country.* **4** honest. *She was open about her feelings.*
open[2] *v* **1** to make or become open. *She opened the door.* **2** to begin. *The story opens in a ruined castle.* **opening** *n.*
openly *adv* **1** honestly. **2** not secretly.
open-minded *adj* willing to consider new ideas.
opera *n* a play in which the words are sung. **operatic** *adj.*
operate *v* **1** to work. *Do you know how to operate the machine?* **2** to perform a surgical operation.
operation *n* **1** the cutting of a patient's body by a surgeon. **2** a carefully planned action. **in operation** working.
operator *n* **1** a person who works a machine. **2** a person who works on a telephone switchboard connecting calls.
opinion *n* what you personally think or believe about something.
opponent *n* a person who is against you in a contest or game.
opportunity *n* a chance to do something.
oppose *v* to be against something. *I am opposed to the testing of cosmetics on animals.* **opposition** *n.*
opposite[1] *adj* **1** facing, across from. *They live on the opposite side of the street from us.* **2** entirely different. *We were going in opposite directions.* **opposite** *prep.*
opposite[2] *n* something that is as different as possible from another thing. *Good is the opposite of bad.*
opt *v* to make a choice. **opt out** to choose not to do something.
optical *adj* to do with the eyes.
optician *n* a person who tests your eyesight and sells glasses.
optimist *n* a person who tends to believe that things will turn out well. **optimism** *n,* **optimistic** *adj,* **optimistically** *adv.*
option *n* a choice.
optional *adj* that may be chosen or not, as you want.
oral *adj* **1** to do with the mouth. **2** spoken. *an oral test.* **orally** *adv.*
orange *n* a round, juicy fruit with a thick skin. **2** the colour of this fruit. **orange** *adj.*
orang-utan *n* a large ape with reddish-brown fur, found in Indonesia.

orbit *n* the path followed by an object in space around a planet or around the Sun. **orbit** *v*, **orbital** *adj*.

orchard *n* an area where fruit trees are grown. *a cherry orchard.*

orchestra *n* a group of musicians who play together. **orchestral** *adj*.

orchid *(or-kid) n* a plant with unusually shaped and often colourful flowers.

ordeal *n* a difficult, painful experience.

order[1] *v* **1** to tell somebody that they must do something. **2** to ask somebody to supply something. *When the waiter came we ordered two salads.*

order[2] *n* **1** a command. **2** a request to somebody to supply something. **3** an arrangement of things. *Put the names in alphabetical order.* **4** tidiness. **5** a peaceful state. *law and order.* **out of order** not working. *The phone is out of order.*

orderly *adj* well-behaved, quiet. *Please form an orderly queue.*

ordinary *adj* normal, usual.

ore *n* rock or earth from which metal can be taken.

organ *n* **1** a part inside the body that does a particular job. *The heart is the organ that pumps blood around the body.* **2** a musical instrument with a keyboard and pipes.

organic *adj* **1** (of plants) grown without the use of artificial fertilizers or pesticides. **2** to do with living things. **organically** *adv*.

organism *n* a living animal or plant.

organization *n* **1** a group of people working together for a purpose. *a charity organization.* **2** the organizing of something.

organize *v* to arrange or prepare for something. *David is organizing a party for his son's birthday.*

oriental *adj* to do with Eastern countries such as China and Japan.

orienteering *n* the sport of finding your way across country with the help of a compass and map.

origin *n* the place or point where something began or first came from. *What is the origin of this word?*

original[1] *adj* **1** earliest or first. *The original town hall burnt down and was then rebuilt.* **2** new, not copied. *This is a really original idea.* **originality** *n*, **originally** *adv*.

original[2] *n* the earliest version, not a copy. *This painting is an original.*

originate *v* to begin.

ornament *n* an object used to decorate a room. *The mantelpiece was full of ornaments.* **ornamental** *adj*.

ornate *adj* richly decorated.

ornithology *n* the study of birds. **ornithologist** *n*.

orphan *n* a child whose parents are dead. **orphaned** *adj*.

orphanage *n* a home for orphans.

ostrich *n* a very large bird that runs very quickly but cannot fly.

ostrich

other *adj, pron* **1** the second of two. *I've found one shoe – do you know where the other one is?* **2** the rest. *Susie is here but where are the others?* **3** different. *The road is closed so we'll have to go some other way.*

otherwise[1] *conj* if not, or else. *Hurry up, otherwise we'll be late.*

otherwise[2] *adv* in all other ways. *She's a bit moody but otherwise she's nice.*

otter *n* an animal that lives near rivers and eats fish.

ought *v* **ought to** should.

ounce *n* an old measure of weight equal to 28.35 grammes.

outback *n* the wild, inland parts of Australia.

outbreak *n* the sudden appearance of something unpleasant. *an outbreak of fighting.*

outburst *n* a sudden expression of a strong feeling, especially anger.

outcast *n* a person who has been driven away from friends, family, etc. *an outcast from society.*
outcome *n* a result.
outdo *v* (outdoes, outdoing, outdid, outdone) to do better than somebody.
outdoors *adv* outside, in the open air. **outdoor** *adj.*
outer *adj* far from the centre, furthest away. *outer space.*
outfit *n* a set of clothes that you wear together.
outgrow *v* (outgrowing, outgrew, outgrown) to get too big or too old for something.
outing *n* a trip.
outlaw *n (old-fashioned)* a person who has broken the law.
outline *n* a line that shows the shape or edge of something.
outlive *v* to live longer than somebody.
outlook *n* **1** your attitude to things. **2** what seems likely to happen.
outnumber *v* to be greater in number than something else.
output *n* **1** the amount produced by a factory, business, person, etc. **2** information produced by a computer.
outrageous *adj* shocking or unacceptable. *outrageous behaviour.*
outright *adv* at once, completely.
outside[1] *n* the outer part of something. **outside** *adj.*
outside[2] *prep, adv* at or to the outside of something.
outskirts *n pl* the edges of a town.
outspoken *adj* saying exactly what you think, even if it upsets people.
outstanding *adj* **1** extremely good. **2** still needing to be paid. *outstanding debts.*
outwit *v* (outwits, outwitting, outwitted) to defeat somebody by being cleverer than they are.
oval *n* a shape like an egg. **oval** *adj.*
oven *n* an enclosed space, especially in a cooker, in which food is baked or roasted.
over[1] *prep* **1** above. *The number is over the door.* **2** across. *We went over the bridge.* **3** more than. *She has won over a million pounds.* **4** on top of. *He lay his coat over the sleeping child.* **5** about. *They quarrelled over money.*
over[2] *adv* **1** finished. **2** down, from an upright position. *I fell over.* **3** so that a different side is on top. *Turn the meat over to cook the other side.* **4** not used. *There is some bread left over from lunch.*
over[3] *n* in cricket, a series of six balls bowled by one person.
over- *prefix* too, too much. *over-excited, overcooked, overweight.*
overall *adj* including or considering everything. *What will the overall cost of the holiday be?*
overalls *n pl* a piece of clothing worn over other clothes to keep them clean.
overboard *adv* over the side of a boat.
overcast *adj* cloudy.
overcome *v* (overcoming, overcame, overcome) **1** to defeat or conquer something. *He has overcome his fear of the dark.* **2** to affect somebody so strongly that they become helpless. *Eleanor was overcome by grief when she heard the news.*
overdue *adj* late.
overflow *v* to flow over the edges of something. *I left my bath water running and it overflowed.*
overhaul *v* to examine something carefully and carry out repairs.
overhead *adj, adv* above, over your head. *overhead lighting.*
overheads *n pl* the general costs involved in running a business, such as wages, rent and electricity.
overhear *v* (overhearing, overheard) to hear what you were not meant to hear.
overlap *v* (overlaps, overlapping, overlapped) to partly cover something. *Each roof tile overlaps the one below it.*
overleaf *adv* on the other side of a piece of paper.
overlook *v* **1** to ignore or not punish something. *He overlooked my mistake.* **2** to miss or fail to notice something. *I think you've overlooked something.* **3** to look down on something. *Our house overlooks the lake.*

overnight *adj, adv* **1** for the night. *Do you want to stay at my house overnight?* **2** sudden or suddenly. *She became a film star overnight.*
overseas *adj, adv* across the sea, abroad.
oversight *n* a mistake, especially due to not noticing something.
overtake *v* (overtaking, overtook, overtaken) to go past another moving vehicle to get in front of it.
overthrow *v* (overthrowing, overthrew, overthrown) to defeat and force somebody out. *The government was overthrown.*
overtime *n* time spent working after your normal hours.
overture *n* a piece of music played as an introduction to an opera or ballet.
overwhelm *v* **1** to defeat somebody completely. **2** to load somebody with too great an amount. *overwhelmed with work.* **3** to have a strong and sudden effect on somebody. *He was overwhelmed by despair.*
owe *v* **1** to need to pay money back to somebody. **2** to have somebody or something to thank for something. *He owes his life to the man who pulled him out of the river.* **owing to** because of.
owl *n* a bird of prey that hunts at night.
own[1] *v* to possess or have something. **own up** to confess. **owner** *n*.
own[2] *adj, pron* belonging to you. *This is my own pen.* **on your own** alone.
ox *n* (*pl* oxen) a male animal of the cattle family, often used for pulling heavy loads.
oxygen *n* a colourless gas found in air.
oyster *n* a flat shellfish. Some oysters are edible and others contain pearls.
ozone *n* a form of oxygen.
ozone layer *n* a layer of ozone in the upper atmosphere that protects the Earth from the Sun's rays.

oyster shell containing a pearl

Pp

pace[1] *n* **1** a step or stride. *She took a pace forward.* **2** a speed of movement. *We were walking at a brisk pace.*
pace[2] *v* to walk backwards and forwards.
pacifist *n* a person who believes that wars are wrong and that you should not fight in them. **pacifism** *n*.
pacify *v* (pacifies, pacifying, pacified) to make somebody who is angry or upset become calm.
pack[1] *n* **1** a packet. *a pack of envelopes.* **2** several things tied or wrapped up together, or put in a bag, especially for carrying. **3** a group of wild animals. *a pack of wolves.* **4** a set of playing-cards.
pack[2] *v* **1** to put things into a bag or other container ready for a journey. **2** to press or crowd together closely. *They packed into the room to hear his speech.*
package *n* things wrapped up or packed in a box for sending.
package holiday *n* a holiday where all the travel and accommodation is organized and included in the price.
packet *n* **1** a small paper or cardboard container in which items are sold. **2** a small parcel.
pact *n* an agreement.
pad[1] *n* **1** a thick piece of soft material, used for protection, to absorb liquids, etc. **2** sheets of paper joined together at one edge.
pad[2] *v* (pads, padding, padded) **1** to walk along softly. **2** to fill or cover something with a pad. **padding** *n*.
paddle[1] *n* a short oar for moving a canoe through water.
paddle[2] *v* to walk about in shallow water.

paddle-steamer *n* a steam-powered boat propelled by two large wheels made up of paddles.

paddle-steamer

paddock *n* small field for horses.
paddy-field *n* a wet field where rice is grown.
padlock *n* a type of lock with a metal loop on one end that you open with a key. **padlock** *v*.
pagan *(pay-gun) n* a person who does not believe in any religion.
page *n* **1** a sheet of paper, or one side of a sheet of paper in a book, etc. **2** (*also* **page-boy**) a small boy who accompanies a bride at her wedding. **3** in earlier times, a boy servant.
pageant *(paj-ent) n* a parade or show in which people wear historical costumes or act out scenes from history.

Chinese pagoda

pagoda *n* an Asian temple in the form of a tower with many storeys.
paid *past of* pay.
pail *n (old-fashioned)* a bucket.
pain *n* suffering, in your body or mind. **take pains** to make a great effort. *She took great pains over the party preparations.* **painful** *adj*, **painfully** *adv*.
painstaking *adj* very careful.
paint[1] *n* a liquid used for colouring surfaces or for making pictures.
paint[2] *v* to use paint to colour a surface or make a picture. **painter** *n*.
painting *n* a painted picture.
pair *n* **1** two things that match or go together. *a pair of socks.* **2** a thing made up of two parts. *a pair of scissors.*
pal *n* a friend.
palace *n* a large, splendid house, especially the home of a king, queen, or bishop.
palate *n* the roof of your mouth.
pale *adj* **1** light or whitish in colour. *pale blue.* **2** not bright. *a pale light.*
palette *n* a board on which an artist mixes paints.
pallid *adj* (of a person's face) pale.
palm *n* **1** the inner surface of your hand. **2** a tree that grows in hot countries, with broad, spreading leaves at the top of its tall trunk.
pamper *v* to take too much care of somebody.
pamphlet *(pam-flit) n* a small, thin book with a paper cover.
pan *n* a metal container with a handle, used for cooking food in.
pancake *n* a flat cake of flour, eggs, etc fried in a pan.
pancreas *n* a gland near your stomach which helps digestion. See **digestion**.
panda *n* (*also* **giant panda**) a large black and white animal similar to a bear, found in China.

panda

pane *n* a sheet of glass in a window.
panel *n* **1** a flat, rectangular piece of wood, etc that is set into a door, wall, ceiling, etc. **2** a group of people chosen, especially to judge a contest or take part in a TV quiz.
panic *n* a sudden feeling of great fear, especially one that spreads quickly from person to person. **panic** *v*.
panorama *n* a wide view of an area. **panoramic** *adj*.
pansy *n* a garden flower.

pant *v* to take short, quick breaths.
panther *n* a leopard, especially the black leopard.
pantomime *n* a type of play with music and dancing, based on a fairy tale and performed around Christmas.
pantry *n* a room or large cupboard where food is kept.
pants *n pl* **1** underpants or knickers. **2** the word for "trousers" in American English.
paper *n* **1** thin, flat sheets of material for writing or printing on, usually made from wood pulp. **2** a newspaper.
paperback *n* a book with a paper cover.
papier-mâché *(pap-ee-ay **mash**-ay) n* a mixture of paper pulp and glue that hardens when it dries and that can be shaped into models, bowls, etc.
papyrus *(pa-**pye**-rus) n* (*pl* papyri *or* papyruses) paper made from the papyrus reed in ancient Egypt.
parable *n* a story that teaches a moral lesson.
parachute *n* an umbrella-shaped device used for floating down from an aircraft. **parachute** *v*, **parachutist** *n*.
parade *n* **1** a line of people, vehicles, etc moving along. *a carnival parade.* **2** soldiers gathered together for inspection. **parade** *v*.
paraffin *n* oil used for burning in jet engines, heaters and lamps.
paragliding *n* the sport of gliding through the air using a kind of parachute.
paragraph *n* a section of a piece of writing. The first word of a paragraph starts on a new line.
parakeet *n* a type of small parrot.
parallel *adj* (of lines) going in the same direction and never meeting, always remaining the same distance apart. *Railway tracks are parallel.*
parallelogram *n* a four-sided shape with opposite sides which are parallel and equal in length.
paralyse *v* to make a person or an animal lose all feeling or movement in a part of their body. **paralysis** *n*.
paraplegic *(pa-ra-**plee**-jik) n* a person who is paralysed in the legs and lower part of the body.
parasite *n* an animal or plant that gets its food by living on or inside another living thing. **parasitic** *adj*.
parasol *n* an umbrella that shades you from the sun.
parcel *n* a package that has been wrapped up in paper, usually for sending through the post.
parchment *n* a material for writing on before paper was invented, made from the dried skin of a sheep or goat.
parch *v* to make something very hot and dry. *earth parched by the sun.*
pardon *v* to forgive or excuse somebody. **pardon** *n*.
parent *n* a mother or father. **parental** *adj*.
parish *n* an area that has its own church.
park[1] *n* a public place with grass and trees.
park[2] *v* to stop and leave a vehicle in a place for a time.
parliament *n* the group of people who are elected to make the laws of a country. **parliamentary** *adj*.
parole *n* the release of a prisoner before the end of their prison sentence, on condition that they behave well.
parrot *n* a brightly coloured tropical bird with a hooked beak.
parsley *n* a herb used in cooking.
parsnip *n* a yellow root vegetable.
part[1] *n* **1** a piece of something, not the whole thing. **2** a character in a play. **take part** to be one of a group of people doing something. *I'm taking part in the school play this year.*
part[2] *v* to divide or separate. **part with** to give something away.

macaw (the world's largest parrot)

partial *adj* **1** not complete. *a partial success.* **2** having a liking for a person or thing. *I'm quite partial to chocolate cake.* **partially** *adv.*
participate *v* to take part. **participation** *n.*
particle *n* a very small piece.
particular *adj* **1** one rather than any other. *I want this particular colour.* **2** difficult to please, fussy. *He's very particular about what he eats.*
particulars *n pl* details.
parting *n* **1** a leaving, a separation. **2** a line in your hair where it is combed in two directions.
partition *n* a structure that divides a room or space into two parts.
partly *adv* not completely.
partner *n* **1** one of a pair of people who do things together or share something. *Alice is my tennis partner.* **2** a husband, wife or permanent lover. **partnership** *n.*
part of speech *n* one of the grammatical groups into which words are divided, eg noun, verb, etc.
partridge *n* a game bird.
party *n* **1** an occasion when a group of people meet to enjoy themselves, especially by eating, drinking and dancing. **2** a group of people travelling together. **3** a group of people sharing the same political ideas.
pass[1] *v* **1** to go by. *I pass the shops on my way to school.* **2** to give from one person to another. *Please pass me the salt.* **3** to spend time. *We passed a few hours in town.* **4** to succeed in an exam. *She passed all her GCSEs.* **pass away** to die. **pass out** to faint.
pass[2] *n* **1** a ticket or card that allows you to do something, such as travel free or enter a building. **2** a road or way through or over mountains.
passage *n* **1** passing. **2** a corridor or alley. **3** a journey by ship or plane.
passenger *n* a person travelling in a vehicle who is not the driver or a member of the crew.
passion *n* a very strong feeling, especially of love or anger. **passionate** *adj.*
Passover *n* a Jewish religious festival at which the escape of the Israelites from Egypt is remembered.
passport *n* a small book that travellers must show to prove who they are when going from one country to another.
password *n* a secret word that allows you to enter a place or use a computer sytem.
past[1] *n* **1** the time before now. **2** the form of a verb that shows that an action is in the past. *Won* is the past of *win.* **past** *adj.*
past[2] *prep, adv* **1** up to and beyond. *You go past the school to get to the hospital.* **2** after. *half past two.*
pasta *n* a food made from flour and eggs, formed into different shapes.

pasta

conchiglie

farfalle

vermicelli

paste[1] *n* **1** a soft, wet mixture. *toothpaste.* **2** glue for sticking paper.
paste[2] *v* to stick something with paste.
pastel[1] *n* a soft crayon.
pastel[2] *adj* pale. *pastel colours.*
pasteurize *v* to treat milk by heating it, in order to kill harmful germs.
pastime *n* what you do in your spare time, a hobby.
past participle *n* a past form of a verb that you use with *have* or *had.*
pastry *n* a mixture of flour, fat and other ingredients, used in making pies.
pasture *n* a field where animals graze.
pasty[1] *(pas-tee) n* a small pie filled with meat or vegetables.
pasty[2] *(**pay**-stee) adj* (of a person) pale.
pat *v* (pats, patting, patted) to touch something lightly with the palm of your hand. *She patted the dog.* **pat** *n.*
patch[1] *n* **1** a part of something that is different from the rest, especially in colour. *a black cat with a white patch on his back.* **2** a small piece of cloth put over a hole to mend it. **3** a small piece of ground.

patch[2] *v* to put a patch over a hole to mend it.
patchwork *n* small pieces of different fabrics sewn together.
patchy *adj* (patchier, patchiest) having patches, uneven.
pâté *n* a paste made from meat, fish or vegetables, spread on bread, etc.
paternal *adj* of or like a father.
path *n* **1** a way across land for people to walk or ride on. **2** the line along which something is moving. *The island is in the path of the hurricane.*
pathetic *adj* **1** making you feel pity. **2** useless, feeble.
patience *n* the ability to be patient.
patient[1] *adj* able to wait a long time and put up with inconvenience without complaining or getting cross.
patient[2] *n* a person who is being treated by a doctor.
patio *n* (*pl* patios) a paved area by a house, where you can sit outside.
patriot *n* a person who loves and is loyal to their country. **patriotic** *adj*, **patriotism** *n*.
patrol *v* (patrols, patrolling, patrolled) to keep guard by moving regularly around an area. *His job is to patrol the factory at night.* **patrol** *n*.
patter *v* to make quick, tapping sounds. *rain pattering on the roof.*
pattern *n* **1** a repeated design on something. *My shirt has a pattern of circles and squares on it.* **2** a thing that is copied to make something else. *a dress pattern.* **patterned** *adj*.
pauper *n* a very poor person.
pause *v* to stop for a short time. *She paused before she spoke.* **pause** *n*.
pave *v* to cover the ground with flat stones, concrete, etc.
pavement *n* a path at the side of a road.
paw *n* the foot of an animal.
pawn[1] *n* the chesspiece that has the lowest value. See **chess**.
pawn[2] *v* to leave a valuable object at a shop called a **pawnbroker's** in exchange for money. When the money is repaid, the object is returned.
pay[1] *v* (paying, paid) **1** to give money in exchange for something. **2** to be useful or beneficial. *It pays to work hard for exams.* **3** to give. *Please pay attention.* **4** to suffer punishment. *She'll pay for her rudeness.*
pay[2] *n* wages.
payment *n* **1** paying. **2** money paid.
pc *short for* personal computer.
PC *short for* police constable.
PE *short for* physical education.
pea *n* a small, round, green vegetable that grows in pods on a climbing plant.
peace *n* **1** a time when there is no war. **2** quiet and calm. **peaceful** *adj*, **peacefully** *adv*.
peach *n* a soft, juicy fruit with a hard stone and furry, orangey-pink skin.
peacock *n* a large male bird with beautiful blue and green tail-feathers.

peacock

peahen *n* the female of the peacock.
peak *n* **1** the top of a mountain. **2** the highest point of something. **3** the pointed front part of a cap that is over your eyes.
peal *v* (of bells) to ring loudly. **peal** *n*.
peanut *n* a nut that grows in a pod under the ground.
pear *n* a green fruit that is round at the base and narrow at the top.
pearl *n* a silver-white gem found in some oysters. See **oyster**.
peasant *n* a person who lives and works on the land, especially in a poor area.
peat *n* a soft, brown substance made of decayed plants, dug from the ground and used as a fuel and in gardening.
pebble *n* a small, round stone.
peck *v* (of birds) to use the beak to hit or pick up something.

peckish *adj* a little hungry.
peculiar *adj* **1** strange, odd. **2** belonging to one particular place, person or thing. *This is a custom peculiar to Scotland.*
pedal[1] *n* a part that you press with your foot to make something move or work.
pedal[2] *v* (pedals, pedalling, pedalled) to use pedals to move or work something.
pedestrian *n* a person walking in the street.
pedigree *adj* (of an animal) from a line of ancestors of the same breed.
peel[1] *n* the skin of a fruit or vegetable.
peel[2] *v* **1** to remove the skin or covering from something. **2** to come off in thin pieces. *The paint on the walls was peeling.*
peep *v* to look at something quickly, or through a small opening. **peep** *n.*
peer[1] *v* to look closely or hard, especially when you cannot see something properly.
peer[2] *n* a nobleman. **peerage** *n.*
peg *n* **1** a small piece of wood or other material, used for hanging things on. *Hang your coat on that peg.* **2** a clip for fastening clothes to a line. **3** a stake. **peg** *v.*
pelican *n* a large water bird with a pouch under its beak for storing fish.
pellet *n* a small, round piece of something.
pelt *v* **1** to throw things at something. **2** to rain very hard.
pen *n* **1** a tool for writing with ink. **2** an enclosed area for animals.
penalty *n* **1** a punishment. **2** in games, an advantage given to the other side when a player breaks a rule.
pencil *n* a tool for writing and drawing containing a thin stick of a soft, black substance called graphite.
pendant *n* an ornament that hangs from a necklace
pendulum *n* a swinging weight on a rod, used in some clocks.
penetrate *v* to go into or through something.
pen-friend *n* a person who you make friends with by writing and receiving letters although you have never met.
penguin *n* a large sea bird which cannot fly, found in the Antarctic.
penicillin *n* a drug used for treating some infections.
peninsula *n* a piece of land that sticks out into the sea.

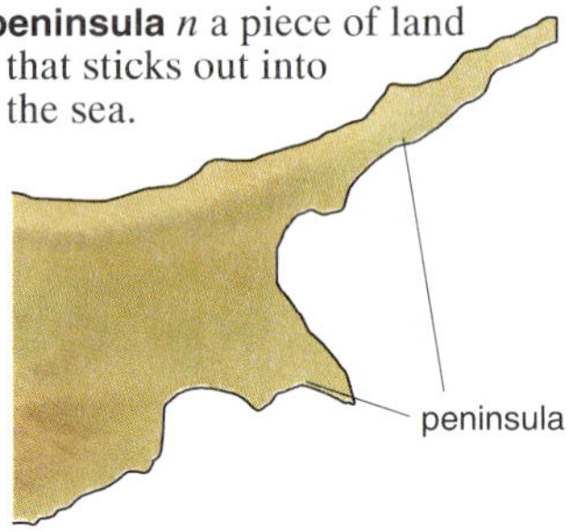

penis *n* the part of the body of a male human or animal used in sexual intercourse and for getting rid of urine.
penknife *n* (*pl* penknives) a small, folding knife.
penny *n* (*pl* pence *or* pennies) a small coin in the UK. There are 100 pence in one pound.
pension *n* money paid regularly to somebody who has retired from work (a **pensioner**).
pentagon *n* a five-sided shape. **pentagonal** *adj.*
pentathlon *n* a sporting competition made up of five athletic events.
people *n pl* human beings.
pepper *n* **1** a hot-tasting powder used to flavour food. **2** a bright-red, green or yellow vegetable containing seeds.
peppermint *n* **1** a plant with strong-smelling leaves used as a flavouring. **2** a sweet flavoured with these leaves.
per *prep* each, for each. *The dinner cost £15 per person.* **per cent** out of every hundred, often written as % with figures. *48 per cent (48%) of children in our school arrive by car.*
percentage *n* a number or rate in each hundred.
perch[1] *n* a resting place for a bird. **perch** *v.*
perch[2] *n* a freshwater fish.
percussion instrument *n* a musical

instrument that is struck or shaken. Drums, tambourines and triangles are percussion instruments.

perennial *adj* lasting for many years. *perennial plants.*

perfect[1] *(**pur**-fikt) adj* so good that it cannot be made better. **perfection** *n.*

perfect[2] *(pur-**fekt**) v* to make perfect.

perforate *v* to make holes in something. **perforation** *n.*

perform *v* **1** to carry out. *A surgeon performs operations.* **2** to give a show in front of an audience. *We performed our play in front of the whole school.* **performance** *n,* **performer** *n.*

perfume *n* **1** a pleasant smell. **2** a pleasant-smelling liquid that you put on your skin. **perfumed** *adj.*

perhaps *adv* possibly, maybe.

peril *n* a great danger. **perilous** *adj.*

perimeter *(pe-**rim**-uh-ter) n* the outside edge of an area.

period *n* **1** a length of time. **2** the natural bleeding from a woman's womb which happens every month.

periodical *n* a magazine that is published regularly.

periscope *n* a tube with mirrors that allows you to look over the top of something. Periscopes are used for seeing out of submarines.

perish *v* **1** to die or be destroyed. *Many people perished in the earthquake.* **2** (of rubber) to rot.

perm *n* (*short for* permanent wave) a long-lasting curly or wavy hairstyle created by a process using chemicals.

permanent *adj* lasting for a long time or for ever. *This is now our permanent address.* **permanence** *n.*

permissible *adj* allowed.

permission *n* allowing somebody to do something. *The teacher gave us permission to go home early.*

permit[1] *(pur-**mit**) v* (permits, permitting, permitted) to allow.

permit[2] *(**pur**-mit) n* a document allowing somebody to do something.

perpendicular *adj* standing exactly upright or at 90° to another line.

perpetual *adj* lasting for ever. **perpetually** *adv.*

persecute *v* to treat somebody cruelly, especially because of their religious or political beliefs. **persecution** *n,* **persecutor** *n.*

persevere *v* to keep trying to do something and not give up. **perseverance** *n.*

persist *v* to keep on doing something in spite of difficulty or opposition. **persistence** *n,* **persistent** *adj.*

person *n* any man, woman or child.

personal *adj* **1** of your own. *personal property.* **2** to do with a person's private business. *These letters are personal – please don't read them.* **3** appearing yourself. *The Prime Minister made a personal appearance on TV.*

personal computer *n* a small computer used in homes and offices.

personality *n* **1** what sort of person you are. **2** a well-known person.

personal stereo *n* a small, portable cassette-player with headphones.

perspective *n* **1** a way of drawing on a flat surface that makes objects that are farther away appear smaller, as they do in real life. **2** a point of view.

perspire *v* to sweat. **perspiration** *n.*

persuade *v* to try to make somebody do something by giving them reasons. **persuasion** *n.*

pessimist *n* a person who tends to believe that things will turn out badly. **pessimism** *n,* **pessimistic** *adj.*

pest *n* **1** a creature that is harmful or that destroys things. **2** a person who keeps annoying you.

pester *v* to keep annoying somebody, especially by asking the same thing many times.

pesticide *n* a chemical used to kill pests, especially insects.

pet *n* **1** a tame animal that you keep in your home. **2** a person who is treated as a favourite.

petal *n* one of the coloured parts of a flower. See **flower**.

petition *n* a written request signed by many people and sent to somebody in authority in order to try to get them to do something.

petrify *v* (petrifies, petrifying, petrified) **1** to make somebody very frightened. **2** to turn to stone.
petrol *n* a liquid fuel made from oil and used to power motor vehicles.
petticoat *n* a piece of clothing worn under a skirt or dress.
petty *adj* not very important, trivial.
pew *n* a bench in a church.
pewter *n* a mixture of lead and tin.
PG (*short for* parental guidance) a certificate given to a film showing that it may not be suitable for children.
pH *n* a measure of how acidic or alkaline a substance is. A pH value of below 7 means that the substance is acidic, and above 7 that it is alkaline.
phantom *n* a ghost.
Pharaoh *(**fair**-oh)* *n* one of the kings of ancient Egypt.
pharmacy *n* a shop where medicines are sold. **pharmacist** *n.*
phase *n* a stage in the development of something. *Phase 2 of the building work is due to start soon.*
pheasant *n* a long-tailed game bird.
phenomenon *(fee-**nom**-in-on)* *n* (*pl* phenomena) something very unusual or remarkable. **phenomenal** *adj.*
philosophical *(fil-o-**sof**-ik-ul)* *adj* **1** to do with philosophy. **2** calm, accepting problems without getting easily upset.
philosophy *(fi-**loss**-o-fee)* *n* **1** the study of the meaning of the universe and human life. **2** what one person thinks or believes. **philosopher** *n.*
phobia *n* a strong fear of something.
phone *short for* telephone.
phoney, phony *adj* fake, false.
photo (*pl* photos) *short for* photograph.
photocopier *n* a machine that copies documents instantly. **photocopy** *n, v.*
photograph *n* a picture taken with a camera and then printed on paper.
photography *n* taking pictures with a camera. **photographer** *n,* **photographic** *adj.*
photosynthesis *n* a process by which green plants use energy from sunlight to turn carbon dioxide and water into food.
phrase *n* a group of words that has a meaning but is not a complete sentence.
physical *adj* **1** to do with the body. *physical exercise.* **2** to do with things that can be seen and felt. *the physical world.* **physically** *adv.*
physics *n* the science which includes the study of light, heat, sound and energy. **physicist** *n.*
pianist *n* a person who plays the piano.
piano *n* (*pl* pianos) a musical instrument with a keyboard.
piccolo *n* (*pl* piccolos) a small flute.
pick *v* **1** to choose, to select. **2** to gather. *We picked some flowers.* **3** to remove small pieces of something from a surface, especially with your fingers. *Don't pick that scab!* **pick on** to be nasty to a particular person. *Stop picking on me!* **pick up 1** to lift. **2** to learn gradually. *She picked up a little Spanish on holiday.* **3** to collect. *I'll pick you up from your house at 6.*
picket *n* a person or group of people who stand outside a place of work to protest and to try to persuade other workers to go on strike. **picket** *v.*
pickle *v* to preserve food in vinegar or salt water. **pickle** *n.*
pickpocket *n* a thief who steals from people's pockets or bags.
picnic[1] *n* a meal eaten out-of-doors away from home.
picnic[2] *v* (picnics, picknicking, picnicked) to have a picnic.
picture[1] *n* a drawing, painting, photograph or other image.
picture[2] *v* to imagine something.
picturesque *(**pik**-chur-esk)* *adj* pretty.
pie *n* meat, vegetables or fruit baked in a pastry case.
piece *n* **1** a part or bit of something. *a piece of cake.* **2** a single object. *a piece of paper.* **3** an artistic work. *a piece of music.* **4** a coin. *a 50p piece.*
pier *n* a long platform stretching from the shore into the sea.
pierce *v* to make a hole in something.
piercing *adj* loud and sharp. *a piercing cry.*
pig *n* a farm animal kept for its meat.

pigeon *n* a grey bird that is very common in towns and cities.
piglet *n* a young pig.
pigment *n* **1** a substance used for colouring dyes, paints, etc. **2** a natural colouring in your skin or hair.
pigsty *n* a building where pigs are kept.
pigtail *n* a plait of hair.
pike *n* a freshwater fish.
pile *n* a number of things lying on top of each other. *a pile of dirty washing.* **pile** *v.*
pilgrim *n* a person who travels to visit a holy place.
pilgrimage *n* a pilgrim's journey.
pill *n* **1** a small tablet of medicine. **2 the pill** a tablet taken regularly by some women to prevent them from getting pregnant.
pillar *n* an upright post, often made of stone, for supporting a building.
pillarbox *n* a tall box in the street where you can post letters.
pillow *n* a large cushion on a bed, where you rest your head.
pillowcase *n* a cover for a pillow.
pilot *n* **1** a person who flies an aircraft. **2** a person who directs a ship in and out of harbours, etc. **pilot** *v.*
pimple *n* a small spot on the skin.
pin *n* a short, pointed piece of metal with a rounded head, used for fastening things together. **pin** *v.*
pinafore *n* **1** a sleeveless dress worn over a shirt or jumper. **2** an apron.
pincer *n* **1** the claw of a crab or lobster. **2 pincers** a tool for gripping things, especially for pulling out nails.

pinch[1] *v* **1** to squeeze somebody's skin between your thumb and finger. **2** *(slang)* to steal something.
pinch[2] *n* **1** pinching. **2** a small amount of something. *a pinch of salt.*
pine[1] *n* **1** a tall evergreen tree that has cones and needle-like leaves **2** the wood from this tree.
pine[2] *v* to feel very sad, especially because you miss somebody or something.
pineapple *n* a large, juicy, tropical fruit with a prickly skin.
ping-pong *n* table-tennis.
pink *n* a pale-red colour. **pink** *adj.*
pint *n* an old measure for liquids, equal to 20 fluid ounces or 0.586 of a litre.
pioneer *n* **1** a person who is among the first to explore a place and start living there. **2** a person who is among the first to do something. *pioneers of television.* **pioneer** *v.*
pious *adj* following a religion very seriously. **piety** *n.*
pip *n* the seed of a fruit.

pipe *n* **1** a tube for carrying water, gas, etc. **2** a tube, usually wooden, for smoking tobacco. **3** a musical instrument made of several tubes joined together, which you play by blowing. *The picture shows a Native American musician from Peru playing the pan-pipes.*
pirate[1] *n* a person who robs ships at sea. **piracy** *n.*
pirate[2] *v* to copy another person's work illegally. *pirated versions of video cassettes.* **piracy** *n.*
pirouette *n* in ballet, a rapid spin on one foot.
pistol *n* a small gun that is held in one hand.
pit *n* **1** a hole in the ground. **2** a coalmine.
pitch[1] *n* **1** an area of ground where a sport is played. *a football pitch.* **2** the highness or lowness of a musical note. **3** a sticky, black substance like tar.

pitch[2] *v* **1** to put up a tent. **2** to throw something.
pitcher *n* **1** a large jug. **2** a person who throws the ball in baseball.
pitchfork *n* a long-handled fork used for lifting hay.
pitfall *n* a hidden difficulty or danger.
pity *n* **1** a feeling of sadness caused by somebody else's troubles or suffering. **2** a cause of sadness or regret. *What a pity Sarah isn't here.* **pity** *v*.
pixy, pixie *n* a small fairy.
pizza *n* a flat piece of dough spread with tomatoes, cheese and other foods, and baked.
placard *n* a notice, especially one that is carried.
place[1] *n* a particular area or position.
place[2] *v* to put something somewhere.
placid *(**plas**-id) adj* calm, not easily upset.
plague *(playg) n* **1** a serious disease that spreads quickly to a lot of people. **2** something bad that comes in large quantities. *a plague of flies.* **plague** *v*.
plaice *n* an edible, flat sea fish.
plain[1] *adj* **1** simple, ordinary, not decorated or fancy. *plain white walls.* **2** easy to understand, see or hear. *It is plain that he is unhappy.*
plain[2] *n* a large, flat area of country.
plain clothes *n pl* ordinary clothes, not a uniform. *The police officers were in plain clothes.*
plait *(rhymes with* flat*) n* a length of hair divided into three and woven together. **plait** *v*.
plan[1] *n* **1** an idea of what you are going to do and how to do it. **2** a drawing of something to show what it will look like when it is built. **3** a map of a town, building, etc as seen from above.
plan[2] *v* (plans, planning, planned) to decide what you are going to do and how to do it.
plane *n* **1** *short for* aeroplane. **2** a tool for making wood smooth. **3** a flat surface.
planet *n* an object in space which moves around the Sun or around another star. Mars, Earth and Venus are planets.
plank *n* a long, flat piece of wood.
plankton *n* tiny plants and animals living in water.
plant[1] *n* **1** any living thing that grows in the ground. Plants usually have a stem, roots and leaves. **2** a factory's buildings and machinery.
plant[2] *v* **1** to put a plant or seed in the ground so that it will grow. **2** to hide something somewhere. *The terrorist planted a bomb on the plane.*
plaque *n* **1** a flat piece of metal, china, etc with words or pictures on it, fixed to a wall. **2** a substance that forms on your teeth and can cause decay.
plaster[1] *n* **1** a substance made of lime, water and sand used for making a smooth surface on walls and ceilings. **2** a small, sticky patch used to cover a wound. **3** a white powder mixed with water, which becomes hard when it dries, used for making models, holding broken bones in place, etc.
plaster[2] *v* **1** to cover a surface with plaster. **2** to cover something thickly with a substance.
plastic *n* a strong, light, chemically produced substance, used to make many different things.
plastic surgery *n* an operation to repair or improve the appearance of a person's skin or part of their body.
plate *n* **1** a flat, round dish for food. **2** a flat piece of metal, glass, etc.
plateau *(**pla**-toe) n (pl* plateaus *or* plateaux) a flat area of land higher than the land around it.
platform *n* **1** a raised pavement beside the lines at a railway station. **2** a raised part of a floor where speakers or performers stand so that they can be seen by the audience.
platinum *n* a valuable, silvery-white metal.
platypus *n* an Australian mammal with fur, a beak and webbed feet. Platypuses lay eggs but they feed milk to their young.

platypus

play[1] *v* **1** to do things for fun, not as work. **2** to take part in a game. **3** to act a part in a play. **4** to make music on an instrument. **player** *n.*
play[2] *n* (*pl* plays) a story that is acted out.
playful *adj* **1** full of fun. **2** not serious.
playground *n* an area where children can play.
playing-card *n* one of a pack of cards used for playing card games.
playwright *n* a person who writes plays.
plc (*short for* public limited company) a company whose shares are owned by members of the public.
plea *n* **1** an urgent request. *a plea for cash.* **2** an accused person's answer to a charge in a law court.
plead *v* **1** to beg somebody to do something. **2** to answer a charge in a law court. *He pleaded guilty to selling drugs.*
pleasant *adj* enjoyable or friendly.
please[1] *v* to give pleasure to somebody.
please[2] a word that you use to ask something politely.
pleasure *n* a feeling of enjoyment or happiness.
pleat *n* a fold in a piece of clothing which has been pressed or sewn in place. **pleated** *adj.*
plectrum *n* a small piece of plastic, metal, etc for plucking the strings of a guitar or similar instrument.
pledge *n* a promise. **pledge** *v.*
plenty *n* a large number or amount. **plentiful** *adj.*
pliable *adj* easily bent.
plight *n* a serious and difficult situation. *The TV programme was about the plight of homeless people.*
plod *v* (plods, plodding, plodded) to walk slowly and with heavy steps.
plot[1] *n* **1** a secret plan to do something, usually bad. *a plot to assassinate the President.* **2** a small piece of ground. **3** the story of a book, film or play.
plot[2] *v* (plots, plotting, plotted) **1** to plan something secretly. **2** to make a chart or graph.
plough *(rhymes with* how*)* *n* a farm tool pulled by a tractor or animal, used to break up the earth to prepare it for planting. **plough** *v.*

plough

pluck *v* **1** to pull feathers off a bird. **2** to pull something sharply. *She plucked a grey hair from her head.* **3** to pick flowers or fruit. **4** to pull on the strings of a musical instrument.
plug[1] *n* **1** an object that fits tightly into a hole to block it. *a bath plug.* **2** a device that connects electrical equipment to an electricity supply.
plug[2] *v* (plugs, plugging, plugged) **1** to block a hole with a plug. **2** to advertise something. **plug in** to put an electrical plug into a socket.
plum *n* a soft fruit with a stone inside.
plumage *n* a bird's feathers.
plumber *(**plum**-er)* *n* a person who fits and repairs water pipes and tanks.
plumbing *(**plum**-ing)* *n* the system of water pipes and tanks in a building.
plump *adj* slightly fat, rounded.
plunder *v* to steal things, usually during a war. **plunder** *n.*
plunge *v* **1** to jump or fall into water. *The man plunged into the river.* **2** to push something suddenly and firmly into something else. *She plunged the knife into the meat.*
plural *n* the form of a word that shows more than one. *Hands* is the plural of *hand,* and *mice* is the plural of *mouse.* **plural** *adj.*
plus *prep* and, added to. *Four plus six equals ten* (4 + 6 = 10).
p.m. *short for* post meridiem (Latin for "after noon"). 1 p.m. is one o'clock in the afternoon.
pneumatic *(new-**mat**-ik)* *adj* **1** worked by air under pressure. *a pneumatic drill.* **2** filled with air.

pneumonia *(new-**moan**-ya) n* a serious disease of the lungs.
poach *v* **1** to cook something gently in liquid. **2** to catch fish or animals illegally. **poacher** *n.*
pocket *n* a small bag sewn into clothes and bags, used for carrying things.
pocket money *n* a regular amount of money that a child gets from its parents.
pod *n* a long case that holds the seeds of many plants, such as peas.
podgy *adj* (podgier, podgiest) slightly fat.
poem *n* a piece of writing with a special rhythm. Poems are often written in short lines with the last word of one line rhyming with the last word of a previous line.
poet *n* a person who writes poems.
poetry *n* poems.
point[1] *n* **1** the sharp end of something, such as a needle. **2** the main purpose of or reason for something. *What's the point of this game?* **3** a mark in a competition. **4** a dot. **5** a particular place or stage. *a meeting-point.*
point[2] *v* to stick out a finger or other thing in the direction of something. *He pointed a gun at her.*
poison *n* a substance that causes illness or death if it is swallowed or breathed in. **poison** *v,* **poisonous** *adj.*
poke *v* to push something sharply with a stick, finger, etc.
poker *n* **1** a rod for stirring up a fire. **2** a card game.
polar *adj* belonging to the North or South Poles.
polar bear *n* a large, white bear that lives near the North Pole.
pole *n* **1** a tall, thin, rounded piece of wood, metal or plastic. **2** one of the two points on the Earth's surface (the North Pole and the South Pole) that are farthest from the equator. **3** one of the opposite ends of a magnet.
pole vault *n* a sport in which you jump over a high bar using a flexible pole.
police *n* the people whose job is to make sure that the law is obeyed.
policy *n* a plan of action.
polish[1] *v* to make something smooth and shiny by rubbing it.
polish[2] *n* a substance used for polishing.
polite *adj* having good manners. **politeness** *n.*
politician *n* a person who is involved in politics.
politics *n pl* the art or study of government. **political** *adj*, **politically** *adv.*
poll *(rhymes with* coal*) n* **1** a survey of people's opinions. **2 polls** a political election.
pollen *n* the powder inside flowers that fertilizes other flowers.
pollinate *v* to fertilize with pollen.
pollution *n* harm to the environment caused by dirty or dangerous substances. **pollute** *v.*
polo *n* a game similar to hockey, played by two teams on horseback.
poltergeist *(**pole**-ter-gyste) n* a kind of ghost believed to move furniture or throw objects around.
poly- *prefix* many. *polygon* (= a flat shape with many sides).
polyester *n* an artificial material used to make clothing.
polystyrene *n* a light, artificial substance used to make packing material and disposable cups.
polythene *n* a light plastic used to make bags.
pompous *adj* behaving in a grand way because you think you are very important.
pond *n* a small area of water, smaller than a lake.
pony *n* a small horse.
poodle *n* a dog with thick, curly hair.
pool *n* **1** a small area of water. **2** a swimming pool. **3** a game in which you use a stick, called a cue, to hit balls into pockets at the edge of a long table. **4 pools** a gambling game in which you bet on football matches.
poor *adj* **1** having very little money. **2** not very good. *poor exam results.* **3** a word you use when you feel sorry for somebody. *Poor Lucy is ill again.*
poorly *adj* ill. *Ben is feeling poorly.*

pop[1] *n* **1** a small bang. **2** a fizzy soft drink. **3** modern, popular music.
pop[2] *v* (pops, popping, popped) **1** to make a pop. **2** to move or put something somewhere quickly. *She popped her head round the door.*
popcorn *n* maize that bursts open when it is heated, eaten as a snack.
Pope *n* the head of the Roman Catholic Church.
poppy *n* a flower with large, usually red, petals.
popular *adj* liked by a lot of people. **popularity** *n.*
populated *v* with people living there.

field poppy

population *n* all the people living in a place.
porcelain *(por-su-lin) n* fine china.
porch *n* a covered entrance to a building.
porcupine *n* a rat-like animal covered with pointed spines.

porcupine

pore *n* one of the tiny holes in your skin, through which you sweat.
pork *n* the meat from a pig.
porous *adj* having lots of tiny holes that allow liquid or gas through.
porpoise *n* a sea animal of the dolphin and whale family.
porridge *n* a breakfast food made from oats boiled in milk or water.
port *n* **1** a harbour, or a town with a harbour. **2** the left side of a ship or aircraft. **3** a strong, sweet, red wine.
portable *adj* easy to carry around. *a portable telephone.*
portcullis *n* a heavy framework of bars that is lowered to protect the entrance to a castle.
porter *n* a person whose job is to carry luggage in a hotel or railway station, or to push hospital trolleys, etc.
port-hole *n* a round window in a ship.
portion *n* a share or part.
portrait *n* a picture of a person.
pose *v* **1** to arrange yourself in a particular position. *We all posed for the photo.* **2** to pretend to be something that you are not. *She was posing as a nurse.* **3** to present a question, problem, etc. **pose** *n.*
position[1] *n* **1** the place where somebody or something is. **2** a way of standing, sitting, etc. **3** a job.
position[2] *v* to put something in position.
positive *adj* **1** completely certain. *Are you positive you saw her steal the money?* **2** meaning or saying "yes". *We got a positive answer.* **3** more than zero. *a positive number.*
possess *v* to have or own something.
possession *n* a thing that you own.
possessive *adj* wanting to keep something all to yourself.
possible *adj* able to happen or be done. **possibility** *n,* **possibly** *adv.*
post[1] *n* **1** the way of sending and receiving letters and parcels. **2** letters and parcels that you send or receive. **3** a tall piece of wood or metal standing in the ground. **4** a job.
post[2] *v* to send a letter or parcel.
post- *prefix* after. *postwar.*
postcard *n* a card that you write a message on and send without an envelope.
postcode *n* numbers and letters added to the end of an address so that post can be sorted by machine.
poster *n* a large notice or picture that can be put up on a wall.
postmark *n* a mark stamped on a letter to show where and when it was posted.

postpone *v* to put something off until later. *The match was postponed because of the rain.* **postponement** *n.*
pot *n* a round container. *a plant pot.*
potato *n* (*pl* potatoes) a round root vegetable that grows underground.
potent *adj* powerful, strong.
potter *n* a person who make pots.
pottery *n* **1** pots and other things made of baked clay. **2** a place where pottery is made.
pouch *n* **1** a small bag. **2** a pocket of skin on the front of kangaroos, etc, where they carry their young.
poultry *n pl* birds kept on farms for their eggs and meat.
pounce *v* to jump on something suddenly. *The cat pounced on the mouse.*
pound[1] *n* **1** an old measure of weight, equal to 16 ounces or 0.454 kilos. **2** the main unit of money in the UK.
pound[2] *v* to hit something many times. *Sam pounded on the door.*
pour *v* to let liquid flow from a jug or other container.
poverty *n* being poor.
powder *n* tiny grains of a substance.
power *n* **1** strength or force. **2** the ability to do something. *This plant has magic powers.* **3** the ability or right to control people. *The police have the power to arrest people.* **4** energy. *nuclear power.* **powerful** *adj*, **powerfully** *adv.*
power station *n* a building where electricity is produced.
practical *adj* **1** to do with doing things rather than with ideas. *The book is a practical guide to finding a job.* **2** useful and likely to work. *Your plan just isn't practical.* **3** good at doing or making things with your hands.
practical joke *n* a trick played on somebody.
practically *adv* **1** in a practical way. **2** almost. *I've practically finished.*
practice *n* **1** the doing of something often so that you get better at it. **2** the doing of something. **3** the business of a doctor or lawyer.
practise *v* **1** to do something often so that you get better at it. **2** to do something regularly. **3** to work as a doctor or lawyer.
prairie *n* a wide, grassy area of land in central North America.
praise *v* to say good things about somebody. **praise** *n.*
pram *n* a small carriage for a baby, pushed along by a person on foot.
prank *n* a trick played on somebody.
prawn *n* a small shellfish like a large shrimp, eaten as food.
pray *v* to speak to God, especially to ask for something or to give thanks.
prayer *n* the words that you use when you pray.
pre- *prefix* before. *prehistoric* (= before history was written down).
preach *v* to give a talk about religious or moral matters.
precaution *n* something that you do in order to prevent something bad happening in the future.
precinct *n* a shopping area in a town, where vehicles are not allowed.
precious *adj* rare and very valuable.
precipice *n* the very steep side of a mountain or cliff.
precise *adj* exact, accurate. **precision** *n.*
predator *n* an animal that hunts other animals. **predatory** *adj.*
predecessor *n* a person who had your job before you started doing it.
predict *v* to say what is likely to happen in the future. **prediction** *n.*
preen *v* (of birds) to clean and tidy feathers with the beak.
preface *(pref-iss) n* an introduction to a book.
prefect *n* a senior pupil in a school who is given certain responsibilities.
prefer *v* (prefers, preferring, preferred) to like something better. **preferable** *adj*, **preference** *n.*
prefix *n* letters added to the beginning of a word to change its meaning. *Un-*, *pre-* and *multi-* are all prefixes.
pregnant *adj* having a baby growing inside the body. **pregnancy** *n.*
prehistoric *adj* from the time before history was written down.
prejudice *n* an unfair opinion that you

have about somebody or something without knowing much about them.

premiere *(**prem**-ee-air)* *n* the first performance of a film or play.

premises *n pl* the building and land that a business uses.

premium *n* money that you pay regularly for an insurance policy.

prepare *v* to get ready. **preparation** *n.*

preposition *n* a word used to show how the words before and after it are related. In the sentence *I walk to school, to* is a preposition.

prescription *n* a written instruction from a doctor to a pharmacist to provide medicine. **prescribe** *v.*

presence *n* being in a place.

present[1] *(**prez**-ent) adj* in a place, there. *The whole class was present for the announcement.*

present[2] *(**prez**-ent) n* **1** the time now. **2** a gift.

present[3] *(pri-**zent**) v* **1** to give something in public. *The mayor presented the trophy to the winner.* **2** to show or offer something. *Please present your passport at the desk.* **3** to introduce something. *She is presenting a new show on TV.* **presentation** *n.*

presently *adv* soon.

preserve *v* to make something last or keep it in good condition. *The ancient Egyptians preserved their dead Pharaohs as mummies.*

president *n* **1** the leader of a republic. **2** the head of a company or organization. **presidential** *adj.*

press[1] *v* **1** to push something. *Press the button.* **2** to iron something. **3** to persuade or force somebody strongly. *They pressed him for an answer.*

press[2] *n* **1** a machine for printing. **2 the press** the newspapers.

pressing *adj* urgent.

pressure *n* **1** the force with which one thing presses on another. *Apply pressure to the cut to stop it bleeding.* **2** strong persuasion or influence. *They put a lot of pressure on me to change my mind.*

presume *v* to believe that something is true without being sure. *I presume you want a pudding.* **presumption** *n.*

pretend *v* to try to make somebody believe something that is not true. **pretence** *n.*

pretext *n* a false reason, an excuse.

pretty[1] *adj* (prettier, prettiest) attractive, pleasant to look at. **prettily** *adv*, **prettiness** *n.*

pretty[2] *adv* fairly, quite.

prevent *v* to stop something from happening. **prevention** *n.*

preview *n* a showing of a film or play before it is seen by the public.

previous *adj* former, coming before.

prey *(pray) n* an animal that is hunted by another animal. **prey** *v.*

price *n* the amount of money that something costs to buy.

priceless *adj* too valuable to have a price. *priceless jewels.*

prick *v* to make a small hole in something with a sharp point.

prickle *n* a sharp point growing on a plant or animal. **prickly** *adj.*

pride *n* the feeling of being proud.

priest *n* a person who performs religious ceremonies, especially in some Christian churches.

prim *adj* too formal and correct.

primary *adj* first. **primarily** *adv.*

primary colours *n pl* in painting, the colours red, yellow and blue, that mix together to make all other colours.

primary school *n* a school for children between the ages of about 5 and 11.

primate *n* a member of the group of mammals that includes monkeys, apes and humans.

prime minister *n* the leader of a government.

primitive *adj* **1** belonging to the earliest times. *primitive societies.* **2** simple and rough. *They made a primitive boat out of pieces of wood.*

primrose *n* a yellow spring flower.

prince *n* a male member of a royal family, especially the son of a king or queen.

princess *n* a female member of a royal family, especially the daughter of a king or queen.

principal *adj* most important, main. **principally** *adv*.

principle *n* a general rule or law.

print *v* **1** to put words or pictures on to paper using a machine. **2** to write without joining up your letters. **print** *n*, **printer** *n*.

print-out *n* printed information produced by a computer.

prior *adj* earlier. *I'm sorry I can't come – I have a prior engagement.* **prior to** before.

priority *n* **1** the right to be first. *Ambulances must have priority over the other traffic.* **2** something that must be done first.

priory *n* a building where a group of monks or nuns live and worship.

prism *n* a transparent glass or plastic object with triangular ends, which splits light into the colours of the rainbow.

prison *n* a building where people are kept as a punishment for committing crimes. **prisoner** *n*.

private *adj* **1** for one person or a few people only, not public. *a private swimming pool.* **2** secret. *a private talk.* **3** not organized or controlled by the government. *a private hospital.*

privilege *n* a special advantage that is given only to certain people. **privileged** *adj*.

prize[1] *n* a reward for winning a competition, game, etc.

prize[2] *v* to value something highly.

pro- *prefix* for, in favour of.

probable *adj* likely to happen or be true. **probability** *n*, **probably** *adv*.

probation *n* **1** a trial period in a new job. **2** a period of time when a prisoner is released on condition that they behave well and are supervised by a social worker called a **probation officer**. **probationary** *adj*.

probe *v* to explore or examine closely.

problem *n* **1** a difficulty to be overcome. **2** a question to be solved.

procedure *n* the way of doing something.

proceed *v* to move forwards or carry on with something.

process *n* a series of actions for doing or making something. *The process of making paper is a complicated one.* **process** *v*.

procession *n* a line of people or vehicles moving along.

proclaim *v* to announce something publicly, to declare. **proclamation** *n*.

prod *v* (prods, prodding, prodded) to poke something. **prod** *n*.

produce[1] *(prod-**yoos**)* *v* **1** to make something. **2** to bring something out to show it. *The magician produced a rabbit from his hat.* **3** to be in charge of putting on a film, play, etc. **producer** *n*, **production** *n*.

produce[2] *(**prod**-yoos)* *n* food grown or produced on a farm or in a garden.

product *n* something that is produced.

profession *n* a job that needs special training, eg that of a doctor or teacher.

professional[1] *n* **1** a person who works in a profession. **2** a person who is paid to do something, not an amateur.

professional[2] *adj* **1** to do with a profession. **2** doing something for money, not as an amateur. **3** skilful. **professionally** *adv*.

professor *n* a head teacher of a university department.

proficiency *n* skill. **proficient** *adj*.

profile *n* **1** a side view of a face. **2** a short description of somebody's life or achievements.

profit *n* the money gained by selling something for a higher price than it cost you to make or buy it. **profit** *v*.

program *n* a set of instructions that control a computer. **program** *v*, **programmer** *n*.

programme *n* **1** a show broadcast on TV or radio. **2** a list of planned events. **3** a booklet giving information about a play, concert, etc.

progress *(proh-**gress**)* *v* **1** to move

forward. **2** to develop or improve. *The building work is progressing well.* **progress** *(**proh**-gress) n,* **progression** *n.*
prohibit *v* to forbid something. *Smoking is prohibited.*
project[1] *(**proj**-ekt) n* **1** a plan or scheme. **2** a piece of study or research. *We are doing a school project on the Middle Ages.*
project[2] *(pro-**jekt**) v* **1** to throw something forwards. **2** to stick out. *The wall projects into the sea.* **3** to show a film or image on a screen. **4** to forecast. *More job losses are projected for next year.* **projection** *n.*
projector *n* machine for showing pictures or films on a screen.
prolong *v* to make something last longer.
promenade *n* a road or path beside the sea.
prominent *adj* **1** standing out, easily seen. **2** famous or important. *a prominent businesswoman.* **prominence** *n.*
promise *v* to say that you will definitely do something. **promise** *n.*
promising *adj* likely to do or turn out well in the future. *a promising young musician.*
promote *v* **1** to move somebody to a more important job. *He was promoted to manager.* **2** to give a lot of publicity to something to try to sell it. *The author is promoting her new book.* **3** to help the progress of something. **promotion** *n.*
prompt *adj* immediate, without delay.
prong *n* one of the points of a fork.
pronoun *n* a word used in place of a noun, such as *he, she, it* and *this.*
pronounce *v* to speak sounds or words in a particular way. **pronunciation** *n.*
proof *n* evidence that shows that something is definitely true.
prop[1] *v* (props, propping, propped) to support something. *Peter propped the ladder against the wall.*
prop[2] *n* **1** a support. *The ceiling was held up with wooden props.* **2** an object used in a play, film, etc.
propaganda *n* ideas spread by a political group or an organization in order to influence people.
propel *v* (propels, propelling, propelled) to drive or push something forward. **propulsion** *n.*
propeller *n* a set of blades that spin round to drive a boat or aircraft.

proper *adj* **1** right or correct. *Put your toys back in the proper place.* **2** real. *We had a proper meal, not just a snack.* **3** respectable, behaving correctly. **properly** *adv.*
proper noun *n* a name for a particular person, place or thing, written with a capital letter. *Sam, York* and *Asia* are proper nouns.
property *n* **1** the things that you own. **2** a building and the land around it.
prophet *n* **1** a person who predicts the future. **2** a religious teacher who tells what they believe to be the will of God. **prophecy** *n.*
proportion *n* **1** a part of something. *A large proportion of the Earth is covered in water.* **2** an amount in relation to another. *The proportion of girls to boys here is two to one.*
propose *v* **1** to suggest something, to put forward an idea. **2** to ask somebody to marry you. **proposal** *n.*
proprietor *n* the owner of a business.
prosecute *v* to accuse somebody in a court of law. **prosecution** *n.*
prospect *n* an idea of what will happen in the future. *There is no prospect of the war ending just yet.*
prosper *v* to do well, to succeed. **prosperity** *n*, **prosperous** *adj.*
prostitute *n* a person who has sexual intercourse in exchange for money.
protect *v* to keep something safe from harm. **protection** *n*, **protective** *adj.*

protein *(pro-teen)* a substance found in foods, such as eggs, meat and milk, that is a necessary part of the diet of humans and animals.
protest *(proh-**test**)* *v* to show that you are strongly against something. *The demonstrators are protesting against the export of live animals.* **protest** *(**proh**-test) n.*
Protestant *n* a member of a part of the Christian Church which separated from the Roman Catholic Church in the 16th century. **Protestant** *adj.*
proton *n* one of the parts of the nucleus of an atom, carrying a positive electrical charge. See **atom**.
protractor *n* an instrument for measuring angles.
protrude *v* to stick out. **protrusion** *n.*
proud *adj* **1** pleased about your or somebody else's achievement. *She is proud of her son's success.* **2** thinking you are more important or better than you really are.
prove *v* to show that something is definitely true.
proverb *n* a well-known saying that gives advice. *"Many hands make light work" is a proverb.*
provide *v* to give something that is needed. *Our teacher provided us with pens and pencils.* **provided that, providing** only if. *I'll go providing you come with me.*
province *n* a region of a country with its own government.
provision *n* **1** providing something. **2 provisions** a supply of food.
provisional *adj* used for the time being, temporary.
provoke *v* to annoy somebody so that they react in an angry way. *The dog might bite if you provoke it.* **provocation** *n,* **provocative** *adj.*
prowl *v* to move around silently and carefully, like an animal waiting to attack.
prune[1] *n* a dried plum.
prune[2] *v* to cut off parts of a plant to control the way it grows.
pry *v* (pries, prying, pried) to look in a nosy way into other people's affairs.
PS written at the end of a letter when you want to add something. *Love from Susie. PS See you soon!*
psalm *(sahm) n* a sacred song.
pseudonym *(**soo**-do-nim) n* a false name, used by a writer.
psychiatrist *(sye-**kye**-a-trist) n* a doctor who treats mental illness. **psychiatric** *(sye-kee-**at**-rik) adj.*
psychic *(**sye**-kik) adj* able to read other people's minds or tell the future.
psycho- *(**sye**-coh) prefix* to do with the mind.
psychologist *(sye-**kol**-o-jist) n* an expert in psychology.
psychology *(sye-**kol**-o-jee) n* the study of the mind and how it works. **psychological** *(sye-ko-**loj**-ik-ul) adj,* **psychologically** *adv.*
pterodactyl *(te-ro-**dak**-til) n* a prehistoric flying reptile.

pterodactyl

PTO *short for* please turn over, written at the bottom of a page.
pub *n* (*short for* public house) a place where people go to drink alcoholic drinks.
puberty *(**pyoo**-ber-tee) n* the time when a child's body develops into that of an adult.
pubic *(**pyoo**-bik) adj* of the lower part of the abdomen. *pubic hair.*
public *adj* to do with or belonging to everybody. *a public library, a public meeting.* **the public** all people. *The palace is open to the public.*
publication *n* **1** the publishing of something. **2** a book, magazine or newspaper.
publicity *n* advertising.
public school *n* in Britain, a secondary school where parents pay for their child's education.
publish *v* to produce a book, newspaper or magazine and make it available to the public. **publisher** *n.*

pudding *n* **1** the sweet course of a meal. **2** a sweet food made from flour, eggs, etc and baked or steamed.
puddle *n* a small pool of water or other liquid on the ground.
puff[1] *n* a small blast of air, wind, etc. *a puff of smoke.*
puff[2] *v* **1** to blow with short puffs. *Smoke was puffing out of the chimney.* **2** to breathe quickly. *She was puffing as she reached the top of the stairs.* **puff out, puff up** to swell up.
puffin *n* a sea bird with a large beak.
pull *v* to move something, especially towards yourself, using force. **pull a face** to make a strange expression with your face. **pull down** to demolish a building. **pull out** to withdraw. **pull up** to stop a vehicle. **pull yourself together** to control your feelings after being upset.
pulley *n* (*pl* pulleys) a wheel with a rope around it, used to lift or move heavy things.
pullover *n* a jumper.
pulp *n* a soft, wet mass produced by crushing something such as fruit, vegetables or wood.
pulpit *n* a raised platform in a church where the priest or minister stands.
pulse *n* **1** the beating of your heart that you can feel in your wrist. **2** a regular beat. **pulse** *v*.
puma *n* a large wild cat found in North and South America.
pump[1] *n* a machine or device for forcing a liquid or gas into or out of something. *a bicycle pump.*
pump[2] *v* to force a liquid or gas with a pump. *Your heart pumps blood around your body.*
pumpkin *n* a large, round, orange-coloured fruit which grows on the ground.

pumpkin

pun *n* a joke based on words that sound the same but that have a different meaning. *"Two pears make a pair" is a pun.*
punch[1] *v* **1** to hit somebody with your fist. **2** to make a hole in something with a punch.
punch[2] *n* **1** a blow with the fist. **2** a tool for making holes in paper, leather, etc. **3** a drink made from fruit juices and sometimes alcohol.
punctual *adj* on time. **punctuality** *n*, **punctually** *adv*.
punctuation *n* marks used in writing, such as full stops, commas and exclamation marks. **punctuate** *v*.
puncture *n* a small hole in a tyre, etc, made by a sharp object. **puncture** *v*.
punish *v* to make somebody suffer because they have done something wrong. **punishment** *n*.
punt *n* a long, flat-bottomed boat, moved by somebody pushing against the bottom of a river with a pole.
puny *adj* (punier, puniest) small and weak.
pupa *(pyoo-pa) n* (*pl* pupae) the stage in an insect's development between the larva and the adult.
pupil *n* **1** a person who is learning from a teacher. **2** the round, dark part of your eye, through which light passes. See **eye**.
puppet *n* a doll that you move by pulling strings or by putting your hand inside and moving your fingers.
puppy *n* a young dog.
purchase[1] *v* to buy something.
purchase[2] *n* a thing you have bought.
pure *adj* clean, not mixed with anything else. **purity** *n*.
purify *v* (purifies, purifying, purified) to make something pure.
purple *n* a reddish-blue colour. **purple** *adj*.
purpose *n* **1** a reason for doing something. **2** what something is used for. **on purpose** deliberately.
purr *n* the low sound made by a cat when it is pleased. **purr** *v*.
purse[1] *n* a small bag for carrying money.

purse[2] *v* to close your lips tightly.
pursue *v* to follow or chase after somebody or something. **pursuit** *n.*
pus *n* a thick, yellowish fluid produced from an infected wound.
push *v* **1** to move something away from you with force. **2** to press on something. *Push the button.* **push** *n.*
pussy *n* a cat.
put *v* (puts, putting, put) **1** to place somewhere. **2** to express in words. *You've got a funny way of putting things!* **put off 1** to delay. **2** to stop somebody liking something. **put up** to let somebody stay in your home overnight. **put up with** not to complain about something even though you do not like it.
putt *v* in golf, to hit the ball gently along the ground towards the hole.
putty *n* a soft paste which hardens when dry and is used for fixing glass into window frames.
puzzle[1] *n* **1** a game that is difficult to solve and that makes you think a lot. *a crossword puzzle.* **2** something that is difficult to understand or explain.
puzzle[2] *v* to make somebody think a lot about something that is difficult to understand or solve.
pyjamas *n pl* a loose jacket and trousers that you wear in bed.
pylon *n* a tall metal tower supporting electric cables.
pyramid *n* **1** a solid shape with sloping sides that come to a point at the top. **2** a building of this shape used as a tomb in ancient Egypt.

pyramids

python *n* a large snake that crushes its prey.

Qq

quack *v* to make a noise like a duck. **quack** *n.*
quad *short for* quadruplet *or* quadrangle.
quadrangle *n* a square courtyard with buildings around it.
quadrant *n* a quarter of the circumference or area of a circle.
quadrilateral *n* a flat shape with four straight sides.
quadruped *n* a four-footed animal.
quadruplet *n* one of four babies born at the same time to the same mother.
quail *n* a small bird similar to a partridge, sometimes shot as game.
quaint *adj* attractively odd and old-fashioned. *a quaint little fishing village in Cornwall.* **quaintness** *n.*
quake *v* to shake, especially with fear.
qualify *v* (qualifies, qualifying, qualified) to reach the required standard so that you can do something, especially by passing tests or exams. *Saleh has qualified as a doctor.* **qualification** *n.*
quality *n* **1** how good something is. *The camera was cheap and of poor quality.* **2** a characteristic of somebody or something. *He has all the qualities of a good father.*
quantity *n* an amount or number of something. *a large quantity of food.*
quarantine *n* a time when an animal or person is kept away from others because they might have a disease.
quarrel *v* (quarrels, quarrelling, quarrelled) to argue. **quarrel** *n,* **quarrelsome** *adj.*
quarry *n* a place where stone is taken out of the ground for building, etc. **2** an animal that is being hunted.
quarter *n* **1** one of four equal parts of something. **2** a part of a town. *the*

Latin quarter of Paris. **3 quarters** a place to stay, especially for soldiers.
quarter-final *n* one of the games or matches of a contest to decide who will take part in the semi-finals.
quartet *n* a group of four singers or musicians.
quartz *n* a hard mineral found in rocks in the form of crystals and used in electronic clocks and watches.

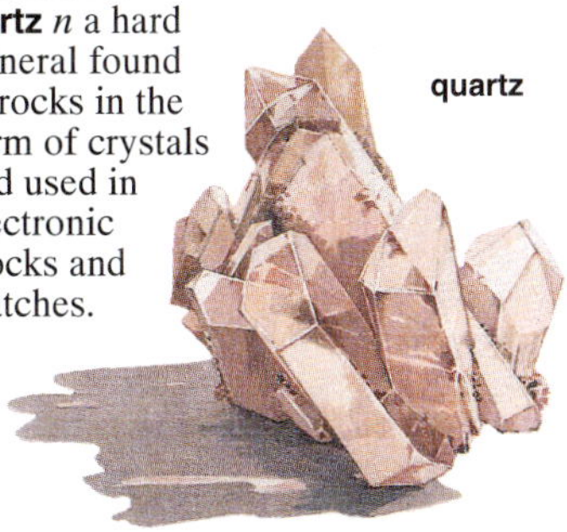

quaver[1] *v* (of a voice) to tremble.
quaver[2] *n* a note in music equal to half a crotchet in length. See **note**.
quay *(kee) n* (*pl* quays) a landing place for boats to load and unload.
queasy *adj* (queasier, queasiest) feeling slightly sick. **queasiness** *n.*
queen *n* **1** the female ruler of a country, or the wife of a king. **2** the playing-card with a picture of a queen on it. **3** the most powerful chesspiece. See **chess**.
queer *adj* strange, odd.
quench *v* **1** to drink enough to take away your thirst. **2** to put out a fire.
query[1] *n* a question.
query[2] *v* (queries, querying, queried) to express doubt about something. *I would like to query this bill.*
quest *n* a long search.
question[1] *n* something that you ask when you need an answer.
question[2] *v* **1** to ask somebody questions. **2** to doubt something. *He questioned the truth of the statement.*
question mark *n* the punctuation mark (?).
questionnaire *n* a list of questions to be answered by several people.
queue[1] *n* (*rhymes with* you*)* a line of people waiting for something.
queue[2] *v* (queues, queuing, queued) to wait in a queue.
quiche *(keesh) n* a pastry case filled with beaten egg, cheese, etc and baked.
quick *adj* **1** done or happening in a short time. **2** moving at speed. **quickness** *n.*
quicksand *n* wet sand that sucks down anybody who stands on it.
quid *n (slang)* a pound in money.
quiet *adj* **1** making little or no noise. **2** calm. *a quiet life.* **quietness** *n.*
quill *n* a large feather, especially one used as a pen.

quilt *n* a bed cover filled with feathers or other soft material.
quilted *adj* made of two layers of material with padding in between. *a quilted jacket.*
quit *v* (quits, quitting, quit *or* quitted) **1** to stop doing something, to give something up. *He has quit smoking.* **2** to leave.
quite *adv* **1** fairly, rather. *Tania can sing quite well.* **2** completely. *You are quite right.*
quiver[1] *v* to tremble.
quiver[2] *n* a long case for arrows.
quiz *n* (*pl* quizzes) a competition in which somebody is asked questions to test their knowledge.
quota *n* a fixed share of something.
quotation *n* words that somebody has spoken or written, repeated by somebody else.
quotation marks *n pl* inverted commas.
quote *v* to repeat words that were first spoken or written by somebody else.

Rr

rabbi ***(rab**-eye)* *n* (*pl* rabbis) a Jewish religious leader.
rabbit *n* a small mammal with long ears and a short tail, that lives in fields and burrows in the wild.
rabble *n* a noisy crowd of people.
rabies *n* a very serious disease caught from the bite of an infected dog or other animal, causing madness and often death. **rabid** *adj*.
raccoon *n* a furry North American mammal with a long striped tail.

raccoon

race[1] *n* **1** a group of people who have the same ancestors and the same physical characteristics, such as skin colour. **2** a competition to find out which person, animal or vehicle is the fastest. *a horse-race.*
race[2] *v* **1** to take part in a race. **2** to run or move very fast.
racial *adj* to do with race. *racial prejudice.* **racially** *adv*.
racist *adj* thinking that some races of people are superior to others, and treating people unfairly or badly because of this. **racism** *n*, **racist** *n*.
rack[1] *n* **1** a kind of frame or shelf made of bars, for holding things. *a letter-rack, a coat-rack.* **2** an instrument for torturing victims by stretching their joints.
rack[2] *v* **rack your brains** to think hard about something.
racket *n* **1** (*also* **racquet**) a bat with strings used in tennis, badminton, squash, etc. **2** a loud, unpleasant noise. **3** an illegal way of making money. *a drugs racket.*
radar *n* a way of finding where an object is by sending out radio waves that hit the object and bounce back.
radiant *adj* **1** sending out rays of heat or light. **2** showing joy and happiness. **radiance** *n*.
radiate *v* **1** to send out rays of heat or light. **2** to spread out from the centre.
radiation *n* the sending out of rays of heat or light or of a radioactive substance.
radiator *n* **1** a metal container through which hot water is pumped, for heating a room. **2** a device in a car through which water is pumped to cool the engine.
radio *n* (*pl* radios) an instrument that sends or receives electrical waves through the air and turns them into sounds that you can hear.
radioactive *adj* giving off powerful and dangerous rays. **radioactivity** *n*.
radiography *n* photography of the inside of the body using X-rays. **radiographer** *n*.
radish *n* a plant with a hot-tasting red or white root, eaten raw in salads.
radius *n* (*pl* radii) a straight line from the centre to the edge of a circle. See **circle**.
raffle *n* a way of raising money by selling numbered tickets, a few of which will win prizes. **raffle** *v*.
raft *n* **1** logs fixed together to make a flat boat. **2** an inflatable boat.
rafter *n* one of the sloping beams of wood supporting a roof.
rag *n* **1** an old or torn piece of cloth. **2 rags** old, torn clothes.
rage[1] *n* great anger.
rage[2] *v* **1** to show violent anger. **2** (of a storm, battle, etc) to be violent.
raid *n* **1** a surprise attack on a place. **2** a surprise visit by the police to search for a criminal, stolen goods, drugs, etc. **raid** *v*.
rail *n* **1** a fixed bar used as a fence or

for hanging things on. *a towel rail.* **2** the railway. **3 rails** the long metal bars that a train runs on.
railings *n pl* a fence made of rails.
railway *n* (*pl* railways) **1** a system of transport using trains that run on tracks. **2** a track that trains run on.
rain *n* drops of water falling from the sky. **rain** *v*, **rainy** *adj*.
rainbow *n* an arch of many colours in the sky, caused by sun shining through rain or mist.
rain-forest *n* a tropical forest where a lot of rain falls.
raise *v* **1** to lift something. *Raise your hand.* **2** to collect a sum of money. *We raised £150 for the appeal.* **3** to grow crops or breed animals for food. **4** to bring up children.
raisin *n* a dried grape.
rake *n* a tool like a comb on a long handle, used for making earth smooth or collecting up leaves, grass, etc. **rake** *v*.
rally *n* **1** a large meeting of people for a special purpose. *a peace rally.* **2** a meeting of cars or motorcycles for a competition or race. **3** in tennis, etc, a long series of shots before a point is scored.
ram[1] *n* a male sheep.
ram[2] *v* (rams, ramming, rammed) **1** to run into something and cause damage to it. *The lorry rammed into the front of the shop.* **2** to hit or push with great force.
Ramadan *n* the ninth month of the Islamic year when Muslims fast between sunrise and sunset.
ramble *v* **1** to walk about in the countryside. **2** to talk for a long time in a confused way.
ramp *n* a sloping path leading from one level to another.
rampage *v* to rush about angrily or violently. *The elephants rampaged through the jungle.*
rampart *n* a mound or wall built as a defence.
ramshackle *adj* falling down, in a bad state of repair.
ran *past of* run.
ranch *n* a large farm for cattle or horses, especially in North America.
random *adj* done without any plan or purpose. *a random collection of objects.*
rang *past of* ring.
range[1] *n* **1** a selection or variety. *The shop sells a wide range of goods.* **2** the distance that an object can be thrown, a sound can be heard, etc. *What is the range of this missile?* **3** a line of mountains. **4** a piece of ground with targets for shooting or archery practice.
range[2] *v* to vary between two limits. *They have five children ranging in age from two to sixteen.*
ranger *n* a person who looks after a forest or park.
rank *n* **1** a title or position that shows how important somebody is. *General is a high rank in the army.* **2** a row or line. *ranks of soldiers.*
ransack *v* to search a place in a chaotic way to try to find or steal something.
ransom *n* money paid to a kidnapper for the release of somebody.
rap *n* **1** a quick knock. *a rap on the door.* **2** a type of music in which the words of a song are spoken in a rhythmical way. **rap** *v*.
rape *v* to force somebody to have sexual intercourse against their will. **rape** *n*, **rapist** *n*.
rapid *adj* quick, fast. **rapidity** *n*.
rapids *n pl* a place in a river where the water flows very fast over rocks.
rapier *n* a light sword with a narrow, double-edged blade.
rare *adj* **1** unusual, not often seen. **2** (of meat) cooked very lightly.
rarity *n* something that is unusual and not often seen.
rascal *n* a naughty person.
rash[1] *n* a lot of spots on your skin.
rash[2] *adj* acting too quickly, without thinking first. **rashness** *n*.
rasher *n* a thin slice of bacon.
raspberry *n* a small, red soft fruit.
rat *n* a rodent with a long tail, similar to a mouse but larger.

rate[1] *n* **1** the number of times that something happens within a given period. *The annual crime rate has risen.* **2** the speed at which something happens. *She works at a fast rate.* **3** a charge or payment. **4** a quality or standard. *first-rate.*

rate[2] *v* to value or estimate. *I don't rate this book very highly.*

rather *adv* **1** fairly, quite. **2** preferably. **3** more correctly.

ratio *(**ray**-shee-oh) n* (*pl* ratios) one size or amount in relation to another. *The ratio of men to women with the disease is eight to one.*

ration *n* a fixed amount of something, especially food, that each person is allowed when there is a shortage. **ration** *v.*

rational *adj* sensible and reasonable. *There must be a rational explanation for the noises you heard in the night.* **rationally** *adv.*

rattle[1] *v* to make repeated short, sharp sounds. *The coins rattled in the tin.*

rattle[2] *n* a baby's toy that makes a rattling noise when you shake it.

rattlesnake *n* a poisonous snake with bony joints on its tail which rattle when shaken.

rattlesnake

rave[1] *v* **1** to talk wildly as if you are mad. **2** to talk very enthusiastically about something. *Everyone is raving about her latest book.*

rave[2] *n* a big party with dancing to fast electronic music.

ravenous *adj* very hungry.

ravine *n* a deep, narrow valley.

raw *adj* **1** uncooked. *raw meat.* **2** in a natural state, not processed or manufactured. *raw materials.*

ray *n* (*pl* rays) **1** a narrow line of light, heat, etc. **2** a flat, edible sea fish with a long tail.

razor *n* an instrument with a sharp blade for shaving hair from the skin.

re- *prefix* again, once more. *redo* (= do again), *revisit* (= visit again).

reach *v* **1** to arrive somewhere. **2** to stretch out your hand to touch or get hold of something. *I'm not tall enough to reach the top shelf.* **3** to be long enough or high enough to come to a certain point. *The curtains reach down to the floor.*

react *v* **1** to behave in a certain way as a result of something. *How did your mum react when you told her the news?* **2** to change chemically when mixed with another substance. *Hydrogen reacts with oxygen to form water.* **reaction** *n.*

reactor *n* an apparatus in which nuclear energy is produced.

read *v* (reading, read) to look at writing and understand it, saying it aloud or to yourself.

readily *adv* **1** willingly. **2** easily. *Fresh fruit is readily available all year round.*

ready *adv* (readier, readiest) **1** prepared. **2** willing.

real *adj* **1** actually existing, not imagined. **2** genuine, not fake.

realistic *adj* showing or seeing things as they really are. *a realistic drawing.* **realistically** *adv.*

reality *n* what is real rather than imaginary.

realize *v* to become aware of something as a fact. *I suddenly realized I was lost.* **realization** *n.*

really *adv* **1** in fact, truly. **2** very.

realm *(relm) n* a kingdom.

reap *v* to cut and collect a crop.

rear[1] *n* the back part. **rear** *adj.*

rear[2] *v* **1** to breed animals. **2** to bring up children. **3** (of an animal) to stand up on its back legs.

reason *n* the cause of or explanation for something.

reasonable *adj* **1** fair. **2** sensible. **reasonably** *adv*.

reassure *v* to take away somebody's doubts and fears. *The doctor reassured her that she would soon feel better.* **reassurance** *n*.

rebel[1] ***(reb**-ul)* *n* a person who fights against the people in power.

rebel[2] *(re-**bel**)* *v* (rebels, rebelling, rebelled) to fight against the people in authority. *She rebelled against her strict upbringing.* **rebellion** *n*, **rebellious** *adj*.

rebound *v* to bounce back.

rebuke *v* to tell somebody off. **rebuke** *n*.

recall *v* **1** to remember something. **2** to order somebody to return.

recede *v* to move back.

receipt *(re-**seet**)* *n* a piece of paper showing that money has been paid.

receive *v* to get something that has been given or sent to you.

receiver *n* **1** the part of a telephone that you speak into and hold to your ear. **2** an apparatus that receives television or radio broadcasts.

recent *adj* happening, done or made a short time ago. *a recent photo.*

reception *n* **1** a formal party. *a wedding reception.* **2** the way in which people react to something. *The film got an enthusiastic reception.* **3** the part of a hotel, hospital, etc where visitors enter and are dealt with. **4** the quality of radio or television signals. *The TV reception is very bad in this area.*

receptionist *n* a person who works in an office, hotel, etc answering the phone and dealing with visitors as they arrive.

recession *n* a time when a country's trade is doing badly and when a lot of people are unemployed.

recipe *(**res**-ip-ee)* *n* instructions on how to prepare or cook a certain dish.

recital *n* a performance of music or poetry by one person or by a small group.

recite *v* to say something aloud that you have learnt by heart.

reckless *adj* done without thinking about the dangerous things that could happen, careless. *reckless driving.* **recklessness** *n*.

reckon *v* **1** to think, to believe something. *I reckon we'll win.* **2** to calculate something.

recline *v* to lie back or lie down.

recognize *v* to know somebody or something because you have seen or heard them before. **recognition** *n*.

recollect *v* to remember something.

recommend *v* to suggest something because you think it is good or suitable. *My friend recommended this book.* **recommendation** *n*.

record[1] *(ri-**kord**)* *v* **1** to put sounds or pictures on a tape or disc so that they can be listened to or watched again. **2** to write something down so that it will be remembered.

record[2] *(**rek**-ord)* *n* **1** the best performance so far in a sport, etc. *He holds the world record for the long jump.* **2** a flat disc that makes sounds when it is turned on a record-player. **3** a written report of facts or events.

recorder *n* a musical instrument you play by blowing into one end and covering the holes with your fingers.

record-player *n* a machine for playing records.

recover *v* **1** to get better after an illness, accident or shock. **2** to get something back. **recovery** *n*.

recreation *n* the sports or hobbies that people do in their spare time.

recruit[1] *n* a person who has just joined an army, club or other group.

recruit[2] *v* to get people to join an army, club or other group. **recruitment** *n*.

rectangle *n* a four-sided shape with opposite sides equal and all its angles right angles. **rectangular** *adj*.

recuperate *v* to get better after an illness, to recover. **recuperation** *n*.

recur *v* (recurs, recurring, recurred) to happen again. *He got better, but unfortunately his illness has since recurred.* **recurrence** *n*, **recurrent** *adj*.

recycle *v* to treat things that have already been used so that they can be used again. *recycled paper.*

red *n* the colour of blood. **red** *adj.*

red herring *n* a false clue that takes people's attention away from what is really happening.

reduce *v* to make something smaller or less. **reduction** *n.*

redundant *adj* **1** without a job because you are not needed any more. *The company has made 30 people redundant.* **2** not needed. **redundancy** *n.*

reed *n* **1** a tall, stiff stalk of grass that grows in or near water. **2** the part of a wind instrument, made of cane or metal, that vibrates and makes a sound when you blow into it.

reef *n* a line of rocks near the surface of the sea.

reek *v* to smell strongly of something unpleasant.

reel[1] *n* **1** a cylinder on which thread, film, fishing lines, etc are wound. **2** a lively Scottish or Irish dance.

reel[2] *v* **1** to stagger. **2** to feel dizzy.

refectory *n* a dining hall in a school, convent or monastery.

refer *v* (refers, referring, referred) **refer to 1** to mention. *The letter refers to your behaviour at school.* **2** to look in a book for information. **3** to be connected with something. *What does this notice refer to?* **4** to pass on to somebody else. *The case was referred to a higher court of law.*

referee *n* a person who controls a sports match and makes sure that the players do not break the rules.

reference *n* **1** a mention. *There is a reference to our town in this book.* **2** a note about somebody's character or ability. *Did your last boss give you a good reference?*

reference book *n* a book, such as a dictionary or an encyclopedia, where you look for information.

referendum *n* (*pl* referenda *or* referendums) a vote by the people of a country about an important matter.

refine *v* to make something pure. *refined sugar.*

refinery *n* a place where something such as sugar or oil is refined.

reflect *v* **1** to send back light, heat or sound. *The white sand reflects the Sun's heat.* **2** to give an image of something. *She saw her face reflected in the mirror.* **reflection** *n*, **reflective** *adj.*

reflection

reflex *n* an action that is automatic, such as jerking your knee when somebody hits your kneecap.

reform *(ri-**form**)* *v* to make something better by making changes to it. **reform** *n*, **reformation** *n.*

refraction *n* the bending of a ray of light when it passes from one substance to another. **refract** *v.*

refrain[1] *v* to stop yourself from doing something. *Passengers are requested to please refrain from smoking in the station.*

refrain[2] *n* a chorus coming at the end of each verse of a song.

refresh *v* to make somebody or something look or feel stronger, cooler, less tired, etc. *I felt refreshed after my long sleep.* **refreshing** *adj.*

refreshments *n pl* food and drink.

refrigerator *n* a kind of cupboard in which food is kept very cold. **refrigerate** *v*, **refrigeration** *n.*

refuel *v* (refuels, refuelling, refuelled) to be filled again with fresh fuel.
refuge *n* a shelter from danger.
refugee *n* a person who has been forced to leave their home or country, for example because there is a war or famine.
refund *(ri-**fund**) v* to pay back money. **refund** *(**ree**-fund) n.*
refuse[1] *(ri-**fyooz**) v* to say that you will not do something. **refusal** *n.*
refuse[2] *(**ref**-yoos) n* rubbish, things that are thrown away.
regal *adj* royal.
regard *v* to consider somebody or something in a certain way. *He is regarded as one of the best novelists alive today.*
regarding *prep* concerning, to do with.
regards *n pl* good wishes. *Please send my regards to your parents.*
reggae *(**reg**-ay) n* a type of music with a strong rhythm, originally from the West Indies.
regiment *n* a large group of soldiers, commanded by a colonel.
region *(**ree**-jun) n* an area or district. **regional** *adj.*
register[1] *n* a book containing a written list or record. *a register of births, marriages and deaths.*
register[2] *v* **1** to enter a name, etc on an official list. *He is registered as disabled.* **2** to show something. *The thermometer registered 90°.* **registration** *n.*
regret *v* (regrets, regretting, regretted) to be sorry about something. **regret** *n*, **regretful** *adj*, **regretfully** *adv.*
regular *adj* **1** happening again and again, with roughly the same amount of space or time in between. *The group meets at regular intervals.* **2** usual. *What are your regular working hours?* **3** even. *His pulse is regular.* **regularity** *n.*
regulate *v* **1** to control something. *Traffic lights regulate the traffic.* **2** to adjust a piece of machinery so that it works properly.
regulation *n* a rule or instruction.
rehearse *v* to practise something before performing in front of an audience. **rehearsal** *n.*
reign *(rain) v* to rule as a king or queen. **reign** *n.*
reindeer *n* (*pl* reindeer) a large deer that lives in cold parts of the world.
reinforce *v* to make something stronger. **reinforcement** *n.*
reins *(rains) n pl* straps fastened to a bridle for guiding a horse.
reject *v* to refuse to accept something. **rejection** *n.*
rejoice *v* to feel or show joy.
relate *v* **1** to form a connection between things. **2** to tell a story.
related *adj* in the same family as somebody. *She's related to John – she's his cousin.*
relation *n* **1** a member of your family. **2** a connection between things.
relationship *n* **1** the way in which people get on together. *She has a good relationship with her parents.* **2** the way in which things or people are connected. *Is there any relationship between violence on TV and violent crime in real life?*
relative[1] *n* a member of your family.
relative[2] *adj* compared with something else. *She used to be rich but now lives in relative poverty.*
relax *v* **1** to rest and become less worried or tense. *You need to relax after a hard day's work.* **2** to become less tight or stiff. *Allow your muscles to relax.* **3** to make something less strict. *The rules were relaxed.* **relaxation** *n.*
relay[1] *(**ree**-lay) n* (*pl* relays) a race in which each member of a team goes part of the distance, starting from where the previous person finished.
relay[2] *(re-**lay**) v* to receive and pass on a message.
release *v* **1** to set a person or an animal free. *The hostages have been released.* **2** to make something available to the public. *The film was released first in the USA.* **release** *n.*

relevant *adj* to do with the subject being discussed. **relevance** *n.*
reliable *adj* able to be trusted and depended upon. **reliability** *n.*
relic *n* something that is left from a past time. *relics of an ancient civilization.*
relief *n* **1** the stopping or lessening of pain or worry. *It was a relief to find that the children were safe and well.* **2** help given to people who need it. *famine relief.*
relief map *n* a map that shows high and low areas of land.
relieve *v* to stop or lessen pain or worry. *The doctor gave her some pills to relieve the pain.*
religion *n* a belief in, or the worship of, a god or gods. **religious** *adj.*
relish[1] *v* to enjoy something very much.
relish[2] *n* a type of pickle or sauce.
reluctant *adj* not willing to do something. *Peter was reluctant to admit he was wrong.* **reluctance** *n.*
rely *v* (relies, relying, relied) to need or have trust in somebody or something. *I am relying on you to help me.* **reliability** *n*, **reliable** *adj.*
remain *v* to be left. *Very little remained of the house after the fire.*
remainder *n* the things, people, etc that remain.
remains *n pl* **1** what is left after the rest has gone or been taken away. **2** a dead body.
remark *v* to make a comment about something. **remark** *n.*
remarkable *adj* worth noticing, extraordinary. **remarkably** *adv.*
remedy *n* a cure for an illness or for something bad. **remedy** *v.*
remember *v* to keep something in your mind or bring it back into your mind.
remind *v* to make somebody remember something. **reminder** *n.*
remnant *n* a small piece or amount that is left over. *a remnant of cloth.*
remorse *n* deep regret for something bad that you have done.
remote *adj* far away, isolated.
remove *v* to take something away. **removal** *n.*
rendezvous *(**ron**-day-voo) n (pl* rendezvous) an arrangement to meet at an agreed time and place.
renew *v* **1** to begin something again. **2** to make something valid for a further period. *I need to renew my travel card.* **3** to replace something old with something new. **renewal** *n.*
renovate *v* to make something as good as new again. *The old house has been renovated.* **renovation** *n.*
renowned *adj* famous.
rent *n* money paid for using a house, shop, etc that is owned by somebody else. **rent** *v.*
rental *n* **1** money paid as rent. **2** the renting of something.
repair *v* to make something that is broken whole again, or to make something work again. **repair** *n.*
repay *v* (repays, repaying, repaid) to pay back. **repayment** *n.*
repeat *v* to say or do something again. **repeat** *n.*
repeatedly *adv* many times.
repel *v* (repels, repelling, repelled) **1** to force somebody or something to move away. *She was able to repel her attackers.* **2** to cause a feeling of disgust in somebody.
repent *v* to be very sorry about the bad things you have done. **repentance** *n*, **repentant** *adj.*
repetition *n* the repeating of something.
repetitive *adj* doing or saying the same thing over and over again.
replace *v* **1** to put something new in place of something old. *You should replace the mug you broke.* **2** to take somebody's place. **3** to put something back where it came from. **replacement** *n.*
replica *n* an exact copy of something.
reply *v* (replies, replying, replied) to answer. **reply** *n.*
report[1] *v* **1** to tell or write about something. *The speech was reported in all the newspapers.* **2** to make a complaint about somebody to a

person in authority. *The man was reported to the police for selling stolen goods.* **3** to announce that you are present and available to do something. *Report for duty at 8 a.m.*

report[2] *n* a description of what has been done. *a school report.*

reporter *n* a person who reports on the news for a newspaper, or for a radio or television programme.

represent *v* **1** to act or speak for other people. *Your MP represents you in Parliament.* **2** to stand for something. *The dots on the map represent forts.* **representation** *n.*

representative *n* **1** a person who acts or speaks for other people. *Each country has sent a representative to the conference.* **2** a travelling salesperson for a company.

reprieve *v* to pardon a criminal or postpone a punishment. **reprieve** *n.*

reprimand *v* to tell somebody off. **reprimand** *n.*

reproach *v* to blame or criticize somebody for a mistake or fault.

reproduce *v* **1** to make a copy of something. **2** to produce young. **reproduction** *n.*

reptile *n* a cold-blooded animal that lays eggs. Crocodiles, snakes and tortoises are all reptiles.

republic *n* a country that elects a president and does not have a king or queen. **republican** *adj.*

repulsive *adj* disgusting.

reputation *n* the opinion that people have of somebody or something. *This restaurant has a reputation for good service.*

request *v* to ask for something politely. **request** *n.*

require *v* **1** to need something. *Do you require any help?* **2** to order somebody to do something. *The law requires all motorcyclists to wear helmets.* **requirement** *n.*

rescue *v* to save somebody or something from danger. **rescue** *n.*

research *n* careful study of a subject to find out new information. *scientific research.* **research** *v.*

resemble *v* to be or look like somebody or something. **resemblance** *n.*

resent *v* to feel angry about something because you think it is insulting or unfair. **resentment** *n.*

reserve[1] *v* to ask for something to be kept so you can use it later.

reserve[2] *n* **1** a piece of land set aside for the protection of animals or plants. *a nature reserve.* **2** an extra player in a team who will play if another player is injured. **3** something kept for later use. *reserves of food.*

reserved *adj* shy.

reservoir *n* an artificial lake where water is stored.

residence *n* a house, especially a grand and impressive one. *the governor's residence.*

resident *n* a person who lives in a particular place.

residential *adj* consisting of houses rather than offices or shops. *a residential area of the city.*

resign *(re-zine)* *v* **1** to give up a job. **2** to accept something even though you are not happy about it. *She had resigned herself to losing the game.* **resignation** *n.*

resin *n* a sticky substance produced by certain trees, such as pines and firs.

resist *v* **1** to fight against something. **2** to stop yourself doing something that you want to do. *I couldn't resist telling her my secret.* **resistance** *n.*

resolute *adj* with your mind made up, determined.

resolution *n* a firm decision to do something.

resolve *v* **1** to make a firm decision to do something. **2** to solve a problem. **resolve** *n.*

resort[1] *n* a place where a lot of people go on holiday. *a beach resort.*

resort[2] *v* **resort to** to do or make use of something because there is no other way to get what you want. *When she became homeless, she resorted to begging on the streets.*

resources *n pl* supplies of things that a country, person, etc has and can use. *The country is rich in natural resources such as oil, coal and gas.*
respect¹ *v* **1** to have a high opinion of somebody. *I respect you for telling the truth.* **2** to treat somebody or something with consideration. *We should respect her wishes.*
respect² *n* **1** a high opinion of somebody. **2** consideration. *She shows no respect for her parents.* **3** a particular detail or part of something. *In some respects, I think the book was better than the film.*
respectable *adj* **1** behaving in a decent, correct way. **2** good enough.
respiration *n* the action of breathing.

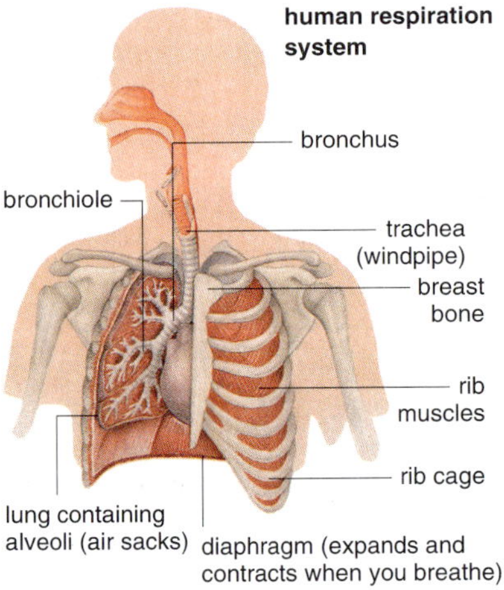

respond *v* **1** to give an answer. *I sent her a letter but she didn't respond.* **2** to do something as a reaction to something else. *Simon responded to my question by laughing.*
response *n* a reply or reaction to something.
responsible *adj* **1** having a duty to make sure that something is done. *I am responsible for checking the equipment.* **2** being the cause of something. *Who was responsible for the accident?* **3** sensible and able to be trusted. **responsibility** *n*.
rest¹ *n* a time of sleeping or relaxing after work or some other activity.
rest² *v* **1** to stop work or another activity for a while. **2** to lean against something. *Her arm rested on the table.* **3** to stay fixed. *Her gaze rested on the pile of money.* **4** to depend. *Our hopes rest on him.*
rest³ *n* **1** what is left after a part has gone. **2** all the other people or things.
restaurant *n* a place where you buy and eat meals.
restless *adj* not able to stay still or calm. **restlessness** *n*.
restore *v* **1** to repair something so that it looks as it was before. **2** to bring or give something back. *The police were called in to restore law and order.* **restoration** *n*.
restrain *v* to hold somebody back. *He had to be restrained from hitting the man.* **restraint** *n*.
restrict *v* to limit. **restriction** *n*.
result *n* **1** what happens because of something that took place before. **2** a final score or mark in a game, contest or examination.
resume *v* to begin again.
resurrection *n* coming back to life after death. **resurrect** *v*.
retail *v* to sell goods to the public. **retail** *n*, **retailer** *n*.
retain *v* to keep something. *Please retain your receipt.* **retention** *n*.
retaliate *v* to do something bad to somebody in return for something bad they have done to you. **retaliation** *n*.
retina *n* (*pl* retinas *or* retinae) the part at the back of your eye that sends a message of what is seen to the brain. See **eye**.
retire *v* **1** to stop working when you reach a certain age. *Jack retired at 65.* **2** to go away to somewhere quiet or private. *She retired to her room.* **3** to stop in the middle of a sports match, race, etc because of injury. **retirement** *n*.
retreat *v* to move back. **retreat** *n*.

retrieve *v* to get back something that was lost. **retrieval** *n*.

return *v* **1** to come or go back. **2** to give, put or send something back. **return** *n*.

return ticket *n* a ticket allowing you to travel to a place and back again.

reunion *n* a meeting of people who have not met for a long time.

rev *v* (revs, revving, revved) to make the engine of a motor vehicle run quickly, eg when starting it up.

reveal *v* to uncover or make something known.

revelation *n* the revealing of something that was secret or hidden. *an amazing revelation.*

revenge *n* harm done to somebody in return for something bad they have done.

revenue *n* the money that a government receives from taxes.

reverse[1] *v* **1** to go backwards in a vehicle. *Mum reversed the car into the garage.* **2** to change something to the complete opposite of what it was. *reverse a decision.* **reversal** *n*.

reverse[2] *n* **1** the opposite. **2** a gear in a vehicle that makes it go backwards. **3** the back of a coin, medal, painting, etc.

review *v* **1** to write a report about a book, film, etc giving your opinion of it. **2** to consider something again. *Let's review our decision.* **review** *n*.

revise *v* **1** to study again work that you have done, to prepare for an exam. **2** to make corrections or improvements to something. **revision** *n*.

revive *v* **1** to bring back to consciousness, strength or health. *He fainted, but the fresh air soon revived him.* **2** to bring back into use. *This ancient custom has recently been revived.* **revival** *n*.

revolt *v* **1** to rebel against somebody or something. *The army revolted against the king.* **2** to make somebody feel horror or disgust. **revolt** *n*.

revolting *adj* horrible and disgusting.

revolution *n* **1** a violent attempt by the people of a country to change the way they are governed. **2** a great change in ideas or ways of doing things. *the Industrial Revolution.* **3** a movement in a circle around a central point. **revolutionary** *adj*.

revolutionize *v* to change something completely. *Computers have revolutionized the way we work.*

revolve *v* to turn around in a circle. *The Earth revolves around the Sun.*

revolver *n* a small gun.

reward *n* a present that you receive in return for something good you have done. **reward** *v*.

rheumatism *(**room**-u-tiz-um) n* a disease that causes stiffness and pain in the joints.

rhinoceros *n* (*pl* rhinoceros *or* rhinoceroses) a large, thick-skinned animal with one or two horns on its nose, found in Africa and Asia.

rhombus *n* (*pl* rhombuses *or* rhombi) a flat shape with four equal sides but no right angles.

rhubarb *n* a plant with long red-skinned stalks that you can eat when cooked.

rhyme[1] *(rime) v* (of two words) to end with the same sound. *"Pale" rhymes with "mail".*

rhyme[2] *n* a short poem.

rhythm *(**rith**-um) n* a regular, repeated pattern of sounds in music, poetry, etc. **rhythmic** *adj*, **rhythmical** *adj*, **rhythmically** *adv*.

rib *n* one of the curved bones of your chest.

ribbon *n* a long, narrow piece of material used for decorating presents, tying up hair, etc.

rice *n* a type of grass grown on wet land in tropical countries, producing seeds that are cooked and eaten.

rich *adj* **1** having a lot of money or valuable possessions. **2** having a lot of something. *Oranges are rich in vitamin C.* **3** (of food) containing a lot of fat, eggs, etc. **4** very beautiful and expensive. *rich fabrics.*

riches *n pl* wealth.
rickety *adj* unsteady, likely to collapse. *a rickety old chair.*
rickshaw *n* a small, two-wheeled carriage pulled by a person, used in some Asian countries.

rickshaw

ricochet *(**rik**-o-shay) v* to hit something and bounce off it at an angle.
rid *v* (rids, ridding, rid) to free somebody from something harmful or annoying. *He finally rid the house of rats.* **get rid of** to remove or free yourself from something.
riddle *n* a puzzling question that has a funny or clever answer.
ride[1] *v* (riding, rode, ridden) to travel along on a horse or bicycle. **rider** *n.*
ride[2] *n* **1** a journey on a horse or bicycle. **2** a journey in a car or other vehicle.
ridge *n* a raised line along the top of something, eg a narrow strip of land along the top of a mountain.
ridicule *v* to make fun of something.
ridiculous *adj* silly enough to be laughed at.
rifle *n* a long gun that you hold up to your shoulder when you fire it.
rift *n* **1** a split or crack. **2** a serious disagreement between people that stops them being friends.
rig[1] *n* an oilrig.
rig[2] *v* (rigs, rigging, rigged) to fit a ship or boat with ropes, sails, etc. **rigging** *n.*
right[1] *adj* **1** of, on or towards the side of you that is towards the east when you are facing north. *I write with my right hand.* **2** correct. **3** good and fair. **right** *adv.*
right[2] *n* **1** what you are allowed to do, especially by law. *Everyone has the right to a fair trial.* **2** what is good and fair. *the difference between right and wrong.* **3** the right side or direction. *Turn to the right.*
right[3] *adv* **1** exactly. *He stood right behind me.* **2** immediately. *I'll go right now.* **3** completely, all the way. *Go right to the end of the road.*
right angle *n* an angle of 90°, like any of the angles in a square. See **triangle**.
right-handed *adj* using your right hand more easily than your left.
right-wing *adj* in politics, having conservative views.
rigid *adj* **1** completely stiff. **2** very strict. **rigidity** *n.*
rim *n* an edge of something rounded. *the rim of a cup.*
rind *n* the hard outer layer of cheese or bacon, or the peel of some fruit.
ring[1] *n* **1** a band of metal worn on your finger. **2** a circle. **3** an enclosed space for boxing or wrestling matches or circus performances. **4** a telephone call.
ring[2] *v* (ringing, rang, rung) **1** to make the sound of a bell. **2** to press or shake a bell so that it makes a sound. **3** to telephone somebody.
ringleader *n* a person who leads others into doing something wrong.
ringlet *n* a long curl of hair.
rink *n* **1** an area of ice for skating. **2** a smooth floor for rollerskating.
rinse *v* to wash in clean water.
riot *n* a noisy, violent protest by a crowd of people. **riot** *v*, **riotous** *adj.*
rip *v* (rips, ripping, ripped) to tear roughly. **rip off** *(informal)* to cheat somebody.
ripe *adj* ready to be picked or eaten. *ripe bananas.* **ripen** *v*, **ripeness** *n.*
ripple *n* a small wave on the surface of water. **ripple** *v.*
rise[1] *v* (rising, rose, risen) **1** to move upwards. **2** to increase. **3** to get up.

rise[2] *n* an increase. *price rises.*

risk *v* **1** to take a chance that something bad might happen. **2** to put something in danger, *She risked her own life to save her child.* **risk** *n,* **risky** *adj.*

ritual *n* a set of actions that are always done in the same way in a particular situation, for example as part of a religious ceremony.

rival *n* a person that you are competing against. **rival** *v*, **rivalry** *n.*

river *n* a large stream of water that flows into a lake or into the sea.

road *n* a wide path with a hard, level surface for vehicles to travel on.

roadworks *n pl* repairs to a road.

roam *v* to wander about.

roar *v* to make a loud, deep sound like the noise a lion makes. **roar** *n.*

roast *v* to cook food in a hot oven.

rob *v* (robs, robbing, robbed) to steal something from a person or place. **robber** *n*, **robbery** *n.*

robe *n* a long, loose piece of clothing.

robin *n* a small bird with a red breast.

robot *n* a machine that can perform some of the actions of a human being. **robotic** *adj.*

robust *adj* strong and healthy.

rock[1] *n* **1** the very hard material that forms part of the surface of the Earth. **2** a large stone. **3** a hard sweet in the shape of a stick. **4** a type of music with a heavy beat and a simple tune.

rock[2] *v* to sway gently backwards and forwards or from side to side.

rocket *n* **1** a tube containing explosive material used for launching missiles and spacecraft. **2** a firework that shoots into the air and explodes.

rod *n* a long, thin stick or bar.

rode *past of* ride.

rodent *n* a mammal with large front teeth for gnawing, for example a rat, beaver or squirrel.

rodeo *n* (*pl* rodeos) a contest in which cowboys show their skill at catching cattle and riding horses.

rogue *(rohg)* *n* a dishonest or mischievous person.

rôle *n* **1** the part played by an actor. **2** the job done by somebody.

roll[1] *v* **1** to move along by turning over and over like a ball or a wheel. *The coin rolled under the table.* **2** to turn something over and over to make a tube or ball. *We rolled up the carpet.* **3** to flatten something by moving a heavy object over it.

roll[2] *n* **1** a tube made by turning something over and over on itself many times. *a roll of film.* **2** a small, round piece of bread made for one person. **3** a long, deep sound. *a roll of thunder.*

rollerblades *n pl* rollerskates with the wheels in a single line.

rollercoaster *n* a fairground ride consisting of a raised railway with steep slopes and sharp curves, which you ride on in small, open carriages.

rollerskates *n pl* boots with wheels for skating on smooth, hard surfaces. **rollerskate** *v*, **rollerskating** *n.*

rolling pin *n* a long tube used to roll out dough or pastry to flatten it.

ROM (*short for* read-only memory) a computer memory storing information that you can read but not change.

Roman Catholic *n* a member of the part of the Christian Church that has the Pope as its leader. **Roman Catholic** *adj.*

romance *n* **1** a relationship between people who are in love. **2** a story about love. **3** a feeling of excitement and adventure. **romantic** *adj.*

Roman numerals *n pl* the letters that are sometimes written to represent numbers, first used in ancient Rome.

Roman numerals

I	II	III	IV	V	X
1	2	3	4	5	10
L	LX	XC	C	D	M
50	60	90	100	500	1,000

roof *n* the covering on top of a building, car, etc.
rook *n* **1** a large, black bird similar to a crow. **2** a chesspiece. See **chess**.
room *n* **1** a part of a building with its own walls, floor and ceiling. **2** space.
roost *n* a perch where a bird settles to sleep. **roost** *v*.
root *n* **1** the part of a plant that grows under the ground. **2** the part of a hair, tooth, etc that attaches it to the rest of the body. **3** the cause of something. *I think I've discovered the root of the problem.*
rope *n* thick, strong cord, made by twisting strands together.
rose[1] *past of* rise.
rose[2] *n* **1** a pleasant-smelling garden flower that grows on a bush with thorns. **2** a deep-pink colour.

rose

rosemary *n* a strong-smelling evergreen shrub used in cooking.
Rosh Hashanah *n* the Jewish New Year.
rosy *adj* (rosier, rosiest) **1** pink. *rosy cheeks.* **2** bright, hopeful. *The future looks rosy.*
rot *v* (rots, rotting, rotted) to go bad, to decay. **rot** *n*.
rota *n* (*pl* rotas) a list showing duties to be done or the people to do them in order.
rotary *adj* turning round like a wheel.
rotate *v* **1** to turn like a wheel. **2** to go through a repeating series of changes. **rotation** *n*.
rotor *n* a blade that turns round fast on the top of a helicopter. See **helicopter**.
rotten *adj* **1** decayed. *rotten wood.* **2** having gone bad. *rotten eggs.* **3** very bad, unpleasant. *rotten luck.*
rough *(rhymes with* cuff*) adj* **1** not smooth or even. *rough ground.* **2** not gentle or calm. *rough seas.* **3** not meant to be exact. *a rough guess.*
round[1] *adj* shaped like a circle or a ball.
round[2] *adv, prep* **1** on all sides. *There's a wall round the garden.* **2** in a circle about something. *The Earth travels round the Sun.* **3** from one person or place to another. *Pass these sweets round the room.* **4** in a different direction. *She turned round.* **5** to somebody's house. *I'm going round to Tim's.*
round[3] *n* **1** one stage of a contest. *Our team was knocked out in the first round.* **2** a series of calls or deliveries. *a doctor's round.* **3** a burst of cheering, shooting, etc. *a round of applause.* **4** a song for two or more singers in which each singer begins at a different time. **5** a number of drinks bought by one person for all the others in the group.
roundabout *n* **1** a moving circular platform with toy horses, cars, etc for children to ride on at a fair. **2** a place where a number of roads meet and the traffic goes round in a circle.
rounded *adj* curved.
rounders *n* a game for two teams played with a bat and ball.
rouse *v* **1** to wake somebody up. **2** to stir up or excite something. *Sue's interest was roused by what he said.*
route *(root) n* the road or path that you follow to get somewhere.
routine *(roo-**teen**) n* a regular, fixed way of doing things. *a daily routine.*
row[1] *(rhymes with* go*) n* a line. *a row of houses.*
row[2] *(rhymes with* go*) v* to use oars to make a boat move through water.
row[3] *(rhymes with* cow*) n* **1** a noisy quarrel. **2** an unpleasant loud noise.
rowdy *adj* (rowdier, rowdiest) noisy and rough.
royal *adj* to do with a king or queen. **royalty** *n*.
rub *v* (rubs, rubbing, rubbed) to move one thing backwards and forwards against another while pressing. *The cat rubbed its head against my leg.* **rub out** to remove pencil or chalk marks with a rubber.

rubber *n* **1** a strong, elastic, waterproof material made from the sap of a tropical plant or from chemicals, used for making tyres, etc. **2** a piece of rubber or some other substance used for removing pencil marks. **rubbery** *adj*.

rubbish *n* **1** things that you throw away because you do not want them any more. **2** nonsense.

rubble *n* broken bricks and stones.

ruby *n* a red precious stone.

rucksack *n* a bag that you carry on your back.

rudder *n* a flat, upright part at the back of a boat or aircraft, used for steering.

rude *adj* bad-mannered, not polite. **rudeness** *n*.

ruffle *v* to make hair, feathers, etc untidy. *The wind ruffled her hair.*

rug *n* **1** a piece of thick, woollen material that covers part of a floor. **2** a blanket.

rugby, rugger *n* a game played with an oval ball which can be kicked, carried or passed from hand to hand.

rugged *(rug-id) adj* **1** rough and rocky. *rugged mountain scenery.* **2** strong and tough. *the film's rugged hero.*

ruin[1] *v* **1** to spoil something completely. **2** to make somebody lose all their money.

ruin[2] *n* **1** the complete loss of all your money. *The company is facing ruin.* **2 ruins** what is left of a building after it has been destroyed.

rule[1] *n* **1** a statement of what you must or must not do. *It is against the school rules to smoke.* **2** government. *This city was once under foreign rule.* **as a rule** usually. *We play football on Sundays, as a rule.*

rule[2] *v* **1** to govern a country. *William the Conqueror ruled England after 1066.* **2** to decide something. *The judge ruled that the new evidence should be heard.*

ruler *n* **1** a long, straight piece of plastic, wood or metal used for drawing lines or measuring. **2** a person who rules a country.

rum *n* an alcoholic drink made from sugar-cane.

rumble *v* to make a deep sound like thunder. **rumble** *n*.

rummage *v* to turn things over while searching for something.

rumour *n* a story that is passed around, but that may not be true.

rump *n* the back part of an animal.

run[1] *v* (runs, running, ran, run) **1** to move fast on your legs. **2** to travel. *This bus doesn't run on Sundays.* **3** to organize or manage something. *Jane runs the local football team.* **4** to flow. *Tears ran down his cheeks.* **5** to work or function. *Our car runs on diesel.* **6** to continue, to go on. *The film runs for an hour and a half.* **run out of** to have no more of something. *We've run out of milk.* **run over** to knock down or drive over a person or an animal in a vehicle.

run[2] *n* **1** an act of running. **2** a point scored in cricket, baseball, etc. **3** an enclosed area in which animals or birds are kept. *a chicken-run.*

rung[1] *past of* ring.

rung[2] *n* a step of a ladder.

runner *n* a person who runs.

runner-up *n* (*pl* runners-up) the person or team that comes second in a race or competition.

runny *adj* (runnier, runniest) liquid or watery.

runway *n* (*pl* runways) a strip of land where an aircraft takes off and lands.

rural *adj* to do with the countryside.

rush[1] *v* to move quickly, to hurry. **rush** *n*.

rush[2] *n* a tall grass that grows near water.

rust *n* the reddish-brown coating that forms on iron and some other metals when they get wet. **rust** *v*, **rusty** *adj*.

rustle *v* to make a soft, whispering or crackling sound, like the sound of dry leaves. **2** to steal cattle or horses. **rustle** *n*.

rut *n* **1** a deep track made by a wheel. **2** a fixed and boring way of life.

ruthless *adj* cruel, without pity.

Ss

Sabbath *n* the day of the week set aside for religious worship and rest.
sabotage *(sab-o-tahj) v* to damage something on purpose. **sabotage** *n.*
sabre *(say-ber) n* a sword with a curved blade.
sachet *(sash-ay) n* a small, sealed packet containing a powder or liquid. *a sachet of shampoo.*
sack[1] *n* a large bag made of strong cloth, paper or plastic. **get the sack** to be dismissed from a job.
sack[2] *v* to dismiss somebody from a job.
sacred *(say-krid) adj* holy.
sacrifice *v* **1** to offer something precious to a god, especially an animal or person that has been killed for this purpose. **2** to give something up for the benefit of another person or to gain something more important. *He sacrificed his job for the sake of his son.* **sacrifice** *n*, **sacrificial** *adj.*
sad *adj* (sadder, saddest) unhappy. **sadden** *v*, **sadness** *n.*
saddle[1] *n* a seat for the rider of a horse or bicycle.
saddle[2] *v* to put a saddle on a horse.
SAE *short for* stamped addressed envelope.
safari *(sa-far-ee) n* an expedition for watching or hunting wild animals.
safe[1] *adj* **1** not in danger. **2** not dangerous. **safety** *n.*
safe[2] *n* a strong box or chest where money and other valuable things can be locked away.
safeguard *v* to protect something.
safety-pin *n* a curved pin with a part that covers its point when it is closed.
sag *v* (sags, sagging, sagged) to droop or hang down. *The bed sags in the middle.*
sage *n* a herb used in cooking.
said *past of* say.
sail[1] *n* **1** a sheet of strong cloth against which the wind blows to drive a ship or boat through the water. **2** the arm of a windmill.
sail[2] *v* **1** to travel in a ship or boat. **2** (of a ship) to start a voyage. **sailing** *n.*
sailor *n* a member of a ship's crew.
saint *n* **1** a title given by the Christian Church to a very good or holy person after their death. **2** a very good, kind person. **saintly** *adj.*
sake *n* **for the sake of 1** in order to help somebody or something. *They stayed together for the sake of their children.* **2** in order to get something. *For the sake of peace, he agreed.*
salad *n* a mixture of cold, raw vegetables, eg tomatoes, lettuce, etc.
salamander *n* a small amphibian similar to a lizard.
salami *n* a type of strong-tasting sausage, eaten cold.
salary *n* a regular payment, usually made once a month, to somebody for the work they do.
sale *n* **1** the selling of something. **2** a time when a shop sells goods more cheaply than usual.
saliva *(sa-lie-va) n* the liquid in your mouth.
salmon *(sam-un) n* (*pl* salmon) a large, edible fish with pink flesh.
salt *n* **1** a white substance found under the ground and in sea water, used for flavouring food. **2** any chemical compound formed from a metal and an acid. **salty** *adj.*
salute *v* to raise your hand to your forehead as a sign of respect, as soldiers do. **salute** *n.*
salvage *v* to save something from loss or destruction. *He salvaged some of his possessions from the fire.*
salvation *n* the saving of somebody or something.
same *adj* exactly alike, not different.
sample[1] *n* a part taken from something to show what the rest of it is like. *a blood sample.*
sample[2] *v* to try something to see if you like it.

samurai *(sam-a-rye) n* (*pl* samurai) in earlier times, a Japanese warrior.

sanction¹ *v* to allow or authorize something.

sanction² *n* **1** permission or approval. **2 sanctions** measures taken by a country to prevent trade with another country that is not obeying international law.

sanctuary *n* **1** a sacred place. **2** a place where somebody is safe from people who want to attack or arrest them. **3** place where wild birds or animals are protected.

sand *n* tiny grains of crushed rock, shells, etc found on beaches and in deserts. **sandy** *adj*.

sandal *n* a type of open shoe with straps to attach it to your foot.

sandwich *n* two slices of bread with food in between.

sane *adj* having a healthy mind. **sanity** *n*.

sang *past of* sing.

sanitary towel *n* a soft, cotton pad worn by women to soak up blood during a period.

sanitation *n* systems for protecting people's health, such as drainage and sewage disposal.

sank *past of* sink.

sap¹ *n* the juice in the stems of plants.

sap² *v* (saps, sapping, sapped) to weaken something gradually. *The long walk sapped our strength.*

sapling *n* a young tree.

sapphire *n* a blue precious stone.

sarcasm *n* remarks that mean the opposite of what they seem to mean, often used to criticize somebody or hurt their feelings. **sarcastic** *adj*, **sarcastically** *adv*.

sardine *n* a small edible fish like a herring, often sold in tins.

sari *(sah-ree) n* a long piece of material draped around the body, traditionally worn by Indian women.

sash *n* a wide band of material worn around the waist or over one shoulder.

sat *past of* sit.

satchel *n* a bag for carrying school books, hung from a strap over your shoulder.

satellite *n* **1** a moon or other natural object orbiting a planet. **2** a manufactured object fired into space to orbit the Earth.

satellite dish *n* a dish-shaped object that receives television broadcasts sent by satellite (**satellite television**).

satire *n* a form of comedy that makes fun of people, groups, etc to show how stupid or bad they are. **satirical** *adj*.

satisfactory *adj* good enough. **satisfactorily** *adv*.

satisfy *v* (satisfies, satisfying, satisfied) to give somebody what they need or want so that they are pleased. **satisfaction** *n*.

saturate *v* to make something so wet that no more can be absorbed. **saturation** *n*.

Saturday *n* the seventh day of the week.

sauce *n* a thick liquid that is served with food.

saucepan *n* a deep metal cooking pot with a handle and sometimes a lid.

saucer *n* a small, curved plate on which a cup stands.

sauna *(saw-na) n* a room filled with steam, where you sit and sweat.

saunter *v* to stroll.

sausage *n* a food made of minced meat stuffed into a tube of edible skin.

savage[1] *adj* **1** wild and fierce. *a savage beast.* **2** extremely violent. *a savage attack.*
savage[2] *v* to attack somebody violently. *The child was savaged by a large dog.*
savanna, savannah *n* a grassy plain with few trees, especially in Africa.
save *v* **1** to rescue from danger. **2** to keep money, etc to use in the future. **3** to not waste something. **4** in football, to stop the opposing team from scoring a goal. **save** *n.*
savings *n pl* money that you have saved.
savoury *adj* salty and spicy, not sweet.
saw[1] *past of* see.
saw[2] *n* a tool with sharp teeth for cutting wood.
saw[3] *v* (sawing, sawed, sawn) to cut something with a saw.
sawdust *n* dust that you get when you saw wood.
saxophone *n* a curved metal musical instrument, played by blowing, often used to play jazz. **saxophonist** *n.*
say *v* (saying, said) **1** to speak words. **2** to give information. *The clock says it's two thirty.*
saying *n* a well-known phrase or proverb.
scab *n* a hard, dry covering that forms over a wound as it heals.
scaffolding *n* a structure of poles and planks used when a building is being put up or repaired.
scald *v* to burn yourself with hot liquid or steam.
scale[1] *n* **1** one of the thin, hard pieces of skin that cover the bodies of fish and reptiles. **2** a series of numbers or values for measuring something. *The company salary scale starts at £10,000 and goes up to £35,000.* **3** a group of musical notes going up or down in order. **4** the measurements on a map compared with the real size of the area shown.
scale[2] *v* to climb up something. *He quickly scaled the wall.*
scalene *n* a triangle with three sides of different lengths. See **triangle**.
scales *n pl* an instrument for weighing people or things.
scalp *n* the skin and hair on your head.
scalpel *n* a small surgical knife.
scamper *v* to run about playfully.
scan *v* (scans, scanning, scanned) **1** to examine something carefully. *We scanned the horizon for any sign of a ship.* **2** to look at something quickly but not in detail. *He scanned the newspaper for news of the accident.* **3** to pass a beam of light, X-rays, etc over something in order to examine it. **scan** *n,* **scanner** *n.*
scandal *n* something that a lot of people think is very shocking or disgraceful. **scandalous** *adj.*
scapegoat *n* a person who gets all the blame for the mistakes of others.
scar *n* the mark left on skin by a wound after it has healed. **scar** *v.*
scarce *adj* in short supply, not enough. *Water is scarce because of the drought.* **scarcity** *n.*
scarcely *adv* only just, barely.
scare *v* to frighten. **scare** *n,* **scary** *adj.*
scarecrow *n* a figure of a person, dressed in old clothes, used to frighten birds away from crops.
scarf *n* (*pl* scarves *or* scarfs) a strip or square of material that you wear around your neck or head.
scarlet *n* bright red. **scarlet** *adj.*
scatter *v* **1** to throw something so that it is spread over a wide area. *Sam scattered crumbs on the bird table.* **2** to go off in different directions.
scavenge *v* to search among rubbish, collecting food or other things for your own use. **scavenger** *n.*
scene *(seen) n* **1** the place where an event happens. *the scene of the crime.* **2** one part of a play or film. **3** a view or painting. *She paints scenes of life in the country.* **4** a public show of anger. *Don't make a scene!*
scenery *(**seen**-er-ree) n* **1** the natural features of a place, such as hills, fields and trees. **2** the painted background of a theatre stage.
scenic *adj* surrounded by beautiful scenery.

scent *(sent) n* **1** a pleasant smell. **2** the trail of a smell, used to track an animal, etc. *The dog picked up the rabbit's scent.* **3** a pleasant-smelling liquid that you put on your skin.

sceptic *(**skep**-tik) n* a person who doubts the truth of what they are told. **sceptical** *adj.*

schedule *(**shed**-yool) n* the time set for doing something.

scheme[1] *(skeem) n* a plan.

scheme[2] *v* to plan something secretly, to plot.

scholar *n* **1** a person who has studied a subject in depth. **2** a person who has won a scholarship. **scholarly** *adj.*

scholarship *n* money given to a student who has done well, to enable them to go to a school or college.

school *n* **1** a place where children go to be taught. **2** a place where you can be taught a particular skill. *a riding school.* **3** a group of fish or other sea creatures swimming together.

schooner *n* a fast sailing ship.

science *n* knowledge gained by studying, observing and experimenting. Biology, chemistry and physics are all branches of science. **scientific** *adj,* **scientifically** *adv.*

science fiction *n* stories about future life on Earth or space travel.

scientist *n* a person who studies science.

scissors *n pl* a cutting tool with two blades joined together.

scoff *v* **1** to mock something. *John scoffed at my idea.* **2** to eat a lot of food quickly.

scold *v* to tell somebody off.

scone *(skon) n* a flat, round cake, usually eaten with butter.

scoop[1] *n* **1** a tool like a large spoon, used for serving food. **2** an important news story that one newspaper reports before its rivals.

scoop[2] *v* to lift something with a scoop or with your hands. *I scooped the rice out of the bag.*

scooter *n* **1** a child's toy made of a board with two wheels and a handlebar, that is moved along by pushing one foot against the ground. **2** a small motorcycle.

scope *n* **1** the opportunity or room to do something. *There is plenty of scope for improvement in your work.* **2** a range, how far something extends. *Foreign words are beyond the scope of this dictionary.*

scorch *v* to burn something slightly.

score[1] *n* **1** the number of points or goals gained in a game. **2** *(old-fashioned)* twenty. **3** a written piece of music. **4 scores** a lot.

score[2] *v* **1** to gain points or goals in a game. **2** to make a cut or scratch on a surface.

scorn *n* a very low opinion of somebody or something, contempt. *She dismissed my suggestion with scorn.* **scorn** *v*, **scornful** *adj*, **scornfully** *adv.*

scorpion *n* a creature of the spider family, with a poisonous sting in its curved tail.

scorpion

scour *v* **1** to clean something by rubbing it hard. **2** to search a place thoroughly for something.

scout *n* **1** a person who is sent ahead to find out about the enemy. **2 Scout** a member of the Scout Association.

scowl *n* to give an angry look. **scowl** *n.*

scramble *v* **1** to climb or crawl up something quickly. *We scrambled to the top of the hill.* **2** to struggle to get hold of something. *They all scrambled for the ball.* **3** to jumble up a message.

scrambled eggs *n pl* eggs mixed up with milk and and cooked in butter.

scrap[1] *n* **1** a small piece of something. **2** old cars or other metal objects that have been thrown away. **3** *(informal)* a fight.

scrap[2] *v* (scraps, scrapping, scrapped) to get rid of something.
scrapbook *n* a blank book where you stick pictures, etc.
scrape *v* **1** to rub against something sharp or rough. *Dad scraped his car on the gate-post.* **2** to clean or peel by rubbing with something sharp. *We scraped the paint off the door.* **scrape through** to only just manage to succeed. *I scraped through the exam.*
scratch[1] *v* **1** to mark or hurt by moving something sharp across a surface. **2** to rub your skin with your fingernails to stop it itching.
scratch[2] *n* a mark made by scratching. **come up to scratch** to be good enough. **start from scratch** to start from the very beginning.
scrawl *v* to write or draw untidily or quickly. **scrawl** *n.*
scream *v* to shout or cry out in a high-pitched voice. **scream** *n.*
screech *v* to make a harsh, high-pitched sound. **screech** *n.*
screen[1] *n* **1** a flat, covered framework used especially to hide or protect something. *She undressed behind a screen.* **2** a flat, white surface on which films are shown. **3** the part of a television or computer on which pictures or data appear.
screen[2] *v* **1** to protect or shelter something with a screen. **2** to test somebody to find out if they have a disease. **3** to show a film on a screen.
screw[1] *n* a nail with a spiral groove, called the thread, which is driven into something by a twisting action.
screw[2] *v* **1** to fasten something with a screw. **2** to fix a lid, etc in place with a twisting action. **screw up** to twist paper or cloth into a tight ball.
screwdriver *n* a tool for driving screws into surfaces.
scribble *v* to make untidy or meaningless marks with a pen, pencil, etc. **scribble** *n.*
script *n* **1** the written version of a play, film or broadcast. **2** a system of writing, an alphabet.
scripture *n* religious writing.

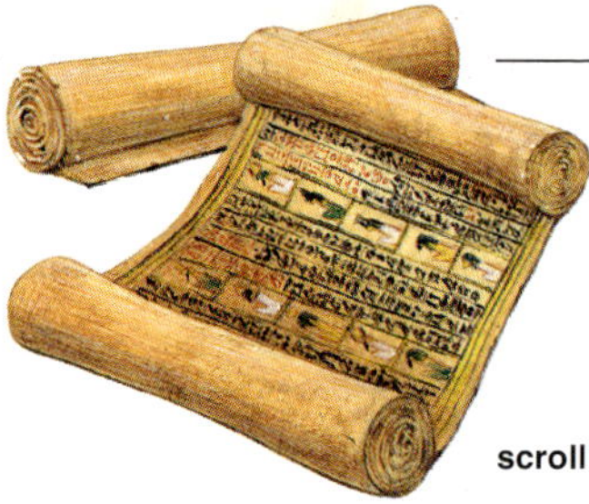
scroll

scroll[1] *n* a roll of paper with writing or pictures on it.
scroll[2] *v* to move text on a computer screen up or down to see different parts of it.
scrounge *v (informal)* to get what you want by begging it from somebody.
scrub[1] *v* (scrubs, scrubbing, scrubbed) to clean something by rubbing it hard, especially with a wet brush.
scrub[2] *n* countryside covered with low bushes.
scruff *n* the back of the neck.
scruffy *adj* (scruffier, scruffiest) untidy. **scruffily** *adv.*
scrum *n* in rugby, a struggle for the ball by a group of players from both sides bunched together.
scuba diving *n* diving using special breathing apparatus.
scuffle *n* a small fight. **scuffle** *v.*
sculptor *n* a person who makes statues or carvings.
sculpture *n* **1** the art of modelling or carving figures or shapes. **2** a figure or shape carved or modelled out of wood, stone, clay, etc. **sculpt** *v.*
scum *n* dirty foam on the surface of a liquid.
scurry *v* (scurries, scurrying, scurried) to run with short, quick steps. *The mouse scurried into its hole.*
scythe *(sythe) n* a large tool with a curved blade for cutting grass or corn.
sea *n* a large area of salt water.
sea anemone *n* a small, plant-like sea creature found on rocks and seaweed.
seagull *n* a large grey or white sea bird.
sea-horse *n* a small fish with a head shaped like a horse's head.
seal[1] *n* a furry sea animal living partly on land.

seal[2] *n* **1** a piece of wax with a design stamped into it, attached to a document to show that it is legal. **2** something that joins tightly or closes up completely. *There is a rubber seal around the lid of the jar.*
seal[3] *v* to close something completely.
sea-lion *n* a large type of seal.
seam *n* the line where two pieces of material are sewn together.
search *v* to look carefully in order to find something. **search** *n.*
seashell *n* the hard covering of a sea creature.
seashore *n* the beach.
seaside *n* a place beside the sea.
season[1] *n* **1** one of the four divisions of the year. *The four seasons are spring, summer, autumn and winter.* **2** the usual time when something takes place. *the mating season.* **seasonal** *adj.*
season[2] *v* to add salt, pepper, herbs or spices to food. **seasoning** *n.*
season ticket *n* a ticket that can be used as many times as you like for a certain period of time.
seat[1] *n* something that you can sit on.
seat[2] *v* **1** to give somebody a seat. **2** to have seats for a certain number of people. *This table seats eight.*
seat-belt *n* a belt fixed to a seat in a car to prevent the passenger being thrown out in an accident.
sea urchin *n* a small sea creature with spines on its shell.
seaweed *n* a plant that grows in the sea.
secluded *adj* quiet and private. *a secluded cottage on the cliff-top.* **seclusion** *n.*

sea urchin

second[1] *adj, adv* next after the first. **second** *n,* **secondly** *adv.*
second[2] *n* one sixtieth of a minute.
second[3] *v* to support somebody's idea or proposal at a meeting.
secondary *adj* **1** coming after and at a higher level than primary. *secondary school.* **2** less important.
second-hand *adj* already used by somebody else, not new.
secret[1] *(see-krit) adj* not known by many people. **secrecy** *n.*
secret[2] *n* a piece of information that is, or must be, kept hidden.
secret agent *n* a spy.
secretary *n* **1** a person whose job is to type letters, keep records and make business arrangements for other people. **2** the head of a government department. *the Education Secretary.*
secrete *(si-**kreet**) v* to produce a liquid. *Your skin secretes sweat when you feel hot.* **secretion** *n.*
secretive *adj* liking to keep things secret.
sect *n* a group of people with strong, especially religious, beliefs, that have separated from a larger group.
section *n* a part of something.
secure[1] *adj* **1** safe, free from danger. **2** firmly fastened. **security** *n.*
secure[2] *v* **1** to make something safe. **2** to fasten something.
seduce *v* to try to persuade or tempt somebody to do something, especially to have sexual intercourse. **seduction** *n,* **seductive** *adj.*
see *v* (seeing, saw, seen) **1** to notice or look at something with your eyes. **2** to understand. *I see what you mean.* **3** to find out. *I'll see what's going on.* **4** to make sure. *See that he eats all his dinner.* **see through** not to be deceived by a trick, lie, etc. **see to** to deal with something.
seed *n* the part of a plant or tree from which a new plant may grow.
seedling *n* a young plant that has just begun to grow from a seed.
seek *v* (seeking, sought) to try to find something.
seem *v* to appear to be. *She seems nice.*
seep *v* to flow slowly. *Blood seeped through his bandage.*
seesaw *n* a plank balanced on a central support, so that when a person sits on either end, one end goes up as the other goes down.
seethe *v* **1** (of a liquid) to boil or bubble. **2** to be very angry.

segment *n* a part of something. *Divide the orange into segments.*
segregate *v* to keep one group of people away from the others. **segregation** *n.*
seize *(seeze)* *v* to take something suddenly or by force. **seize up** to become stuck. **seizure** *n.*
seldom *adv* not often, rarely.
select *v* to choose from a number of things. **selection** *n.*
selective *adj* choosing carefully.
self *n* (*pl* selves) your own personality and nature.
self-confident *adj* believing in your own abilities. **self-confidence** *n.*
self-conscious *adj* embarrassed or worried about what other people think of you.
self-defence *n* protecting yourself against attack.
selfish *adj* caring only about yourself, rather than about other people. **selfishness** *n.*
self-service *adj* where customers serve themselves. *a self-service restaurant.*
self-sufficient *adj* needing no help or support from anybody else.
sell *v* (selling, sold) to give something in exchange for money. **sell out** to sell all of something.
selves *plural of* self.
semaphore *n* a way of signalling using your arms or flags to form different positions for each letter.
semen *(see-men)* *n* the liquid that carries sperm.
semi- *prefix* half. *semicircle, semi-detached.*
semibreve *n* in music, a whole note equal to four crotchets in length. See **note**.
semicircle *n* half of a circle.
semicolon *n* the punctuation mark (;).
semi-detached *adj* (of a house) joined to another house on one side only.
semi-final *n* one of the games or matches of a contest to decide who will take part in the final.
send *v* (sending, sent) to make somebody or something go somewhere. *Send me a postcard.* **send for** to ask somebody to come. *We had to send for the doctor.*
senile *adj* having the weaknesses and diseases of old age. **senility** *n.*
senior *adj* **1** older. **2** higher in rank. **seniority** *n.*
sensation *n* **1** a feeling. *I've got a tingling sensation in my toes.* **2** a state of great excitement. *The news caused a sensation.*
sensational *adj* causing great excitement or interest.
sense[1] *n* **1** one of the ways that your body has of telling you what is going on around you. The senses are sight, hearing, touch, smell and taste. **2** meaning. *The word "bat" has more than one sense.* **3** the ability to feel or understand something. *She's got no sense of direction.* **4** the ability to think carefully about something and do the right thing. *I'm glad you had the sense to call a doctor.*
sense[2] *v* to feel something. *He sensed that she was angry with him.*
senseless *adj* **1** stupid and pointless. *a senseless act.* **2** unconscious.
sensible *adj* **1** able to behave in an intelligent way and not do stupid things. **2** practical. *sensible shoes.* **sensibly** *adv.*
sensitive *adj* **1** easily affected by something, or easily damaged. *sensitive skin.* **2** reacting to something. *Photographic film is sensitive to light.* **3** easily feeling hurt or offended. **sensitivity** *n.*
sensor *n* a device that detects and measures light, heat, pressure, etc.
sent *past of* send.
sentence[1] *n* **1** a group of words which together make a complete statement. **2** a punishment given to a criminal by a law court.
sentence[2] *v* to announce in a law court the punishment that a criminal will receive.
sentimental *adj* **1** to do with the emotions. *This ring has sentimental value – it used to belong to my grandmother.* **2** showing or causing

too much emotion. *I didn't like the film – I thought it was sentimental.* **sentimentality** *n*, **sentimentally** *adv*.

sentry *n* a soldier who stands outside a building in order to guard it.

separate[1] *(**sep**-er-ut) adj* divided, not joined.

separate[2] *(**sep**-er-ate) v* **1** to set or keep apart. *Separate the clean clothes from the dirty ones.* **2** to go in different directions. *We walked along together and separated at the crossroads.* **3** to start living apart by choice. *His parents have separated.* **separation** *n*.

September *n* the ninth month of the year.

septic *adj* (of a wound) infected with germs.

sequel *n* a story that is a continuation of an earlier story.

sequence *n* a series of things coming after one another in a particular order.

serene *adj* calm, peaceful. **serenity** *n*.

serf *n* a medieval slave who was bought and sold with the land on which he or she worked. **serfdom** *n*.

sergeant *(**sar**-junt) n* an officer in the armed forces or in the police force.

serial *n* a story told in parts instead of all at once. *a television serial.*

serial number *n* a number that identifies one in a series of things that were produced.

series *n* (*pl* series) **1** a number of similar things coming one after the other. *a series of accidents.* **2** a set of television or radio programmes.

serious *adj* **1** solemn and thoughtful. **2** not laughing or joking. **3** important. **4** very bad or worrying.

sermon *n* a serious talk given during a religious service.

serpent *n* a snake.

serrated *adj* having notches or teeth along one edge, like a saw.

servant *n* a person who works in somebody else's home, doing cooking, cleaning, etc.

serve *v* **1** to work for somebody. **2** to bring food to somebody at the table. **3** to help a customer in a shop. **4** to be able to be used as something. *The cave served as a shelter.* **5** in tennis and other games, to throw up the ball and hit it with the racket to start play.

service *n* **1** the serving of customers in a restaurant, shop, etc. **2** help, or work that you do for somebody. **3** a business or organization that provides something for the public. *the ambulance service.* **4** a religious ceremony. **5** a check of a car, machine, etc to make sure that it is working properly. **6 services** the armed forces.

serviette *n* a piece of cloth or paper for wiping your lips and hands at meals.

session *n* **1** a time spent doing a particular activity. *an aerobics session.* **2** a meeting of a court, council, etc.

set[1] *n* **1** a group of things that belong together. *a set of tools.* **2** the scenery for a play or film. **3** a group of six or more games that form part of a match in tennis.

set[2] *v* (sets, setting, set) **1** to put. *He set the tray down on the table.* **2** to give somebody a task to do. *Our teacher has set us some questions for homework.* **3** to become firm and solid. *Has the jelly set yet?* **4** to adjust. *I'll set my alarm for six thirty.* **5** to arrange or fix. *Will you set the table for lunch, please?* **6** (of the Sun) to go down below the horizon. **set off, set out** to start on a journey.

set-square *n* a flat, triangular drawing instrument with one right angle.

settee *n* a sofa.

setting *n* a background. *The castle is the perfect setting for a ghost story.*

settle *v* **1** to go to live somewhere. *My uncle went to Canada to settle.* **2** to make yourself comfortable. *I settled down in the armchair.* **3** to decide or sort something out. *settle an argument.* **4** to come to rest. *Dust had settled on the books.* **5** to pay a bill. **settle in** to become used to new surroundings. **settler** *n*.

settlement *n* **1** an agreement. **2** a small community.

sever *v* to cut or break something off.

several *adj* more than one or two, but not many. **several** *pron.*
severe *adj* **1** very bad, serious. *a severe drought.* **2** strict or harsh. *a severe punishment.* **severity** *n.*
sew *v* (sewing, sewed, sewn) to use a needle and thread to join pieces of cloth together or join something to cloth.
sewage *(soo-wij)* *n* waste matter carried away in sewers.
sewer *(soo-wer)* *n* an underground pipe for carrying away waste matter from drains.
sex *n* **1** being male or female. **2** sexual intercourse. **sexual** *adj*, **sexually** *adv.*
sexist *n* discriminating against people of the opposite sex. **sexism** *n.*
sexual intercourse *n* the physical act between a man and a woman in which the man's penis is put into the woman's vagina.
shabby *adj* (shabbier, shabbiest) old and worn out. *shabby clothes.* **shabbily** *adv*, **shabbiness** *n.*
shack *n* a roughly built hut.
shade[1] *n* **1** an area of slight darkness caused by blocking out the light. *The dog sat in the shade where it was cool.* **2** something which protects against light or heat. *a lampshade.* **3** how dark or light a colour is. *a darker shade of green.* **shady** *adj.*
shade[2] *v* **1** to shelter from the sun or light. **2** to make a part of a drawing darker by filling it in. **shading** *n.*
shadow[1] *n* a dark shape caused by a person or thing blocking the light.
shadow[2] *v* to follow somebody closely.
shaft *n* **1** the long, straight part or handle of a tool, weapon, etc. **2** a revolving rod which turns a machine or an engine. **3** a deep, narrow hole leading to a mine. **4** a ray of light.
shaggy *adj* (shaggier, shaggiest) covered with thick, rough hair or fur.
shake *v* (shaking, shook, shaken) to move vigorously from side to side or up and down. *I was shaking with fear. Shake the bottle.* **shaky** *adj.*
shallow *adj* not deep. *This part of the river is quite shallow.*
shame *n* **1** a feeling of sadness, guilt and regret at something bad or stupid you have done. **2** a pity. *What a shame you can't come to our party.*
shampoo *n* liquid for washing your hair. **shampoo** *v.*
shamrock *n* a plant like clover with three leaves on each stem, used as the national symbol of Ireland.
shan't shall not.
shanty *n* **1** a roughly built hut. **2** a sailor's song.
shape[1] *n* **1** the form or outline of something. **2** condition. *He's in good shape because he works out every day.*
shape[2] *v* **1** to give a certain shape to something. **2** to develop. *Our plans are shaping up well.*
share[1] *v* to divide something among two or more people.
share[2] *n* **1** one part of something that is divided among several people. **2** one of the parts into which the money of a company is divided.
shark *n* a large sea fish with sharp teeth and a pointed fin on its back.
sharp[1] *adj* having an edge or point that cuts things easily. **2** sudden, quick. *a sharp bend in the road.* **3** clear and easy to see. *These photos are very sharp.* **4** sour. **5** angry, severe. *a sharp voice.* **6** able to see, hear or learn well. *a sharp mind.*
sharp[2] *adv* punctually. *one o'clock sharp.*
sharp[3] *n* a sign (♯) in music which indicates that a note should be played higher by half a tone.
sharpen *v* to make something sharper.
shatter *v* to break into many small pieces. *The glass shattered.*
shave *v* to cut away hair with a razor.
shawl *n* a large piece of material worn by a woman around her shoulders.
sheaf *n* (*pl* sheaves) a bundle, especially of corn or of papers.
shear *v* (shearing, sheared, shorn) to cut the wool from a sheep.
shears *n pl* a tool like large scissors.
sheath *n* a cover for a sword or dagger.
shed[1] *n* a small hut used for storing things or as a shelter for animals.

shed[2] *v* (sheds, shedding, shed) to let something fall or drop off. *Some trees shed their leaves in the autumn.*
sheen *n* brightness, shine.
sheep *n* (*pl* sheep) a farm animal kept for its wool and meat.
sheer *adj* **1** very steep. *a sheer drop to the sea.* **2** complete. *sheer nonsense.* **3** (of material) very thin and almost transparent.
sheet *n* **1** a thin, rectangular piece of material used on a bed. **2** a thin, flat piece of paper, metal, glass, ice, etc.
sheikh *(shake) n* an Arab chief.
shelf *n* (*pl* shelves) a flat board fixed to a wall or inside a cupboard, for putting things on.
shell *n* **1** the hard outer covering of a shellfish, egg, nut, etc. **2** a metal case filled with explosive, fired from a gun.
shellfish *n* (*pl* shellfish) a soft-bodied water creature covered with a shell. Mussels, oysters and whelks are shellfish.
shelter *n* **1** a place where you are protected from bad weather, or kept safe from harm. **2** being protected or kept safe. **shelter** *v*.

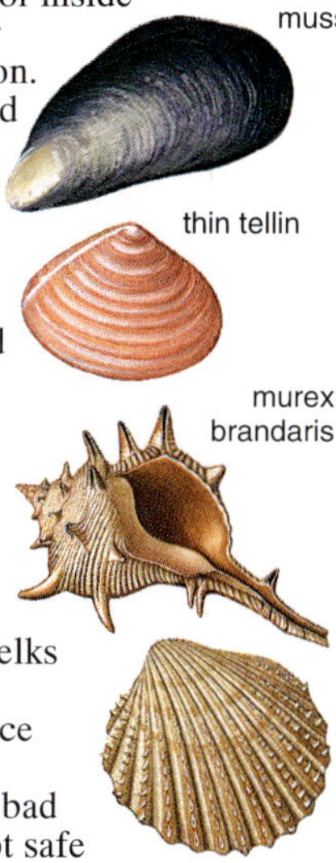

shells

shepherd *n* a person who looks after sheep.
sheriff *n* in the USA, the chief law officer of a county.
sherry *n* a strong type of wine.
shield[1] *n* **1** a wide piece of metal, wood, etc used to protect the person carrying it against attack. **2** something that protects. *a heat shield.*
shield[2] *v* to cover or protect something.

shield

shift[1] *v* to move something. *Can you help me shift the sofa?*
shift[2] *n* a period of time that a group of people are working, ending when another group comes to take their place. *The night shift begins at 10.*
shilling *n* a coin formerly used in the UK.
shimmer *v* to shine with an unsteady light. *The moonlight shimmered on the lake.* **shimmer** *n*.
shin *n* the front part of your leg below the knee.
shine *v* (shining, shone) to give out or reflect light, to be bright. **shiny** *adj.*
shingle *n* small pebbles.
ship[1] *n* a large boat for travelling on the sea.
ship[2] *v* (ships, shipping, shipped) to transport something by ship.
shipwreck *n* **1** an accident in which a ship is sunk or badly damaged at sea. **2** a wrecked ship.
shipyard *n* a place where ships are built or repaired.
shirk *v* to avoid doing something that you should do, especially work.
shirt *n* a piece of clothing worn on the top half of the body. A shirt usually has a collar, sleeves and buttons down the front.
shiver *v* to shake with cold or fear. **shiver** *n*, **shivery** *adj*.
shoal *n* a group of fish swimming together.
shock[1] *n* **1** a sudden, unpleasant surprise. **2** the effect on your body of an electric current passing through it. *I got a slight shock when I touched the wire.* **3** a violent shaking. *earthquake shocks.* **4** an unhealthy condition of the body caused by a bad shock or physical injury. *She was suffering from shock.* **shocking** *adj.*
shock[2] *v* to upset or horrify somebody. *Everyone was shocked by her death.*

shoddy *adj* (shoddier, shoddiest) of poor quality.
shoe *n* an outer covering for your foot.
shoelace *n* a string for tying up a shoe.
shone *past of* shine.
shook *past of* shake.
shoot[1] *v* (shooting, shot) **1** to fire a bullet from a gun, an arrow from a bow, etc. **2** to move quickly. *She shot out of the room.* **3** to kick or hit a ball at a goal, etc. **4** to photograph. **5** (of a plant) to grow new buds.
shoot[2] *n* a new growth on a plant.
shooting star *n* a meteor.
shop[1] *n* a place where goods are sold.
shop[2] *v* (shops, shopping, shopped) to visit shops and buy things. **shopper** *n.*
shopkeeper *n* a person who owns or looks after a shop.
shoplifter *n* a person who steals from a shop. **shoplifting** *n.*
shop steward *n* a person elected by workers as their representative.
shore *n* the land along the edge of a sea or lake.
shorn *past participle of* shear.
short *adj* **1** not long. **2** not tall. **3** not taking a lot of time. **4** not enough, less than it should be. *When I checked my change, I found I was 20 pence short.* **short of** not having enough of something. *We're short of bread.* **short** *adv*, **shortness** *n.*
shortage *n* a lack of something.
shortbread *n* a crumbly biscuit made from flour, butter and sugar.
shortcoming *n* a fault.
short cut *n* a short way of getting somewhere or doing something. *We took a short cut across the field.*
shorten *v* to make or become shorter.
shorthand *n* a way of writing quickly using strokes and dots to show sounds.
shortly *adv* soon, before long.
shorts *n pl* short trousers that come to just above your knees.
short-sighted *adj* seeing clearly only things that are near to you.
short-tempered *adj* easily made angry.
shot[1] *past of* shoot.
shot[2] *n* **1** the firing of a gun. *We heard a shot in the distance.* **2** a throw, hit, kick or turn in a game or competition. *a shot at goal.* **3** a photograph. **4** lead bullets used in cartridges. **5** an attempt to do something. **6** an injection.
shot put *n* a sports event in which the competitors throw a heavy metal ball as far as possible with one hand.
should *v* **1** *past of* shall. **2** used to say or ask what is the right thing to do. *You should phone her.* **3** used to say what is likely. *They left ages ago so they should be home by now.*
shoulder *n* the part of your body between your neck and the top of your arm.
shoulderblade *n* the wide, flat bone of your shoulder.
shout *v* to call out or speak loudly. **shout** *n.*
shove *v* to push somebody roughly. **shove** *n.*
shovel *n* a tool like a large spade with curved sides, for moving sand, coal, snow, etc. **shovel** *v.*
show[1] *v* (showing, showed, shown) **1** to let something be seen. *Show me what you have written.* **2** to explain how to do something. *Can you show me how to print from this computer?* **3** to be visible. *Her anger showed in her face.* **show off 1** to display something. **2** to try to impress people.
show[2] *n* **1** a play or other entertainment. **2** a public display or exhibition. *a horse show.*
shower *n* **1** a short fall of light rain. **2** a device that sprays water on you from above, used for washing yourself. **3** a lot of things falling or coming at one time. *a shower of bullets.* **shower** *v.*
shrank *past of* shrink.
shrapnel *n* small pieces of metal from an exploding bomb.
shred *n* a narrow piece torn off something. *My skirt was torn to shreds.* **shred** *v.*
shrew *n* an animal similar to a small mouse with a long nose.
shrewd *adj* clever, cunning.
shriek *v* to make a high-pitched scream or laugh. **shriek** *n.*

shrill *adj* (of a sound) piercing.
shrimp *n* a small, edible shellfish with a long tail.
shrine *n* a sacred place.
shrink *v* (shrinking, shrank, shrunk) **1** to become smaller. *Wool often shrinks in hot water.* **2** to move back because you are afraid, disgusted, etc. *He shrank back in horror.*
shrivel *v* (shrivels, shrivelling, shrivelled) to dry up or wither. *The plants shrivelled up in the heat.*
shrub *n* a small bush.
shrug *v* (shrugs, shrugging, shrugged) to raise your shoulders to show doubt or a lack of interest. **shrug** *n.*
shrunk *past participle of* shrink.
shudder *v* to shake suddenly with cold or fear. **shudder** *n.*
shuffle *v* **1** to mix playing-cards before a game. **2** to move your feet slowly along the ground without lifting them. **shuffle** *n.*
shun *v* (shuns, shunning, shunned) to avoid or keep away from somebody.
shut *v* (shuts, shutting, shut) to move a door, window, lid, etc so that it is no longer open.
shutter *n* **1** a wooden or metal cover for a window. **2** the moving cover over the lens of a camera, which opens when a photograph is taken.
shuttle *n* **1** a device used in weaving for carrying a thread backwards and forwards across the other threads. **2** a bus, plane, etc that travels regularly between two places.
shuttlecock *n* a cork ball with feathers or a light plastic frame fixed round it, used in badminton.

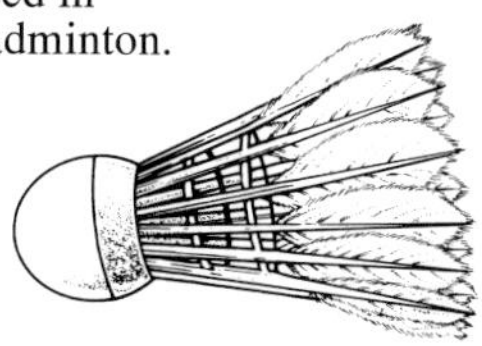

shuttlecock

shy[1] *adj* nervous about talking to people you do not know. **shyness** *n.*
shy[2] *v* (shies, shying, shied) to turn away in sudden fear.
sick *adj* **1** vomiting. *I was sick twice this morning.* **2** needing to vomit. *I feel sick.* **3** not well, ill. **4** tired of something. *I'm sick of telling you to tidy your room.* **sickness** *n.*
sicken *v* to disgust somebody.
sickle *n* a tool with a curved blade for cutting grain, etc.
sickly *adj* (sicklier, sickliest) unhealthy. *a sickly child.*
side *n* **1** an edge. *the side of the field.* **2** a surface of something. *An octagon has eight sides.* **3** one of the two parts of something that are not the top, bottom, front or back. *the side of the house.* **4** the right or left part of the body. **5** a team or group that is opposing another.
side effect *n* an additional, often bad, effect of taking a drug.
sidetrack *v* to distract somebody from what they were going to do or say.
sideways *adv* to or towards one side. *Crabs move sideways.*
siding *n* a short track beside a railway line where trains can stand when they are not being used.
siege *(seej) n* the surrounding of a building, town, etc with armed forces until the people inside surrender.
siesta *(see-es-ta) n* a short sleep taken in the afternoon.
sieve *(rhymes with* give*) n* a container made of a wire or plastic net attached to a ring, used to separate liquids from solids, or small pieces from large pieces. **sieve** *v.*
sift *v* to put something through a sieve. *Sift the flour into a bowl.*
sigh *(rhymes with* die*) v* to breathe out loudly, especially to show tiredness, boredom or relief. **sigh** *n.*
sight *n* **1** the ability to see. **2** seeing something. **3** something that you see. **4 sights** the interesting places worth visiting in a town or city.
sightseeing *n* visiting the famous and interesting places and buildings in a town or city. **sightseer** *n.*
sign[1] *n* **1** a board with words or pictures giving information. **2** a symbol that stands for something. *+ is the sign meaning "plus".* **3** a

movement to show a meaning. *She made a sign to me to be quiet.* **4** a clue that shows something. *There was no sign of a break-in.*

sign[2] *v* to write your name in your own way on something.

signal *n* **1** a sign, for example a hand movement or a light or sound giving a command or warning. *Car drivers have to signal before they turn.* **2** the wave of sound received or sent out by a radio, etc. **signal** *v*.

signature *n* a person's name written in their own writing.

signature

significant *n* important, meaning a lot. **significance** *n*.

signify *v* (signifies, signifying, signified) to mean something, to be a sign of something. *A nod signifies agreement.*

signpost *n* a post with a sign on it, showing the direction and distance of places.

Sikh *(seek)* *n* a member of an Indian religion, called **Sikhism**, based on a belief in a single god. **Sikh** *adj*.

silent *adj* without any sound. **silence** *n*.

silhouette *(sil-oo-**et**)* *n* the dark outline of something seen against the light.

silicon *n* a chemical element found in sand and rocks and used in making electronic equipment.

silk *n* very fine, smooth cloth made from fibres produced by caterpillars called **silkworms**. **silky** *adj*.

sill *n* the ledge along the bottom of a window.

silly *adj* (sillier, silliest) foolish, not sensible. **silliness** *n*.

silt *n* fine sand and mud left behind by flowing water.

silver *n* **1** a precious, shiny, grey metal, used for making jewellery, coins, etc. **2** money made of silver or of a metal that looks like silver. **3** cutlery or other objects made of silver. **4** the colour of silver. **silver** *adj*.

similar *adj* alike, almost the same. **similarity** *n*.

simmer *v* to boil very gently.

simple *adj* **1** not difficult, easy. **2** not complicated. *a simple design.* **simplicity** *n*, **simply** *adv*.

simplify *v* (simplifies, simplifying, simplified) to make something simpler. **simplification** *n*.

simulate *v* **1** to pretend. *She already knew, but she simulated surprise at the news.* **2** to recreate a real situation, especially by using computers and moving machines. *The equipment simulates the experience of flying an aeroplane.* **simulation** *n*, **simulator** *n*.

simultaneous *adj* happening at the same time.

sin *n* a wicked act, especially one that breaks a religious or moral law. **sin** *v*, **sinful** *adj*, **sinner** *n*.

since *conj* **1** from the time that. *I haven't seen her since she moved house.* **2** because. *Since Harry is away, I'll do it myself.* **since** *prep*.

sincere *adj* meaning what you say, honest. **sincerely** *adv*, **sincerity** *n*.

sing *v* (singing, sang, sung) to make musical sounds with your voice. **singer** *n*.

singe *v* (singeing, singed) to burn something slightly.

single *adj* **1** one only. *a single-storey house.* **2** for one person only. *a single bed.* **3** not married. *a single man.* **4** for one direction of a journey. *a single ticket.*

singular *adj* the form of a word that shows only one. *Foot* is the singular of *feet*. **singular** *adj*.

sinister *adj* seeming or suggesting evil. *a sinister disappearance.*

sink[1] *v* (sinking, sank, sunk) **1** to go down under the surface of a liquid. *The stone sank to the bottom of the pool.* **2** to make a ship sink. **3** to go down slowly. *The sun sank slowly behind the hills.*

sink[2] *n* a basin with a drain and water supply connected to it.

sinus *n* one of the hollow spaces in the bones of your head at the top of your nose.
sip *v* (sips, sipping, sipped) to drink in very small mouthfuls. **sip** *n.*
siphon *(sigh-fon) n* a tube for flowing liquid from one container into to another at a lower level. **siphon** *v.*
sir *n* **1** a polite way of speaking or writing to a man, without using his name. **2 Sir** the title placed before the name of a knight.
siren *n* a device that makes a loud wailing noise as a warning or signal.
sister *n* **1** a girl or woman who has the same parents as you. **2** a senior female nurse. **3** a nun.
sit *v* (sits, sitting, sat) **1** to rest on your bottom. **2** to take an exam.
site *n* a place where a building, town, etc is, was or will be built. *the site for a new factory.*
sitting-room *n* a room in a house where people sit to relax, read or watch television.
situated *v* **be situated** to be in a particular place. *The library is situated in the city centre.*
situation *n* a set of circumstances at a certain time. *I was in an embarrassing situation.*
size *n* how large something is.
sizzle *v* to make a hissing sound. *meat sizzling in a frying-pan.*
skate *n* an ice skate or rollerskate. **skate** *v.*
skateboard *n* a narrow board on four wheels, that you stand and ride on.
skeleton *n* the framework of bones in the body of an animal or human.
sketch[1] *n* **1** a rough drawing. **2** a short, funny play.
sketch[2] *v* to draw roughly and quickly.
ski[1] *n* (*pl* skis) one of a pair of long, narrow strips of metal or wood that are fixed to boots for moving on snow.
ski[2] *v* (skis, skiing, skied) to move on skis. **skier** *n.*
skid *v* (skids, skidding, skidded) to slide sideways on a slippery surface.
skill *n* the ability to do something very well. **skilful** *adj,* **skilfully** *adv.*
skim *v* (skims, skimming, skimmed) **1** to remove something from the surface of a liquid. *Skim the fat off the gravy.* **2** to move lightly and quickly over a surface.
skin *n* **1** the natural outer covering of an animal or person. **2** the outer layer of a fruit.
skinny *adj* (skinnier, skinniest) very thin.
skip[1] *v* (skips, skipping, skipped) **1** to move along with a little hop on each foot in turn. **2** to jump over a rope that is turning under your feet and over your head. **3** to miss something out. *I skipped the second chapter.*
skip[2] *n* a large, open, metal container used for transporting rubbish.
skipper *n* the captain of a boat or of a sports team.
skirt *n* a piece of clothing worn by women and girls, that hangs down from the waist.
skittles *n* a game in which you try to knock down a set of bottle-shaped objects, called skittles, with a ball.
skull *n* the bony part of your head.
skunk *n* a small, North American mammal which defends itself by giving off a bad smell.

skunk

sky *n* the part of space above the Earth, where you can see the Sun, Moon and stars.
skyscraper *n* a very tall building with many floors.
slab *n* a thick, flat slice.
slack *adj* **1** loose, not pulled tight. **2** lazy and careless. **3** not busy.
slain *past participle of* slay.
slam *v* (slams, slamming, slammed) to shut or put something down with force, making a loud noise. **slam** *n.*
slang *n* words and phrases that you use in conversation, especially with people of your own age, but not when you are writing or being polite.

slant *v* to slope. *His handwriting slants to the left.* **slant** *n.*
slap *v* (slaps, slapping, slapped) to hit something with the palm of your hand. **slap** *n.*
slapstick *n* a type of comedy that uses actions, not words, to make you laugh.
slash *v* to make long cuts in something. **slash** *n.*
slate *n* **1** a blue-grey stone which can be split into thin, flat sheets. **2** a piece of this, used as a roof tile.
slaughter *v* **1** to kill animals for food. **2** to kill large numbers of people brutally. **slaughter** *n.*
slave *n* a person who is owned by somebody and forced to work for them without pay. **slavery** *n.*
slay *v* (slays, slaying, slew, slain) *(old-fashioned)* to kill somebody.
sled, sledge *n* a small vehicle with rods underneath instead of wheels, used for travelling on snow or ice.
sleek *adj* smooth and shiny. *sleek fur.*
sleep *v* (sleeping, slept) to rest with your eyes closed in a state of natural unconsciousness. **sleep** *n.*
sleepless *adj* unable to sleep, without sleep. *a sleepless night.*
sleepy *adj* (sleepier, sleepiest) tired and feeling ready to sleep. **sleepily** *adv*, **sleepiness** *n.*
sleet *n* rain mixed with snow.
sleeve *n* the part of a piece of clothing that covers your arm.
sleigh *(rhymes with* ray*)* *n* a large sledge, usually pulled by animals.
slender *adj* thin or narrow.
slept *past of* sleep.
slew *past of* slay.
slice *n* a thin piece cut from something. *a slice of bread.* **slice** *v.*
slick *n* a patch of oil floating on water.
slide[1] *v* (sliding, slid) to move smoothly over a surface.
slide[2] *n* **1** a structure in a playground with a smooth, sloping surface for children to slide down. **2** a small, transparent photograph for projecting onto a screen. **3** a piece of glass on which you put things to examine under a microscope.
slight *adj* small or not important.
slim *adj* (slimmer, slimmest) **1** thin. **2** very small. *a slim chance.*
slime *n* unpleasantly wet, slippery stuff. **slimy** *adj.*
sling[1] *n* **1** a piece of cloth used to support an injured arm. **2** a strap with a string attached to either end, used for throwing stones,
sling[2] *v* (slinging, slung) *(informal)* to throw something.
slip[1] *v* (slips, slipping, slipped) **1** to slide accidentally and lose your balance. **2** to move quietly and easily. *She slipped out of the room.* **3** to do something with a quick, light movement. *I slipped off my shoes.*
slip[2] *n* **1** a small mistake. **2** a small piece of paper. **3** a petticoat.
slipper *n* a soft shoe worn indoors.
slippery *adj* so smooth or wet that it causes slipping.
slit *v* (slits, slitting, slit) to make a long, narrow cut in something. **slit** *n.*
slither *v* to slide or slip.
slog *v* (slogs, slogging, slogged) to work hard. **slog** *n.*
slogan *n* an easily remembered phrase used in advertising.
slope *n* a surface that has one end higher than the other, such as the side of a hill. **slope** *v.*
sloppy *adj* (sloppier, sloppiest) **1** careless. *sloppy work.* **2** half-liquid. *sloppy food.* **3** sentimental. *a sloppy love story.*
slot *n* a small, narrow opening to push something into. *Insert a coin in the slot.* **slot** *v.*
sloth *(rhymes with* both*)* *n* **1** a slow-moving South American mammal that lives in trees. **2** laziness. **slothful** *adj.*

sloth

slouch *v* to stand or sit with your shoulders rounded and your head hanging forward.
slow *adj* **1** not fast. **2** showing a time earlier than the right time. *That clock is slow.* **slow** *v*, **slowness** *n*.
slug *n* a creature like a snail with no shell.
sluggish *adj* moving slowly.
slum *n* an area with old, overcrowded houses in a poor condition.
slump *v* to fall suddenly or heavily.
slung *past of* sling.
sly *adj* cunning and secretly deceitful. **slyness** *n*.
smack *v* to hit somebody with the palm of your hand. **smack** *n*.
small *adj* little, not big or much.
smart[1] *adj* **1** well-dressed, neat. **2** clever. **smartness** *n*.
smart[2] *v* to have a sharp, stinging feeling. *The smoke made his eyes smart.*
smash *v* to break something to pieces.
smear *v* to spread something sticky or oily over a surface. **smear** *n*.
smell[1] *v* (smelling, smelt *or* smelled) **1** to notice something through your nose. *I can smell smoke.* **2** to give out a smell. *My hands smell of onions.*
smell[2] *n* **1** the ability to smell things. **2** something that you notice through your nose. **smelly** *adj*.
smile *v* to turn up the corners of your mouth as a sign of pleasure or amusement. **smile** *n*.
smog *n* smoke mixed with fog.
smoke[1] *n* the cloud-like gases and bits of soot given off by something that is burning. **smoky** *adj*.
smoke[2] *v* **1** to give off smoke. **2** to have a cigarette, pipe, etc in your mouth and breathe the smoke in and out. **3** to preserve ham, fish, etc by hanging it in smoke.
smooth *adj* **1** having an even surface, not rough or lumpy. **2** without problems or difficulties. *a smooth journey.* **smooth** *v*, **smoothness** *n*.
smother *(rhymes with* mother*)* *v* **1** to kill somebody by covering their face so they cannot breathe. **2** to cover something thickly. *She smothered the toast with butter.*
smoulder *v* to burn very slowly, without bursting into flame.
smudge *n* a dirty mark. **smudge** *v*.
smug *adj* (smugger, smuggest) too pleased with yourself.
smuggle *v* to take goods into or out of a country illegally. **smuggler** *n*.
snack *n* a small, quick meal.
snag *n* a small difficulty.
snail *n* a small creature with a soft body and a hard, protective shell.
snake *n* a long, thin reptile without legs. Some snakes are poisonous.
snap[1] *v* (snaps, snapping, snapped) **1** to break suddenly with a sharp noise. **2** to bite at somebody suddenly. **3** to speak in a sharp, angry way.
snap[2] *n* **1** the noise made by snapping. **2** a photograph. **3** a card game.
snare *n* a trap for animals. **snare** *v*.
snarl *v* to growl angrily, showing the teeth. **snarl** *n*.
snatch *v* to seize something quickly. *She snatched my bag and ran off.*
sneak[1] *v* to go somewhere quietly and secretly. *He sneaked out of the room.*
sneak[2] *n* a person who tells tales.
sneer *v* to curl your upper lip at one side in a kind of smile that shows scorn. **sneer** *n*.
sneeze *v* to blow out air suddenly and noisily through your nose and mouth. **sneeze** *n*.
sniff *v* to draw in air quickly and noisily through your nose. **sniff** *n*.
snigger *v* to laugh quietly in an unpleasant way. **snigger** *n*.
snip *v* (snips, snipping, snipped) to cut something sharply and quickly.
sniper *n* a person who shoots at people from a hidden position.
snippet *n* a small piece.
snob *n* a person who looks down on people of a lower social class. **snobbery** *n*, **snobbish** *adj*.
snooker *n* a game in which you use a stick, called a cue, to hit balls into pockets at the edge of a long table.
snoop *v* to look around a place secretly to try to find out something.

snooze *v* to sleep lightly. **snooze** *n.*
snore *v* to make a snorting noise through your nose or mouth when you are asleep. **snore** *n.*
snorkel *n* a tube for breathing air through when you are underwater.
snort *v* to make a noise by forcing air through your nostrils. **snort** *n.*
snout *n* the nose and mouth of an animal such as a pig.
snow *n* flakes of frozen water that fall from the sky in cold weather. **snow** *v*, **snowy** *adj.*
snowball *n* snow pressed into a ball.
snowboard *n* a single board used as a ski on snow. **snowboarding** *n.*
snowdrop *n* a small, white flower.
snowplough *n* a vehicle for clearing snow from roads or railways.
snug *adj* (snugger, snuggest) warm and comfortable.
snuggle *v* to get close to somebody for warmth or love.
soak *v* **1** to put something in a liquid and leave it there. **2** to make something very wet. **soak up** to take in liquid, to absorb.
soap *n* a substance used with water for washing. **soapy** *adj.*
soap opera *n* a television series about the daily lives of a group of characters.
soar *v* **1** to fly high in the sky. **2** to rise high and quickly.
sob *v* (sobs, sobbing, sobbed) to cry noisily. **sob** *n.*
sober *adj* **1** not drunk. **2** serious. **3** not bright. *a sober grey dress.*
soccer *n* Association football.
social *adj* **1** to do with people in communities, and how they live. *social problems.* **2** living in communities. *Ants are social insects.* **3** to do with meeting and being friendly with other people. *a social club.* **socially** *adv.*
social security *n* money paid by the government to people who are unemployed, ill, etc.
social worker *n* a person whose job is to help people in the community who have special needs.
society *n* **1** all the people who live in a group or country, and the way they live and meet. **2** a club.
sock *n* a piece of clothing that you wear on your foot, inside your shoe.
socket *n* a hole or set of holes into which something fits. *an electrical socket* (= for a plug).
soda *n* **1** fizzy water. **2** any of several substances formed from sodium, eg baking soda (sodium bicarbonate).
sodium *n* a metallic chemical element found in many substances including salt.
sofa *n* a long, soft seat with arms and a back, for two or more people.
soft *adj* **1** not hard or firm. *a soft pillow.* **2** smooth and pleasant to touch. *soft fur.* **3** (of a sound) not loud. *a soft voice.* **4** (of a colour) not bright. **5** not strict. *Her dad is too soft.*
soft drink *n* a cold drink that does not contain alcohol.
soften *v* to make or become softer.
software *n* computer programs.
soggy *adj* (soggier, soggiest) very wet and soft.
soil[1] *n* the earth in which plants grow.
soil[2] *v* to make something dirty.
solar *adj* **1** to do with the Sun. **2** powered by energy from the Sun's rays.
solar system *n* the Sun and the planets that revolve around it.
sold *past of* sell.
soldier *n* a member of an army.
sole[1] *n* **1** the underneath of your foot or your shoe. **2** a flat, edible sea fish.
sole[2] *adj* only. *She was the sole survivor of the crash.*
solemn *adj* very serious. **solemnity** *n.*
solicitor *n* a lawyer who advises people about legal matters.
solid[1] *adj* **1** hard, not like a liquid or gas. **2** not hollow. **solidity** *n.*
solid[2] *n* a substance that is solid.
solidify *v* (solidifies, solidifying, solidified) to become solid.
solitary *adj* alone.
solo *n* (*pl* solos) a performance by a single person, especially of a musical piece. **soloist** *n.*
soluble *adj* capable of dissolving.

solution *n* **1** the answer to a problem, or puzzle. **2** a liquid with something dissolved in it.
solve *v* to find the answer to a problem or puzzle.
sombre *(**som**-ber) adj* gloomy.
somebody, someone *pron* a person.
somehow *adv* in some way. *I'll get there somehow.*
somersault *n* a rolling movement in which your heels go over your head. **somersault** *v*.
something *pron* a thing.
sometime *adv* at an unknown time in the past or future. *Let's meet sometime this week.*
sometimes *adv* occasionally, not often.
somewhere *adv* in or to some place.
son *n* somebody's male child.
sonar *n* a system that uses sounds and their echoes to find objects in deep water.
sonata *n* a piece of music, usually with three movements, for one or two instruments.
song *n* **1** a piece of music with words that you sing. **2** singing. *bird-song.*
sonnet *n* a poem of 14 lines with a fixed pattern of rhymes.
soon *adv* in a short time.
soot *n* the black powder left by something that has burnt. **sooty** *adj*.
soothe *v* **1** to calm or comfort somebody. **2** to make something less painful. **soothing** *adj*.
sophisticated *adj* **1** knowing a lot about the world and about what is fashionable to do or wear. **2** able to do difficult and complicated things. *sophisticated machinery.* **sophistication** *n*.
sorcerer *(**saw**-ser-er) n* a person who casts magic spells. **sorcery** *n*.
sore[1] *adj* painful. **soreness** *n*.
sore[2] *n* a painful, infected place on your skin.
sorrow *adj* sadness. **sorrowful** *adj*.
sorry *adj* feeling sadness, regret or sympathy.
sort[1] *n* a type or kind.
sort[2] *v* to arrange things into groups. *He sorted the washing into two piles.* **sort out** to put something in order, to deal with something.
SOS *n* a signal calling for urgent help or rescue.
sought *past of* seek.
soul *n* **1** the part of a person that is often thought to continue after they die. **2** a person. *a poor old soul.*
sound[1] *n* something that you hear.
sound[2] *v* **1** to give a certain impression. *You sound excited.* **2** to resemble something in sound. *That sounded like a train.* **3** to make a noise with something. *She sounded her horn.*
sound[3] *adj* **1** strong, in good condition. *sound teeth.* **2** reliable and sensible. *sound advice.* **3** deep. *a sound sleep.* **4** thorough. *a sound beating.*
soup *n* a liquid food made from meat or vegetables cooked in water.
sour *adj* sharp-tasting like lemons. **sourness** *n*.
source *n* **1** the place, person or thing from which something comes. **2** the place where a river starts.
south *n* one of the points of the compass. When you face the rising Sun, south is on your right. **south** *adj, adv*.
southern *adj* in or of the south part of a place. *southern Africa.*
souvenir *(**soo**-ve-neer) n* an object that you keep to remind you of a place, person or event.
sovereign *(**sov**-rin) n* a king or queen.
sow[1] *(rhymes with* how*) n* a female pig.
sow[2] *(rhymes with* so*) v* (sowing, sowed, sown) to put seeds in the ground so that they grow.
soya bean *n* a bean containing a lot of protein, used instead of animal products in some foods.
space *n* **1** an empty place. **2** the area beyond the Earth's atmosphere, where all the stars, planets, etc are.
spacecraft *n* (*pl* spacecraft) a vehicle for travelling in space.
spacious *adj* having plenty of room.
spade *n* **1** a tool for digging the ground. **2 spades** one of the four suits in a pack of cards, with the symbol ♠ on them.

spaghetti

spaghetti *n* long, thin strips of pasta.
span¹ *v* (spans, spanning, spanned) to reach from one side of something to the other. *A bridge spans the river.*
span² *n* **1** the distance between the tip of your little finger and your thumb when your hand is spread out. **2** the length of something. **3** the time for which something lasts.
spaniel *n* a dog with large, droopy ears.
spank *v* to hit somebody, especially on the bottom, with the palm of your hand.
spanner *n* a tool for turning nuts on bolts.
spare¹ *adj* extra, not in use. *a spare tyre.*
spare² *v* **1** to have something available. *I can't spare any time today.* **2** to treat somebody with mercy. *They begged the king to spare them.*
spark *n* a tiny, red-hot piece thrown off by something burning.
sparkle *v* to shine with a lot of tiny, bright flashes of light. **sparkle** *n.*
sparrow *n* a small, brown bird.
sparse *adj* thinly scattered, not much.
spat *past of* spit.
spawn *n* the eggs of fish, frogs, etc.
speak *v* (speaking, spoke, spoken) to talk, to say words.
speaker *n* **1** a person who speaks. **2** a part of a radio, stereo system, etc that turns electrical waves into sound.
spear *n* a weapon that is thrown, consisting of a sharp point on the end of a long pole.
special *adj* **1** not ordinary or usual. *a special occasion.* **2** for a particular purpose. *a special tool.* **specially** *adv.*
specialist *n* a person who knows a lot about a particular subject.
speciality *n* something that you make or do particularly well.
specialize *v* to work or study in a particular field. *a doctor specializing in natural medicine.*
species *n* (*pl* species) a group of animals or plants that are alike in some way. *Mice are a species of rodent and so are rats.*
specific *adj* **1** particular. **2** clear and detailed. **specifically** *adv.*
specify *v* (specifies, specifying, specified) to name or state something in a clear and detailed way. *She specified what colour she wanted.* **specification** *n.*
specimen *n* a sample.
speck *n* a tiny piece of something, for example dust.
speckled *adj* covered with small spots. *a speckled hen.*
spectacles *n pl* lenses set into a frame, that you wear to improve your eyesight.
spectacular *adj* impressive, splendid.
spectator *n* a person who watches an event.
spectrum *n* (*pl* spectra *or* spectrums) all the different colours that are produced when light goes through a prism, a drop of water, etc.
speculate *v* to guess. **speculation** *n.*
speech *n* **1** speaking. **2** a talk given to a group of people.
speed¹ *n* how fast something is moving.
speed² *v* (speeding, sped) to travel very fast, or faster than is allowed by law.
speedometer *n* an instrument in a vehicle that shows how fast you are travelling.
spell¹ *v* (spelling, spelt *or* spelled) to write or say the letters of a word in the correct order. **spelling** *n.*
spell² *n* **1** magic words that are supposed to make something happen. **2** a period of time. *a spell of fine weather.*
spend *v* (spending, spent) **1** to use money to buy things. **2** to pass time.
sperm *n* one of the cells produced by males that can fertilize a female egg.
sphere *(sfeer)* *n* a round object like a ball. **spherical** *adj.*

Sphinx *(sfinks) n* in mythology, a monster with a lion's body and a woman's head.
spice *n* a substance obtained from part of a plant, used to flavour food. *The picture shows a selection of spices.* **spicy** *adj*.

spices

spider *n* a small creature with eight legs that spins webs.
spike *n* a sharp point. **spiky** *adj*.
spill *v* (spilling, spilt *or* spilled) to pour out accidentally. *I spilt some milk on the table.*
spin *v* (spins, spinning, spun) **1** to turn around quickly on the spot. **2** to make thread by twisting fibres together.
spinach *n* a plant with dark-green leaves used as a vegetable.
spinal *adj* to do with the spine.
spine *n* **1** the line of bones down the middle of your back. **2** a prickle. **3** the narrow part of a book, where the pages are joined together.
spiral *adj* winding round and round, like the thread of a screw. **spiral** *n*.

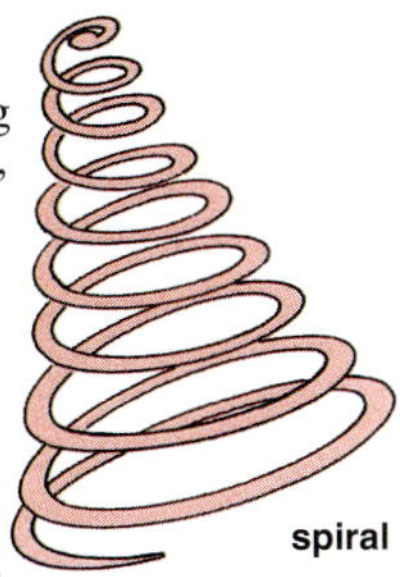
spiral

spire *n* a tall pointed part on the top of a church tower.
spirit *n* **1** a person's soul. **2** a ghost. **3** a strong, alcoholic drink, such as whisky or gin. **4** liveliness or courage. *She showed a lot of spirit in overcoming her disability.* **5 spirits** a person's feelings. *He's in high spirits* (= cheerful) *today.*
spiritual *adj* to do with the soul or religion. **spirituality** *n,* **spiritually** *adv.*
spit *v* (spits, spitting, spat) to send out saliva from your mouth. **spit** *n.*
spite *n* the wish to hurt or upset somebody. **spiteful** *adj*, **spitefully** *adv*. **in spite of** taking no notice of something. *They set off in spite of the bad weather.*
splash *v* to make something wet with drops of liquid. **splash** *n.*
splendid *adj* very good or very impressive. *a splendid palace.*
splint *n* a piece of wood, plastic, etc, used to keep a broken bone in a fixed position while it heals.
splinter *n* a thin, sharp, broken piece of wood, etc. **splinter** *v.*
split *v* (splits, splitting, split) to break or divide into parts. **split** *n.*
spoil *v* (spoiling, spoilt *or* spoiled) **1** to make something less good than before. **2** to let children always have what they want so that they become selfish.
spoke[1] *n* one of the rods connecting the centre to the rim of a wheel.
spoke[2] *past of* speak.
spoken *past participle of* speak.
sponge *n* **1** a sea creature with a light, soft skeleton full of holes, that soaks up water. **2** a piece of a sponge or similar material used for washing or cleaning. **3** a light cake. **spongy** *adj*.
sponsor *n* **1** a person or company that pays for an event as a form of advertising. **2** a person who promises to pay money if another person completes a task, eg a walk for charity. **sponsor** *v,* **sponsorship** *n.*
spontaneous *adj* not planned beforehand. *a spontaneous act of kindness.* **spontaneity** *n.*
spoon *n* a tool with a handle and a small, shallow bowl for eating soup, cereals, etc.
sport *n* games or competitions involving physical activity.
spot[1] *n* **1** a small, round mark. **2** a small, red mark on your skin. **3** a place. *a nice spot for a picnic.*
spot[2] *v* (spots, spotting, spotted) to notice something. *Can you spot the mistake in this picture?*

spotless *adj* very clean.
spotlight *n* a strong beam of light that is used to light up a small area.
spouse *n* a husband or wife.
spout *n* the part of a kettle, jug, etc where the liquid is poured out.
sprain *v* to twist a joint, for example your ankle, and injure it. **sprain** *n.*
sprang *past of* spring.
sprawl *v* **1** to sit or lie with your arms and legs spread out widely. **2** to spread out untidily. *a huge, sprawling city.*
spray *n* (*pl* sprays) a mist of small, flying drops of liquid. **spray** *v.*
spread *v* (spreading, spread) **1** to cover a surface with something. *I spread the bread with butter.* **2** to open out. *Spread the map out on the table.* **3** to reach a wider area or a larger number of people. *The disease is spreading.* **4** to distribute over a wider area or to a larger number of people. *Spread the news!* **spread** *n.*
sprig *adj* a small piece of a plant.
spring¹ *v* (springing, sprang, sprung) to jump or move suddenly.
spring² *n* **1** the season of the year when plants begin to grow again after winter. **2** a wire coil that returns to its original shape after being pressed down. **3** a small stream flowing out from the ground.
sprinkle *v* to scatter in small drops or bits. *He sprinkled salt on his food.*
sprint *v* to run very fast. **sprinter** *n.*
sprout¹ *v* to start to grow.
sprout² *n* a small, round, green vegetable.
spun *past of* spin.
spur¹ *n* a sharp point on a rider's boot, used to dig into the horse's side to make it go faster. **on the spur of the moment** without planning it.
spur² *v* (spurs, spurring, spurred) to encourage somebody to do something. *The thought of the prize spurred her into action.*
spurt *v* to burst out in a sudden stream. *Water spurted from the pipe.* **spurt** *n.*
spy¹ *n* a person who tries to get secret information, eg about the military operations of another country.
spy² *v* (spies, spying, spied) **1** to be a spy. **2** to notice something.
squabble *v* to quarrel. **squabble** *n.*
squad *n* a small group of soldiers or other people working.
squalid *adj* filthy. **squalor** *n.*
squander *v* to waste something. *She squanders all her money on gambling.*
square¹ *n* **1** a shape with four equal sides and four right angles. **2** an open space with buildings on all sides. **square** *adj.*
square² *v* to multiply a number by itself. *Three squared is nine.*
square root *n* the number which, when multiplied by itself, gives a certain other number. *4 is the square root of 16.*
squash¹ *v* to press or crush something so that it becomes flat.
squash² *n* **1** a game for two players in a walled court using rackets and a rubber ball. **2** a crowd of people in a small space. **3** a fruit drink that you mix with water.
squat *v* (squats, squatting, squatted) **1** to sit on your heels. **2** to occupy a building without permission. **squat** *n.*
squawk *v* to make a loud, harsh cry. **squawk** *n.*
squeak *v* to make a short, high-pitched sound like a mouse. **squeak** *n.*
squeal *v* to make a long, high-pitched sound. **squeal** *n.*
squeeze *v* **1** to press something tightly. **2** to force somebody or something into a small space. **squeeze** *n.*
squid *n* a sea creature with tentacles.
squint *v* **1** to look at something with your eyes half-closed, especially in bright light. **2** to have eyes that look in two directions at once. **squint** *n.*
squirrel *n* a small grey or red mammal with a bushy tail.

grey squirrel

squirt *v* to shoot out a narrow jet of liquid. **squirt** *n.*
St 1 *a short way of writing* saint. *St Patrick.* **2** *a short way of writing* street. *Oxford St.*
stab *v* (stabs, stabbing, stabbed) to push a knife or pointed object into somebody. **stab** *n,* **stabbing** *n.*
stable[1] *n* a building where horses are kept.
stable[2] *adj* **1** firm and steady. *This chair isn't very stable.* **2** firmly established, not changing. *a stable government.* **3** sensible, not easily upset. *a stable personality.*
stack *n* a large pile. **stack** *v.*
stadium *n* (*pl* stadiums *or* stadia) a large sports ground with seats for spectators.

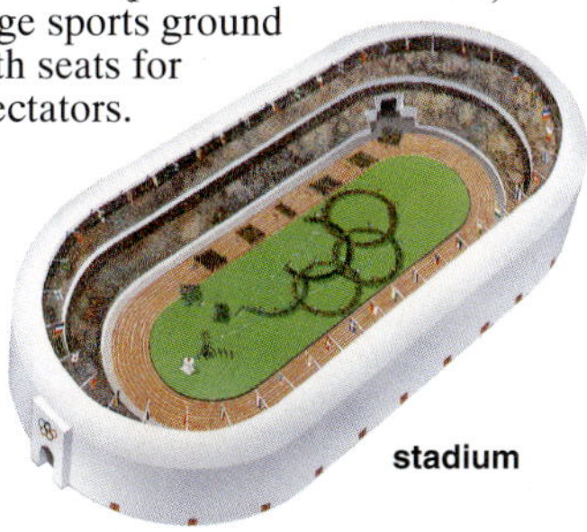

stadium

staff *n* **1** all the people employed by an organization. **2** a thick stick.
stag *n* an adult male deer. See **deer**.
stage[1] *n* **1** a raised platform in a theatre on which people perform plays. **2** a point in the development of something.
stage[2] *v* to organize an event. *The residents are staging a protest.*
stage-coach *n* in earlier times, a horse-drawn vehicle carrying passengers and mail on regular routes.
stagger *v* **1** to walk unsteadily. **2** to shock somebody deeply. *I was staggered by his rudeness.* **3** to arrange events so that they do not begin or end at the same time. *The staff were asked to stagger their holidays.*
staggering *adj* astonishing.
stagnant *adj* (of water) standing still instead of flowing, and therefore not pure. **stagnate** *v.*
stain *n* a mark that is difficult to remove. **stain** *v.*
stained glass *n* coloured glass cut into shapes and fixed together with lead, used in windows.
stairs *n pl* a set of steps in a building.
stake *n* **1** a strong stick, pointed at one end, used for example as part of a fence. **2** a sum of money that you risk or gamble. **3** an investment in a company. **at stake** at risk. **stake** *v.*
stalactite *n* an icicle-shaped rock formation hanging from the roof of a cave, caused by water dripping.
stalagmite *n* an icicle-shaped rock formation rising up from the floor of a cave, caused by water dripping.
stale *adj* no longer fresh.
stalemate *n* a situation in an argument or in a game of chess where neither side can win.
stalk[1] *adj* the main stem of a plant, or one of the stems that hold a leaf, flower or fruit.
stalk[2] *v* **1** to follow an animal or person closely and secretly. **2** to walk stiffly and proudly. *She stalked out of the room in fury.*
stall[1] *n* **1** a table or open-fronted shop with goods for sale. **2** a part of a barn or stable for one animal. **3 stalls** theatre seats on the ground floor.
stall[2] *v* **1** to stop a car engine by mistake. *He stalled at the lights.* **2** to delay doing something.
stallion *n* a male horse.
stamen *n* one of the thread-like parts in the centre of a flower, that hold the pollen. See **flower**.
stamina *n* strength to go on exercising or working for a long time.
stammer *v* to have difficulty saying the first letter of words when you are speaking. **stammer** *n.*
stamp[1] *n* **1** a small piece of printed paper that you stick to a letter or parcel to show that you have paid to send it. **2** a small object that you use to print a design or mark on paper. *a date stamp.*
stamp[2] *v* **1** to bring your foot down with force. **2** to print on something

with a stamp. **3** to put a postage stamp on something.

stand[1] *v* (standing, stood) **1** to be upright. *Helen stood at the top of the stairs.* **2** to get up on your feet. *I stood up when Ian came into the room.* **3** to put something somewhere. *Stand the ladder against the wall.* **4** to remain unchanged. *My decision still stands.* **5** to put up with something, to bear. *I can't stand rudeness!* **stand for** to represent. *"GP" stands for "general practitioner".* **stand in** to take somebody's place. **stand out** to be easily noticed. **stand up for** to support or defend somebody. **stand up to** to defend yourself against somebody.

stand[2] *n* **1** an object for holding or supporting something. *a hat-stand.* **2** a stall where goods are displayed. **3** a structure at a sports ground with seats for spectators.

standard[1] *n* **1** a level against which things can be judged or measured. *His work does not reach the required standard.* **2** a flag.

standard[2] *adj* usual or ordinary. *a standard-sized box of cereals.*

stank *past of* stink.

staple[1] *n* a U-shaped piece of wire that is forced through pieces of paper to fasten them together. **staple** *v*, **stapler** *n.*

staple[2] *adj* chief, main. *Rice is the staple food in many countries.*

star[1] *n* **1** any of the bodies in the sky which are distant suns, appearing as small, bright lights. **2** a shape with a number of points, usually five or six. **3** a famous actor or performer.

star[2] *v* (stars, starring, starred) to have the main part in a play or film.

starboard *n* the right side of a ship or aircraft if you are facing the front.

starch *n* **1** a substance found in foods such as potatoes and rice. **2** a substance used for making clothes stiff. **starch** *v.*

stare *v* to look hard at something for a long time. *Everyone stared at her green hair.* **stare** *n.*

starfish *n* (*pl* starfish) a small sea creature with five points or arms.

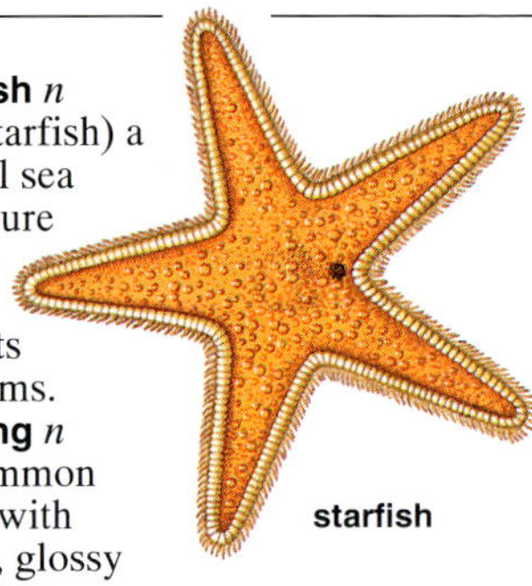

starfish

starling *n* a common bird with dark, glossy feathers.

starry *adj* full of stars. *a starry sky.*

start *v* **1** to begin. **2** to make a machine go. **3** to jump in surprise or fright. **start** *n.*

startle *v* to give somebody a shock or fright.

starve *v* to suffer or die from hunger. **starvation** *n.*

state[1] *n* **1** how somebody or something is. *The house is in an untidy state.* **2** a country or part of a country with its own government and laws.

state[2] *v* to say something clearly and definitely.

stately home *n* a grand old house that the public may visit.

statement *n* **1** something that is stated. **2** a record of all the money paid into and out of an account.

static *adj* not moving or changing.

static electricity *n* electric sparks caused by friction.

station *n* **1** a place where trains or buses stop so that passengers can get on and off. **2** a headquarters or centre. *a fire station, a police station.*

stationary *adj* standing still, not moving.

stationery *n* paper, pens and other materials used for writing.

statistics *n pl* figures that give information about something. **statistical** *adj*, **statistically** *adv.*

statue *n* a model of a person or animal made of stone, metal, clay, etc.

status *n* a position or rank.

stay *v* **1** to continue to be. **2** to live for a time somewhere. **stay** *n.*

steady[1] *adj* (steadier, steadiest) **1** firm,

not shaking or moving. *Hold the camera steady.* **2** regular, even, or not changing. *a steady pace.* **steadily** *adv.*
steady[2] *v* (steadies, steadying, steadied) to make something steady.
steak *n* a thick slice of meat or fish.
steal *v* (stealing, stole, stolen) **1** to take something that does not belong to you, without permission. **2** to move secretly and quietly. *He stole out of the room.*
steam[1] *n* the hot gas that water turns into when it boils. **steamy** *adj.*
steam[2] *v* **1** to give off steam. **2** to cook by steam.
steam-engine *n* an engine, especially a railway engine, powered by steam.

steam-engine

steamroller *n* a steam-driven vehicle with wide, heavy wheels, used for flattening road surfaces.
steel *n* a strong, very hard metal made from iron and carbon.
steep *adj* sloping sharply. **steepness** *n.*
steeple *n* a church tower with a spire.
steer *v* to control the direction of a vehicle.
stem *n* the part of a plant from which the leaves and flowers grow.
stench *n* a strong, unpleasant smell.
stencil *n* a sheet of card, metal, etc with a pattern cut out of it. The pattern is applied to a surface by painting over the stencil. **stencil** *v.*
step[1] *n* **1** the movement of lifting your foot and putting it down again when walking, dancing, etc. **2** one of the places to put your feet when going up or down stairs, a ladder, etc. **3** one stage in doing something.
step[2] *v* (steps, stepping, stepped) to take a step, to walk.
step- *prefix* related through one parent. *stepfather* (= a man married to your mother but who is not your father), *stepsister* (= a female child of your stepmother or stepfather from a previous marriage).
stereo *n* (*pl* stereos) a system for playing recorded music in which different instruments or voices are transmitted through different speakers.
stereotype *n* a fixed idea about a type of person or thing. **stereotypical** *adj.*
sterile *adj* **1** completely clean and free from germs. **2** unable to produce young. **sterility** *n,* **sterilize** *v.*
sterling *n* British money.
stern[1] *adj* serious and severe.
stern[2] *n* the back part of a ship.
stethoscope *n* an instrument used by a doctor to listen to a patient's breathing or heartbeat.

stethoscope

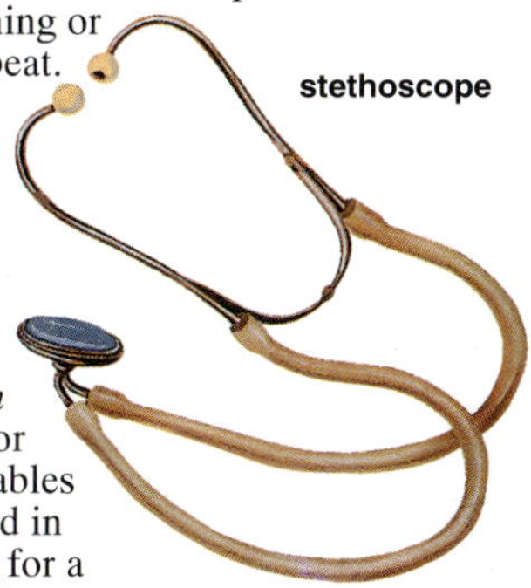

stew[1] *n* meat or vegetables cooked in liquid for a long time.
stew[2] *v* to cook by boiling slowly.
steward *n* **1** a person who looks after passengers on an aeroplane or ship. **2** a person who helps to organize a large public event, race, etc.
stewardess *n* a female steward.
stick[1] *n* **1** a long, thin piece of wood. **2** a long piece of something. *a stick of rock.*
stick[2] *v* (sticking, stuck) **1** to push something pointed into something else. **2** to fix something to something else using glue, etc. **3** to become fixed. *My boot got stuck in the mud.* **stick out 1** to be farther out than something else. *His front teeth stick out.* **2** to be very noticeable. **stick up for** to support or defend somebody.

sticker *n* a sticky label with a picture or words on it.
sticky *adj* (stickier, stickiest) capable of sticking to things.
stiff *adj* **1** not easy to bend. *stiff cardboard.* **2** moving with difficulty or pain. *I woke up with a stiff neck.* **3** severe, harsh. *a stiff punishment.* **4** too formal in behaviour. **stiffen** *v.*
stifle *v* to suffocate.
still[1] *adj* **1** not moving. **2** not fizzy.
still[2] *adv* **1** continuing until now. *Is it still snowing?* **2** even so. *Alice was ill but she still went out.* **3** even. *It was cold earlier and it's colder still now.*
stilts *n pl* **1** long poles with parts where you put your feet to walk high above the ground. **2** tall poles on which a house is built.
stimulate *v* to make a person or thing more active. **stimulation** *n.*
sting[1] *n* **1** the part of some animals and plants that can prick your skin. **2** the wound or pain caused by a sting.
sting[2] *v* (stinging, stung) **1** to wound with a sting. **2** to feel or cause pain like a sting. *The soap made my eyes sting.*
stingy *(**stin**-jee) adj* (stingier, stingiest) mean, not generous. **stinginess** *n.*
stink *v* (stinking, stank, stunk) to smell very unpleasant. **stink** *n.*
stir[1] *v* (stirs, stirring, stirred) **1** to move liquid around with a spoon, etc. **2** to move slightly. *She stirred in her sleep.* **3** to arouse somebody.
stir[2] *n* a disturbance or fuss.
stirrup *n* a metal loop hung from a horse's saddle as a support for the rider's foot.
stitch[1] *n* **1** the loop made in wool or thread by a needle in knitting or sewing. **2** a sudden pain in your side.
stitch[2] *v* to sew something.
stock[1] *n* **1** the store of goods in a shop or warehouse. **2** a share in the value of a company. **3** a liquid used to make soups, sauces, etc. **4 stocks** in earlier times, a wooden structure with holes for the feet, where criminals were put as a punishment.
stock[2] *v* to keep a supply of goods for sale.
stocking *n* a close-fitting piece of clothing that covers your foot and leg.
stocky *adj* (stockier, stockiest) short and stout.
stodgy *adj* (stodgier, stodgiest) (of food) heavy and not easily digested.
stole *past of* steal.
stolen *past participle of* steal.
stomach *n* the part inside your body where food is digested. See **digestion**.
stone *n* **1** a hard, solid substance found in the ground. **2** a piece of this. **3** the hard seed inside some fruits, such as plums and peaches. **4** an old measure of weight equal to 14 pounds or 6.35 kilogrammes.
stony *adj* (stonier, stoniest) full of, or covered with, stones.
stood *past of* stand.
stool *n* a seat without a back.
stoop *v* to bend your body forward and down.
stop *v* (stops, stopping, stopped) **1** to finish moving or happening. **2** to finish doing something. **3** to prevent. **4** to fill a hole or gap. **stop** *n.*
stopwatch *n* a watch that you can stop and start, used in timing races.
store[1] *v* to keep things until they are needed. **storage** *n.*
store[2] *n* **1** a large shop. **2** a supply of something that you keep for future use. **3** a place where things are kept.
storey *n* (*pl* storeys) one level of a building.
stork *n* a large, white bird with a long beak, neck and legs.

stork

storm[1] *n* very bad weather, with strong winds, heavy rain, and often thunder and lightning.
storm[2] *v* **1** to move somewhere in an angry and noisy way. *Dad stormed out of the room.* **2** to attack a place suddenly. *They stormed the castle.*
story *n* an account of people and events that are real or imaginary.

stout *adj* **1** quite fat. **2** strong.
stove *n* an apparatus for cooking or for heating a room.
stowaway *n* (*pl* stowaways) a person who hides in a ship, aircraft, etc in order to travel in secret or without paying.
straight[1] *adj* **1** not bent or curved. *a straight line.* **2** level. *That picture isn't straight.* **3** honest. *a straight answer.* **4** neat and tidy. *It took hours to get the room straight.* **straighten** *v*.
straight[2] *adv* **1** in a straight line. **2** directly.
straightaway *adv* immediately.
straightforward *adj* **1** simple, without difficulties. *a straightforward task.* **2** honest and open. *a straightforward person.*
strain[1] *v* **1** to try very hard to do something. *He had to strain his ears to hear her.* **2** to injure a part of your body by using it too much or stretching the muscles. **3** to separate solid matter from a liquid by using a sieve or something similar.
strain[2] *n* **1** straining something. **2** the bad effect of too much work or worry.
strait *n* a narrow strip of sea between two pieces of land.
strand *n* a length of something, especially hair or thread.
stranded *adj* left helpless somewhere.
strange *adj* **1** odd, unusual. **2** not known, seen, etc before.
stranger *n* **1** a person you do not know. **2** a person who is in a place for the first time. *I'm a stranger in this town.*
strangle *v* to kill somebody by squeezing their throat hard. **strangulation** *n*.
strap[1] *n* a strip of leather, cloth, etc used to fasten or hold things.
strap[2] *v* (straps, strapping, strapped) to fasten something with straps.
strategy *n* a plan for achieving something. **strategic** *adj*, **strategically** *adv*.
straw *n* **1** dry stalks of corn. **2** a thin tube for drinking through.
strawberry *n* a small, red, soft fruit.
stray[1] *v* to wander away.
stray[2] *n* a lost cat or dog.
streak[1] *n* a long mark or stripe.
streak[2] *v* to run fast.
stream[1] *n* **1** a small river. **2** a flow of anything.
stream[2] *v* to move or flow fast.
streamer *n* a long strip of coloured paper, used for decorating a place.
streamline *v* to shape a vehicle so that it can cut through air or water easily.
street *n* a road with buildings along it.
strength *n* being strong. **strengthen** *v*.
strenuous *adj* needing a lot of effort. *a strenuous climb.*
stress[1] *n* the effect of too much worry or work.
stress[2] *v* to give special emphasis or importance to something.
stretch[1] *v* **1** to make or become longer or bigger, especially by pulling. **2** to reach or extend. *The beach stretches for several kilometres.*
stretch[2] *n* **1** stretching. **2** a length of time or a distance. *a stretch of road.*
stretcher *n* a light, folding bed for carrying sick or injured people.
strict *adj* **1** not allowing people to break rules or behave badly. **2** exact. *the strict truth.* **strictness** *n*.
stride *v* (striding, strode, stridden) to walk with long steps. **stride** *n*.
strife *n* trouble or fighting.
strike *v* (striking, struck) **1** to hit hard. **2** to stop work as a protest. **3** to make a ringing sound. *The clock struck two.* **4** to impress. *I was struck by her beauty.* **5** to make a flame by rubbing. *He struck a match.* **strike** *n*.
striker *n* an attacking player in football.
striking *adj* noticeable, impressive.
string *n* **1** thin cord or rope. **2** a piece of thin wire, nylon, etc on a musical instrument. **3 the strings** the musical instruments in an orchestra that have strings.
strip[1] *n* a long, narrow piece.
strip[2] *v* (strips, stripping, stripped) **1** to take off all your clothes. **2** to tear off.
stripe *n* a band of colour. **striped** *adj*, **stripy** *adj*.
strive *v* (striving, strove, striven) to try hard, to struggle.

strode *past of* stride.
stroke[1] *v* to move your hand gently over something.
stroke[2] *n* **1** stroking something. **2** a hit. *a stroke of the axe.* **3** a sudden occurrence of something. *a stroke of luck.* **4** a sudden illness that can paralyse part of a person's body or leave them unable to speak properly. **5** one movement of a pen, paintbrush, etc. **6** one movement in swimming.
stroll *v* to walk along slowly, for pleasure. **stroll** *n.*
strong *adj* **1** powerful, not weak. **2** not easily broken or damaged. **3** very noticeable, intense. *a strong smell.*
strove *past of* strive.
struck *past of* strike.
structure *n* **1** something that has been built. **2** the way the parts of something are arranged.
struggle *v* **1** to try hard to do something difficult. *Lauren is struggling with her homework.* **2** to fight with somebody to escape. **struggle** *n.*
strut[1] *v* (struts, strutting, strutted) to walk along in a stiff, proud way.
strut[2] *n* a wooden or metal bar that supports something.
stub[1] *n* the short, blunt end piece, for example of a cigarette or pencil.
stub[2] *v* (stubs, stubbing, stubbed) to hit your toe against something.
stubborn *adj* not willing to change, or to do what other people want. **stubbornness** *n.*
stuck *past of* stick.
student *n* a person who is studying, usually at a college or university.
studio *n* (*pl* studios) **1** a room where an artist or photographer works. **2** a place where films, CDs, etc are made.
studious *adj* spending a lot of time studying.
study[1] *v* (studies, studying, studied) **1** to spend time learning about something. **2** to look carefully at something. *We studied the map.*
study[2] *n* a room where somebody reads, writes or studies.
stuff[1] *n* any material or substance.
stuff[2] *v* to pack or fill something tightly. *The pillow is stuffed with feathers.* **stuffing** *n.*
stuffy *adj* (stuffier, stuffiest) **1** full of stale air. *a stuffy room.* **2** too formal and old-fashioned.
stumble *v* **1** to trip and almost fall, or walk unsteadily. **2** to make mistakes or hesitate when speaking.
stump *n* **1** the part of something that is left when the rest has been cut or broken off. *a tree stump.* **2** one of the three upright wooden poles at which the ball is bowled in cricket.
stun *v* (stuns, stunning, stunned) **1** to make a person or an animal unconscious by a blow on the head. **2** to shock somebody.
stung *past of* sting.
stunk *past participle of* stink.
stunning *adj* very attractive or impressive.
stunt[1] *n* something daring or spectacular, done to attract attention.
stunt[2] *v* to stop something growing or developing properly.
stupid *adj* silly or not intelligent. **stupidity** *n.*
sturdy *adj* (sturdier, sturdiest) strong, well-built.
stutter *v* to stammer. **stutter** *n.*
sty *n* **1** (*also* **stye**) a painful, red swelling on your eyelid. **2** a pen in which pigs are kept.
style *n* **1** the way something is done or made. *different styles of architecture.* **2** elegance in dress, behaviour, etc. *He's got style.* **stylish** *adj.*
sub- *prefix* under, below. *sub-zero temperatures, substandard.*
subdue *v* to bring somebody or something under control.
subdued *adj* quiet or sad. *John is very subdued today.*
subject[1] *(sub-jekt) n* **1** the thing or person being talked or written about. **2** an area of study at school, etc. **3** a citizen. *a British subject.*
subject[2] *(sub-**jekt**) v* to make somebody suffer something. *She was subjected to cruel treatment.*
submarine *n* a type of boat that can travel underwater.

submerge *v* to put something under water.
subscribe *v* to pay for a magazine or newspaper to be sent to you regularly. **subscription** *n.*
subside *v* **1** to sink lower. *The flood gradually subsided.* **2** to become quieter. *She waited until the applause subsided before she spoke.*
subsidy *n* money paid by a government, etc to keep the price of something low. **subsidize** *v.*
substance *n* anything that can be seen or touched, a material.
substantial *adj* **1** large. *a substantial meal.* **2** solid, strong.
substitute *v* to put something in the place of something else. *You can substitute margarine for butter in this recipe.* **substitute** *n.*
subtle *(sut-ul) adj* not very noticeable or obvious. *a subtle difference.* **subtlety** *n,* **subtly** *adv.*
subtract *v* to take one number or quantity away from another. **subtraction** *n.*
suburb *n* an area on the edge of a large town or city where people live. **suburban** *adj.*
subway *n* (*pl* subways) **1** a tunnel under a road or railway where people can walk. **2** in American English, an underground railway.
succeed *v* **1** to manage to do something that you were trying to do. **2** to follow after somebody and take their place. *Who will succeed John Fraser as manager of the club?* **success** *n*, **successful** *adj.*
suck *v* **1** to draw liquid or air into your mouth. **2** to hold a sweet, etc in your mouth and lick it hard. **3** to draw something in. *Vacuum cleaners suck up dust.* **suction** *n.*
sudden *adj* happening quickly and unexpectedly. **suddenness** *n.*
sue *v* to start a legal case, usually in order to get money from somebody.
suede *(swade) n* a type of leather with a soft surface like velvet.
suffer *v* to experience pain or unhappiness. **suffering** *n.*
sufficient *adj* enough.
suffix *n* a letter or letters added to the end of the word to make another word, such as *-ness* to *good* to make *goodness* and *-ly* to *quick* to make *quickly.*
suffocate *v* **1** to die because you cannot breathe. **2** to kill somebody by preventing them from breathing. **suffocation** *n.*
sugar *n* a sweet substance obtained from plants such as sugar-cane and sugar-beet. **sugary** *adj.*
suggest *v* to put forward an idea. **suggestion** *n.*
suicide *n* the act of killing yourself deliberately. **suicidal** *adj.*
suit[1] *n* **1** a jacket with trousers or a skirt, made to be worn together. **2** one of the four sets of playing-cards (hearts, diamonds, clubs and spades). **3** a case in a law court.
suit[2] *v* **1** to look good on somebody. *That colour really suits you.* **2** to be convenient or suitable. *Would Friday suit you for a meeting?*
suitable *adj* right or convenient for somebody or something. **suitability** *n.*
suitcase *n* a case with flat sides, for carrying your clothes in when you are travelling.
suite *(sweet) n* **1** a set of pieces of furniture. *a three-piece suite* (= a sofa and two armchairs). **2** a set of rooms in a hotel.
sulk *v* to show anger by being silent. **sulky** *adj,* **sulkily** *adv.*
sullen *adj* bad-tempered and silent.
sulphur *n* a yellow chemical element with a strong, unpleasant smell, used to make matches, gunpowder, etc.
sultan *n* a Muslim ruler.
sultana *n* a dried, seedless grape.
sum[1] *n* **1** the total made by adding two or more numbers together. **2** an amount of money. **3** a problem in arithmetic.
sum[2] *v* (sums, summing, summed) **sum up** to give the main points of something.
summary *n* a short description of the main points. *The newspaper printed a summary of her speech.* **summarize** *v.*

summer *n* the warmest season of the year, between spring and autumn.
summit *n* **1** the top of a mountain. **2** an important meeting of world leaders.
summon *v* to order somebody to come.
sumo *n* a Japanese form of wrestling. See **wrestling**.
sun *n* **1 Sun** the star that shines during the day and gives us heat and light. **2** light and heat from the Sun. **3** any star. **sunny** *adj.*
sunbathe *v* to lie or sit in sunshine to get a suntan.
sunburn *n* red, sore skin caused by being in sunshine for too long.
Sunday *n* the first day of the week.
sundial *n* an instrument for telling the time from the shadow of a rod cast on its surface by the sunlight.
sunflower *n* a tall, large, yellow flower.
sung *past participle of* sing.
sunglasses *n pl* glasses with dark lenses to protect your eyes in bright sunlight.
sunk *past participle of* sink.

sunflower

sunrise *n* the rising of the Sun in the morning.
sunset *n* the going down of the Sun in the evening.
sunshine *n* bright light from the Sun.
suntan *n* a brown colour of the skin caused by spending time in the sunshine.
super *adj* extremely good, wonderful.
super- *prefix* above, over, more than. *super-fit* (= extremely fit).
superb *adj* excellent, magnificent.
superficial *adj* on the surface only. *The cut is only superficial – it will soon heal.* **superficially** *adv.*
superior *adj* **1** better. **2** higher in rank. **3** thinking that you are better than others. **superiority** *n.*
supermarket *n* a large shop selling food and other goods.
supernatural *adj* not capable of being explained by the laws of nature. *a supernatural being.*
supersonic *adj* faster than the speed of sound.
superstition *n* a belief in powers that cannot be explained, especially a belief that certain things bring good or bad luck. **superstitious** *adj.*
supervise *v* to be in charge of work and see that it is properly done. **supervision** *n,* **supervisor** *n.*
supper *n* an evening meal.
supple *adj* able to bend and stretch easily. *Exercise will keep your body supple.* **suppleness** *n.*
supplement *n* something that is added to something else. **supplementary** *adj.*
supply *v* (supplies, supplying, supplied) to give or provide something. **supplier** *n,* **supply** *n.*
support *v* **1** to carry the weight of something. *That bridge won't support heavy lorries.* **2** to give somebody money, help or encouragement. *Her family supported her in her decision.* **3** to be a fan of a particular sports team. **support** *n,* **supporter** *n.*
suppose *v* to think that something is true, but not be sure.
suppress *v* **1** to stop something by using force. *The army suppressed the rebellion.* **2** to keep back feelings, etc. *She suppressed a yawn.*
supreme *adj* greatest, most important or best. **supremacy** *n.*
sure *adj* having no doubt, certain.
surf[1] *n* the foam that is produced as waves break on the shore.
surf[2] *v* to ride on surf, using a long, narrow board called a **surfboard**. **surfer** *n.*
surface *n* the outside or top part of something.
surgeon *(ser-jun) n* a doctor who performs operations.
surgery *n* **1** a place where a doctor or dentist sees patients. **2** treating a disease or injury by operating. **surgical** *adj,* **surgically** *adv.*

surly *adj* (surlier, surliest) rude and unfriendly. **surliness** *n.*
surname *n* a person's last name or family name.
surplus *n* what is left over.
surprise *n* **1** the feeling that you have when something unexpected happens. **2** an unexpected event. **surprise** *v.*
surrender *v* to give up, to admit that you are defeated. **surrender** *n.*
surround *v* to be all around something.
surroundings *n pl* everything that is around somebody or something.
survey[1] *(ser-**vay**)* *v* **1** to look at the whole of something. *She surveyed the garden from her window.* **2** to measure and make a map of an area of land. **surveyor** *n.*
survey[2] *(**ser**-vay)* *n* (*pl* surveys) **1** surveying something. **2** a study of something, especially of people's opinions.
survive *v* to continue to live or exist. **survival** *n,* **survivor** *n.*
suspect[1] *(sus-**pekt**)* *v* **1** to believe that something may be true. *I suspect that she's unhappy.* **2** to believe that a person is guilty of something.
suspect[2] *(**sus**-pekt)* *n* a person who is thought to be guilty of a crime.
suspend *v* **1** to hang something up. **2** to stop something for a while. **3** to stop somebody doing their job, etc for a while, as a punishment. **suspension** *n.*
suspense *n* a state of uncertainty or worry.
suspicion *n* the suspecting of somebody or something.
suspicious *adj* **1** feeling or showing suspicion. **2** causing suspicion.
swallow[1] *v* to make food or drink go down your throat.
swallow[2] *n* a small bird with long, slim wings and a forked tail.
swam *past of* swim.
swamp *n* wet, marshy ground.
swan *n* a large, white, long-necked water bird.
swap *v* (swaps, swapping, swapped) to exchange one thing for another. *We swapped phone numbers.* **swap** *n.*
swarm *n* a large group of bees or other insects moving together. **swarm** *v.*
swat *v* (swats, swatting, swatted) to kill an insect by hitting it with something flat.
sway *v* to move from side to side.
swear *v* (swearing, swore, sworn) **1** to make a solemn promise. **2** to use rude words.
sweat *n* the liquid that comes out of your skin when you are hot or nervous. **sweat** *v,* **sweaty** *adj.*
sweater *n* a jumper.
sweatshirt *n* a thick, cotton sweater.
swede *n* a large, yellow turnip.
sweep *v* (sweeping, swept) **1** to clean by removing dirt, dust, etc with a broom. **2** to move quickly and with force. *The boat was swept out to sea by the huge waves.*
sweet[1] *adj* **1** tasting like sugar, not salty or sour. **2** pleasant, lovely. *a sweet smell.* **sweetness** *n.*
sweet[2] *n* **1** a small piece of sweet food. **2** a dessert.
sweetcorn *n* yellow grains of maize that are eaten as a vegetable.
swell *v* (swelling, swelled, swollen) to become bigger or fatter. *The insect bite made her finger swell up.* **swelling** *n.*
sweltering *adj* very hot.
swept *past of* sweep.
swerve *v* to change direction suddenly. *The driver swerved to avoid the dog.*
swift[1] *adj* quick. **swiftness** *n.*
swift[2] *n* a bird similar to a swallow.
swim *v* (swims, swimming, swam, swum) to use your arms and legs to move yourself through water. **swim** *n,* **swimmer** *n.*
swindle *v* to cheat somebody out of money.
swing[1] *v* (swinging, swung) to move backwards and forwards or from side to side.
swing[2] *n* a seat for swinging, hung on ropes or chains from a support.
swirl *v* to move round and round.
switch *n* **1** a device for turning a light or other electrical appliance on and off. **2** a sudden change. **switch** *v.*

switchboard *n* the place in a large office, hotel, etc where all the telephone calls are connected.
swivel *v* (swivels, swivelling, swivelled) to turn on a central point.
swollen *past participle of* swell.
swoop *v* to rush or fly downwards. *The eagle swooped on its prey.* **swoop** *n.*
swop *another spelling of* swap.
sword *(sord) n* a weapon with a handle and a long blade.
swore *past of* swear.
sworn *past participle of* swear.
swot *v* (swots, swotting, swotted) to study hard.
swum *past participle of* swim.
swung *past of* swing.
syllable *n* a word or part of a word spoken with one breath. *Ambulance has three syllables: am-bu-lance.*
syllabus *n* (*pl* syllabuses *or* syllabi) a list of subjects to be studied.
symbol *n* a thing that stands for or represents something. *The cross is a symbol of Christianity.* **symbolic** *adj*, **symbolize** *v.*
symmetrical *adj* having the same shape and size on both sides of a central line. **symmetry** *n.*

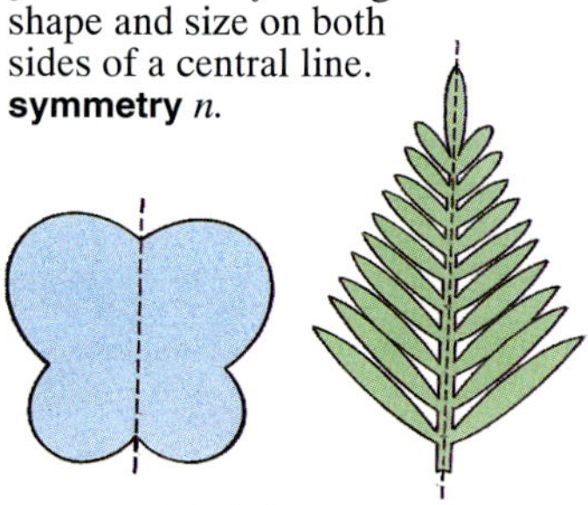

symmetrical shapes

sympathy *n* an understanding of other people's feelings and problems. **sympathetic** *adj*, **sympathetically** *adv*, **sympathize** *v.*
symphony *(sim-fa-nee) n* a long piece of music for a large orchestra.
symptom *n* a sign that you have an illness. *Sneezing, a fever and headache are the symptoms of flu.*
synagogue *(sin-a-gog) n* a Jewish place of worship.
synonym *n* a word that has the same meaning as another word.
synthesizer *n* an electronic keyboard instrument that can make many different sounds.
synthetic *adj* created artificially.
syringe *n* an instrument with a tube and a needle, used to take blood, inject drugs, etc.
syrup *n* a sticky, sweet liquid, made from sugar.
system *n* **1** an arrangement of several parts which work together. *the railway system.* **2** a way of organizing something. *a system of education.*

Tt

tab *n* a small piece of metal, paper, cloth, etc attached to something, so it can be pulled, identified, etc.
tabby *n* a grey or brown striped cat.
table *n* **1** a piece of furniture with a flat top on legs. **2** a list of facts or figures arranged in columns.
tablespoon *n* a large spoon used for serving or measuring food.
tablet *n* **1** a small, hard piece of medicine that you swallow. **2** a flat block of stone with words cut into it.
table tennis *n* a game played on a table with small bats and a light ball.
tabloid *n* a small-sized newspaper.
taboo *n* anything forbidden for religious reasons or by social custom.
tack[1] *n* a small, flat-headed nail.
tack[2] *v* **1** to attach something with tacks. *They tacked the carpet down.* **2** to sew with long, loose stitches. **3** to sail a boat on a zigzag course into the wind.
tackle[1] *v* **1** to deal with a difficulty. *We still have several problems to tackle.* **2** to try to stop or take the ball from

another player in a game such as football.
tackle[2] *n* equipment for a sport or another activity. *fishing tackle.*
tact *n* skill in dealing with people so that you do not upset them. **tactless** *adj*, **tactful** *adj.*
tactics *n pl* plans or methods used to win a game, contest, battle, etc. **tactical** *adj.*
tadpole *n* a young frog or toad at the stage between the egg and the adult.
tag *n* **1** a small label. **2** a chasing game.
tail *n* **1** the part of a creature that sticks out behind the rest of its body. **2** the end part. *the tail of a plane.*
tailor *n* a person who makes suits, coats and other clothes.
take *v* (taking, took, taken) **1** to reach out for something and grasp or hold it. *Take this money.* **2** to carry or lead to another place. *I took the books back to the library.* **3** to accept. *Do you take credit cards?* **4** to need or require. *It takes a long time to learn the piano.* **5** to travel by bus, train, etc. *We're taking the next bus to Oxford.* **6** to do an action. *They decided to take a walk.* **take after** to be or look like somebody in your family. *Doesn't Ella take after her mum?* **take off 1** to remove clothes. **2** (of a plane) to leave the ground. **3** to copy the way somebody talks or behaves. **take over** to take control of something. *Ann took over the business when her father retired.*
take-away *n* (*pl* take-aways) food prepared and bought in a restaurant and eaten at home.
talcum powder *n* a fine powder used for rubbing on your body after a bath.
tale *n* **1** a story. **2** a lie.
talent *n* a special ability or skill. *He has a talent for music.* **talented** *adj.*
talk[1] *v* to say things, to speak.
talk[2] *n* **1** a conversation or discussion. **2** a short lecture.
talkative *adj* talking a lot.
tall *adj* high, or higher than average.
talon *n* a sharp claw.
tambourine *n* a musical instrument shaped like a shallow drum, with tinkling metal discs around it.
tame *adj* used to living with people, not wild or dangerous. **tame** *v.*
tamper *v* to interfere with or touch something when you should not. *Someone has tampered with this lock.*
tampon *n* a plug of cotton wool that a woman inserts into her vagina to soak up blood during a period.
tan[1] *n* **1** light brown. **2** a suntan.
tan[2] *v* (tans, tanning, tanned) **1** to go brown in the sun. **2** to make animal skin into leather by treating it with chemicals.
tandem *n* a bicycle for two people.

tandem

tang *n* a sharp taste or smell. **tangy** *adj.*
tangent *n* a straight line that touches a circle or curve without crossing it.
tangerine *n* a small, loose-skinned orange.
tangle *n* an untidy, twisted mass of threads, etc. **tangle** *v.*
tank *n* **1** a large container for liquids. **2** a heavy, steel-covered military vehicle armed with guns.
tanker *n* a ship or lorry for carrying liquids, especially oil.
tantrum *n* a sudden fit of bad temper.
tap[1] *n* a device for controlling the flow of a liquid or gas.
tap[2] *v* (taps, tapping, tapped) **1** to knock lightly. *I tapped on the door.* **2** to attach a listening device secretly to a telephone wire.
tapdance *n* a dance done with special shoes that make a tapping sound.
tape[1] *n* **1** a strip of magnetic material used for recording sound or pictures, contained in a plastic box. **2** a strip of cloth, paper, plastic, etc.

tape² *v* **1** to record something on tape. **2** to fasten something with tape.
tape-measure *n* a narrow strip of paper, plastic, etc used for measuring length.
taper *v* to become thinner at one end.
tape-recorder *n* an instrument for recording sound on tape and playing it back again.
tapestry *n* a cloth with pictures or designs woven into it.
tar *n* a thick, black, sticky liquid that comes from oil, used for covering the surface of roads.
tarantula *n* a large, poisonous spider.
target *n* **1** a person or thing that you aim at when shooting or attacking. **2** a result that you are trying to achieve.
tarmac *n* a mixture of tar and small stones used for making the surface of roads.
tarpaulin *n* strong, waterproof cloth.
tart¹ *n* an open pie, usually filled with something sweet such as fruit.
tart² *adj* sharp, sour. **tartness** *n.*
tartan *n* a traditional Scottish woollen cloth with squares of different colours.
task *n* a job, a piece of work.
tassel *n* a bunch of hanging threads used to decorate a cushion, hat, etc.
taste¹ *n* **1** the ability to recognize the flavour of food and drink. **2** the feeling a food or drink gives you in your mouth. *This cheese has a salty taste.* **3** the ability to know what is good, fine or beautiful. *He has good taste in clothes.*
taste² *v* **1** to recognize the flavour of something. *Can you taste ginger in this cake?* **2** to try a little of a food or drink. *Taste this and tell me if it's too salty.* **3** to have a particular flavour. *Honey tastes sweet.*
tattoo *n* a coloured design on a person's skin, made by pricking with needles and putting in dyes.
tatty *adj* (tattier, tattiest) in bad condition.
taught *past of* teach.
taunt *v* to tease somebody in a cruel way. **taunt** *n.*
taut *(tawt) adj* stretched tight.
tavern *n* in earlier times, a pub.
tawny *adj* yellowish-brown in colour.
tax *n* money paid to the government by people and businesses to help pay for public services. **tax** *v*, **taxation** *n.*
taxi¹ *n* (*pl* taxis) a car with a driver that can be hired for short journeys.
taxi² *v* (taxies, taxiing, taxied) (of an aeroplane) to travel on the runway before or after takeoff.
tea *n* **1** a drink made from the dried leaves of a plant grown in Asia and Africa. **2** a meal eaten in the afternoon or early evening.

tea picker

teach *v* (teaching, taught) to give somebody knowledge or a skill. **teacher** *n.*
teak *n* a tree that grows in Asia, or its very hard wood.
team *n* **1** a group of people who play a sport or game together on the same side. **2** a group of people who work together.
teapot *n* a pot with a spout for making and pouring out tea.
tear¹ *(rhymes with* where*) v* (tearing, tore, torn) **1** to pull something apart or make a hole in something with a sudden pulling action. *She tore the photo to pieces.* **2** to rush. *He went tearing down the road.* **tear** *n.*
tear² *(rhymes with* here*) n* a drop of liquid from your eye.
tease *v* to annoy or laugh at somebody playfully and often unkindly. *The*

other children teased Will because of his accent.

teaspoon *n* a small spoon that is used for stirring drinks.

teat *n* **1** an animal's nipple, through which it feeds milk to its young. **2** a rubber part shaped like this, attached to a baby's feeding bottle.

technical *adj* **1** to do with a science or practical skill. *They have the technical knowledge to build permanent space stations.* **2** to do with a particular subject. *There are a lot of technical words connected with computing.* **technically** *adv*.

technique *n* the way in which something is done, a method.

technology *n* the practical use of science. **technological** *adj*.

teddy, teddybear *n* a stuffed toy bear.

tedious *adj* long and boring.

teem *v* **1** to be full of moving people or animals. *The river was teeming with fish.* **2** to rain heavily.

teenager *n* a person between the ages of 13 and 19. **teenage** *adj*.

teens *n pl* the years of your life between the ages of 13 and 19.

tee-shirt *n* a cotton shirt that you pull on over your head, usually with short sleeves and no collar or buttons.

teeth *plural of* tooth.

teethe *v* to grow your first teeth.

teetotal *adj* never drinking alcohol.

telecommunications *n pl* the sending of information by telephone, radio, television, satellite, etc.

telegram *n* a message sent by telegraph or radio.

telegraph *n* a system of sending messages by the use of an electrical current along wires.

telephone *n* an instrument for talking to people over long distances by using an electrical current travelling along wires, or radio waves. **telephone** *v*.

telescope *n* a tube-shaped instrument which makes distant things appear larger and nearer.

televise *v* to broadcast on television.

television *n* **1** an apparatus with a screen that shows moving pictures with sound. **2** the sending of pictures and sounds for people to watch on their televisions.

tell *v* (telling, told) **1** to give information to somebody. *Tell me about your holiday.* **2** to order somebody to do something. **3** to know or see something. *I can't tell the difference between the twins.* **tell off** to speak angrily to somebody because they have done something wrong.

telly *short for* television.

temper *n* a tendency to get angry easily. *She has a terrible temper.* **lose your temper** to show that you are angry.

temperament *n* the way you feel and behave.

temperamental *adj* easily getting upset or excited, moody.

temperate *adj* (of climate) neither very hot nor very cold.

temperature *n* **1** a measure of how hot or cold something is. **2** a fever.

tempest *n* a violent storm.

template *n* a pattern that you draw around and use as a guide for cutting paper, cloth, metal, etc.

temple *n* **1** a building used for worship. **2** the small, flat area on each side of your forehead.

temple

tempo *n* (*pl* tempos) the speed at which a piece of music is played.

temporary *adj* lasting only for a time, not permanent. **temporarily** *adv*.

tempt *v* to make somebody want to do something, especially something they ought not to do. **temptation** *n*.

tenant *n* a person who rents a house, flat, etc.

tend *v* **1** to be likely to behave in a certain way. *She tends to get angry easily.* **2** to look after something.
tendency *n* the way a person or thing tends to be or behave. *She has a tendency to get angry.*
tender *adj* **1** soft, not hard or tough. *This meat is very tender.* **2** sensitive or sore. *My leg still feels quite tender where I banged it.* **3** loving and gentle. *tender looks.* **tenderness** *n.*
tendon *n* a tough cord joining a muscle to a bone.
tennis *n* a game for two or four players using rackets to hit a ball to each other over a net in a specially marked area (a **tennis court**).
tenor *n* the highest natural adult male singing voice.
tense[1] *adj* **1** nervous or worried. **2** tightly stretched. *tense muscles.* **tense** *v*, **tension** *n.*
tense[2] *n* the form of a verb that shows when an action happened, such as the past tense and the present tense.
tent *n* a shelter made of canvas or nylon, stretched over a frame of poles and held up with ropes.
tentacle *n* a long, thin part of an animal used to feel or grasp. *Octopuses have tentacles.*

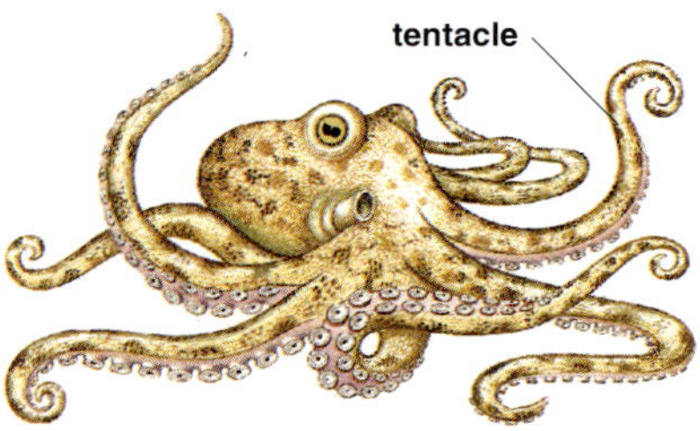

tepee *(**tee**-pee)* *n* a tent made from animal skins by Native Americans.
tepid *adj* slightly warm.
term *n* **1** a length of time. **2** a part of the school year. **3 terms** the conditions of an agreement. **4** a word or phrase.
terminal[1] *n* **1** a building where passengers arrive and depart by plane, bus, etc. **2** a computer monitor connected to a network.
terminal[2] *adj* (of an illness) not able to be cured, fatal.
terminate *v* to end or stop. *The train terminates here.*
terrace *n* **1** a row of houses built as a single block. **2** a level area cut into the side of a slope. **3** an open, paved area next to a restaurant, house, etc where people can sit. **4 terraces** steps in a sports stadium where people stand to watch matches.
terracotta *n* a brownish-red clay used for making pots, tiles, etc.
terrapin *n* a small kind of turtle.
terrestrial *adj* to do with the Earth.
terrible *adj* very bad, dreadful. **terribly** *adv.*
terrier *n* a breed of small dog.
terrific *adj* **1** marvellous, wonderful. *terrific news.* **2** very great or powerful. *a terrific storm.* **terrifically** *adv.*
terrify *v* (terrifies, terrifying, terrified) to make somebody very frightened.
territory *n* **1** an area of land. **2** an area of land controlled by one country or ruler. **territorial** *adj.*
terror *n* very great fear.
terrorist *n* a person who tries to frighten people or governments into doing what they want by using violence or threats. *The bomb was planted by terrorists.* **terrorism** *n.*
terrorize *v* to frighten very much.
test[1] *v* **1** to try out or examine something to see what it is like. *Do you believe drugs should be tested on animals?* **2** to ask somebody questions or set them exercises to find out what they know or what they can do.
test[2] *n* **1** a set of questions or exercises to find out what you know or what you can do. **2** a medical examination. *an eye test.* **3** trying out or examining something to see what it is like.
testicles *n pl* one of the two glands in a man's body that produce sperm.
testify *v* (testifies, testifying, testified) to give evidence in a law court.
test tube *n* a glass tube closed at one end, used in chemical tests.
tether *n* a rope for tying an animal to a post, etc. **tether** *v.*

text *n* the main written part of a book, newspaper, etc.
textbook *n* a book used for teaching a subject in a school or college.
textile *n* a woven cloth or fabric.
texture *n* the way something feels when you touch it.
thank *v* to tell somebody that you are grateful to them. **thanks** *n.*
thankful *adj* grateful or happy. **thankfully** *adv.*
thatch *n* a roof covering made from straw or reeds. **thatched** *adj.*
thaw *v* to make or become soft or liquid again after freezing. *Take the meat out of the freezer to thaw.*
theatre *n* **1** a place where plays are performed. **2** a room in a hospital where surgical operations take place.
theatrical *adj* to do with the theatre.
theft *n* stealing.
their *adj* belonging to them. *This is their house.* **theirs** *pron.*
theme *n* the main subject.
theme park *n* a park with many different amusements that are all based on a single idea.
then *adv* **1** at that time. **2** after that, next. **3** in that case.
theology *n* the study of religion. **theological** *adj.*
theory *n* **1** an explanation that has not been proved. *There are many theories about the origin of life.* **2** the main ideas about a subject, rather than its practice. **theoretical** *adj.*
therapy *n* a treatment of a mental or physical illness. **therapeutic** *adj,* **therapist** *n.*
there *adv* in, at or to that place.
therefore *adv* for that reason. *Lucy is ill and therefore can't come.*
thermal *adj* **1** to do with heat. *thermal currents.* **2** keeping you warm by stopping heat from escaping. *thermal underwear.*
thermometer *n* an instrument for measuring temperature.

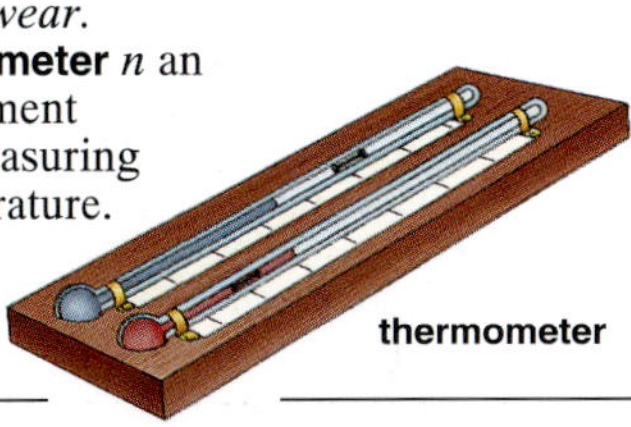
thermometer

thermostat *n* a device for automatically controlling the temperature in a room.
thesaurus *n* (*pl* thesauri *or* thesauruses) a book that has lists of words with similar meanings grouped together.
thick *adj* **1** having a long distance from one side to the other, not thin. *thick walls.* **2** having a certain distance between the opposite sides. *The glass is 2 cm thick.* **3** having a lot of things close together, dense. *a thick forest.* **4** (of a liquid) not flowing easily. *thick soup.* **5** *(informal)* stupid. **thicken** *v,* **thickness** *n.*
thicket *n* a group of small trees or bushes growing close together.
thief *n* (*pl* thieves) a person who steals. **thieve** *v.*
thigh *(rhymes with* my*)* *n* the top part of your leg between your hip and knee.
thimble *n* a small metal or plastic object worn on the end of your finger to avoid pricking it when sewing.
thin *adj* (thinner, thinnest) **1** not very wide between its two sides, not thick. *thin paper.* **2** slim, not fat. **3** not dense. *His hair is getting thin.* **4** (of a liquid) watery. *thin soup.* **thin** *v,* **thinness** *n.*
thing *n* **1** any object that is not living. **2 things** belongings.
think *v* (thinking, thought) **1** to use your brain. **2** to believe, to have an opinion.
third[1] *adj* next after second. **third** *adv, n.*
third[2] *n* one of three equal parts of something.
thirst *n* **1** the dry feeling you have in your mouth and throat when you need to drink. **2** a strong desire for something. *the thirst for knowledge.* **thirsty** *adj.*
thistle *n* a prickly wild plant with purple flowers.
thorax *n* **1** the middle section of an insect's body. See **insect**. **2** the chest of a person or an animal.

thistle

thorn *n* a sharp point sticking out from the stem of a plant such as a rose.
thorough *adj* careful, attending to every detail. *Ned gave his room a thorough clean.* **thoroughness** *n*.
thoroughfare *n* a passage or way through.
thoroughly *adv* **1** in a careful way, attending to every detail. **2** completely. *I'm thoroughly bored.*
though[1] *conj* although. *Though it's sunny, it's a bit cold.*
though[2] *adv* however. *I bought it. It was expensive, though.*
thought[1] *past of* think.
thought[2] *n* **1** an idea. **2** thinking about something.
thoughtful *adj* **1** thinking carefully. **2** thinking about other people, considerate. **thoughtfully** *adv*.
thoughtless *adj* not thinking about other people, inconsiderate. **thoughtlessness** *n*.
thrash *v* **1** to hit many times with a stick or whip. **2** to defeat easily. **3** to move about violently. *She was thrashing her arms about in the water.*
thread[1] *n* **1** a long, thin piece of cotton, silk, etc, used for sewing. **2** the spiral ridge around a screw.
thread[2] *v* to put a thread through a hole, such as the eye of a needle.
threadbare *adj* worn thin. *His clothes were old and threadbare.*
threat *n* **1** a warning that you are going to hurt or punish somebody. **2** a sign of something dangerous or unpleasant in the future. *the threat of war.* **3** something that is likely to cause harm. *Nuclear weapons are a threat to our children's future.*
threaten *v* **1** to make a threat. **2** to be about to come. *A storm is threatening.*
three-dimensional, 3-D *adj* having length, width and height, not flat. *A cube is a three-dimensional shape.*
thresh *v* to beat stalks of corn in order to separate out the grain.
threshold *n* **1** a piece of wood or stone under the door of a building. **2** a beginning. *She is on the threshold of a brilliant career.*
threw *past of* throw.
thrifty *adj* (thriftier, thriftiest) careful about how you spend your money.
thrill *n* a sudden, strong feeling of excitement or pleasure. **thrill** *v*.
thriller *n* a book, film or play with an exciting plot, usually about a crime.
thrive *v* to grow strong and healthy. *The business is thriving.*
throat *n* the front of your neck, and the tubes inside that take food and air into your body.
throb *v* (throbs, throbbing, throbbed) to beat strongly and regularly. *Her toe throbbed with pain.*
throne *n* a special chair for a king, queen, emperor, etc.
throng *n* a large crowd. **throng** *v*.
throttle[1] *v* to strangle somebody.
throttle[2] *n* a device that controls the flow of fuel into a vehicle's engine.
through *prep* **1** from one side or end to the other. *The train went through the tunnel.* **2** from the beginning to the end. *They are travelling through the night.* **3** because of, by way of. *You caused the accident through your own carelessness.* **through** *adv*.
throughout *prep* **1** in all parts of. *The band is known throughout Europe.* **2** from the start to the finish of. *He interrupted me throughout my talk.*
throw *v* (throwing, threw, thrown) **1** to send something through the air with force. *Throw the ball to me.* **2** to puzzle or confuse somebody. *The question really threw me.* **throw up** *(slang)* to vomit. **throw** *n*.
thrush *n* a songbird with a speckled brown breast.
thrust *v* (thrusting, thrust) to push something with force. *They thrust their way through the crowd.* **thrust** *n*.
thud *n* the dull sound made by a heavy object falling to the ground. **thud** *v*.
thug *n* a violent, brutal person.
thumb[1] *n* the short, thick finger on each hand.
thumb[2] *v* to turn over the pages of a book with your thumb and fingers.
thunder[1] *n* the deep, rumbling sound you hear after a flash of lightning.

thunder[2] *v* to make the sound of, or a sound like, thunder.
thunderstorm *n* a storm with thunder and lightning.
Thursday *n* the fifth day of the week.
thus *conj* in this or that way, therefore.
thyme *(time)* *n* a herb used in cooking.
tiara *n* a small crown decorated with jewels.
tick[1] *n* **1** the short, light, regular sound made by a clock or watch. **2** a small mark, like this ✓, used to show that something is correct. **3** a tiny, blood-sucking insect.
tick[2] *v* **1** to make short, light, regular sounds like a clock or watch. **2** to mark something with a tick.
ticket *n* a piece of printed card or paper that shows you have paid to travel on a train or bus, go into a cinema, etc.
tickle *v* to touch somebody's skin lightly. *I tickled the baby's feet and made her laugh.* **tickle** *n.*
tide *n* the regular rise and fall of the sea. **tidal** *adj.*
tidings *n pl (old-fashioned)* news.
tidy *adj* (tidier, tidiest) in good order, neat. **tidily** *adv*, **tidiness** *n*, **tidy** *v.*
tie[1] *v* (ties, tying, tied) **1** to fasten with string, rope, etc. **2** to score the same number of points in a game or contest. *Two people tied for first place.*
tie[2] *n* **1** a thin piece of cloth worn knotted around the neck of a shirt. **2** an equal score or result in a game or competition. **3** a game or match to be played. *a cup tie.*
tier *(rhymes with* ear*)* *n* one of a number of rows or levels set one above the other. *The wedding cake had four tiers.* **tiered** *adj.*
tiger *n* a large wild cat with a striped coat, found in Asia.

tiger

tight *adj* **1** fitting very closely. *My trousers are too tight.* **2** firmly fastened or fixed, hard to move or undo. *This knot is too tight.* **3** firmly stretched. *Make sure the rope is tight.* **tight** *adv*, **tighten** *v.*
tightrope *n* a tightly stretched rope or wire on which acrobats balance high above the ground.
tights *n pl* a close-fitting piece of clothing that covers your feet, legs and body up to your waist.
tigress *n* a female tiger.
tile *n* one of the flat pieces of baked clay or other material used to cover floors, walls or roofs. **tile** *v.*
till[1] *n* a container or drawer for money in a shop.
till[2] *v* to plough.
till[3] *conj, prep* until.
tiller *n* the handle that turns a boat's rudder from side to side.
tilt *v* to lean to one side.
timber *n* cut wood used for building.
time[1] *n* **1** the passing of minutes, days, years, etc. **2** a particular hour, shown on a clock. *What time is it?* **3** a particular point or period connected with an event. *breakfast time.* **4** an amount of minutes, hours, etc. *I haven't got time to help you now.* **5** an occasion. *She won four times.*
time[2] *v* **1** to measure how long something takes. *She timed the drive to school.* **2** to choose the right time to do something.
times *prep* multiplied by.
timetable *n* a list of the times of trains, lessons at school, etc.
timid *adj* easily frightened, shy.
tin *n* **1** a silvery metal. **2** a metal container for food, a can.
tingle *v* to have a slight prickling feeling. *My fingers were tingling with cold.* **tingle** *n.*
tinkle *v* to make a sound of, or like, the ringing of small bells.
tinned *adj* in a tin.
tinsel *n* strings of glittering, sparkling material used for decoration.
tint *n* a shade of a colour. **tinted** *adj.*
tiny *adj* (tinier, tiniest) very small.

tip[1] *n* **1** the top or point of something. **2** a piece of useful information. **3** a small gift of money to a waiter, etc. **4** a rubbish dump.
tip[2] *v* (tips, tipping, tipped) **1** to fall or lean over. **2** to empty something from a container. *I tipped the water down the drain.* **3** to give a waiter, etc a small gift of money.
tipsy *adj* slightly drunk.
tiptoe *v* to walk quietly on your toes.
tire *v* **1** to become tired. **2** to make somebody tired.
tiresome *adj* annoying or boring.
tissue *n* **1** thin, soft paper. **2** a paper handkerchief. **3** the mass of cells that make up an animal or plant.
title *n* **1** the name of a book, play, film, etc. **2** a word put in front of a name to show the person's rank, occupation, etc, eg Mr, Ms, Sir, Lady, Dr.
toad *n* an amphibian similar to a frog, with a rough skin.
toadstool *n* a type of fungus similar to a mushroom and often poisonous.
toast[1] *n* grilled bread. **toast** *v.*
toast[2] *v* to hold up your glass and wish somebody good luck, happiness, etc before you drink. **toast** *n.*
tobacco *n* a plant whose dried leaves are smoked in cigarettes, cigars and pipes.
toboggan *n* a long, light sledge. **toboggan** *v.*
today *adv, n* **1** (on) this day. **2** (at) the present time.
toddler *n* a child who has only just learned to walk.
toe *n* one of the five finger-like parts of your foot.
toffee *n* a sticky, chewy sweet made from boiled sugar and butter.
toga *n* a loose robe worn by men in ancient Rome.
together *adv* with each other, with another person or thing.
toil *v* to work very hard and for a long time. **toil** *n.*
toilet *n* **1** a kind of bowl into which you get rid of urine and faeces, with a water supply for washing this into a drain. **2** a room with a toilet in it.
toiletries *n pl* soap, toothpaste and other things that you use when you are getting washed, doing your hair, etc.
token *n* **1** a sign or symbol. *Please accept this gift as a token of my thanks.* **2** a piece of printed paper, plastic, etc used in place of money. *a book token.*
told *past of* tell.
tolerate *v* to put up with or endure something. *I couldn't tolerate his rudeness.* **tolerance** *n*, **tolerant** *adj.*
toll[1] *n* a tax charged for crossing a bridge, using a certain road, etc. **take its toll** to cause damage or loss.
toll[2] *v* to ring slowly and solemnly. *The bell tolled for the dead soldiers.*
tomato *n* (*pl* tomatoes) a round, red, juicy fruit often eaten in salads.
tomb *(toom) n* a grave.
tombstone *n* a block of stone placed over a grave that shows who is buried there.
tomcat *n* a male cat.
tomorrow *adv, n* **1** (on) the day after today. **2** (in) the future.
ton *n* **1** an old measure of weight, equal to 2,240 pounds or about 1,016 kilogrammes. **2 tons** *(informal)* a lot.
tone *n* **1** the quality of a sound. *He spoke in a gentle tone.* **2** a shade of a colour. *various tones of green.*
tongs *n pl* a tool with two parts joined at one end, used for picking things up.
tongue *n* the flap of muscle inside your mouth that you use for tasting, swallowing and speaking.
tongue-twister *n* a phrase that is not easy to say quickly, such as *She sells sea shells on the sea shore.*
tonight *adv, n* (on) the night of this day.
tonne *n* a measure of weight equal to 1,000 kilogrammes.
tonsillitis *n* an infection of the tonsils which makes them red and painful.
tonsils *n pl* a pair of soft, fleshy lumps at the back of your throat.
too *adv* **1** as well, also. *Can I come too?* **2** more than is required, wanted, etc. *This coat is too small for me now.*
took *past of* take.
tool *n* a piece of equipment that you use to do a particular job.

tooth *n* (*pl* teeth) **1** one of the hard, bony parts in your mouth, used for chewing food. **2** one of the pointed parts on a saw, comb, etc.

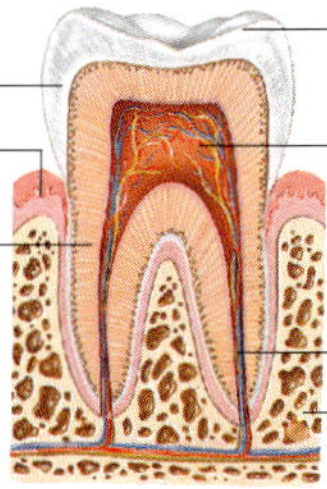

tooth

toothache *n* pain in a tooth.
toothpaste *n* a paste used to clean your teeth.
top *n* **1** the highest point of something. **2** the upper surface of something. **3** a lid. **4** a piece of clothing that you wear on the top part of your body. **5** a spinning toy. **top** *adj*.
topic *n* a subject that you speak or write about.
topical *adj* interesting and important at the present time.
topple *v* to become unsteady and fall.
torch *n* **1** a small, portable light that is powered by batteries. **2** a flaming piece of wood or rope carried as a light in processions.
tore *past of* tear.
torment *v* **1** to make somebody suffer very much. *He was tormented by worry.* **2** to annoy somebody on purpose. **torment** *n*.
torn *past participle of* tear.
tornado *n* (*pl* tornadoes) a violent, whirling storm that causes great damage.
torpedo *n* (*pl* torpedoes) a tube-shaped bomb that is fired underwater. **torpedo** *v*.
torrent *n* **1** a rushing stream. **2** a heavy flow of something. **torrential** *adj*.
torso *n* (*pl* torsos) the main part of your body, not including your head or limbs.
tortoise *n* a slow-moving land reptile with a hard shell.
torture *v* to treat somebody cruelly as a punishment or in order to force them to confess something. **torture** *n*.
Tory *n* a member of the British Conservative Party.
toss *v* **1** to throw something carelessly. **2** to turn restlessly from side to side. *She tossed and turned all night.* **3** to decide by throwing a coin into the air to see which side faces upwards when it falls.
total[1] *adj* counting everything, complete.
total[2] *n* the number or amount that you get when you add numbers or amounts together. **total** *v*.
totem pole *n* a pole carved with characters from traditional Native American stories.

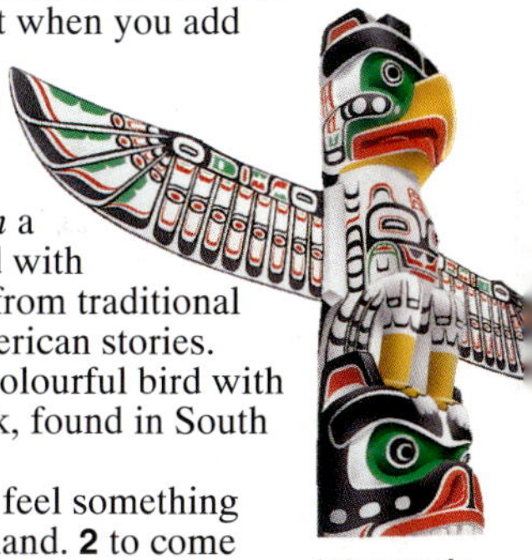
totem pole

toucan *n* a colourful bird with a large beak, found in South America.
touch *v* **1** to feel something with your hand. **2** to come into contact with something. **3** to affect the feelings of somebody. *I was touched by her kindness.* **touch** *n*, **touching** *adj*.
touchline *n* in football, the line that marks the edge of the pitch.
touchy *adj* easily upset or offended.
tough *(tuff) adj* **1** not easily broken or damaged. **2** able to bear hardship, illness, etc. **3** difficult to chew. *This meat is tough!* **4** difficult. *a tough decision.* **toughen** *v*.
tour *n* a journey on which you visit a number of different places. **tour** *v*.
tourist *n* a person who travels for pleasure, visiting places of interest. **tourism** *n*.
tournament *n* a contest in which many players or teams play games against each other.
tow *v* to pull a vehicle along by a rope or chain.
towards, toward *prep* in the direction of. *The car was coming towards us.*

towel *n* a piece of thick cloth or paper for drying things.
tower *n* **1** a tall, narrow building. **2** a tall, narrow part of a building.
town *n* a place with many houses, shops, etc that is larger than a village but smaller than a city.
toxic *adj* poisonous.
toy[1] *n* (*pl* toys) an object for a child to play with.
toy[2] *v* to play with something carelessly. *He wasn't hungry and just sat toying with his food.*
trace[1] *v* **1** to find out where somebody or something is. **2** to copy a picture by covering it with very thin paper and drawing around the outline.
trace[2] *n* **1** a small sign or mark left by something. *She vanished without trace.* **2** a small amount. *Traces of poison were found in the cup.*
track[1] *n* **1 tracks** a series of marks left behind by a person, animal, vehicle, etc. **2** a path or rough road. **3** a racecourse for runners, cyclists, etc. **4** a railway line. **5** one song or piece of music on a CD, tape or record.
track[2] *v* to follow something by looking for the signs or tracks it has left behind.
tracksuit *n* a pair of loose trousers and a top that you wear for sports.
tractor *n* a strong vehicle used to pull farm machinery.
trade[1] *n* **1** the buying and selling of goods. **2** a person's job.
trade[2] *v* **1** to buy and sell. **2** to exchange. *I traded my computer game for some rollerblades.*
trademark *n* a special mark or sign used to show who made something and to prevent illegal copying.
trade union *n* an organization of workers who join together to bargain with employers for fair wages, etc.
tradition *n* a belief, custom, etc that is handed down from one generation to another. **traditional** *adj*, **traditionally** *adv*.
traffic[1] *n* moving vehicles.
traffic[2] *v* (traffics, trafficking, trafficked) to buy and sell something illegally. *drug trafficking.*
traffic warden *n* a person whose job is to control the parking of vehicles in towns.
tragedy *n* **1** a play about unhappy events, with a sad ending. **2** a very sad event. **tragic** *adj*, **tragically** *adv*.
trail[1] *n* **1** a series of marks left by somebody or something as they pass. *He left a trail of footprints behind him.* **2** a path through the country.
trail[2] *v* **1** to drag or be dragged along. *Your scarf is trailing on the ground.* **2** to walk slowly and wearily. **3** to follow the trail of somebody or something. **4** (of a plant) to grow over a surface.
trailer *n* **1** a vehicle used for carrying things, towed by a car or lorry. **2** a series of short pieces taken from a film, used to advertise it.
train[1] *n* **1** a railway engine with carriages or trucks. **2** a part of a long dress that trails behind the wearer. *The bride wore a dress with a train.* **3** a series of connected thoughts, events, etc.
train[2] *v* **1** to learn how to do something. *She's training to be a solicitor.* **2** to teach a person or an animal how to do something. *They train guide dogs for the blind.* **3** to prepare for a sports event by practising or exercising.
trainer *n* **1** a person who trains people or animals. **2** a soft sports shoe with a thick sole.
traitor *n* a person who betrays their country or friends.
tram *n* a kind of bus that runs on rails like a train, powered by electricity.
tramp[1] *v* **1** to walk with heavy footsteps. **2** to go for a long walk.
tramp[2] *n* a person with no permanent home or job, who travels from place to place by foot.
trample *v* to tread heavily on something.
trampoline *n* a piece of equipment for gymnasts to bounce on, made of a sheet of strong material attached to a framework by springs.
tranquil *(**tran**-kwil) adj* calm and peaceful. **tranquility** *n*.

trans- *prefix* across, through. *transatlantic.*
transaction *n* a business deal.
transfer[1] *(trans-**fur**)* *v* (transfers, transferring, transferred) to move something from one place to another.
transfer[2] *(**trans**-fur)* *n* **1** transferring somebody or something. **2** a design or picture that can be transferred from one surface to another.
transform *v* to change completely. *A witch had transformed him into a frog.* **transformation** *n.*
transfusion *n* the injection of blood into somebody who is very ill or who has lost a lot of blood in an accident.
transistor *n* **1** a small device that controls the flow of an electrical current. **2** a portable radio.
translate *v* to put something into another language. **translation** *n,* **translator** *n.*
transmit *v* (transmits, transmitting, transmitted) **1** to pass something on. *Some insects transmit diseases.* **2** to send out television or radio signals. **transmission** *n.*
transparent *adj* able to be seen through, like glass. **transparency** *n.*
transplant *v* **1** to remove a plant from where it is growing and plant it somewhere else. **2** to remove a part of somebody's body, such as a heart or kidney, and put it into the body of a person who is very ill. **transplant** *n.*
transport[1] *(trans-**port**)* *v* to carry people, animals or goods from one place to another.
transport[2] *(**trans**-port)* *n* **1** transporting people, animals or goods. **2** a vehicle or a way of travelling.
trap[1] *n* **1** a device for catching animals. **2** something that tricks you.
trap[2] *v* (traps, trapping, trapped) to catch in a trap or by a trick.
trapdoor *n* a door in a floor or ceiling.
trapeze *n* a bar hung on ropes high above the ground, on which acrobats and gymnasts perform.
trapezium *n* (*pl* trapeziums *or* trapezia) a four-sided shape with two sides parallel.
trash *n* rubbish.
travel *v* (travels, travelling, travelled) to go from one place to another. **travel** *n,* **traveller** *n.*
trawler *n* a fishing boat that drags a wide, bag-shaped net along the bottom of the sea. **trawl** *v.*

trawler

tray *n* (*pl* trays) a flat piece of plastic, metal, etc for carrying food and drinks.
treacherous *(**trech**-er-us)* *adj* **1** betraying people who trust you. **2** dangerous. *treacherous road conditions.* **treachery** *n.*
treacle *n* thick, dark syrup, produced from sugar when it is being refined.
tread[1] *v* (treading, trod, trodden) to put your foot down on something.
tread[2] *n* the raised pattern on the outside of a tyre.
treason *n* betrayal of your country, especially by giving away important information to an enemy.
treasure[1] *n* a store of valuable things, such as gold and jewels.
treasure[2] *v* to value something very highly.
treasury *n* **1 Treasury** the government department that controls a country's money. **2** a place where treasure is stored.
treat[1] *v* **1** to deal with somebody or something in a certain way. *The Smiths treat Ali like their own son.* **2** to try to make a sick or injured person well again. **3** to put something through a process, especially to protect or preserve it. *The wood is treated with chemicals to stop it rotting.* **4** to buy a meal, present, etc for somebody. **treatment** *n.*
treat[2] *n* something that gives you special pleasure. *Mum took us to the cinema as a treat.*

treaty *n* a written agreement made between countries.
treble[1] *adj, adv* three times as much or as many. **treble** *v.*
treble[2] *adj* high in pitch. *a treble recorder.*
tree *n* the tallest type of plant with a thick, wooden trunk.
trek *n* a long journey. **trek** *v.*
tremble *v* to shake with fear, cold, excitement, etc.
tremendous *adj* **1** very great or large. **2** very good, excellent.
trench *n* a long, narrow ditch.
trend *n* **1** a general direction or course. **2** a fashion.
trendy *adj* (trendier, trendiest) fashionable.
trespass *v* to go illegally on somebody else's land. **trespasser** *n.*
tri- *prefix* three.
trial *n* **1** the examination of an accused person in a law court. **2** a test. *Trials of the new drug will begin shortly.*
triangle *n* **1** a flat shape with three sides. **2** a triangular metal musical instrument. **triangular** *adj.*

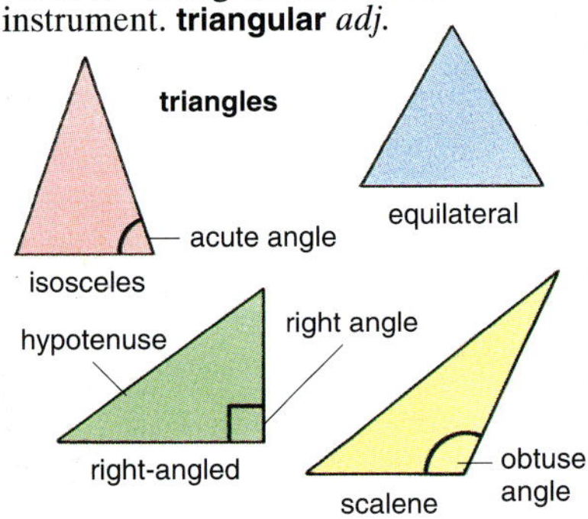

tribe *n* a group of people who have the same ancestors, customs and language. **tribal** *adj,* **tribesman** *n,* **tribeswoman** *n.*
tributary *n* a stream that flows into a river or another stream.
trick *n* **1** something done to cheat or deceive somebody **2** a clever or skilful action done to amuse people. *a magic trick.* **trick** *v.*
trickle *v* to flow in a thin stream.
tricky *adj* (trickier, trickiest) difficult.
tricycle *n* a three-wheeled cycle.
trifle *n* **1** a dessert made from cake, custard, jelly, fruit and cream. **2** something that is not important.
trifling *adj* not very important.
trigger *n* the lever on a gun that you pull to fire it.
trim *v* (trims, trimming, trimmed) to cut the edges or ends of something. **trim** *n.*
trimming *n* something added as a decoration. *a dress with lace trimming.*
trinket *n* a small ornament or piece of jewellery of little value.
trip[1] *v* (trips, tripping, tripped) to catch your foot on something and fall, or almost fall.
trip[2] *n* a journey. *Have a good trip.*
triple *adj* **1** three times as much or as many. **2** made of three parts. **triple** *v.*
triplet *n* one of three babies born to the same mother at the same time.
tripod *n* a three-legged stand, especially for a camera.
triumph *n a* great success or victory. **triumph** *v,* **triumphant** *adj.*
trivial *adj* of very little importance.
troll *n* in stories, an ugly, bad-tempered dwarf or giant that lives in a cave.
trolley *n* (*pl* trolleys) **1** a small cart used for carrying things. *a shopping trolley.* **2** a table on wheels. **3** a bed on wheels in a hospital.
trombone *n* a brass musical instrument with a sliding tube.
troops *n pl* soldiers.
trophy *(troh-fee) n* a prize such as a silver cup won in a competition.
tropic *n* **1** one of the two imaginary circles running around the Earth at about 23 degrees north and south of the equator. **2 tropics** the hot regions between these circles. **tropical** *adj.*
trot *v* (trots, trotting, trotted) to run with short steps like the slow run of a horse. **trot** *n.*
trouble[1] *n* difficulty, problems or worry.
trouble[2] *v* **1** to cause somebody worry or problems. *She was troubled by the news.* **2** to bother somebody. *Sorry to trouble you, but have you got the time?*

trough *(troff)* *n* a long, narrow container for animals' food or water.
trousers *n pl* a piece of clothing for the lower part of the body which covers each leg separately.
trout *n* (*pl* trout) an edible freshwater fish.
trowel *n* **1** a garden tool like a small spade. **2** a tool with a flat blade for spreading mortar, plaster, etc.
truant *n* a pupil who stays away from school when he or she is supposed to be there. **truancy** *n.*
truce *n* a rest from fighting or quarrelling, agreed by both sides.
truck *n* **1** a lorry. **2** a wagon for carrying goods on a railway.
trudge *v* to walk with slow, heavy steps. *They trudged through the snow.*
true *adj* **1** that really happened. *a true story.* **2** correct, not invented or wrong. *It's true that the Earth is round.* **3** real, genuine. *true love.* **truly** *adv.*
truffle *n* **1** an edible fungus that grows underground. **2** a soft sweet made of a chocolate mixture.
trumpet *n* a brass musical instrument, played by pressing valves.
truncheon *n* a short, thick stick carried by police officers as a weapon.
trunk *n* **1** the main stem of a tree. **2** the main part of your body, not including your head or limbs. **3** a large box for storing or carrying clothes and other things. **4** the long nose of an elephant. **5** in American English, the boot of a car. **6 trunks** shorts worn by men and boys for swimming.
trust *v* to believe that somebody is honest or reliable. *Can I trust you to behave while I'm out?* **trust** *n.*
trustworthy *adj* able to be trusted.
truth *n* the true facts. *I'm telling you the truth.* **truthful** *adj*, **truthfully** *adv.*
try[1] *v* (tries, trying, tried) **1** to make an effort to do something. *I tried to open the window but I couldn't.* **2** to test something by using it. *Have you tried this new shampoo?* **3** to judge somebody in a law court.
try[2] *n* **1** an effort or attempt. **2** in rugby football, a way of scoring by placing the ball over the other team's goal line with your hand.
trying *adj* making you annoyed or impatient. *He is a very trying person!*
tsar *(zar)* *n* an emperor of Russia.
T-shirt *another spelling of* tee-shirt.
tub *n* **1** a plastic container for food. **2** a wide, open container used for washing clothes, etc.
tuba *n* a large brass musical instrument that gives a low note.
tubby *adj* short and fat.
tube *n* **1** a long, hollow cylinder. **2** an underground railway. **tubular** *adj.*
tuber *n* a swelling on the underground stem of a plant such as a potato.
tuck *v* to fold or push something into or under a place. *She tucked her shirt into her trousers.* **tuck in 1** to push bedclothes tightly around somebody in bed. **2** to eat with enjoyment.
tuck shop *n* a shop in a school where sweets, cakes, etc are sold.
Tuesday *n* the third day of the week.
tuft *n* a bunch or clump of grass, hair, etc.
tug[1] *v* (tugs, tugging, tugged) to pull something hard. **tug** *n.*
tug[2], **tugboat** *n* a small boat that tows large ships in and out of port.
tuition *(tyoo-**ish**-un)* *n* teaching.
tulip *n* a plant with brightly coloured, cup-shaped flowers, which grows from a bulb.

tulip

tumble *v* to fall down suddenly.
tumbler *n* a tall drinking glass with straight sides.
tummy *n (informal)* the stomach.
tumour *n* a lump or swelling in the body made up of abnormal cells.
tuna *n* (*pl* tuna *or* tunas) a large sea fish eaten as food.
tundra *n* a level, treeless plain in Arctic regions.
tune[1] *n* a pattern of musical notes. **in tune** singing or playing the right notes.
tune[2] *v* **1** to adjust a musical instrument to the correct pitch. **2** to

adjust a radio or television to a particular station.
tunic *n* **1** a close-fitting jacket, often part of a uniform. **2** a loose robe without sleeves.
tunnel[1] *n* an underground passage.
tunnel[2] *v* (tunnels, tunnelling, tunnelled) to dig under the ground.
turban *n* a long piece of cloth wound round the head, worn especially by Muslim and Sikh men.
turbine *n* an engine with curved blades, turned by the action of water, steam, hot air, etc.
turf *n* grass and the soil below it.
turkey *n* (*pl* turkeys) a large bird kept on farms for its meat.
turmoil *n* a state of wild confusion.
turn[1] *v* **1** to go round, to revolve. *Turn the wheel.* **2** to change direction. *I turned to face her.* **3** to change. *Water turns into ice when it freezes.* **4** to become. *Her hair turned white.* **5** to find a certain page in a book. *Turn to page 23.* **6** to adjust the switch on a television, heater, etc. *I'll just turn the radio off. Can you turn the fire up?* **turn down** to refuse. *She turned down the offer.* **turn up** to arrive. *Emma turned up just before dinner.*
turn[2] *n* your chance or duty to do something. *It's your turn to wash up.*
turnip *n* a plant with a large, round root used as a vegetable.
turnstile *n* a gate that turns, allowing only one person to pass at a time.
turquoise *n* **1** a greenish-blue precious stone. **2** the colour of this.
turret *n* a small tower on a castle or other building.
turtle *n* a sea reptile with a round shell.
tusk *n* a long, curved tooth sticking out from the mouth of animals such as the elephant and the walrus.
tutor *n* a teacher who teaches individual students or small groups.
tutu *n* a ballet dancer's short skirt, made of layers of stiff material that stick out.
TV *short for* television.
twice *adv* two times.
twig *n* a small, thin branch.
twilight *n* the dim light between sunset and night.
twin *n* one of two children born to the same mother at the same time.
twinkle *v* to shine with little flashes of light. **twinkle** *n.*
twirl *v* to turn or spin round and round. **twirl** *n.*
twist *v* **1** to turn or bend. *The path twists and turns through the forest.* **2** to wind around or together. *He twisted the pieces of string to make a rope.* **twist** *n*, **twisted** *adj.*
twitch *v* to make slight jerking movements.
tycoon *n* a rich, powerful businessman.
type[1] *n* a kind or sort.
type[2] *v* to use a typewriter or computer keyboard to write something.
type[3] *n* the letters used to print words.
typewriter *n* a machine with keys that you press to print letters on paper.
typhoon *(tie-**foon**)* *n* a violent tropical storm of wind and rain.
typical *adj* having the usual characteristics. *a typical English village.* **typically** *adv.*
tyrant *n* a cruel and unfair ruler. **tyrannical** *adj*, **tyranny** *n.*
tyre *n* an air-filled rubber ring around the wheel of a car, bicycle, etc.

Uu

udder *n* the bag-like part of a female mammal, such as a cow, from which milk comes.
UFO *n* (*short for* unidentified flying object) a flying object that cannot be identified and that is therefore thought to come from outer space.
ugly *adj* (uglier, ugliest) unpleasant to look at, not attractive. *an ugly, modern building.* **ugliness** *n.*

ulcer *n* a sore area on your skin or inside your body. *a mouth ulcer.*
ultimate *adj* **1** last, final. *Our ultimate goal is to win the championship.* **2** the greatest. *the ultimate achievement.*
ultimatum *n* a final warning that if somebody does not do as you ask, you will take action against them.
ultra- *prefix* extremely. *ultra-light, ultra-modern.*
ultraviolet light *n* a type of light which cannot be seen by the human eye, but which causes your skin to tan.
umbilical cord *n* a cord connecting an unborn mammal to its mother before it is born.
umbrella *n* a folding, covered framework on a stick with a handle, used to keep you dry in the rain.
umpire *n* a person who watches a game of tennis, baseball or cricket to see that it is played according to the rules.
un- *prefix* **1** not, opposite. *unequal, unhappy, unlucky.* **2** used to show the opposite of an action. *unfasten, undo.*
unanimous *(yoo-**nan**-im-us) adj* agreed by everybody. *a unanimous decision.*
uncanny *adj* strange, mysterious. **uncannily** *adv.*
uncle *n* the brother of your mother or father, or the husband of your aunt.
uncouth *adj* rough and rude.
uncover *v* **1** to take the cover off something. **2** to discover something.
under *prep* **1** lower than or below. **2** less than. *prices under £5.* **3** controlled or ruled by. *The hotel is under new management.* **4** having or using. *She travelled under a false name.* **under** *adv.*
under- *prefix* **1** below. *underground.* **2** not enough, too little. *underweight.*
undercarriage *n* an aircraft's wheels and their supports.
underclothes *n pl* clothes worn next to your skin, under your other clothes.
undercover *adj* acting or done in secret. *an undercover agent* (= a spy).
underdog *n* a person or team that is expected to lose a contest, fight, etc.
underestimate *v* **1** to think that somebody or something is not as strong as they really are. **2** to guess that the amount of something is less than it really is.
undergo *v* (undergoes, undergoing, underwent, undergone) to suffer or experience something.
underground[1] *adj, adv* below the surface of the ground.
underground[2] *n* a railway which runs mainly underground.
undergrowth *n* bushes and plants growing among trees.
underline *v* **1** to draw a line under a word or words. **2** to stress something to show it is especially important.
undermine *v* to make something weaker.
underneath *adv, prep* under or below.
underpants *n pl* underwear worn by men and boys over the bottom.
underpass *n* a road passing under another road.
underprivileged *adj* not having normal living standards or rights. *a charity for underprivileged children.*
understand *v* (understanding, understood) **1** to see the meaning of something. **2** to know the reasons for something. *I don't understand why you're so angry.* **3** to know somebody or something well. **4** to believe that something is true. *I understand you're moving house.* **understanding** *adj, n.*
understudy *n* an actor who learns the part of another actor and is able to take his or her place if necessary.
undertake *v* (undertaking, undertook, undertaken) to agree to do something. **undertaking** *n.*
undertaker *n* a person who arranges funerals.
underwater *adj, adv* under the surface of the water.
underwear *n pl* clothes worn next to your skin, under your other clothes.
undo *v* (undoes, undoing, undid, undone) **1** to open something that was fixed or tied. *Can you undo this knot?* **2** to reverse or remove the effects of something.
undress *v* to take clothes off.

undue *adj* too great, more than is necessary.
unearth *v* to dig up or discover something after searching.
uneasy *adj* anxious, worried. **uneasily** *adv*, **uneasiness** *n.*
unemployed *adj* without a paid job. **unemployment** *n.*
unfold *v* **1** to open and spread out a map, newspaper, etc. **2** (of a story) to gradually become known.
unfounded *adj* not based on fact, not true. *Your doubts are unfounded.*
uni- *prefix* one. *unicycle* (= a cycle with only one wheel).

unicorn

unicorn *n* in stories, an animal like a horse with a single horn in the middle of its forehead.
uniform[1] *n* a set of clothes worn by all the members of a group of people, such as a school or an army.
uniform[2] *adj* all the same, not changing or varying in any way. *The sky was a uniform grey.*
unify *v* (unifies, unifying, unified) to join several things together to form a single whole.
union *n* **1** the joining together of things or people. **2** a trade union.
unique *(yoo-**neek**)* *adj* being the only one of its kind.
unisex *adj* for both men and women. *unisex clothing.*
unison *n* **in unison** together. *They answered in unison.*
unit *n* **1** a single thing that is complete in itself. *The building is divided into ten different apartments or living units.* **2** a quantity that is used as a standard. *A metre is a unit of length.*
unite *v* to join together. **unity** *n.*
universal *adj* to do with or affecting everybody or everything.
universe *n* everything that exists, including all the stars and planets.
university *n* a place where people study for degrees and do research.
unkempt *adj* untidy.
unleaded *adj* (of petrol) not containing lead.
unless *conj* if not. *I'm not going unless you come too.*
unload *v* to remove things from a ship, vehicle, etc.
unravel *v* (unravels, unravelling, unravelled) to undo threads that are tangled, woven or knitted.
unruly *adj* badly behaved, not obeying laws or rules. **unruliness** *n.*
unscathed *adj* not harmed.
unscrupulous *adj* having no moral principles, not honest or fair.
unsightly *adj* ugly.
untie *v* (unties, untying, untied) to undo something that was tied.
until *prep* up to a particular time. *We stayed until one o'clock.* **until** *conj.*
unusual *adj* strange or remarkable, not usual. **unusually** *adv.*
unwieldy *adj* difficult to move or handle.
unwind *v* (unwinding, unwound) **1** to undo something that was wound in a ball or around something. **2** to relax.
unwrap *v* (unwraps, unwrapping, unwrapped) to take the wrapping off something.
up *adv, prep* **1** from a lower to a higher level, amount, etc. **2** from a lying position to sitting or standing. *What time did you get up today?* **3** completely, so that it is finished. *Who used all the milk up?* **4** as far as. *He came up to me and shook my hand.* **5** along. *I was walking up the road.* **6** into pieces. *He tore the letter up.*
upbringing *n* the way that a child is brought up.
update *v* to bring up to date by including all the latest information. *This dictionary is updated regularly to include new words.* **update** *n.*
upheaval *n* a great change or disturbance.
uphill *adv* up a hill or slope.

upholstery *n* the padding and covering of chairs and sofas.
upkeep *n* the keeping of something in good condition, or the cost of this. *The museum charges an entrance fee to pay for the upkeep of the building.*
upon *prep* on.
upper *adj* higher, further up.
upright *adj* **1** standing straight up, vertical. *a row of upright posts.* **2** honest and decent. *an upright citizen.* **upright** *adv*.
uprising *n* a fight against the people in power, a revolt.
uproar *n* a lot of shouting or protest, especially because people are angry. *The MP's speech caused uproar in parliament.*
upset[1] *v* (upsets, upsetting, upset) **1** to make somebody unhappy or worried. **2** to knock something over.
upset[2] *adj* unhappy or worried.
upside down *adv* with the top part underneath. **upside-down** *adj.*
uptight *adj* nervous, tense.
up-to-date *adj* **1** modern. **2** having the latest information. *up-to-date reports.*
uranium *n* a radioactive metal.
urban *adj* to do with a town or city.
urge[1] *v* to encourage somebody strongly. *We urged him to go home.*
urge[2] *n* a strong, sudden desire to do something.
urgent *adj* so important that it needs immediate action. **urgency** *n.*
urine *(**yoor**-in)* *n* the waste liquid that people and animals get rid of from their bodies.
urn *n* **1** a vase, especially one for holding the ashes of a dead person. **2** a large, metal container with a tap, for hot drinks.

urn

usage *n* **1** the way that something is used. **2** the way in which the words of a language are used.
use[1] *(yooz)* *v* **1** to do a job with something. *May I use your pen?* **2** to take something. *I've used all the coffee.* **3** to treat somebody badly in order to get what you want.
use[2] *(yoos)* *n* **1** using something. **2** the way that something is used. *Plastics have many different uses.*
used *(yoozd)* *adj* not new. *used cars.*
used to *(**yoos** too)* words that refer to something that happened often or that was true in the past. *We used to go there every year.* **be used to** to know something well. *She's used to children because she's got two young nephews.*
useful *adj* helpful, serving a purpose. **usefully** *adv*, **usefulness** *n.*
useless *adj* **1** not useful. **2** very bad. *I'm useless at chess.* **uselessness** *n.*
user *n* a person who uses something.
user-friendly *adj* easy to understand and use.
usher, usherette *n* a person who shows other people to their seats in a theatre, etc.
usual *adj* happening or used most often. **usually** *adv*.
utensil *n* a tool or container, especially one used in cooking.
utter[1] *v* to say something or make a sound. *She uttered a sigh of relief.*
utter[2] *adj* complete, total. *There was utter silence.*
U-turn *n* **1** a turn in the shape of a U, made by a vehicle in order to go back the way it has come. **2** a complete change of plan or policy.

Vv

vacant *adj* **1** empty, not occupied. *Does the hotel have any rooms vacant?* **2** (of a person's expression) showing no intelligence or interest.
vacate *v* to leave a place empty.

vacation *n* a holiday.
vaccinate *(**vak**-sin-ate) v* to protect somebody from a disease, usually by giving them an injection. **vaccination** *n.*
vacuum[1] *n* a space from which all air or other gas has been removed.
vacuum[2] *v* to clean with a vacuum cleaner.
vacuum cleaner *n* a machine that cleans carpets by sucking up dirt.
vacuum flask *n* a container with double walls enclosing a vacuum, for keeping liquids hot or cold.
vagina *(va-**jye**-na) n* the passage in a woman's body leading to her womb.
vague *adj* not clear, not definite. *Through the fog we saw the vague outline of a ship.* **vagueness** *n.*
vain *adj* **1** too proud of what you look like, what you can do, etc. **2** unsuccessful. *They made a vain attempt to find the dog.*
valentine *n* **1** a card sent to the person you love on St Valentine's Day, 14 February. **2** the person that you send a valentine to.
valiant *adj* brave.
valid *adj* **1** legally acceptable. *My passport is valid for one year only.* **2** reasonable and acceptable. *I hope you've got a valid excuse for being so late.* **validity** *n.*
valley *n* (*pl* valleys) an area of low land between hills or mountains, often with a river running through it.
valuable *adj* of great value.
valuables *n pl* belongings that are worth a lot of money.
value[1] *n* **1** the usefulness or importance of something. *His experience is of great value to the company.* **2** the amount of money that something is worth.
value[2] *v* **1** to decide how much something is worth. *The painting has been valued at over £200,000.* **2** to think of something as good or important. *She values her freedom.*
valve *n* a device that controls the flow of liquid, air, gas, etc, allowing it to go in one direction only.
vampire *n* in stories, a dead person who rises from the grave at night to suck the blood of living people.
van *n* a covered vehicle for carrying goods.
vandal *n* a person who deliberately destroys or damages things for no purpose. **vandalism** *n,* **vandalize** *v.*
vanilla *n* a sweet-smelling substance produced from the pods of a type of orchid, used for flavouring ice-cream, cakes, etc.
vanish *v* to disappear suddenly.
vanity *n* too much pride in what you look like, what you can do, etc.
vanquish *(**van**-kwish) v* to defeat.
vapour *n* the gas-like form into which a substance can be changed by heating. *Steam is water vapour.*
variable *adj* changing a lot, not staying the same.
varied *adj* full of variety.
variety *n* **1** a number of different types of thing. *The shop sells a huge variety of toys.* **2** a type. *a variety of apple.*
various *adj* several different. *The shirt is available in various colours.*
varnish *n* a clear liquid that is painted onto wood, etc to give it a glossy surface. **varnish** *v.*
vary *v* (varies, varying, varied) **1** to make or become different, to change. **2** to be different from each other. *These books vary in price from 99p to £6.99.* **variation** *n.*
vase *n* a jar of pottery, glass, etc used as an ornament to hold cut flowers.
vast *adj* very large. **vastness** *n.*
vat *n* a large container for liquids.
VAT (*short for* value-added tax) a tax charged on goods and services.
vault[1] *v* to jump over or onto something, using your hands or a pole for support.
vault[2] *n* **1** an underground room, often used to store valuable things. **2** a room beneath a church, used for burials. **3** an arched roof.
VCR *short for* videocassette recorder.
VDU (*short for* visual display unit) a screen on which information from a computer is displayed.
veal *n* the meat from a calf.

veer *v* to change direction suddenly. *The car veered across the road.*
vegan *(vee-gan) n* a person who does not eat or use any animal products. **vegan** *adj*, **veganism** *n*.
vegetable *n* any part of a plant grown as food, except for its fruit or seeds.
vegetarian *n* a person who does not eat meat or fish. **vegetarian** *adj*, **vegetarianism** *n*.
vegetation *n* all the plants growing in a certain place.
vehicle *(vee-i-kul) n* something, especially a machine with an engine, that transports people or goods.
veil *(vale) n* a piece of thin cloth worn over a woman's face to hide it.
vein *(vane) n* **1** one of the tubes that carry blood back to the heart. **2** a line on a leaf.
velvet *n* cloth with a thick, soft surface on one side.
vendetta *n* a long-lasting, bitter quarrel between people or groups.
vending machine *n* a machine selling sweets, drinks or other things, operated by putting coins in a slot.
veneer *n* a thin layer of good quality wood covering a cheaper material.
vengeance *n* harm done to somebody in return for something bad they have done, revenge.
venison *n* the meat from a deer.
venom *n* the poison of some snakes and spiders. **venomous** *adj*.
vent *n* a hole to allow air, smoke, gas, etc to pass in or out.
ventilate *v* to allow fresh air to pass through a room or building. **ventilation** *n*.
ventriloquist *n* a person who can speak without seeming to move their lips so that it seems as if their voice is coming from a dummy or puppet. **ventriloquism** *n*.
venture[1] *v* to dare to go somewhere or do something.
venture[2] *n* a project that involves risk. *a business venture.*
venue *(ven-yoo) n* the place where an event, such as a concert, sports match, etc takes place.
veranda, verandah *n* a covered platform around the side of a house.
verb *n* a word or words showing what somebody or something does in a sentence. In the sentence *I saw her*, *saw* is the verb.
verbal *adj* **1** spoken, not written. **2** to do with words. **verbally** *adv*.
verdict *n* **1** the decision of a judge or jury at the end of a trial in a law court. **2** somebody's opinion of something.
verge *n* a grass edge to a road. **on the verge of** about to do something. *He was on the verge of laughing.*
verruca *n* (*pl* verrucas *or* verrucae) a wart, especially on the foot.
versatile *adj* **1** having many different uses. *a versatile tool.* **2** having many different skills. *a versatile entertainer.*
verse *n* **1** one section of a song or poem, made up of several lines. **2** poetry.
version *n* **1** a thing that is based on something else but that is different in some way. *I haven't read* The Jungle Book, *but I have seen the film version.* **2** one person's description of an event. *Her version of what happened was different from mine.*
versus *prep* against. *the England versus Wales rugby match.*
vertebra *n* (*pl* vertebrae) one of the bones of your spine.
vertebrate *n* an animal with a backbone.
vertical *adj* straight up and down, upright. **vertically** *adv*.
vessel *n* **1** a ship or boat. **2** a container for liquids.
vest *n* a piece of clothing that you wear under your other clothes on the top part of your body.
veteran *n* **1** a person with a lot of experience of something. **2** a person who has served in the armed forces, especially during a war.
veterinary surgeon, vet *n* a doctor for animals.
veto *n* (*pl* vetoes) the power to forbid something. *The President used his veto to prevent the changes.* **veto** *v*.

vex *v* (vexes, vexing, vexed) to annoy or irritate somebody.
via *(vy-a) prep* by way of. *We drove from London to Oxford via Reading.*
viable *adj* capable of succeeding. *I don't think your plan is viable.*
viaduct *n* a long bridge that carries a railway or road over a valley.
vibrate *v* to shake very quickly. **vibration** *n.*
vicar *n* a priest of the Church of England.
vicarage *n* a vicar's house.
vice *n* **1** evil or immoral actions. **2** a bad habit or serious moral fault. *Lying and greed are vices.* **3** a tool that holds an object in one place while you are working on it.
vice- *prefix* next in rank to. *vice-president, vice-captain.*
vice versa *adv* the other way round. *I needed his help and vice versa* (= he needed mine).
vicinity *n* the area surrounding a particular place. *They live in the vicinity of the park.*
vicious *adj* violent and spiteful. *a vicious attack.* **viciousness** *n.*
victim *n* a person who is harmed or killed by somebody or something.
victor *n* the winner of a contest or battle.
victory *n* success in a battle, contest, etc. **victorious** *adj.*
video *n* (*pl* videos) **1** (*also* **videocassette recorder**) a machine for recording and playing back television programmes. **2** (*also* **videocassette**) a plastic box containing videotape. **video** *v.*
videotape *n* magnetic tape for recording and playing back sound and pictures in a videocassette recorder.
vie *v* (vies, vying, vied) to compete with somebody.
view[1] *n* **1** what you can see from a certain place. *a wonderful view of the sea.* **2** an opinion. *What are your views on capital punishment?*
view[2] *v* to look at something. **viewer** *n.*
vigilant *adj* watching carefully. **vigilance** *n.*
vigorous *adj* strong and energetic. *vigorous exercise.* **vigour** *n.*
vile *adj* horrible, disgusting.
villa *n* a detached house with a garden, usually in a warm country, used especially as a holiday home.
village *n* a group of houses and other buildings that is smaller than a town.
villain *n* a wicked person. **villainy** *n.*
villein *n* in the Middle Ages, a slave who was bought and sold with the land on which he or she worked.
vindictive *adj* spiteful.
vine *n* **1** a climbing plant that grapes grow on. **2** any climbing or trailing plant.
vinegar *n* a sour-tasting liquid made from wine, cider, etc, used for flavouring and preserving food.
vineyard *(vin-yard) n* a piece of land where grapes are grown.
vintage *n* the wine that was made in a particular year, particularly when it is of high quality.
vintage car *n* an old car, built between 1919 and 1930.
vinyl *n* a type of strong plastic.
viola *n* a stringed musical instrument larger than a violin.
violent *adj* **1** using physical force, often to hurt or kill somebody. *a violent man.* **2** very strong, uncontrolled. *a violent storm.* **violence** *adj.*
violet *n* **1** a small, purple flower with a pleasant smell. **2** a bluish-purple colour. **violet** *adj.*
violin *n* a stringed musical instrument played with a bow. **violinist** *n.*
VIP *short for* very important person.
viper *n* a poisonous snake, an adder.
virgin *n* a person who has never had sexual intercourse. **virginity** *n.*
virtually *adj* almost. *I've virtually finished this book.*
virtual reality *n* the creation on computer of an environment which gives the user the impression that it is real.
virtue *n* **1** goodness of character. **2** a good quality. *Honesty and generosity are virtues.* **virtuous** *adj.*

virus *n* **1** a tiny living thing, smaller than bacteria, that can cause disease. **2** hidden instructions written into a computer program which are intended to destroy data. **viral** *adj.*
visa *(vee-za) n* a stamp in a passport allowing a person to enter a country.
viscount *(vie-count) n* a nobleman.
visible *adj* able to be seen. *The ship was visible on the horizon.* **visibility** *n.*
vision *n* **1** the power to see, sight. **2** something that you see in your imagination. **3** the ability to see or plan into the future.
visit *v* to go to see a person or place. **visit** *n*, **visitor** *n.*
visor *n* **1** a part of a helmet that you pull down to cover your eyes. **2** a shade that protects your eyes from the sun.
visual *adj* to do with sight and seeing. **visually** *adv.*
visualize *v* to form a clear picture of something in your mind. *I tried to visualize what the room would look like with no furniture.*
vital *adj* very important or necessary. **vitally** *adv.*
vitality *n* liveliness and energy.
vitamin *n* one of a group of substances found in food that we need in order to stay healthy.
vivid *adj* **1** bright. *vivid colours.* **2** producing a clear picture in your mind. *vivid memories.*
vivisection *n* the use of live animals in scientific experiments.
vixen *n* a female fox.
vocabulary *n* **1** all the words used in a particular language. **2** all the words used by a particular person or group.
vocal *adj* to do with the voice.
vocalist *n* a singer.
vocation *n* **1** a strong wish to do a particular job, such as medical work, teaching, or caring for people in some way. **2** an occupation or profession of this kind. **vocational** *adj.*
vodka *n* a strong, colourless, alcoholic drink made from grain.
vogue *n* the fashion at a particular time.
voice *n* the sounds that come from your mouth when you speak or sing.
void *adj* an empty space.
volcano *n* (*pl* volcanoes) a mountain with an opening, called a crater, in the top, through which molten rock, ashes, etc erupt. **volcanic** *adj.*
vole *n* a small rodent.
volley *n* (*pl* volleys) **1** in tennis or football, the hitting or kicking of a ball before it has bounced. **2** a number of shots fired, or missiles thrown, at the same time. **volley** *v.*
volleyball *n* a game in which two teams try to hit a ball over a high net using their hands.
volt *n* a unit for measuring the force of electricity.
voltage *n* an electrical force measured in volts.
volume *n* **1** the amount of space that something takes up or contains. *What is the volume of the petrol tank?* **2** a large book, especially one of a set. **3** loudness.
voluntary *adj* **1** done by choice, not by accident and not because you are asked or forced. *a voluntary agreement.* **2** done or working without payment. *Jane does voluntary work at the local hospital.* **voluntarily** *adv.*
volunteer *v* to offer to do something without being asked or forced. **volunteer** *n.*
vomit *v* to be sick, to bring food up from your stomach through your mouth. **vomit** *n.*
vote *v* to make a choice in an election, debate, etc by raising your hand or writing on a piece of paper. **vote** *n.*
voucher *n* a piece of paper that can be exchanged for money or goods.
vow *v* to make a serious promise. **vow** *n.*
vowel *n* any of the letters a, e, i, o and u.
voyage *n* a journey, especially by sea.
vulgar *adj* having bad manners, rude. **vulgarity** *n.*
vulnerable *adj* unprotected against attack, and easily hurt or damaged.
vulture *n* a large bird that feeds on dead animals.

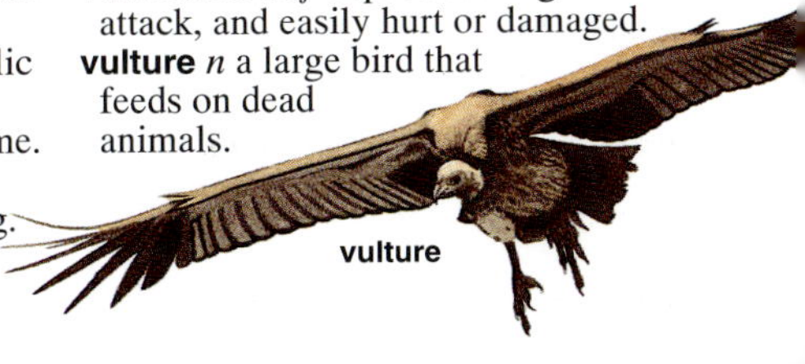
vulture

Ww

waddle *v* to walk with short, unsteady steps, moving from side to side as a duck does.
wade *v* to walk through water.
wader *n* **1** a long-legged bird that wades through shallow water in search of food. **2 waders** high, waterproof boots worn by anglers.
wafer *n* a thin, light type of biscuit.
waffle[1] *n* a type of crisp, square pancake.
waffle[2] *v* to talk or write for a long time without saying anything important.
wag *v* (wags, wagging, wagged) to move from side to side or up and down. *The dog wagged its tail.*
wage *v* to carry on or take part in something. *They waged war for five years.*
wages *n pl* the money that you get for working, usually paid weekly.
waggle *v* to move from side to side.
wagon *n* **1** an open cart with four wheels. **2** an open railway carriage for goods.
wail *v* to let out a long, loud cry of sorrow. **wail** *n.*
waist *n* the narrow part of your body between your chest and your hips.
waistcoat *n* a jacket without sleeves.
wait *v* to stay where you are, expecting something to happen. **wait on** to serve food and drinks to somebody. **wait** *n.*
waiter *n* a person who serves food and drinks in a restaurant.
waitress *n* a woman who serves food and drinks in a restaurant.
wake[1] *v* (waking, woke, woken) **1** to stop sleeping. **2** to stop somebody sleeping.
wake[2] *n* **1** the track left in water by a ship. **2** a night spent watching over a dead body.
walk *v* to move along on your feet. **walk** *n,* **walker** *n.*
walk-over *n* an easy victory.
wall *n* **1** a structure made of brick or stone used to enclose or separate an area of land. **2** a side of a building or room. **walled** *adj.*
wallaby *n* a small type of kangaroo.
wallet *n* a small, folding case for holding money and credit cards.
wallow *v* **1** to roll about with enjoyment in mud or water. **2** to enjoy something greatly. *He wallowed in self-pity.*
walnut *n* **1** a tree whose wood is used for making furniture. **2** the edible nut produced by this tree. See **nut**.
walrus *n* a large sea animal found in the Arctic, similar to a seal with two long tusks.

walrus

waltz *n* a type of ballroom dance.
wand *n* a long, thin rod used by a magician, fairy, etc.
wander *v* to go from place to place with no definite plan or purpose.
wane *v* to become smaller or less. *The Moon is waning.*
wangle *v* get something by being clever or cunning. *Sam has wangled a free ticket to the concert.*
want *v* **1** to wish to have or do something. **2** to need something. *Your boots want a good clean!* **want** *n.*
wanted *adj* being searched for, especially by the police.
war *n* armed fighting between countries or groups of people.
ward[1] *n* **1** a room with beds for patients in a hospital. **2** one of the parts into which a town is divided for voting in elections. **3** a child who is under the legal control and care of a person who is not their parent, or of a law court.
ward[2] *v* **ward off** to defend yourself against something.

warden *n* a person who is in charge of a building such as a hostel or college.
warder *n* a person who guards prisoners in a jail.
wardrobe *n* a cupboard where you hang clothes.
warehouse *n* a large building where goods are stored.
warm *adj* **1** fairly hot. **2** keeping you warm. *a warm coat.* **3** friendly and kind. **warm** *v*, **warmth** *n*.
warn *v* to tell somebody about a danger or about something bad that may happen. **warning** *n*.
warp *v* to become twisted or bent because of heat or dampness.
warrant *n* a document that gives somebody the right to do something. *a search warrant.*
warren *n* a group of rabbit burrows.
warrior *n* a fighter.
wart *n* a small, hard lump on your skin.
wary *adj* (warier, wariest) cautious. **warily** *adv*.
wash *v* **1** to clean something with water, soap, etc. **2** to flow over or against something. *I let the waves wash over my feet.* **wash** *n*. **wash up** to wash dishes, cutlery and pans after a meal. **washing-up** *n*.
washer *n* a flat ring used to make a joint tight, such as on a tap.
washing *n* clothes that need to be washed or that have been washed.
wasp *n* a flying insect with yellow and black stripes and a sting.
waste[1] *v* to use more than you need of something, or not use something in a useful way.
waste[2] *n* **1** wasting something. **2** unwanted material that you throw away or get rid of. **waste** *adj*, **wasteful** *adj*.
watch[1] *v* **1** to look carefully at somebody or something. **2** to be careful about something. **3** to guard or take care of somebody or something.
watch[2] *n* a small clock that you wear on your wrist.
water[1] *n* clear liquid that falls as rain.
water[2] *v* **1** to give water to plants. **2** (of the eyes or mouth) to produce tears or saliva. *Chopping onions often makes your eyes water.*
water-colour *n* **1** a paint that you mix with water. **2** a painting done with this paint.
waterfall *n* a natural fall of water from a height, such as from a rock or cliff.
waterlogged *adj* completely soaked or flooded with water.
watermark *n* a faint design on paper which can be seen when it is held up to the light.
watermelon *n* a large melon with red, juicy flesh and green skin.
water polo *n* a ball-game played in a pool between teams of swimmers.
waterproof *adj* not allowing water to pass through. *a waterproof jacket.*
water-skiing *n* the sport of skiing on water, towed by a motor-boat.
watertight *adj* so closely fitted that water cannot pass through. *a watertight seal.*
waterwheel *n* a wheel that uses the force of falling water to run machines.
watt *n* a unit of electrical power.
wattage *n* electrical power measured in watts.
wattle and daub *n* twigs woven and held together with mud or clay, used in earlier times for building houses.
wave[1] *n* **1** a moving ridge on the surface of water, especially the sea. **2** a curve or curl in your hair. **3** a vibration travelling through the air carrying light, sound, etc. **4** waving with your hand. **5** a sudden, strong increase. *a wave of emotion.*
wave[2] *v* **1** to move your hand from side to side in the air, usually to say hello or goodbye. **2** to move from side to side in the air. *They were waving flags.*
wavelength *n* **1** the distance between two sound, radio, etc waves. **2** the wavelength used by a radio station for broadcasting its programmes.
waver *v* to be uncertain, to hesitate.
wavy *adj* having curves. *a wavy line.*
wax[1] *n* **1** a substance made from fat or oil that is used to produce candles, furniture polish and other things. **2** a substance like wax, found in your ears.

wax[2] *v* to grow or increase. *The Moon is waxing.*
way *n* (*pl* ways) **1** a road or path that you follow to get somewhere. *Do you know your way home?* **2** a direction. *Which way is north?* **3** how to do something. *What's the best way to cook rice?* **4** a distance. *Australia is a long way from Britain.* **5 ways** habits.
WC *n* (*short for* water-closet) a toilet.
weak *adj* not strong. **weakness** *n.*
weaken *v* to make or become weak.
weakling *n* a weak person or animal.
wealth *n* **1** riches. **2** a large quantity. *a wealth of information.*
wealthy *adj* (wealthier, wealthiest) rich.
wean *v* to gradually make a child or young animal used to food other than its mother's milk.
weapon *n* an object, such as a gun or sword, used for fighting.
wear *v* (wearing, wore, worn) **1** to be dressed in or have something on your body. **2** to become thin or damaged through use. *The carpet in the hall is beginning to wear.* **wear off** to gradually become less. **wear out 1** to make or become so damaged or thin that it cannot be used any more. **2** to make somebody very tired. **wear** *n.*
weary *adj* (wearier, weariest) tired. **wearily** *adv*, **weariness** *n.*
weasel *n* a small wild animal with a long, slender body, that feeds on mice, rabbits and other small animals.
weather *n* the conditions in the atmosphere, for example heat, coldness, cloudiness, etc.
weathercock, weathervane *n* a flat piece of metal that swings in the wind to show the way it is blowing.
weave *v* (weaving, wove *or* weaved, woven *or* weaved) **1** to pass threads over and under each other to make cloth on a loom. **2** to pass strips of a material over and under each other to make baskets, etc. **3** to move in and out between things or people.
web *n* a net made by a spider.
webbed *adj* (of feet) with skin between the toes. Ducks have webbed feet.
wedding *n* a marriage ceremony.
wedge[1] *n* a piece of wood, etc with one end thicker than the other.
wedge[2] *v* **1** to keep something in place using a wedge. **2** to push something firmly into a small space.
Wednesday *n* the fourth day of the week.
weed[1] *n* a wild plant that grows where it is not wanted.
weed[2] *v* to pull up weeds.
week *n* **1** a period of seven days, especially from Sunday to Saturday. **2** the working days of the week, not Saturday and Sunday. **weekly** *adj, adv.*
weekend *n* Saturday and Sunday.
weep *v* (weeping, wept) to have tears falling from your eyes, to cry.
weigh *v* **1** to measure how heavy something is on scales. **2** to have a certain weight. *This box weighs 2 kg.*
weight *n* **1** how heavy something is. **2** a piece of metal weighing a certain amount.
weird *adj* very odd, strange.
welcome[1] *v* to show that you are happy to see somebody or have something. *She welcomed us at the door.* **welcome** *n,* **welcoming** *adj.*
welcome[2] *adj* received with pleasure. *The extra money was very welcome.* **welcome to** allowed to do something.
weld *v* to join pieces of metal, usually by heating and pressing them together.
welfare *n* a person's health and happiness.
well[1] *adj* healthy, not ill.
well[2] *adv* **1** in a good or right way. *Amy can swim very well.* **2** thoroughly. *I don't know him very well.*
well[3] *n* a deep hole in the earth from which you can get water, oil or gas.
wellingtons *n pl* high, rubber boots that you wear to keep your legs dry.
well-known *adj* known by many people.
well-off *adj* rich.
went *past of* go.
wept *past of* weep.
were *past of* be.
we're we are.
werewolf *n* in stories, a person who can change into a wolf when there is a full Moon.

west *n* **1** one of the points of the compass, the direction that you face to see the Sun set. **2 the West** Europe and North America. **west** *adj, adv.*
western[1] *adj* in or of the west part of a place.
western[2] *n* a film or book about cowboys in the west of the USA.
wet[1] *adj* (wetter, wettest) **1** soaked or covered in water or another liquid. **2** rainy. *wet weather.*
wet[2] *v* (wets, wetting, wet *or* wetted) to make something wet.
whack *v* to hit somebody or something hard. **whack** *n.*
whale *n* a very large sea mammal that looks like a fish.

blue whale

whaling *n* the hunting of whales.
wharf *n* (*pl* wharfs *or* wharves) a place where ships are loaded and unloaded.
what *adj, pron* **1** used in questions. *What time is it?* **2** the thing that. *Tell me what you want.* **3** used to show surprise or to express something strongly. *What a stupid thing to say!*
whatever *adj, pron* **1** anything that. *Show me whatever you have.* **2** no matter what. *Whatever he may say, I still don't believe him.*
wheat *n* the grain from which most flour is made.
wheel[1] *n* a circular object that turns around an axle in its centre.
wheel[2] *v* to push something along on wheels.
wheelbarrow *n* a small cart with one wheel in front, pushed along by two handles.
wheelchair *n* a chair on wheels for a person who is not able to walk.
wheeze *v* to breathe with difficulty, making a whistling sound. **wheezy** *adj.*
when *adv, conj* **1** at what time? **2** at the time that. *Call me when you get in.*
whenever *adv, conj* **1** at any time. *You can come whenever you like.* **2** every time that. *Whenever I hear this song I feel happy.*
where *adv, conj* **1** in or to what place. *Where have you been?* **2** at or to the place that. *Sit where she tells you to.*
whereas *conj* but. *Polly is blonde, whereas I've got dark hair.*
wherever *adv, conj* at or to any place.
whether *conj* if. *I don't mind whether you come or not.*
which *adj, pron* **1** what person or thing. *Which flavour do you want?* **2** used to refer to a particular person or thing. *This is the book which you asked for.*
whichever *adj, pron* no matter which.
while[1] *n* a period of time. *She'll be back in a while.*
while[2], **whilst** *conj* **1** during the time that. *Did anyone phone while I was out?* **2** although. *While I sympathize, I can't do much to help.*
while[3] *v* to pass time. *We whiled away the hours playing card games.*
whim *n* a sudden idea or change of mind.
whimper *v* to make little, soft, crying sounds. **whimper** *n.*
whine *v* **1** to make a long, high-pitched, unpleasant sound. **2** to complain in an annoying way.
whip[1] *n* a long rope or strip of leather joined to a handle, used for hitting animals.
whip[2] *v* (whips, whipping, whipped) **1** to hit with a whip. **2** to beat cream, eggs, etc until they are thick. **3** to move quickly and suddenly. *She whipped out a gun from her bag.*
whirl *v* to turn around fast in circles. **whirl** *n.*
whirlpool *n* a place in a river or sea where the current moves in a circle.
whirlwind *n* a very strong wind that blows in circles.
whisk[1] *n* a kitchen tool made of wire, used for beating eggs, cream, etc.
whisk[2] *v* **1** to beat eggs, cream, etc with a fork or whisk. **2** to move quickly and suddenly. *The waiter whisked our plates away.*

whisker *n* **1** one of the long, stiff hairs that grow near the mouth of animals such as cats and mice. **2 whiskers** hair on the sides of a man's face.
whisky, whiskey *n* a strong, alcoholic drink made from grain.
whisper *v* to speak very quietly and softly. **whisper** *n.*
whist *n* a card game for four players.
whistle[1] *v* to make a high-pitched sound by blowing through your tightened lips.
whistle[2] *n* an instrument that you blow through to make a whistling sound.
white[1] *n* the colour of pure snow.
white[2] *adj* **1** with the colour of pure snow. **2** light-coloured. *white wine.* **3** with light-coloured skin. **4** with milk. *white coffee.*
white[3] *n* the clear liquid in an egg, around the yolk.
whiz, whizz *v* (whizzes, whizzing, whizzed) to move very quickly, often making a buzzing sound.
who *pron* **1** what person or people? *Who did that?* **2** used to refer to a certain person. *I know who he is.*
whoever *pron* **1** any person or people. *Invite whoever you want to the party.* **2** any person that. *Whoever rings, tell them I'm out*
whole *adj* complete, with nothing missing. *Tell me the whole story.* **whole** *n,* **wholly** *adv.*
wholemeal *adj* made from flour that contains all the grain, with nothing removed.
wholesale *n* the buying and selling of goods in large quantities.
wholesome *adj* healthy, good for you.
whom *pron* who.
whooping-cough *(**hoo**-ping koff)* *n* an infectious disease that makes you cough and make a loud noise as you breathe in.
who's who is, who has.
whose *adj, pron* **1** belonging to whom. *Whose book is this?* **2** of whom. *She's the girl whose mum is a model.*
why *adv* for what reason?
wick *n* the thread in a candle, which you light.
wicked *adj* evil. **wickedness** *n.*
wicket *n* in cricket, a set of three stumps at which the ball is bowled.
wide *adj* **1** far from one side to the other. *a wide road.* **2** measuring a certain amount from side to side. *five metres wide.* **3** great, large. *a wide range of choices.* **widen** *v.*
widespread *adj* found or happening in many places.
widow *n* a woman whose husband is dead, and who has not married again.
widower *n* a man whose wife is dead, and who has not married again.
width *n* the distance from one side to the other.
wife *n* (*pl* wives) the woman that a man is married to.
wig *n* an artificial covering of hair, made to fit the head.
wiggle *v* to move from side to side.
wigwam *n* a dome-shaped hut or tent made by Native Americans.
wild *adj* **1** natural, not tamed or cultivated by humans. **2** uncontrolled, especially because of anger or excitement. *The spectators went wild.*
wilderness *n* an area of wild land where nobody lives.
wildlife *n* wild animals and plants
will[1] *v* (would) used to talk about future actions and events.
will[2] *n* **1** determination. *She has the will to succeed.* **2** what you want. *They did it against my will.* **3** a document that says what will happen to somebody's property when they die.
willing *adj* ready and happy to do what is wanted or needed.
willow *n* a tree with long, thin branches.
wilt *v* (of a plant) to start to droop.
wily *adj* (wilier, wiliest) cunning, sly.
win *v* (wins, winning, won) **1** to come first in a contest or game. **2** to get a prize. **3** to get something by working or trying hard. **win** *n,* **winner** *n.*
winch *n* a machine for lifting things, worked by winding a rope around a revolving cylinder.
wind[1] *(rhymes with* kind*)* *v* (winding, wound) **1** to wrap something round and round another thing. **2** to turn a

key or handle round and round to make something work. *Wind up the clock.* **3** to twist and turn. *a winding road.* **wind up** *(informal)* to annoy or tease somebody.
wind[2] *(rhymes with* tinned*)* *n* moving air. **windy** *adj.*
wind instrument *n* a musical instrument played by blowing into it.
windmill *n* a mill powered by wind blowing against its sails.
window *n* an opening, usually covered by glass, in the wall of a building to let in light and air.

windmill

windpipe *n* the tube leading from your mouth to your lungs.
windscreen *n* the front window of a car.
windsurfing *n* the sport of moving across water on a long board with a sail attached to it. **windsurfer** *n.*
wine *n* an alcoholic drink, usually made from grapes.
wing *n* **1** one of the parts of a bird or insect used for flying. **2** one of the wing-like parts on the side of an aircraft that it uses to fly. **3** a part of a building that sticks out to the side. **4** one of the sides of a football pitch.
wink *v* to open and close one eye quickly.
winter *n* the coldest season of the year, between autumn and spring. **wintry** *adj.*
wipe *v* to rub something to make it clean or dry. **wipe out** to destroy completely. *Disease has wiped out the entire village.*
wire *n* a long, very thin piece of metal that can be bent and twisted.
wisdom *n* knowledge, experience and good sense.
wisdom tooth *n* one of the four back teeth that grow after childhood.
wise *adj* having a lot of knowledge and experience and able to use it well, sensible.
wish *v* **1** to want or desire something. *I wish we could go to the beach.* **2** to say that you hope somebody will have something. *I wished Ben a happy birthday.* **wish** *n.*
wit *n* **1** the ability to say clever and funny things. **2** intelligence, common sense.
witch *n* a woman who is supposed to have magic powers.
witchcraft *n* the use of magic powers.
with *prep* **1** accompanying. *I walk to school with my sister.* **2** using. *Cut it with a knife.* **3** having something. *the boy with red hair.* **4** because of. *He was shaking with fear.*
withdraw *v* (withdrawing, withdrew, withdrawn) **1** to move back or away. *The general has withdrawn his troops.* **2** to decide not to take part in something. *Leavis has withdrawn from the race.* **3** to remove something, to take something out or away. *I withdrew £20 from my bank account.* **withdrawal** *n.*
withdrawn *adj* quiet, not liking to talk to people.
wither *v* to dry up and die. *The plant withered in the hot sun.*
withhold *v* (withholding, withheld) to refuse to give something. *She withheld her permission.*
within *adv, prep* inside.
without *prep* not having something.
witness *n* a person who sees something happen and who can describe it later, especially in a law court. **witness** *v.*
witty *adj* (wittier, wittiest) funny in a clever way. *a witty remark.* **wittily** *adv.*
wizard *n* a man who is supposed to have magic powers.
wobble *v* to move unsteadily from side to side. **wobbly** *adj.*
woe *n* great sadness. **woeful** *adj.*

woke *past of* wake.
woken *past participle of* wake.
wolf *n* (*pl* wolves) a wild animal similar to a dog, that hunts in a pack.
woman *n* (*pl* women) a fully grown female human.
womb *n* the part of the body of a female mammal where her young develop before they are born.
wombat *n* a small Australian animal that lives in burrows. A female wombat has a pouch.
won *past of* win.
wonder[1] *v* **1** to ask yourself something. **2** to be amazed at something.
wonder[2] *n* **1** a feeling of amazement and admiration. **2** something that gives you this feeling.
wonderful *adj* excellent, marvellous.
won't will not.
wood *n* **1** a number of trees growing together in one place. **2** the substance that forms the trunk and branches of trees. **wooden** *adj.*
woodlouse *n* (*pl* woodlice) a small creature like an insect with a hard shell, that feeds on decaying wood.
woodpecker *n* a bird that pecks holes in the bark of trees in search of insects.
woodwind *n* musical instruments, made of wood or metal, that you play by blowing through a mouthpiece and into a hollow tube. Flutes and clarinets are woodwind instruments.
woodwork *n* **1** making things out of wood. **2** the parts of a building that are made from wood.
wool *n* the natural covering found on sheep. **woollen** *adj.*
word *n* **1** a sound, spoken or written, that has a meaning. **2** a short conversation. **3** news. **4** a promise.
word processing *n* using a computer to write letters, reports, etc.
wore *past of* wear.
work[1] *n* **1** the effort made to achieve or make something. **2** employment. **3** a painting, book, play, etc. **4** anything that you have made or done by working. **5** the place where you work. **6 works** a factory.
work[2] *v* **1** to put effort into doing something. **2** to do a job. **3** to function correctly. **work out 1** to solve something. **2** to have the result you hoped for. **3** to do physical exercises, especially in a gym, to keep fit.
workshop *n* a place where things are made or mended.
world *n* **1** the Earth and everything on it. **2** a particular area of activity. *the world of fashion.*
worm *n* a small, creeping creature with no backbone.
worn *past participle of* wear.
worry *v* (worries, worrying, worried) to be anxious about something. **worry** *n,* **worrier** *n.*
worse *adj, adv* less good or well.
worsen *v* to make or become worse.
worship *v* (worships, worshipping, worshipped) **1** to praise God or a god. **2** to love or admire somebody greatly. **worship** *n.*
worst *adj, adv* least good or well.
worth *adj* **1** having a value of. *This ring is worth thousands of pounds.* **2** good enough for. *The museum is worth a visit.* **worth** *n.*
worthless *adj* having no value.
would *v* **1** *past of* will. **2** used to talk about things that are possible. *It would be nice to see you.*
wound[1] *(rhymes with* spooned*) n* an injury or cut. **wound** *v.*
wound[2] *(rhymes with* round*) past of* wind.
wove *past of* weave.
woven *past participle of* weave.
wrap *v* (wraps, wrapping, wrapped) to fold or roll something around somebody or something.
wrapper *n* a plastic or paper cover in which something is wrapped.
wrath *(roth) n* great anger.
wreath *n* a ring of flowers or leaves.
wreck *v* to damage something so badly that it cannot be used again. **wreck** *n.*
wreckage *n* the remains of something that has been wrecked.
wren *n* a small, brown bird.
wrench[1] *v* to pull or twist something with force. *He wrenched the steering wheel from her hand.*

wrench² *n* a strong tool for turning nuts and bolts.

wrestle *v* **1** to fight by getting hold of your opponent and trying to throw them to the ground. **2** to struggle.

wrestling *n* the sport in which two people try to throw each other to the ground. **wrestler** *n.*

sumo wrestling

wretched *adv* very unhappy, miserable.

wriggle *v* to twist and turn your body.

wring *v* (wringing, wrung) to twist and squeeze wet cloth to remove the water.

wrinkle *n* a small crease in your skin or in paper or cloth. **wrinkle** *v.*

wrist *n* the joint that connects your arm and your hand.

write *v* (writing, wrote, written) **1** to form letters, especially with a pen or pencil on paper. **2** to compose a book, piece of music, etc. **writer** *n,* **writing** *n.*

writhe *v* to twist backwards and forwards, especially in pain. *He was writhing in agony.*

wrong *adj* **1** not correct, not right. **2** bad or evil. **3** not suitable. **wrong** *adv.*

wrote *past of* write.

wrung *past of* wring.

Xx

Xmas *a short way of writing* Christmas.

X-ray *n* **1** a ray that can pass through solid things. **2** a photograph produced by X-rays on film, used for showing the inside of something, especially a part of the body. **X-ray** *v.*

xylophone *(zy-lo-fone) n* a musical instrument made up of a row of bars that you strike with small hammers.

Yy

yacht *(yot) n* **1** a light sailing boat. **2** a large motor-driven boat used for cruising. **yachting** *n.*

yak *n* a long-haired ox found in Tibet.

yam *n* the edible root of a tropical plant similar to the potato.

yank *v* to pull something suddenly and with force. **yank** *n.*

yap *v* (yaps, yapping, yapped) to give a high-pitched bark, as small dogs do. **yap** *n.*

yard *n* **1** an old measure of length, equal to 3 feet or 0.914 metres. **2** an enclosed piece of ground beside a building. **3** in American English, a garden.

yarn *n* **1** wool or cotton spun into thread. **2** a long, exaggerated story.

yashmak *n* a veil covering the lower part of the face, worn by Muslim women.

yawn *v* to open your mouth wide and take a deep breath when you are tired or bored. **yawn** *n.*

year *n* **1** the amount of time that it takes the Earth to travel around the Sun, about 365 days. **2** the period from 1 January to 31 December. **3** any period of twelve months.

yearn *(yurn) v* to long for something. *She yearned to see her children again.* **yearning** *n.*

yeast *n* a substance used for making bread rise, and for making beer.

yell *v* to shout loudly. **yell** *n.*

yellow *n* the colour of lemons and egg-yolks. **yellow** *adj*.
yelp *n* a sudden, sharp cry. **yelp** *v*.
yesterday *n*, *adv* (on) the day before today.
yet[1] *adv* **1** up till now, so far. *I haven't met her new boyfriend yet.* **2** even. *He asked for yet more money.*
yet[2] *conj* but, nevertheless.
yield *v* **1** to give in, to surrender. **2** to produce something. *How much milk does that herd of cows yield?* **yield** *n*.
yodel *v* (yodels, yodelling, yodelled) to sing in a voice that constantly changes between an ordinary and a very high-pitched sound. **yodel** *n*.
yoga *n* a system of exercises to help relax the body and mind, based on an ancient Hindu system of philosophy and meditation.
yoghurt, yogurt *n* a semi-liquid food made from soured milk.
yoke *n* a wooden frame placed over the necks of oxen to keep them together when they are pulling a cart or plough.
yolk *(rhymes with* oak*)* *n* the yellow part inside an egg.
Yom Kippur *n* a Jewish holy day of fasting and prayer.
young[1] *adj* not old.
young[2] *n pl* young animals.
youngster *n* a young person.
your *adj* belonging to you.
you're you are.
youth *n* **1** the time when you are young. **2** a young man.
youthful *adj* seeming or looking young.
yo-yo *n* a toy consisting of a reel that winds and unwinds from a string.
Yuletide *n* *(old-fashioned)* Christmas time.

zebra

Zz

zany *(zay-nee) adj* funny in a crazy way. **zanily** *adv*.
zap *v* (zaps, zapping, zapped) to strike or shoot something suddenly.
zeal *(zeel) n* enthusiasm, eagerness. **zealous** *(zel-us) adj*.
zebra *n* an African animal like a horse with black and white stripes.
zebra crossing *n* a place marked with black and white stripes where pedestrians can cross the road.
zero *n* (*pl* zeros) nought, the figure 0.
zest *n* **1** enthusiasm, lively enjoyment. **2** the outer skin of an orange or lemon.
zigzag *n* a line with sharp bends or angles. **zigzag** *adj*, *v*.
zinc *n* a bluish-white metal.
zip *n* a fastener with two sets of teeth that fit together when a sliding tab is pulled between them. **zip** *v*.
zodiac *n* in astrology, an imaginary strip across the sky divided into 12 equal parts called the **signs of the zodiac**. Each sign is named after a group of stars.
zombie *n* a dead body that is brought back to life by witchcraft.
zone *n* an area that is made separate from the rest of a building, town, etc for a particular purpose. *This is a no-parking zone.*
zoo *n* a place where wild animals are kept for people to look at them.
zoology *(zoo-**ol**-o-jee) n* the scientific study of animals. **zoological** *adj*, **zoologist** *n*.
zoom *v* to move fast with a low, humming or buzzing noise.
zoom lens *n* a lens on a camera that you adjust to make a distant object appear gradually nearer.